EASTERN EUROPE
PHRASEBOOK

Eastern Europe phrasebook
3rd edition – February 2001

Published by
Lonely Planet Publications Pty Ltd ABN 36 005 607 983
90 Maribyrnong St, Footscray, Victoria 3011, Australia

Lonely Planet Offices
Australia Locked Bag 1, Footscray, Victoria 3011
USA 150 Linden St, Oakland CA 94607
UK 10a Spring Place, London NW5 3BH
France 1 rue du Dahomey, 75011 Paris

Cover illustration
'Go Home, Your Igloo is on Fire' by Patrick Marris

ISBN 1 86450 227 4

text © Lonely Planet Publications Pty Ltd 2001
cover illustration © Lonely Planet Publications Pty Ltd 2001

10 9 8 7 6 5   3 2 1

Printed by The Bookmaker International Ltd
Printed in China

About the Authors

Dr Angel Pachev wrote and updated the Bulgarian chapter, which originally appeared in Lonely Planet's *Eastern Europe phrasebook*. He also updated the Albanian chapter, based on Lonely Planet's *Mediterranean phrasebook*, and written by Stephen Schwartz and Gjon Sinishta. To complete the hat trick, he updated Romanian, from Lonely Planet's *Eastern Europe phrasebook*, written by Daniel Condratov.

Angel is a Senior Researcher and Senior Lecturer in General Linguistics, Sociolinguistics and Ethnolinguistics. He is Head of the Department of General and Applied Linguistics at the Institute for the Bulgarian Language with the Bulgarian Academy of Sciences in Sofia.

Pavlinka Georgiev updated the Croatian and Macedonian chapters, which were based on chapters of Lonely Planet's *Mediterranean phrasebook*, written by Lily Stojanovska. Pavlinka is a professional translator of English, German, French, Macedonian, Serbian and Croatian languages. Her translations and essays have been published in Europe, USA and Australia.

Katarina Steiner updated the Czech chapter, originally written by Richard Nebeský. She also wrote and updated the Slovakian chapter based on the second edition of Lonely Planet's *Eastern Europe phrasebook*. Katarina is a Sydney based freelance translator and interpreter of the Czech, German and Slovak languages.

German was updated by Gunter Mühl. Gunter teaches German at the University of Canterbury in Christchurch, New Zealand, and works as a freelance translator. This chapter was based on Lonely Planet's *German phrasebook*, written by Franziska Buck and Anke Munderloh.

Katalin Koronczi wrote and updated Hungarian (Magyar). A Budapester born and bred, Katalin Koronczi has worked in the tourism profession for 23 years. She also finds time to run her own translation bureau.

Krzysztof Dydyński wrote the Polish chapter. Born and raised in Warsaw, Poland, he is the author of several Lonely Planet guidebooks, including *Poland*, *Kraków*, *Colombia* and *Venezuela*.

Mirjana Djukic updated Serbian, which was based on the Serbian chapter of Lonely Planet's *Mediterranean phrasebook*, written by Lily Stojanovska. Mirjana was born in Yugoslavia and lives in Sydney, Australia, and works as a translator and librarian.

Slovene was updated by Miran Hladnik, a professor of Slovene literature at the University of Ljubljana, Slovenia. The original chapter was written by Draga Gelt, and appeared in Lonely Planet's *Mediterranean phrasebook*. Once upon a time, Miran was a Slovene lecturer in the USA and, using his teaching experience, he wrote a phrasebook, *Slovene for Travelers*.

From the Authors

Dr Angel Pachev is grateful to Zoya Kostadinova for her work on the Albanian chapter, and is very much obliged to Dr E. Kaldieva for her contribution to the Romanian chapter.

Pavlinka Georgiev is grateful to Ofelija Kovilovska and Aleksandar Georgiev for their participation in this project.

Katalin Koronczi thanks all those who helped her in compiling the Hungarian (Magyar) section, especially her young son Peter who gave her just enough peace and quiet to complete the work to deadline.

Warmest thanks from Krzysztof Dydyński to Angela Melendro, Ela Lis, Beata Wasiak, Basia Meder, Tadek Wysocki, Kuba Leszczyński, Majka and Marek Bogatek, and Grażyna and Jacek Wojciechowicz for help with the Polish chapter.

Miran Hladnik wishes you a joyful start in acquisition of the Slovene language and a pleasant stay in Slovenia.

From the Publisher

The skilful team behind this book are: Lou Callan who edited, Vicki Webb and Karin Vidstrup Monk who co-edited and Fleur Goding, Haya Husseini and Emma Koch who proofed. Brendan Dempsey, Yukiyoshi Kamimura and Patrick Marris laid out and Patrick also illustrated book and cover. Natasha Velleley provided the map, Fabrice Rocher supervised design and Karin Vidstrup Monk the rest. Peter D'Onghia checked layout and Sally Steward made the book a reality.

CONTENTS

INTRODUCTION

The Eastern European languages covered in this book are Albanian, Bulgarian, Croatian, Czech, Hungarian, Macedonian, Polish, Romanian, Serbian, Slovak and Slovene. These languages come from three different language families.

1. Slavonic languages form a branch of the large Indo-European language family. These languages, which originated north of the Carpathians, share a large amount of basic vocabulary. They're now divided into Northern, Southern and Western subgroups, however, within the Slavonic-speaking region, national and linguistic boundaries don't neatly line up.

   Slavonic languages are now written in either Cyrillic or Roman script. Those languages traditionally associated with the Eastern Orthodox Church use Cyrillic, while those influenced by the Catholic Church use Roman.

   • Czech, Polish and Slovak belong to the West Slavonic sub group

   • Bulgarian, Croatian, Macedonian, Serbian and Slovene are all South Slavonic languages

   Croatian and Serbian are still often referred to as one language (with various titles such as Serbo-Croat or Croato-Serbian); until recent events in the former Yugolsavia, Bosnian was also classified within the general 'Serbo-Croatian' moniker.

2. Albanian, also an Indo-European language, is the only surviving member of a branch from the Balkan Peninsula

3. Hungarian, a Finno-Ugric language, is unique in Europe. It's closest European relative is Finnish, although today the two languages are no longer mutually intelligible.

4. Romanian is a Romance language, related to, among others, French, Italian, Portuguese and Spanish

Transliterations

Simplified transliterations have been provided in **purple** throughout the book. Italics is used to indicate where to place stress in a word.

Arthur or Martha?

When a word has both masculine and feminine forms, they're indicated in one of three ways, with the masculine form always appearing first:

- with a slash separating a masculine form and its feminine ending:

  I'm a student.   (eu) sînt **stu-dent/**ă   *(Eu) sînt student/ă.*

- with a slash separating the masculine and feminine word within a sentence:

I'm happy.	ysehm *shtyahst*-nee/	*Jsem št'astný/*
	shtyahst-naa	*št'astná.* (m/f)

- when the distinction between masculine and feminine is more complex, each word is given in full:

scientist	*vyeh*-dehts	*vědec* (m)
	vyeht-ki-nyeh	*vědkyně* (f)

Polite Forms

When a language has polite and informal forms of the singular pronoun 'you', the polite form has been used in most cases. However, where the informal form of 'you' is used, this is indicated in brackets.

ABBREVIATIONS USED IN THIS BOOK

f	feminine	pl	plural
inf	informal	pol	polite
m	masculine	sg	singular
neut	neuter		

ALBANIAN

QUICK REFERENCE

Hello.	toon-gya-tye-ta/ahlo	*Tungjatjeta./Allo.*
Goodbye.	lam-too-meer	*Lamtumirë.*
Yes./No.	po/yo	*Po./Jo.*
Excuse me.	me-fal-nee	*Me falni.*
Sorry.	me vyen kech	*Më vjen keq.*
Please.	yu lu-tem	*Ju lutem.*
Thank you.	yu fal-em ndereet	*Ju falem nderit.*
You're welcome.	ska per-seh	*S' ka përse.*
What time is it?	sah ahsht ora?	*Sa është ora?*
How much is it?	sah koosh-ton?	*Sa kushton?*
Where's ...?	ko ahsht ...?	*Ku është ...?*

Where are the toilets?		
koo ahsht ne-voy-tor-ya?		*Ku është nevojtorja?*
How do I get to ...?		
se moond t' ve-teh-teh ...?		*Si mund të vete te ...?*
Turn left/right.		
kthe-hoo mai-tas/dya-thtas		*Kthehu majtas/djathtas.*

at the ...	nye kyo-shen ...	në qoshen ...
next corner	tye-tr t' roogs	*tjetër të rrugës*
traffic lights	te dree-ta eh	*te drita e*
	tra-fee-koot/	*trafikut/*
	say-mah-fo-ree	*semafori*

I (don't) understand.		
oon (nook) koop-toy		*Unë (nuk) kuptoj.*
Do you speak English?		
ah flees-nee an-glisht?		*A flisni Anglisht?*

I'd like a ... ticket.	d'sheeroy nye bee-let ...	*Dëshiroj një biletë ...*
one-way	vai-tyeh	*vajtje*
return	kthee-mee	*kthimi*

I'd like a single/	oo-n' dwa nyethom' me	*Unë dua një dhomë*
double room.	me nye/du kre-vat	*me një/du krevat.*

1	nyeh	*një*	6	gyasht	*gjashtë*
2	du	*dy*	7	shtaht	*shtatë*
3	trey	*tre*	8	tet	*tetë*
4	ka-t'r	*katër*	9	nent	*nëntë*
5	pes	*pesë*	10	thyet	*dhjetë*

ALBANIAN

The Albanians, descendants of the ancient Illyrians, speak one of the oldest Indo-European languages. Albanian is not directly related to any other language. Some nine million speakers live in five main areas: within the borders of the Albanian state (3.5 million), in the neighbouring areas of Kosovë, Montenegro (*Mal të Zi*), and Macedonia (3 million), in Greece and Italy (500,000), in Turkey (1 million), and in the USA (300,000, including Italo-Albanians or *Arbëresh*). They possess a rich cultural and literary tradition.

The Albanian language has been traditionally spoken and written in two variants, Gheg (northern) and Tosk (southern). However, the Communist regime, which ruled from 1944 to 1990, attempted to standardise the language in a single form based on Tosk. This so-called 'unified' speech has been used in this phrasebook.

Albanians are characterised by warm family life and by an unparalleled habit of hospitality. *Besa*, meaning 'customary law', requires that wayfarers be protected and helped in their journey. Travellers will find attempts to speak Albanian welcome. Many Albanian speakers, particularly in Kosovë and other regions outside the post-1912 borders of the Albanian state, have travelled and worked in Europe, particularly in Germany and Switzerland. In addition, many will have studied foreign languages in school. German, Italian, Serbian and Greek are more widely known as second languages than English, although this is expected to change.

ALBANIAN

PRONUNCIATION

Albanian is written as it's pronounced. Sounds not described here are pronounced as in English.

Vowels

ë	a/uh	at the beginning of a word, as the 'a' in 'father' or the 'u' in 'nut'
	e	sometimes as the 'a' in 'soda';
'		silent when in a final, unstressed syllable (note that at the end of a word, *ë* is a feminine gender marker)
aj	ai	as the 'y' in 'fly'

Consonants

Remember that some consonants present in English are pronounced differently in Albanian. These include:

c	ts	as the 'ts' in 'hats'	'		as the sound made
ç	ch	as the 'ch' in 'church'			between the words
dh	<u>th</u>	as the 'th' in 'this'			'uh-oh'
gj	gy	as the 'gy' in 'big yeti'	*th*	th	as the 'th' in 'thistle'
j	y	as the 'y' in 'yellow'	*x*	ds	as the 'ds' in 'lads'
nj	ny	as the 'ny' in 'canyon'	*xh*	dj	as the 'dj' in 'badge'
q	ky	as the 'cu' in 'cure';			
	chy	sometimes as the 'chi' as the in Italian 'chiao'			

SUBJECT PRONOUNS		
SG		
I	u-nah	*unë*
you (inf/pol)	ti/ju	*ti/ju*
he/she	ay/ayo	*ai/ajo*
it (m/f)	ay/ayo	*ai/ajo*
PL		
we	ne	*ne*
you	ju	*ju*
they (m/f)	a-ta/a-to	*ata/ato*

Stress

For the vast majority of words, the main stress falls on the last word of a phrase, on the last stem of a compound word and on the last syllable of a word.

GREETINGS & CIVILITIES
Top Useful Phrases

Hello.	toon-gya-tye-ta/ahlo	*Tungjatjeta./Allo.*
Goodbye.	lam-too-meer	*Lamtumirë.*
	mir-oo-paf-shim	*Mirupafshim.* (inf)
Yes./No.	po/yo	*Po./Jo.*
Excuse me.	me-fal-nee	*Me falni.*
Please.	yu lu-tem	*Ju lutem.*
Thank you.	yu fal-em ndereet	*Ju falem nderit.*
That's fine.	ahsht eh-meer	*Eshtë e mirë.*
You're welcome.	ska per-seh	*S' ka përse.*

ALBANIAN

Greetings

Good morning.	meer-men-gyes	*Mirëmëngjes.*
Good afternoon.	meer dee-tah	*Mirdita.*
Good evening.	meer'-mbra-hma	*Mirëmbrëma.*
Good night.	nat'n-e-meer	*Natën e mirë.*
How are you?	see ye-nee?	*Si jeni?*
Well, thanks.	yam meer, yu fal-em	*Jam mirë,*
	nede-reet	*ju falem nderit.*

QUESTION WORDS		
How?	si?	*Si?*
When?	kur?	*Kur?*
Where?	ku?	*Ku?*
Which?	tsi-li?	*Cili?*
Who?	kush?	*Kus?*
Why?	pseh?	*Pse?*

ALBANIAN

Forms of Address

Madam/Mrs	zo-nya	*Zonjë*
Sir/Mr	zo-te-ree	*Zotëri*
Miss	zo-ny-ush	*Zonjushë*
companion/friend	meek/mee-keh	*mik* (m)/*mike* (f)

SMALL TALK
Meeting People

What's your name?
  see chyu-he-nee yu lu-tem?   *Si quheni ju lutem?*
My name's ...
  oon chyu-hem ...   *Unë quhem ...*
  moo-am' chwain ...   *Mua më quajnë ...*
Pleased to meet you.
  yam-ee loom-toor   *Jam i lumtur*
  t'yu nyoh   *t'ju njoh.*
How old are you?
  ch' mosh ke-nee?/   *Ç'moshë keni?/*
  sa vyech ye-nee?   *Sa vjeç jeni?*

Nationalities

Where are you from?
  (prey) nga je-nee?   *(Prej) Nga jeni?*

I'm from ...	yam nga ...	*Jam nga ...*
Australia	aoos-trah-leea	*Australia*
Canada	ka-na-da-yah	*Kanadaja*
England	an-glia	*Anglia*
Ireland	ir-lan-da	*Irlanda*
New Zealand	zay-lan-da eh-ray	*Zelanda e Re*
Scotland	skot-lan-da	*Skotlanda*
the USA	shte-tet eh	*Shtetet e*
	bahsh-koo-ah-ra	*Bashkuara*
Wales	ooels	*Uells*

Occupations

What do you do?	ch poon benee?	Ç' punë bëni?
I'm a/an ...	yam ...	Jam ...
business person	treg-tar	tregtar
journalist	ga-ze-tar	gazetar (m)
	ga-ze-ta-reh	gazetare (f)
manual worker	poon-tor/kra-hoo	punëtor/krahu
nurse	in-fehr-my-ehr	infermier (m)
	in-fehr-my-ehr-reh	infermiere (f)
office worker	ne-poons	nëpunës (m)
	ne-poon-seh	nëpunëse (f)
scientist	shken-ts-tar	shkencëtar (m)
	shken-ts-ta-reh	shkencëtare (f)
teacher	mu-soos	mësues (m)
	mu-soo-seh	mësuese (f)
waiter	ka-meh-ry-ehr	kamerier (m)
	ka-meh-ry-eh-reh	kameriere (f)
writer	shkrim-tar	shkrimtar (m)
	shkrim-ta-reh	shkrimtare (f)

Religion

I'm ...	yam ...	Jam ...
Buddhist	bood-ist	Budist (m)
	bood-ist-eh	Budiste (f)
Catholic	ka-to-lik	Katolik (m)
	ka-to-lik-eh	Katolike (f)
Christian	ee kreesh-ter	I krishter (m)
	eh kreesh-ter-eh	E krishtere (f)
Hindu	hin-du	Hindu (m/f)
Jewish	chee-foot	Çifut (m)
	chee-foo-teh	Çifute (f)
Muslim	mus-li-man	Musliman (m)
	mus-li-ma-neh	Muslimane (f)

ALBANIAN

What's your religion?
    ch fay ke-nee?   *Ç' fe keni?*
I'm not religious.
    nook yam fe-tar/fe-ta-reh   *Nuk jam fetar/fetare.* (m/f)

Family

Are you married?
    ah ye-nee ee/eh marr-too-ahr? *A jeni i/e martuar?* (m/f)
I'm single.
    s' yam ee/eh marr-too-ahr   *S' jam i/e martuar.* (m/f)
I'm married.
    yam ee/eh marr-too-ahr   *Jam i/e martuar.* (m/f)
How many children do you have?
    sa f'-mee ke-nee?   *Sa fëmijë keni?*

brother	v'-la	*vëlla*
children	f'-mee-yuh	*fëmijë*
daughter	bee-yuh	*bijë*
family	fa-mi-li-eh	*familje*
father	ba-ba	*baba*
grandfather	gyush	*gjysh*
grandmother	gyush-eh	*gjyshe*
husband	bahsh-k'-short/boor	*bashkëshort/burrë*
mother	ma-ma/na-na	*mëmë/nënë*
sister	mo-ter	*motër*
son	beer/dyal	*bir/djalë*
wife	bahsh-k'-shor-teh/grua	*bashkëshorte/grua*

Feelings

I like ...		
meh pel-kyen ...		*Më pëlqen ...*
I (don't) like ...		
(s')meh pel-kyen ...		*(S')më pëlqen ...*
I'm in a hurry.		
kam poon/yam ee ngoo-toor		*Kam punë./Jam i ngutur.*
I'm sorry. (condolence)		
m' vyen kech		*Më vjen keq.*
I'm grateful.		
yam mee-r'-nyo-h's		*Jam mirënjohës.*

I'm ...	kam ...	*Kam ...*
cold	te ftoh-te	*të ftohtë*
hot	te ndzeh-te	*të nxehtë*
hungry	ooree	*uri*
thirsty	etye	*etje*
right	te drey-te	*të drejtë*
sleepy	gyoo-me	*gjumë*

Useful Phrases

Sorry. (forgive me)	me vyen kech	*Më vjen keq.*
Excuse me.	me falnee	*Më falni.*
Sure.	si-gu-risht	*Sigurisht.*
Good luck!	me fat mee-r!	*Me fat te mirë!*
Just a minute.	veh-tam par	*Vetëm për një*
	nya mi-nut	*minutë*

ALBANIAN

BODY LANGUAGE

When Albanians meet, they touch their cheeks together three times while shaking hands. In Kosovë, where the population is predominantly Muslim, men usually walk several steps in front of women.

Men and women don't usually shake hands – women are greeted by a nod. Albanians signify 'yes' by shaking their head from side to side and 'no' by nodding their head up and down.

BREAKING THE LANGUAGE BARRIER

Do you speak English?
   ah flees-nee an-glisht?   *A flisni Anglisht?*
Does anyone speak English?
   ah flet nye-ree an-glisht?   *A flet njeri Anglisht?*
I (don't) understand.
   oon (nook) koop-toy   *Unë (nuk) kuptoj.*
Could you speak
more slowly please?
   flees-nee m'n'ga-dahl   *Flisni më ngadalë,*
   yu lu-tem?   *ju lutem?*
Please repeat that.
   pur-s'-ree-te-ni yu lu-tem   *Përsëriteni, ju lutem.*
How do you say ...?
   see eh tho-nee ...?   *Si e thoni ...?*
What does ... mean?
   ch' do t' tho-t' ...?   *Ç' do të thotë ...?*

PAPERWORK

address	ad-re-sa	*adresa*
age	mo-sha	*mosha*
birth certificate	cher-ti-fi-ca-ta	*çertifikata*
	eh leen-dyes	*e lindjes*
border	koo-fee-ree	*kufiri*
car owner's title	ti-too-lee ee	*titulli i*
	pro-na-reet t'	*pronarit të*
	au-to-mo-bi-lit	*automobilit*
car registration	re-gyi-stree-mee ee	*regjistrimi i*
	au-to-mo-bi-lit	*automobilit*
customs	do-ga-na	*dogana*
date of birth	da-t'-leen-dya	*datëlindja*
driver's licence	le-ya e t' nga-reet t'	*leja e të ngarit të*
	au-to-mo-bi-lit	*automobilit*
identification	kahr-tuh	*kartë*
	ee-den-tee-te-tee	*identiteti*

ALBANIAN

immigration	e-mee-gree-mee	*emigrimi*
marital status	gyen-dya tsi-vee-leh	*gjendja civile*
name	em-ree	*emri*
passport	pa-sa-por-ta	*pasaporta*
passport number	noom-ree ee	*numri i*
	pa-sa-ports	*pasaportës*
place of birth	v'nd-leen-dya	*vendlindja*
profession	my-esh-tri-a	*mjeshtria*
reason for travel	ar-sy-eya eh	*arsyeja e*
	uth'-tee-meet	*udhëtimit*
religion	fe-ya	*feja*
single	pa-mar-too-ar	*pamartuar*
tourist card	car-ta tu-ri-sti-ca	*karta turistike*
visa	vi-za	*viza*
sex	sek-see	*seksi*
feminine	fe-m'r	*femër*
masculine	mah-shkool	*mashkul*

ALBANIAN

GETTING AROUND

What time does	n'chor nee-set/	*Në ço'rë*
the ... leave/arrive?	arr-een ...?	*niset/arrin ...?*
aeroplane	ae-ro-plah-nee	*aeroplani*
boat	bar-ka/loon-dra	*barka/lundra*
bus	au-to-boo-see	*autobusi*
train	tre-nee	*treni*
tram	tram-vai-ee	*tramvaji*

Directions

Where's ...?
  ko ahsht ...?   *Ku është ...?*
How do I get to ...?
  se moond t' ve-teh-teh ...?   *Si mund të vete te ...?*
Is it far from/near here?
  a ahsht larg/afur nga k'-tu?   *A është larg/afër nga këtu?*

ALBANIAN

Can you show me (on the map)?

	ah moond t' mah	*A mund të ma*
	tregonee (n' hart)?	*tregoni (në hartë)?*

Go straight ahead.

	shkoh dreyt	*Shko drejt.*

Turn left/right ...	kthe-hoo mai-tas/	*Kthehu majtas/*
	dya-thtas ...	*djathtas ...*
at the next	nye kyo-shen	*në qoshen*
corner	tye-tr t' roogs	*tjetër të rrugës*
at the traffic	te dree-ta eh	*te drita e*
lights	tra-fee-koot/	*trafikut/*
	say-mah-fo-ree	*semafori*

behind	pra-hpa	*prapa*
in front of	pur-bahl/n' front t'	*përballë/në front të*
near	afur	*afër*
opposite	koon-dreyt	*kundrejt*

north	veh-ri	*veri*
south	yugh	*jug*
east	lin-dyeh	*lindje*
west	peh-ran-dim	*perëndim*

Booking Tickets

Where can I buy a ticket?

	koo moond ta blay nye bi-let?	*Ku mund të blej një biletë?*

Do I need to book?

	a doo-het ta byeh	*A duhet të bëj*
	re-zer-veem-in?	*rezervimin?*

I'd like to book a seat to ...

	duh-shee-roy t'	*Dëshiroj të*
	rez-er-voy nyevend per ...	*rezervoj një vend për ...*

Is it completely full?

	ahsht mboo-shoor plot?	*Eshtë mbushur plot?*

I'd like ...	d'sheeroy ...	Dëshiroj ...
a one-way ticket	nye bee-let vai-tyeh	një biletë vajtje
a return ticket	nye bee-let kthee-mee	një biletë kthimi
two tickets	doo bee-leta	dy bileta
a student's fare	nye bee-let me	një biletë me
	zbree-ye-tye	zbrietje
	per stu-dent	për student
1st class	klahss ee par	klas i parë
2nd class	klahss ee doot	klas i dytë

Bus & Tram

Where's the bus/tram stop?
  koo nda-let au-to-bu-see/   *Ku ndalet autobusi/*
  tram-vai?   *tramvaj?*
Which bus goes to ...?
  tsee-lee au-to-bus ve-teh-teh ...?   *Cili autobus vete te ...?*
Does this bus go to ...?
  ah ve-teh koo au-to-boos te ...?   *A vete ky autobus te ...?*
Could you let me know
when we get to ...?
  moond t' m'tre-gon-ee   *Mund të më tregoni*
  koort zbre-sseem te ...?   *kur të zbresim te ...?*
I want to get off!
  dwa teh zbress!   *Dua të zbres!*

What time's	n' ch' koh vyen/	Në ç' kohë vjen
the ... bus?	au-to-bu-see ...?	autobusi ...?
first	ee par	i parë
last	ee fun-dit	i fundit
next	tye-tr	tjetër

ALBANIAN

Train

Is this the right platform for ...?
    ah ahsht kyo   *A është kjo platforma për ...?*
    plat-for-ma per ...?
How long will it be delayed?
    per sah koh doht vo-no-het?   *Për sa kohë do të vonohet?*

THEY MAY SAY ...

tre-ni ni-set mga plat-for-ma ...
    The train leaves from platform ...
pa-sa-gye-rt (or u-the-tart) doo-et te nd'rroyn
tre-nat/plat-for-mat
    Passengers must change trains/platforms.
tre-ni vyen me vo-nes/ahsht ah-noo-loo-ahr
    The train is delayed/cancelled.
doht vo-no-het nya ... ohr
    There's a delay of ... hours.

Taxi

Please take me to ...
    yu lu-tem m'shpee-nee te ...   *Ju lutem më shpini te ...*
How much does it cost to go to ...?
    sah koosh-ton per t'   *Sa kushton për të*
    vai-toor ne ...?   *vajtur/në ...?*
Continue!
    vee-yo-nee!   *Vijoni!*
The next corner, please.
    n' kyo-shen tye-tr yu lu-tem   *Në qoshen tjetër, ju lutem.*
Stop here!
    ndahl k'-too!   *Ndal këtu!*

THEY MAY SAY ...
    ahsht plot   It's full.

The next street to the left/right.
   n' rroo-g'n tye-tr n' t'
   mung-yur/n' t' dyatht
       Në rrugën tjetër në të
       mëngjër/në të djathtë.

Here's fine, thanks.
   yu fa-lem nder-eet
   k'-too ahst meer
       Ju falem nderit,
       këtu është mirë.

Car

Where can I rent a car?
   ku mund ta mahrr meh
   ky-irah nya veh-tu-ra?
       Ku mund të marrë me
       qira një veturë?

How much is it daily/weekly?
   sah ku-shton par di-ta/
   par ya-va?
       Sa kushton për ditë/
       për javë?

Does that include insurance?
   ah a-shta par-fshir
   si-ghu-rah-tsi-o-ni?
       A është përfshirë
       siguracioni?

Where's the next petrol station?
   ku ahsht sta-tsi-on-ee
   tye-tr ee ben-zeens?
       Ku është stacioni
       tjetër i benzinës?

It's not working.
   nook poo-non
       Nuk punon.

ALBANIAN

air (for tyres)	ai-er	*ajër*
battery	ba-te-ri-a	*bateria*
brakes	fre-nat	*frenat*
clutch	lev kon-tro-lee	*levë kontroli*
drivers licence	leya eh sho-fe-reet	*leja e shoferit*
engine	mo-to-ree	*motori*
lights	dree-tat	*dritat*
oil	vai-ee	*vaji*
petrol	ben-zeen	*benzinë*
puncture	vree-muh	*vrimë*
radiator	ra-di-at-or-ee	*radiatori*
road map	hart rroo-gsh	*hartë rrugësh*
tyres	go-mat	*gomat*
windscreen	pen-ges eh-reh	*pengesë ere*

ACCOMMODATION
At the Hotel

Do you have any rooms available?

ah ke-nee ndo-ny'		A keni ndonjë
<u>th</u>om t' leer?		dhomë të lirë?

I'd like ...	oo-n' dwa ...	Unë dua ...
a single room	nye<u>th</u>om' me	një dhomë me
	nye kre-vat	një krevat
a double room	nye<u>th</u>om' me	një dhomë me
	du kre-vat	dy krevat
a room with	nye<u>th</u>om' me	një dhomë me
a bathroom	bah-ny'	banjë
to share a dorm	nye<u>th</u>o-m per	një dhomë për
	doo ve-tah	dy veta

I'm staying	doht kyen-droy	Do të qëndroj
for ...	per ...	për ...
one day	nye de-et	një ditë
two days	du de-et	dy ditë
one week	nye yah-v'	një javë

How much per night/person?

sah koosh-ton per nye naht/	Sa kushton për një natë/
nye-ree?	njeri?

Can I see it?

a moond tah show?	A mund ta shoh?

Are there any others?

a kah tetyehr?	A ka të tjerë?

Is there a discount
for students/children?

ah b'-nee zbree-tyeh	A bëni zbritje
per stu-dent/f mee?	për studentë/fëmijë?

Is there hot water all day?

a kah nyet ndzeht tre deet'n?	A ka një të nxehtë tërë ditën?

It's fine, I'll take it.

mee-r' ahsht po eh marr	Mirë është, po e marr.

Requests & Complaints

Do you have a safe where I can leave my valuables?

	ah ke-nee ny ark' si-gu-ree-mee koo t' l' gye-raht eh koosh-too-shmeh?	*A keni një arkë sigurimi ku të lë gjërat e kushtueshme?*

Is there some place to wash clothes?

	ah kah vend pur tuh lahr rro-baht?	*A ka vënd për të larë rrobat?*

I'd like to pay the bill.

	dwat pah-goo-ai fah-too-ram/ llog-har-eem	*Dua të paguaj faturën/llogarimë.*

It's too ...	dgho-mah a-shta shu-ma eh ...	*Dhoma është shumë e ...*
dark	eh-rrat eh	*errët e*
dirty	eh fa-lyi-kyur	*e fëliqur*
noisy	eh zhurm-shmeh	*e zhurmshme*
small	eh vo-ghal	*e vogël*

AROUND TOWN
At the Post Office

I'd like to send a/an ...	dwat post-ai nye ...	*Dua të postoj një ...*
aerogram	ai-ro-gram	*aerogram*
letter	le-t'r	*letër*
parcel	pa-ko	*pako*
postcard	kart-pos-ta-le	*kartpostale*
telegram	te-le-gram	*telegram*

ALBANIAN

ALBANIAN

I'd like some stamps.
    dwat sa poo-la pos-teh   *Dua ca pulla poste.*
How much is the postage?
    sah koosh-ton pos-tee-mee?   *Sa kushton postimi?*

airmail	le-t'r ai-ro-reh	*letër ajrore*
envelope	zarf	*zarf*
mail box	koo-tee pos-teh	*kuti poste*
parcel	pa-ko/ko-lee-post	*pako/kolipostë*
registered mail	le-t'r re-ko-man-deh	*letër rekomande*
surface mail	let-r'h thy-esht	*letër e thjeshtë*

Telephone

I want to ring ...
    dwat te-le-fo-noy ...   *Dua të telefonoj ...*
The number is ...
    noom-ree ahsht ...   *Numri është ...*
How much does a three-minute
call cost?
    sah koosh-toyn tree   *Sa kushtojnë tri*
    mi-noo-ta meh te-le-fon?   *minuta me telefon?*
How much does each extra
minute cost?
    sah koosh-ton chdo   *Sa kushton çdo*
    mi-noot eh ta-purt?   *minutë e tepërt?*
I'd like to speak to (Mr Perez).
    dwat flahs me (zoh-teen   *Dua të flas me (Zotin*
    pe-re-zin)   *Perezin).*
I want to make a
reverse-charges phone call.
    dwat bee nye te-le-fon du-keh   *Dua të bëj një telefon duke*
    pa-goor eth-eh per-gyee-gyen   *paguar edhe përgjigjen.*
It's engaged.
    ahsht zen   *Eshtë zënë.*
I've been cut off.
    ma pren te-le-fo-neen   *M' a prenë telefonin.*

SIGNS

DALJE	EXIT
DOGANA	CUSTOMS
E NDALUAR	PROHIBITED
E REZERVUAR	RESERVED
HAPUR/MBYLLUR	OPEN/CLOSED
HYRJE	ENTRANCE
HYRJE E LIRË	FREE ADMISSION
INFORMIM	INFORMATION
NDALOHET HYRJA!	NO ENTRY
NDALOHET	NO SMOKING
TË PIRIT E DUHANIT!	
NEVOJTORJA	TOILETS/RESTROOMS
NXEHTË/FTOHTË	HOT/COLD
ORAR	TIMETABLE
POLICIA	POLICE
STACIONI I POLICISË	POLICE STATION
TELEFONI	TELEPHONE
URGJENTE/DALJE E	EMERGENCY EXIT
JASHTZAKONSHME	
ZYRË BILETASH	TICKET OFFICE

ALBANIAN

Internet

Where can I get Internet access?
> kur mund ta kehm mun-da-si
> khu-ya-eh na in-tehr-neht?   *Kur mund të kem mundësi hyrjeje në internet?*

How much is it per hour?
> sah pah-ghu-kheht par
> nya o-ra?   *Sa paguhet për një orë?*

I want to check my email.
> du-ah ta kon-tro-loy pos-tan
> ti-meh eh-lehk-tro-ni-keh
> (em-al-in tim)   *Dua të kontrolloj postën time elektronike (emailin tim).*

ALBANIAN

At the Bank

Can I have money transferred
here from my bank?
    ah mund ta ma
    trahns-fehr-oyn pah-rah
    nghah bahn-kah I-meh?

*A mund të më transferojnë
para nga banka ime ?*

How long will it take to arrive?
    par sah ko-kha do ta
    ah-rriy-na pah-raht?

*Për sa kohë do të
arrijnë parat?*

I want to exchange some money/
travellers cheques.
    dwat t' hoo-ehee tsa (t' ho-lla/
    tsa che-keh uth-tarsh)

*Dua të thyej ca (të holla/
ca çeke udhëtarësh).*

What's the exchange rate?
    sah asht koor-see?

Sa është keersi?

How many leks per dollar?
    sah lek per nye do-llar?

Sa lekë për një dollar?

banknotes	pa-reh let-reh	*pare letre*
cashier	ark-tar	*arkëtar*
coins/currency	mo-ne-<u>tha</u>	*monedha*
credit card	kart kre-dee-yeh	*kartë kredije*
exchange	shk'm-beem	*shkëmbim*
signature	nen-shkreem	*nënshkrim*

INTERESTS & ENTERTAINMENT
Sightseeing

Do you have a
(guidebook/local map)?
    ah keh-nee nye
    (lee-b'r uth-zee-mesh/
    hart lo-ka-le)?

A keni një
(libër udhëzimesh/
hartë lokale)?

What are the main attractions?
    tsee-lat yahn gye-rat
    me t'rhe-kye-seh?

Cilat janë gjërat
më tërheqëse?

What's that?
    chahsht ai-oh?

Ç'është ajo?

How old is it?
    sah ee vyetr ahsht?

Sa i vjetër është?

Can I take photographs?
    ah moond tuh bay
    fo-to-gra-fee?

A mund të bëj
fotografi?

What time does it open/close?
    ne-chor ha-pet/mboo-let?

Në ç' orë hapet/mbyllet?

ancient	ahn-teek	*antik*
archaeological (site)	lok-ahl ar-ke-ho-lo-gheek	*lokal arkeologjik*
architecture	ar-kee-tek-too-ruh	*arkitekturë*
art gallery	ga-leh-ree eh ar-teet	*galeri e artit*
cathedral	kah-te-dral	*katedral*
excavations	gur-mee-meh	*gërmime*
mosque	djah-mee	*xhami*
museum	moo-zeh	*muze*
square	shehsh	*shesh*

Going Out

What's there to do in the evenings?
    chfa-rah mund tah bah-ni
    gya-tah mbra-hmi-jes

Çfarë mund të bëhet
gjatë mbrëmjes?

Are there any clubs around here?
    a ka clu-be?

A ka klube?

ALBANIAN

ALBANIAN

Are there places where you can
hear local folk music?

a ca ven-de cu mund tah
de-gyosh mu-zi-cah
po-pu-lore shqhip-ta-re?

*A ka vende ku mund të
degjosh muzikë
popullore shqiptare?*

How much is it to get in?

sa kush-ton bi-le-ta?

Sa cushton bileta?

cinema	ci-ne-ma	*kinema*
concert	con-cert	*koncert*
nightclub	dis-co	*disko*
theatre	te-at-ahr	*teatër*

Public Holidays

New Year's Day	vi-ti i ri	*Viti i Ri*
Christmas Day	krish-tah-lind-jet	*Kirishtlindjet*
Easter	pash-cat	*Pashkat*
Independence Day	di-ta e	*Dita e*
(28 Nov)	pa-va-rah-si-sah	*Pavarësisë*
Teacher's Day	di-ta e	*Dita e*
(7 Mar)	mah-sue-sit	*Mësuesit*

Sports & Interests

What sports do you play?

me chfa-rah sport me-re-ni?

Me cfarë sport merreni?

What interests do you have?

chfa-rah ja-nah
in-te-re-sat tu-ah-ya?

Çfarë janë interesat Tuaja.

art	art	*art*
basketball	bas-ket-bol	*basketboll*
chess	shah	*shah*
collecting things	ko-lek-tso-noy gya-hra	*koelkcionoj sende*
dancing	vall-zi-me	*vallzime*
food	ush-chi-me	*ushqim*
football	fut-bol	*futboll*
hiking	tu-riz-ahm	*turizëm*
martial arts	ar-te lu-fta-ra-ke	*arte luftarake*
meeting friends	tah ta-ko-hem me mich	*të takohem me miq*
movies	ci-ne-ma	*kinema*
music	mu-zi-cah	*muzikë*
nightclubs	lo-ca-le tah na-tah	*lokale të natës*
photography	pho-tog-ra-phy	*fotografi*
reading	tah led-zoj	*të lexoj*
shopping	tah bahy pa-zar	*të bëjë pazar*
skiing	ski sport	*ski sport*
swimming	tah no-toy	*të notoj*
tennis	te-nis	*tenis*
travelling	tah uth-ah-toy	*të udhetoj*
TV/videos	te-le-vi-zion/vi-de-o	*televizion/video*
visiting friends	tah bahy vi-ziah te micht	*të bëj vizitë te miqt*
walking	tah she-tis	*të shetis*

ALBANIAN

IN THE COUNTRY
Weather

Will it be ...	ah mos doht	*A mos të*
tomorrow?	yet ... nesr?	*jetë ... nesër?*
cloudy	vr'ret	*vrërët*
cold	fto-ht'	*ftohtë*
hot	ndze-ht'	*nxehtë*
raining	meh shee	*me shi*
snowing	meh bor	*me borë*
sunny	meh dyell	*me diell*
windy	meh ehr	*me erë*

ALBANIAN

What's the weather like?
   see ahsht klee-ma?   *Si është klima?*
The weather's ... today.
   ko-ha ahsht ... sot   *Koha është ... sot.*

Camping

Am I allowed to camp here?
   ah moond t' kyen-droy   *A mund të qëndroj*
   k'too per fu-sheem?   *këtu për pushim?*
Is there a campsite nearby?
   akah k'-too a-fer nye   *A ka këtu afër një*
   vend fu-shee-mee?   *vend pushimi?*

backpack	rruk-sak	*rruksak*
can opener	chel-see koo-tee-yash	*çelësi kutijash*
compass	kom-pas	*kompas*
firewood	droo zee-ya-ree	*dru zjarri*
gas cartridge	fee-shek ga-zee	*fishek gazi*
mattress	doo-shek	*dyshek*
penknife	breesk dje-pee	*brisk xhepi*
rope	li-tar	*litar*
tent	chah-der	*çadër*
tent pegs	pook cha-dreh	*pykë çadre*
torch/flashlight	pee-shtar	*pishtar*
sleeping bag	thes gyoo-mee	*thes gjumi*
stove	stoof/so-buh	*stufë/sobë*
water bottle	shee-sheh oo-yee	*shishe uji*

FOOD

breakfast	men-gyes	*mëngjes*
lunch	drek	*drekë*
dinner	dark	*darkë*

Vegetarian

I'm a vegetarian.
  yam veg-ye-ta-ri-an *Jam vegjetarian.*
I don't eat meat.
  nook hah meesh *Nuk ha mish.*

Breakfast Menu

bread	book	*bukë*
butter	gyal-p'	*gjalpë*
jam	mar-me-lahd	*marmeladë*
omelette	om-let	*omlet*

... eggs	vehz ...	*vezë ...*
fried	t' f'r-goo-ra	*të fërguara*
hardboiled	t' zi-eh-ra fort	*të ziera fort*
scrambled	t' ra-hoo-rah	*të rrahura*
softboiled	pahk t' zi-eh-ra	*pak të ziera*

Meat Dishes

shishquebap	grilled meat on a skewer
romstek	minced meat patties
çomlek	meat and onion stew
fërges	a rich beef stew
rosto me salcë kosi	roast beef with sour cream
tavë kosi	mutton with yogurt

Non-Alcoholic Drinks

coffee	ka-feh	*kafe*
fruit juice	lahng froo-tahsh	*lëng frutash*
mineral water	ooye mi-ner-ah-lee	*ujë minerali*
tea	chai	*çaj*
(boiled) water	u-ya (i vlyu-ahr)	*ujë (i vlur)*

ALBANIAN

ALBANIAN

Alcoholic Drinks

beer	beer	*birrë*
brandy	ra-kee	*raki*
cognac	kon-yak	*konjak*
wine	vehr	*verë*
red/white wine	veh-ra eh	*verë e*
	(kyuu-cheh/bahr-tha)	*(kuqe/bardhë)*

Staple Foods & Condiments

black pepper	pee-behr	*piber*
bread	book	*bukë*
butter	gyal-p'	*gjalpë*
cheese	dyah-th'	*djathë*
dessert	em-b'l-seer	*ëmbëlsirë*
eggs	vehz	*vezë*
flour	mi-el	*miel*
olive oil	vai-oo-lee-ree	*vaj ulliri*
macaroni	ma-ka-ro-na	*makarona*
pastries	pas-ta	*pasta*
rice	or-ees	*oriz*
salad	sa-laht	*salatë*
salt	kroop	*krypë*
soup	soop	*supë*
sugar	she-cher	*sheqer*
vinegar	oo-thool	*uthull*
yogurt	kos	*kos*

Meat & Fish

beef	meesh kaoo/lope	*mish kau/lope*
chicken	meesh poo-le	*mish pule*
fish	peshk	*peshk*
ham	pahr-shu-tah	*përshutë*
mutton	meesh dah-shee/deh-leh	*mish dashi/dele*
pork	meesh de-rree	*mish derri*
prosciutto	pro-shoot	*proshutë*
sardines	sar-de-leh	*sardele*
sausage	sa-lam	*sallam*
veal	meesh vee-chee	*mish viçi*

Vegetables

beans	grohsh	*groshë*
eggplant	paht-lee-djahn	*patlixhan*
onions	kyep	*qepë*
peppers	spe-tza/pee-pehr-kah	*speca/piperka*
potatoes	pa-ta-teh/k'r-to-la	*patate/kërtolla*
tomatoes	mo-la-ta-reh	*mollatare*

Fruit & Nuts

apple	moll	*mollë*
figs	feek	*fiq*
grapes	roosh	*rrush*
lemon	li-mon	*limon*
orange	por-to-ka-la	*portokalla*
peaches	pyeshk	*pjeshkë*
pear	darth	*dardhë*
tangerines	man-da-ri-na	*mandarina*
walnuts	ar-ra	*arra*

ALBANIAN

SHOPPING

How much is it?	sah koosh-ton?	*Sa kushton?*
general store	doo-kyan ee perg-yeeth-shem/ bah-kah-lan	*dyqan i përgjithshëm/ bakallanë*
grocer	pe-ree-mo-reh	*perimore*
laundry	lar-yeh ro-bash	*larje rrobash*
market	pa-zar	*pazar*
newsagency/ stationers	agyen-see-ah eh lai-me-veh/ kar-to-le-ree	*agjensia e lajmeve/ kartoleri*
chemist	far-maht-see	*farmaci*
supermarket	su-per-mar-ket	*supermarketë*

Do you accept credit cards?
  ah prah-no-ni kar-ta kreh-di-ti? *A pranoni karta krediti?*

ALBANIAN

Essential Groceries

I'd like ...	ma jyep-ni ...	*Më jepni ...*
bread	book	*bukë*
butter	gyalp	*gjalpë*
cheese	thja-tah	*dhjatë*
chocolate	cho-ko-la-tah	*çokollatë*
eggs	vez	*vez*
honey	mjalt	*mjalt*
margarine	mar-ga-rin	*margarin*
marmelade	re-chel	*reçel*
matches	shkrep-sah	*shkrepsë*
milk	chy-mahsht	*qumësht*
shampoo	sham-poo	*shampo*
soap	sa-pun	*sapun*
toilet paper	leahr hi-gye-ni-ke	*letër higjenike*
toothpaste	pas-tah thahm-bahsh	*pastë dhëmbësh*
washing powder	plu-hur la-rahs	*pluhur larës*

Clothing

clothing	vehsh-yeh	*veshje*
coat	pahl-to	*palto*
dress	fus-tahn	*fustan*
jacket	djah-ko vehn-to	*xhakovento*
jumper (sweater)	pu-lo-vehr	*pulover*
shirt	ka-mi-sha	*këmishë*
shoes	ka-pu-tsa	*këpucë*
skirt	fund	*fund*
trousers	pahn-to-lah	*pantolla*

Materials

cotton	pahm-buk	*pambuk*
handmade	pu-nim do-reh	*punim dore*
leather	la-nu-ra	*lëkurë*
brass	meh-singh	*mesing*
gold	ah-ri	*ari*
silver	ahr-ghehn-ti	*argjenti*
silk	mehn-dah-fa	*mendafsh*
wool	lehsh	*esh*

Souvenirs

alabaster vases	va-zo prej al-ab-as-tre	*vazo alabastre*
ashtrays	ta-vah-la du-ha-ni	*taveëll duhani*
copper utensils	ie-ne prej bak-ry	*ene prej bakri*
trays	ta-ka-bah	*tabakë*
Turkish coffeepots	djze-zve	*xhezve*
vases	va-zo	*vazo*
silver jewellery	biz-hu-te-ri argj-yen-ti	*bizhuteri argjenti*

Colours

black	zee	*zi*
blue	kahl-tert	*kaltërt*
brown	boy ka-feh	*bojë kafe*
green	gyel-ber	*gjelbër*
red	kooch	*kuq*
white	barth	*bardhë*
yellow	vehrth	*verdhë*

Toiletries

comb	kre-h'r	*krëhër*
condoms	pro-fee-lak-teks	*profilakteks*
deodorant	ehr-past-roo-eseh	*erëpastruese*
razor	breesk rrooes	*brisk rrues*
sanitary napkins	m's-al hee-gye-ni-ka	*mësallë higjenike*
shampoo	sham-poo/l'ng	*shampu/lëng*
	sa-poo-nee per flok	*sapuni për flokë*
shaving cream	sa-poon rroyeh	*sapun rroje*
soap	sa-poon	*sapun*
sunscreen	krehm ku-nar	*krem kundër*
	di-eh-gyehs sa	*djegjes së*
	ahs-eh-llit	*djellit*
tampons	lahmsh pam-boo-koo	*lëmsh pambuku*
	hee-gye-nik	*higjenik*
tissues	let-ra hee-gye-ni-ka	*letra higjenike*
toothbrush	foortz <u>th</u>em-b'sh	*furcë dhëmbësh*

ALBANIAN

ALBANIAN

Stationery & Publications

map	hart	*hartë*
(English-language) newspaper	ga-zet	*gazetë*
	ga-zet (ang-lisht)	*gazetë (anglisht)*
paper	le-t'r	*letër*
pen (ballpoint)	stee-lo-lahps	*stilolaps*

Photography

How much is it to process this film?
> sah ku-shton lah-rya eh   *Sa kushton larja e*
> na-tiy fil-mi?   *këtij filmi?*

When will it be ready?
> kur do ta yeh-ta ghah-ti?   *Kur do të jetë gatti?*

B&W (film)	film	*film*
camera	kah-meh-rah	*kamera*
colour (film)	film meh ngha-u-rah	*film me ngjyra*
film	film	*film*
flash	blits	*blic*
lens	o-byeh-ktiv	*objektiv*
light meter	mah-tas i dri-tas	*matës i dritës*

Smoking

A pack of cigarettes, please.
> nye pak-yet tsin-ga-reh   *Një paqetë cigare,*
> yu lu-tem   *ju lutem.*

Do you have a light?
> ah ke-nee shkrep-seh?   *A keni shkrepse?*

cigarette papers	le-t'r tsin-ga-ryeh	*letër cigareje*
cigarettes	tsin-ga-reh	*cigare*
filtered	fil-ter	*filter*
lighter	chak-mak	*çakmak*
matches	shkrep-seh	*shkrepse*
menthol	kam-foor/kya-foor	*kamfur/qafur*
tobacco	doo-hahn	*duhan*

Sizes & Comparisons

small	vo-gel	*vogël*
big	mahth	*madh*
heavy	rend	*rendë*
light	leyt	*lehtë*
more	me-shoom	*më shumë*
less	me-pahk	*më pak*
too much/many	te-p'r/se tep-rmee	*tepër/së tepërmi*

HEALTH

Where's a ...?	koo ahsht nye ...?	*Ku është një ...?*
chemist	kee-mist	*kimist*
dentist	den-tist/<u>th</u>em-tar	*dentist/dhëmbtar*
doctor	dok-tor	*doktor*
hospital	spi-tal	*spital*

ALBANIAN

Parts of the Body

arm	do-rah	*dorë*
back	shpi-nah	*shpinë*
chest	krah-nor	*krahnor*
ear	vesh	*vesh*
eye	syj	*sy*
finger	gisht	*gisht*
foot	kahm-bah	*këmbë*
hand	pah-lahm-bah	*pëllëmbë*
head	ko-kah	*kokë*
heart	ze-mahr	*zemër*
leg	kahm-bah	*këmbë*
mouth	go-jah	*gojë*
nose	hun-dah	*hundë*
skin	lah-ku-rah	*lëkurë*
spine	shty-la ku-riz-ore	*shtylla kurizore*
stomach	sto-mah	*stohah*
teeth	thahm-ba-la	*dhëmballa*
throat	gry-kah	*gjrykë*

ALBANIAN

Ailments

I have ...

a cold	yam fto-hoor	*Jam ftohur.*
constipation	me ka-zen bar-koo	*Më ka zënë barku.*
diarrhoea	mesh-kon bar-koo	*Më shkon barku.*
fever	kam eth-eh	*Kam ethe.*
headache	me themb	*Më dhëmb*
	ko-ka/kru-et	*koka/kryet.*
indigestion	me themb	*Më dhëmb*
	bar-ku	*barku.*
influenza	kam gree-peen	*Kam gripin.*
low/high	kam pre-si-on	*Kam presion*
blood	gya-koo t' oolt/t'	*gjaku të ulët/të*
pressure	lart	*lartë.*
sore throat	muh them groo-kah	*Më dhëmb gryka.*
sprain	kahm perd-rethoor	*Kam përdredhur.*
sunburn	oo do-gya nkah	*U dogja nga*
	dye-llee	*dielli.*
temperature	kahm tem-pe-ra-toor	*Kam temperaturë*
	t lart	*të lartë.*
toothache	kahm them-byeh	*Kam dhëmbje*
	them-bee	*dhëmbi.*

MAN IS NOT A CAMEL!

Albanian white wine is generally better than the vinegary red. That said, the red *Shesi e Zi* from either Librazhd or Berat is an excellent drop.

Raki, a clear brandy distilled from grapes, is taken as an apertif. There's also *konjak*, 'cognac', and various fruit liqueurs. *Fërnet* is a medicinal apertif containing herbal essences, made at Korça.

At the Chemist

I need medication for ...
    kam ne-voy per nye bar ...   *Kam nevojë për një bar ...*
I have a prescription.
    kam nye ret-set   *Kam një recetë.*

antiseptic	an-ti-sep-tik	*antiseptik*
bandage	lee<u>th</u>-seh	*lidhëse*
contraceptive	hah-pye koon-d'r	*hapje kundër*
	pye-lyes	*pjelljes*
medicine	me-det-seen/bar	*medicinë/bar*

ALBANIAN

At the Dentist

I have a toothache.
    ma thehmb tha-mbi   *Më dhemb dhëmbi.*
I've lost a filling.
    ma rah mbu-shya   *Më ra mbushja.*
My gums hurt.
    ma tha-mbin tha-mby-laht   *Më dhëmbin dhëmballat.*
I don't want it extracted.
    nuk du-ah shah ndzir-ni   *Nuk dua ta nxirrni.*

ALBANIAN

TIME & DATES

What date is it today?		
chasht dah-tah sot?		*Ç'është data sot?*
What time is it?		
sah ahsht ora?		*Sa është ora?*
It's ... am/pm.		
orahsht ... pa-ra-dre-keh/		*Ora është ... para dreke/*
pas-dre-keh		*pas dreke.*

in the morning	ne-mengyes	*në mëngjes*
in the afternoon	pah-sdre-keh	*pas dreke*
in the evening	nem-bre-myeh	*në mbrëmje*

Days

Monday	e hen	*e hënë*
Tuesday	eh mart	*e martë*
Wednesday	e mer-koor	*e mërkurë*
Thursday	eh ahn-y't-eh	*e ënjte*
Friday	eh prem-teh	*e premte*
Saturday	eh shtoon	*e shtunë*
Sunday	eh dyel	*e diel*

Months

January	yan-ar/kal-noor	*janar/kallnor*
February	shkoort	*shkurt*
March	mars	*mars*
April	pril	*prill*
May	mai	*maj*
June	kyer-shor	*qershor*
July	ko-rik	*korrik*
August	goosht	*gusht*
September	shtah-tor	*shtator*
October	te-tor	*tetor*
November	nen-tor	*nëntor*
December	<u>thye</u>-tor	*dhjetor*

Seasons

spring	prahn-vehr	*pranverë*
summer	vehr	*verë*
autumn	vyesht	*vjeshtë*
winter	dee-mer	*dimër*

Present

today	sot	*sot*
this morning	k't men-gyes	*këtë mëngjes*
tonight	sonteh	*sonte*
this week/year	k't veet	*këtë vit*
now	ta-nee	*tani*

Past

yesterday	dyeh	*dje*
(two) days ago	(du) deet m' par	*(dy) ditë më parë*

Future

tomorrow	nesr	*nesër*
in (two) days	pahsdu deet	*pas dy ditë*
last night	mbram	*mbrëm*
tomorrow night	neh-sar mbra-myeh	*nesër mbrëmje*
next week/year	ya-van eh ahrd-shmeh/	*javën e ardhshme/*
	vi-tin eh ard-sham	*vitin e ardhshëm*

During the Day

afternoon	pahs-dre-keh	*pas dreke*
day	deet	*ditë*
midnight	mes-naht	*mesnatë*
morning	men-gyes	*mëngjes*
night	naht	*natë*
noon/midday	drek	*drekë*
sunset	pren-dee-mee ee	*perëndimi i*
	dye-llit	*diellit*
sunrise	lind-ya eh die-llit	*lindja e diellit*

ALBANIAN

NUMBERS & AMOUNTS

0	ze-ro	*zero*
1	nyeh	*një*
2	du	*dy*
3	trey	*tre*
4	ka-t'r	*katër*
5	pes	*pesë*
6	gyasht	*gjashtë*
7	shtaht	*shtatë*
8	tet	*tetë*
9	nent	*nëntë*
10	<u>thy</u>et	*dhjetë*
20	nye-zet	*njëzet*
100	nye-kyint	*njëqind*
1000	nye-mee	*njëmijë*
one million	nye-milion	*një milion*

ALBANIAN

Useful Words

Enough!	myahft!	*Mjaft!*
a little (amount)	pahk	*pak*
few	pahk	*pak*
more	me-shoom	*më shumë*
some	dee-sah	*disa*
too much	tepr	*tepër*

ABBREVIATIONS

SIDA	AIDS
pd/md	am/pm
Z./Zonjës/Zonjushës	Mr/Mrs/Ms
V/J	Nth/Sth

EMERGENCIES

Help!	n'deem!	*Ndihmë!*
Go away!	zhdoo-koo nee!	*Zhduku ni!*
Thief!	hai-doot!	*Hajdut!*

There's been an accident.
    kan-do-thoor nye ak-si-dent   *Ka ndodhur një aksident.*
Call a doctor!
    thee-reh-nee dok-to-rin!   *Thirrni doktorin!*
Call an ambulance!
    thee-reh-nee am-bu-lan-tsin!   *Thirrni ambulancën!*
Call the police!
    thee-reh-nee po-lee-sin!   *Thirrni policinë!*
I've been raped.
    m' kahn pur-thoon-oor   *Më kanë përdhunuar.*
I've been robbed.
    m' kahn plah-chkee-toor   *Më kanë plaçkitur.*
Where's the police station?
    koo ahsht stat-si-on-ee ee   *Ku është stacioni i*
    po-lit-sees?   *policisë?*
I'm lost.
    yam hoom-boor rrug'n   *Jam humbur rrugën.*
Where are the toilets?
    koo ahsht ne-voy-tor-ya?   *Ku është nevojtorja?*
Could you help me please?
    ah moond te me   *A mund të më*
    ndee-mo-nee yu lu-tem?   *ndihmoni, ju lutem?*
Could I please use the telephone?
    ah moond ta pur-dor   *A mund ta përdor*
    te-le-fo-neen yu lu-tem?   *telefonin, ju lutem?*
I'm sorry. I apologise.
    m' vyen shoom kech.   *Më vjen shumë keq.*
    yu ker-koy nd'yess   *Ju kërkoj ndjesë.*

I'm ill.	yam ee smoor	*Jam i sëmurë.*
I didn't do it.	oon se bera	*Unë s' e bëra.*

ALBANIAN

ALBANIAN

I didn't realise I was doing anything wrong.

nook m' vai-tee neh mend se po bya kech

Nuk më vajti në mend se po bëja keq.

I want to contact my embassy/consulate.

d'shee-roy te bey li-thya me am-ba-sa-din/kon-su-la-tin

Dëshiroj të bëj lidhje me ambasadën/konsullatën.

I speak English.

oon flahss ahn-gleesht

Unë flas anglisht.

My possessions are insured.

oon ee kam plach-kat t' si-gu-roo-ra

Unë i kam plaçkat të siguruara.

My friend is ill.

mee-koo eem ahsht ee smoor

Miku im është i sëmurë.

I have medical insurance.

oon kam si-gu-rim myek-sor

Unë kam sigurim mjekësor.

I've lost my ...	kam hoom-boor ...	*Kam humbur ...*
baggage/ suitcases	trahs-tat/va-lee-djer	*trastat/valixher*
handbag	chahnt-'n pah-leeg-yen	*çantën paligjen*
money	t' hol-laht	*të hollat*
travellers cheques	chek-yet e uth-'tee-meet	*çeqet e udhëtimit*
passport	pa-sa-por-ten	*pasaportën*

BULGARIAN

QUICK REFERENCE

Hello.	zdrah-*vehy*-teh	Здравейте.
Goodbye.	do-*vizh*-dah-neh	Довиждане.
Yes./No.	dah/neh	Да./Не.
Excuse me.	iz-vi-*neh*-teh	Извинете.
Sorry.	sa-zhah-*lya*-vahm	Съжалявам
(excuse me)	(pro-*shtah*-vahy-the)	(прощавайте).
Please.	*mo*-lya	Моля.
Thank you.	blah-gho-dah-*rya* mehr-*si*	Благодаря мерси.
You're welcome.	*nya*-mah zah-*shto*	няма защо.
Where's ...?	ka-deh seh nah-mi-rah ...?	Къде се намира ...?

What time is it?
kol-ko eh chah-*sat*?   Колко е часът?

Where are the toilets?
ka-*deh* i-mah to-ah-*leh*-tni?   Къде има тоалетни?

Do you speak English?
gho-*vo*-ri-teh li ahn-*ghliy*-ski?   Говорите ли английски?

How much is it?
kol-ko stru-vah?   Колко струва?

I'd like a ...	bikh zheh-*lahl* ...	Бих желал ...
single room	*stah*-ya s eh-*dno*	стая с едно
	leh-*ghlo*	легло

I'd like a ...	*mo*-lya dahy-teh-mi	Моля, дайте ми
ticket.	bi-*leht* ... f eh-*dnah*	билет ... в една.
one-way	po-so-kah	посока
return ticket	zah o-*ti*-vah-neh	за отиване
	i vra-shtah-neh	и връщане

How do I get to ...?
kahk dah sti-ghnah do ...?   Как да стигна до ...?

Turn left/right	zah-*viy*-teh nah-*lya*-vo/	Завийте наляво/
at the ...	nah-dya-sno ...	надясно ...
next corner	nah slehd-*vah*-	на следва-
	shti-ya a-ghal	щия ъгъл
traffic lights	pri sfeh-to-fah-rah	при светофара

1	eh-*din*	един	6	shehs	шест
2	dvah	два	7	*seh*-dehm	седем
3	tri	три	8	o-sehm	осем
4	*cheh*-ti-ri	четири	9	*deh*-veht	девет
5	peht	пет	10	*deh*-seht	десет

BULGARIAN

BULGARIAN

Modern Bulgarian belongs to the group of South Slavonic languages. It is the descendant of the oldest Slavonic literary language, Old Bulgarian (also called Old Slavic or Old Church Slavonic). Originally formulated in connection with the missionary work of the Salonica brothers, Cyril and Methodius, during the 9th century AD, Old Bulgarian flourished in the Bulgarian lands for several centuries, giving rise to an original literary and cultural tradition which continues to thrive.

Today Bulgarian is the native language of more than nine million speakers who make up the Slavonic ethnic majority of the Republic of Bulgaria. It is the second language of several linguistic minorities in the country, including speakers of Turkish, Romany, Armenian, Greek and Romanian. While Contemporary Standard Bulgarian is the official language of the Republic of Bulgaria, historical and social factors have given rise to regional varieties in neighbouring areas. In Bulgaria itself, a number of regional dialects are common, and Bulgarian is spoken by sizable groups in the former USSR, Canada, Argentina and in some other countries.

Bulgarian has affinities with all other Slavonic languages. It's losely related to Russian, which also uses the Cyrillic alphabet (with a few minor differences). But unlike Russian, Polish, Czech and other Slavonic languages, Modern Bulgarian has lost its grammatical case endings. A number of similarities with other Balkan languages within the Balkan Sprachbund (Greek, Albanian and Romanian) also gives Bulgarian a unique place among the Slavonic languages.

Bulgarians are generally friendly and very approachable. If you don't have the time to learn the intricacies of local etiquette and body language, rest assured that the use of the polite forms, accompanied by a friendly smile, will take you a long way in Bulgaria. Have a great time!

PRONUNCIATION

To a great extent, Bulgarian is written as it's spoken, with almost every letter corresponding with only one sound. Most Bulgarian sounds also occur in the English, with some slight differences. With a little practice, you'll have no problems making yourself understood. Following are the transliterations used in this chapter.

а	ah		м	m
е	eh		н	n
о	o		п	p
и	i		р	r
ъ	a		с	s
у	u		т	t
б	b		ф	f
в	v		х	kh
г	gh		ц	ts
д	d		ч	ch
ж	zh		ш	sh
з	z		щ	sht
й	y		ю	yu
к	k		я	ya
л	l			

BULGARIAN

Transliterations
Vowels

Contemporary Standard Bulgarian has six vowels. They are more rounded and tense in articulation than English vowels. They are of medium length, whereas English has two distinct classes of short and long vowels.

All vowels occur in stressed and in non-stressed syllables. Non-stressed vowels are shorter and weaker.

a	as the 'a' in 'soda'
ah	as the 'a' in 'father' but shorter
eh	as the 'e' in 'bet'
o	as the 'o' in 'pot'
i	as 'i' in 'it'
u	as the 'u' in 'pull'

Consonants

Consonants not described here are pronounced as in English, but much less emphatically.

ch	as the 'ch' in 'chop'
gh	as the 'g' in 'goat'
kh	as the 'ch' in Scottish 'loch'
r	trilled
s	as the 's' in 'sin'
sht	as the 'shed' in 'pushed'
ts	as the 'ts' in 'bets'
y	as 'y' in 'yes'
ya	as 'ya' in 'yard', but shorter
yu	as 'yu' in 'youth', but shorter
zh	as the 's' in 'pleasure'

The pronunciation of some letters changes at the end of a word or when they appear before a voiceless consonant (one where the vocal chords don't vibrate. For example, 'f' is unvoiced while 'v' is voiced). The following voiced consonants become voiceless:

б	b	sounds like	п	p
в	v	sounds like	ф	f
г	gh	sounds like	к	k
ж	zh	sounds like	ш	sh
з	z	sounds like	с	s
д	d	sounds like	т	t

snow	snyagh	сняг
sounds like ...	snyak	

to sign	pod-*pi*-shah	подпиша
sounds like ...	pot-*pi*-shah	

At the end of a word, 't' is dropped. For example:

the back	*ghar*-bat	гърбът
sounds like ...	*ghar*-ba	

night	nosht	нощ
sounds like ...	nosh	

Stress

There's no general rule as to where stress should fall on a word. The position of stress of each word can change with the different grammatical forms of a word. In this chapter, stressed syllables are given in italics in transliterations.

QUESTION WORDS		
How?	kahk?	Как?
When?	ko-*ghah*?	Кога?
Where?	ka-*deh*?	Къде?
Which?	*koy*?	Кой?
Who?	koy?	Кой?
Why?	za-*shto*?	Защо?

SUBJECT PRONOUNS		
SG		
I	ahz	аз
you (inf)	ti	ти
you (pol)	vi-eh	Вие
he/she/it	toy/tya/to	той/тя/то
PL		
we	ni-eh	ние
you	vi-eh	вие
they	teh	те

GREETINGS & CIVILITIES
Top Useful Phrases

Hello.	zdrah-*vehy*-teh	Здравейте.
Goodbye.	do-*vizh*-dah-neh	Довиждане.
Yes./No.	dah/neh	Да./Не.
Excuse me.	iz-vi-*neh*-teh	Извинете.
Please.	*mo*-lya	Моля.

May I? Do you mind?
   mo-ghah li. *i*-mah-teh
   li *neh*-shto pro-*tif*?
Мога ли. Имате
ли нещо против?

Sorry. (excuse me, forgive me)
   sa-zhah-*lya*-vahm
   (pro-*shtah*-vahy-the)
Съжалявам
(прощавайте).

Thank you.
   blah-gho-dah-*rya* mehr-*si*
Благодаря мерси.

Many thanks.
   mno-*gho* (vi) blah-gho-dah-*rya*
Много (ви) благодаря.

That's fine. You're welcome.
   mo-lya, *nya*-mah zah-*shto*
Моля, няма защо.

BULGARIAN

Greetings

Good morning.	do-*bro u*-tro	Добро утро.
Good afternoon.	*do*-bar dehn	Добър ден.
Good evening/	*do*-bar *veh*-chehr	Добър вечер
night.	*leh*-kah nosh	лека нощ.
How are you?	kahk steh?	Как сте?
Well, thanks.	blah-gho-dah-*rya*,	Багодаря,
	do-*breh* sam	добре съм.

Forms of Address

Madam/Mrs	ghos-*po*-zho	госпожо
Sir/Mr	ghos-po-*di*-neh	господине
Miss	ghos-*po*-zhi-tseh	госпожице
friend	pri-*ya*-tel-yu	приятелю

BULGARIAN

DID YOU KNOW ...

An ancient Greek myth ascribed a Thracian origin to Orpheus and the Muses. Bulgarians today are renowned singers and the country's Orthodox religious chants are the equivalent of classical music in the West.

Bulgarian ecclesiastic music dating back to the 9th century played a key role in the 19th-century Bulgarian National Revival.

SMALL TALK
Meeting People

What's your name?
  kahk seh *kahz*-vah-teh?   Как се казвате?

My name's ...
  kahz-vahm seh ...   Казвам се ...

I'd like to introduce you to ...
  poz-vo-*leh*-teh dah vi   Позволете да ви
  preht-*stah*-vya nah ...   представя на ...

Pleased to meet you.
  pri-*ya*-tno mi eh dah she   Приятно ми е да се
  zah-poz-*nah*-ya z vahs   запозная с Вас.

How old are you?
  nah *kol*-ko ste gho-*di*-ni?   На колко сте години?

I am ... (years old).
  nah ... (gho-*di*-ni sam)   На ... (години съм).

Nationalities

Where are you from?
  ot-ka-*deh* steh?   Откъде сте?

I am from ...	ahs sam ot ...	Аз съм от ...
Australia	ahf-*strah*-li-ya	Австралия
Canada	kah-*nah*-dah	Канада
England	*ahn*-ghli-ya	Англия
Ireland	ir-*lahn*-di-ya	Ирландия
New Zealand	*no*-vah zeh-*lahn*-di-ya	Нова Зеландия
Scotland	sho-*tlahn*-di-ya	Шотландия
the USA	sa-eh-di-*neh*-ni-teh *shtah*-ti	Съединените Щати
Wales	u-*ehls*	Уелс

Occupations

What is your occupation?
   kah-*kaf* steh po   Какъв сте по
   pro-*feh*-si-ya?   професия?

I'm unemployed.
   behz-ra-*bo*-tehn/   Безработен/
   bez-ra-*bot*-na sam   Безработна съм.   (m/f)

I'm a/an ...	ahs sam ...	Аз съм ...
artist	khu-*dozhnk*	художник (m)
	khu-*dozh*-nich-kah	художничка (f)
business person	bi-zneh-*smehn*	бизнесмен
computer	kom-*pyu*-ta-rehn	компютърен
programmer	pro-ghra-*mist*	програмист
doctor	*leh*-kahr	лекар (m)
	leh-kah	лека (f)
engineer	in-zheh-*nehr*	инженер
farmer	*fehr*-mehr	фермер
journalist	zhur-nah-*lis*	журналист (m)
	zhur-nah-*lis*-kah	журналистка (f)
lawyer	ahd-vo-*kaht*	адвокат
manual worker	fi-*zi*-cheh-ski	физически
	rah-*bo*-tnik	работник
mechanic	meh-*khah*-nik	механик
nurse	meh-di-*tsin*-skah	медицинска
	sehs-*trah*	сестра (f)
office worker	chi-*no*-vnik	чиновник (m)
	chi-*no*-vnich-kah	чиновничка (f)
scientist	*u*-chehn	учен
student	stu-*dehnt*	студент (m)
	stu-*dehnt*-kah	студентка (f)
teacher	u-*chi*-tel	учител (m)
	u-*chi*-tel-kah	учителка (f)
waiter	*kehl*-nehr	келнер (m)
	kehl-nehr-kah	келнерка (f)
writer	pi-*sah*-tel	писател (m)
	pi-*sah*-tel-kah	писателка (f)

Religion

What's your religion?
kai-ghi-yahk-vah *re*-l
is-po-vya-*dah*-teh?

Каква религия
изповядате?

I'm not religious.
neh sam *vyar*-vahsh/
vyar-vah-shtah

Не съм вярващ/
вярваща. (m/f)

I'm ...	ahs sam ...	Аз съм ...
Buddhist	bu-*dist*	будист (m)
	bu-*dist*-kah	будистка (f)
Christian	khris-ti-*ya*-nin	християнин (m)
	khris-ti-*yan*-kah	християнка (f)
Hindu	in-*dus*	индус (m)
	in-*dus*-kah	индуска (f)
Jewish	eh-*vreh*-in	евреин (m)
	eh-*vrehy*-kah	еврейка (f)
Muslim	myu-syul-*mah*-nin	мюсюлманин (m)
	myu-syul-*mahn*-kah	мюсюлманка (f)
Orthodox	pra-vo-*slah*-vehn	православен (m)
	pra-vo-*slahv*-na	православна (f)

BULGARIAN

Family

Are you married?
zheh-nehn/o-*ma*-zheh-nah
li ste?

Женен/Омъжена
ли сте? (m/f)

I'm single.
neh *sam zheh*-nehn/
o-*ma*-zheh-nah

Не съм женен/
омъжена. (m/f)

I'm married.
zheh-nehn/
o-*ma*-zheh-nah sam

Женен/Омъжена
съм. (m/f)

How many children do you have?
kol-ko deh-*tsah* i-mah-teh?

Колко деца имате?

I don't have any children.
nya-mahm de-*tsah*

Нямам деца.

I have a daughter/son.
i-mahm da-shteh-*rya*/sin

Имам дъщеря/син.

Is your husband/wife here?
sa-*pru*-ghat/sa-*pru*-
ghah-tah vi tuk li eh?

Съпругът/съпругата
Ви тук ли е?

Do you have a boyfriend/
girlfriend?
i-mah-teh li pri-*ya*-tehl/
pri-*ya*-tehl-kah?

Имате ли приятел/
приятелка?

brother	braht	брат
children	deh-*tsah*	деца
daughter	da-shteh-*rya*	дъщеря
family	seh-*mehy*-stvo	семейство
father	bah-*shtah*	баща
grandfather	*dya*-do	дядо
grandmother	*bah*-bah	баба
husband	sa-*pruk*	съпруг
mother	*mahy*-kah	майка
sister	seh-*strah*	сестра
son	sin	син
wife	sa-*pru*-ghah	съпруга

Feelings

I (don't) like ...
    (neh) khah-*rehs*-vahm ...   (Не) харесвам ...

I'm ...	... sam	... съм.
angry	*ya*-do-sahn	Ядосан (m)
	ya-do-sah-nah	Ядосана (f)
grateful	blah-gho-dah-rehn	Благодарен (m)
	blah-gho-dahr-nah	Благодарна (f)
happy	*rah*-do-stehn	Радостен (m)
	rah-do-snah	радостна (f)
hungry	*ghlah*-dehn	Гладен (m)
	ghlah-dnah	Гладна (f)
right	prahf/*prah*-vah	Прав/Права (m/f)
thirsty	*zhah*-dehn	Жаден (m)
	zhah-dnah	Жадна (f)
tired	iz-mo-*rehn*	Изморен (m)
	iz-mo-*reh*-nah	Изморена (f)
well	do-*breh* sam	Добре

I'm ...		
cold	stu-*deh*-no mi eh	Студено ми е.
hot	gho-*reh*-shto mi eh	Горещо ми е.
sad	*ta*-zhno mi eh	тъжно ми е.
sleepy	spi mi seh	Спи ми се.
sorry	sa-zhah-*lya*-vahm	Съжалявам.
(condolence)		

Useful Phrases

Sure.	dah, rahz-*bi*-rah seh	Да, разбира се.
Just a minute.	*sah*-mo zah mo-*mehnt*	Само за момент.
It's important.	*vah*-zhno eh	Важно е.
It's not	neh eh *vah*-zhno	Не е важно.
important.		
It's possible .	va-*zmo*-zhno eh	възможно е.
It's not possible.	neh *eh* va-*zmo*-zhno	Не е възможно.
Wait!	po-*chah*-kahy-teh!	Почакайте!
Good luck!	us-*pehkh*!	Успех!

BREAKING THE LANGUAGE BARRIER

Do you speak English?
  gho-*vo*-ri-teh li
  ahn-*ghliy*-ski?

Говорите ли
английски?

Does anyone speak English?
  nya-koy gho-*vo*-ri li
  ahn-*ghliy*-ski?

Някой говори ли
английски?

I (don't) understand.
  (neh) rahz-*bi*-rahm

(Не) разбирам.

Could you speak more
slowly please?
  bikh-*teh li mo*-ghli *dah*
  gho-vo-*ri-teh* po bah-*vno*
  mo-*lya?*

Бихте ли могли да
говорите по-бавно,
моля?

Could you repeat that?
  bikh-*teh li mo*-ghli *dah*
  pof-*to-ri-teh to*-vah?

Бихте ли могли да
повторите това?

How do you say ...?
  kahk kahz-*vah-teh* ...?

Как казвате ...?

What does ... mean?
  kahk-vo o-*znah*-chah-
  vah ...?

Какво означава ...?

BODY LANGUAGE

Bulgarians don't normally confine themselves to mere speech. As speaking usually involves at least two parties in sight of each other, a great deal of meaning is conveyed by facial expression, tone of voice and movements and postures of the whole body – especially of the hands.

There are few, if any, aspects of body language that are likely to cause confusion, with one important exception: Bulgarians shake their head from side to side to signify 'yes', and nod their head up and down to indicate 'no'. As is common elsewhere, the shrugging of shoulders means 'I don't know'.

PAPERWORK

name	*i*-meh	име
address	ahd-*rehs*	адрес
date of birth	*dah*-tah nah *rahzh*-dah-neh	дата на раждане
place of birth	meh-sto-rozh-*deh*-ni-eh	месторождение
age	va-zrahs	възраст
sex	pol	пол
nationality	nah-*ro*-dnos	народност
next of kin	*nahy bli*-zak ro-*dni*-nah	най-близък роднина
religion	veh-ro-is-po-veh-*dah*-ni-eh	вероизповедание

reason for travel	tsehl na pa-*tu*-vah-neh-to	цел на пътуването
profession	pro-*feh*-si-ya	професия
marital status	seh-*mehy*-no po-lo-zheh-ni-eh	семейно положение
passport	pahs-*port*	паспорт
passport number	*no*-mehr nah pahs-*por*-tah	номер на паспорта
visa	*vi*-zah	виза
identification	do-ku-*mehnt* zah sah-mo-*li*-chnos	документ за самоличност
birth certificate	svi-*deh*-tehl-stvo zah *rah*-zhdah-neh	свидетелство за раждане
driver's licence	svi-*deh*-tehl-stvo zah prah-vo-u-prah *vleh*-ni-e	свидетелство за правоупра вление

BULGARIAN

BULGARIAN

SIGNS

ЗАТВОРЕНО	CLOSED
АВАРИЕН ИЗХОД	EMERGENCY EXIT
ВХОД	ENTRANCE
ИЗХОД	EXIT
ВХОД СВОБОДЕН	FREE ADMISSION
ГОРЕЩО/СТУДЕНО	HOT/COLD
ИНФОРМАЦИЯ	INFORMATION
ВХОД ЗАБРАНЕН	NO ENTRY
ПУШЕНЕТО ЗАБРАНЕНО	NO SMOKING
ОТВОРЕНО	OPEN
ЗАБРАНЕНО	PROHIBITED
ЗАПАЗЕНА	RESERVED
ТЕЛЕФОН	TELEPHONE
ТОАЛЕТНИ	TOILETS

GETTING AROUND

What time does the ... leave/arrive?	f *kol*-ko chah-*sa zah-mi-nah-vah pri-sti-ghah* ...?	В колко часа заминава пристига ...?
aeroplane	sah-mo-*leh*-tah	самолетът
bus (city)	*ghraht*-ski-ya ah-fto-*bus*	градския автобус
bus (intercity)	mehzh-du-*ghraht*-ski-ya ah-fto-*bus*	междуград-ският автобус
train	*vlah*-kah	влакът
tram	trahm-*vah*-ya	трамваят

Directions

Where's ...?
ka-deh *seh* nah-mi-*rah* ...?   Къде се намира ...?
How do I get to ...?
kahk dah sti-*ghnah do* ...?   Как да стигна до ...?

Is it far/close by?
dah-leh-*cheh*/bli-*zo*
li eh ot tuk?

далече/близо
ли е от тук?

Can I walk there?
mo-*ghah* li dah sti-*ghnah*
peh-shah do tahm?

Мога ли да стигна
пеша до там?

Can you show me (on the map)?
mo-*zheh*-teh li dah mi
po-kah-*zheh*-teh (na
kahr-*tah*-tah)?

Можете ли да ми
покажете (на
Картата)?

I want to go to ...
is-*kahm* dah o-ti-*dah* do ...

Искам да отида до ...

Go straight ahead.
var-veh-teh nah-prah-*vo*

Вървете направо.

It's farther down.
po-*nah*-do-*lu eh*

По-надолу е.

BULGARIAN

Turn left/right ...	*zah*-viy-*teh*	Завийте
	nah-lya-*vo*/	наляво/
	nah-dya-*sno* ...	надясно ...
at the next corner	*nah* slehd-	на следващия
	vah-shti-ya a-*ghal*	ъгъл
at the traffic lights	*pri sfeh-to-fah-rah*	при
		светофара

behind	zaht	зад
in front of	preht	пред
far	dah-*leh*-cheh	далече
near	*bli*-zo	близо
opposite	*sreh*-shtu	срещу

north	*seh*-vehr	север
south	yuk	юг
east	*i*-stok	изток
west	*zah*-pat	запад

Booking Tickets

Where can I buy a ticket?
ka-*deh* *mo*-ghah dah si
ku-pya bi-*leht*?

Къде мога да си
купя билет?

I want to go to ...
is-kahm dah
pa-*tu*-vahm do ...

Искам да
пътувам до ...

Do I need to book?
tryab-vah li dah si *ku*-pya
prehd-vah-*ri*-tehl-no
bi-*leht*?

Трябва ли да си
купя предварително
билет?

I'd like to book a seat to ...
bikh *is*-kahl bi-*leht* saz
zah-*pah*-zeh-no *myas*-to
do ...

Бих искал билет
със запазено
място до ...

I'd like ...	*mo*-lya *dahy*-teh-mi ...	Моля, дайте ми ...
a one-way ticket	bi-*leht* f eh-*dnah* po-*so*-kah	билет в една посока
a return ticket	bi-*leht* zah o-*ti*-vah-neh i *vra*-shtah-neh	билет за отиване и връщане
two tickets	dvah bi-*leh*-tah	два билета
tickets for all of us	bi-*leh*-ti zah *fsich*-ki nahs	билети за всички нас
a student's fare	u-cheh-*ni*-cheh-ski stu-*dehn*-ski bi-*leht*	ученически студентски билет
a child's/ pensioner's fare	*deht*-ski/ pehn-si-o-*nehr*-ski bi-*leht*	детски/ пенсионерски билет
1st class	*par*-vah *klah*-sah	първа класа
2nd class	*fto*-rah *klah*-sah	втора класа

BULGARIAN

Bus

Where's the bus stop?
  ka-*deh* eh ahf-to-*bu*-
  snah-tah *spir*-kah?

Къде е автобусната
спирка?

Which bus goes to ...?
  koy ahf-to-*bus* o-*ti*-vah
  do ...?

Кой автобус отива
до ...?

Does this bus go to ...?
  to-zi ahf-to-*bus*
  o-*ti*-vah li do ...?

Този автобус
отива ли до ...?

How often do buses pass by?
  nah *kol*-ko *vreh*-meh
  mi-*nah*-vaht ahf-to-*bu*-si?

На колко време
минават автобуси?

Could you let me know
when we get to ...?
  bikh-teh li mi *kah*-zah-li,
  ko-*ghah*-to *sti*-ghnehm
  do ...?

Бихте ли ми
казали, когато
стигнем до ...?

I want to get off!
  is-kahm dah *slya*-zah!

Искам да сляза!

What time's the   f *kol*-ko chah-*sa*   В колко часа
... bus?   eh ... *ahf*-to-*bus?*   е ... автобус?
  first   *par*-vi-ya   първият
  last   po-*sleh*-dni-ya   последният
  next   slehd-vah-*shti*-ya   следващият

Train & Metro

Which line takes me to ...?
  s ko-*ya li*-ni-ya shteh
  sti-gnah do ...?

С коя линия ще
стигна до ...?

What's the next station?
  ko-*ya* eh *slehd*-vah-shtah-tah
  spir-kah *stahn*-tsi-ya?

Коя е следващата
спирка станция?

Is this the right platform for ...?
  to-*vah* li eh peh-*ro*-na
  zah ...?

Това ли е перонът
за ...?

Is that seat taken?
  to-*vah myas*-to *zah-eh*-to li eh?

Това място заето ли е?

dining car	vah-*ghon* rehs-to-*rahnt*	вагон-ресторант
express	ehks-*prehs* barz vlahk	експрес бърз влак
local	krahy-*graht*-ski vlahk	крайградски влак
passenger train	pa-tni-chehs-ki vlahk	пътнически влак
sleeping car	*spah*-lehn vah-*ghon*	спален вагон

THEY MAY SAY ...

pa-tni-tsi-teh   Passengers must ...
tryab-vah dah ...
  smeh-*nyat vlah*-kah   change trains
  o-*ti*-daht nah druk   change platforms
  peh-*rohn*

vlah-kah zah-mi-*nah*-vah ot peh-*rohn* ...
  The train leaves from platform ...
vlah-kat i-mah zah-ka-*sneh*-ni-eh/eh o-tmeh-*nehn*.
  The train is delayed/cancelled.
i-mah ... chah-sah zah-ka -*sneh*-ni-eh
  There's a delay of ... hours.

BULGARIAN

Taxi

Can you take me to ...?
  mo-zheh-teh li dah meh
  zah-*kah*-rah-teh do ...?

Можете ли да ме
закарате до ...?

Please take me to ...
  mo-lya zah-*kah*-rahy-teh
  meh do ...

Моля, закарайте
ме до ...

How much does it cost
to go to ...?
  kol-ko *stru*-vah do ...?

Колко струва до ...?

Here's fine, thank you.
  tuk eh do-*breh*,
  blah-gho-dah-*rya*

Тук е добре,
благодаря.

The next corner, please.
  nah *slehd*-vah-shti-ya
  a-gal *mo*-lya

На следващия
ъгъл, моля.

Continue!
  pro-dal-*zhah*-vahy-teh!

Продължавайте!

The next street to the left/right.
  slehd-vah-shtah-tah
  u-li-tsah nah-lya-vo/
  nah-*dya*-sno

Следващата
улица наляво/
надясно.

Stop here!
  spreh-teh tuk!

Спрете тук!

Please slow down.
  mo-lya nah-mah-*leh*-teh

Моля, намалете.

Please wait here.
  mo-lya *chah*-kahy-teh tuk

Моля, чакайте тук.

Car

Where can I hire a car?
  ka-*deh mo*-ghah dah
  nah-*eh*-mah ko-*lah*?

Къде мога да
наема кола?

How much is it daily/weekly?
  kol-ko *stru*-vah nah dehn/
  nah *seh*-dmi-tsah?

Колко струва на
ден/на седмица?

Does that include insurance/
mileage?
   to-*vah fklyuch*-vah li
   zah-strah-*khof*-kah-tah/
   pro-beh-gah?

Това включва ли
застраховката/
пробега?

Where's the next petrol station?
   ka-*deh* seh nah-*mi*-rah
   slehd-vah-shtah-tah
   behn-zi-no-*stahn*-tsi-ya?

Къде се намира
следващата
бензиностанция?

How long can I park here?
   zah *kol*-ko *vreh*-meh
   mo-ghah dah
   pahr-*ki*-rahm tuk?

За колко време
мога да
паркирам тук?

Does this road lead to ...?
   to-zi pat *vo*-di li do ...?

Този път води ли до ...?

I need a mechanic.
   tryab-vah mi mon-*tyor*

Трябва ми монтьор.

SIGNS

БЕЗОЛОВЕН	UNLEADED
ВХОД ЗАБРАНЕН	NO ENTRY
ГАРАЖ	GARAGE
ДАЙ ПРЕДИМСТВО	GIVE WAY
ДИЗЕЛОВО ГОРИВО	DIESEL
ЕДНОПОСОЧНО ДВИЖЕНИЕ	ONE WAY
ЗАБРАНЕНО ПАРКИРАНЕТО	NO PARKING
ИНВАЛИДИ	DISABLED
МАГИСТРАЛА	FREEWAY
МОНТЬОР	MECHANIC
НА САМООБСЛУЖВАНЕ	SELF SERVICE
ОБИКНОВЕН	NORMAL
ОТКЛОНЕНИЕ	DETOUR
СЕРВИЗ	REPAIRS
СПРИ	STOP
СУПЕР	SUPER

BULGARIAN

air (for tyres)	*vaz*-dukh pot nah-*lya*-ghah-neh	въздух под налягане
battery	a-ku-mu-*lah*-tor	акумулатор
brakes	spi-*rahch*-ki	спирачки
clutch	ahm-bri-*ahsh*	амбриаж
driver's licence	sho-*fyor*-skah *knish*-kah	шофьорска книжка
engine	dvi-*ghah*-tel	двигател
lights	sveh-tli-*ni*	светлини
oil	mah-*slo*	масло
petrol	*behn*-zin	бензин
puncture	*spuk*-vah-neh nah *ghu*-mah	спукване на гума
radiator	rah-di-*ah*-tor	радиатор
road map	*pa*-tnah *kahr*-tah	пътна карта
tyres	*van*-shni *ghu*-mi	външни гуми
windscreen	*preh*-dno sta-*klo*	предно стъкло

ACCOMMODATION

Where's a ...?	ka-deh i-mah ...?	Къде има ...?
cheap hotel	*ehf*-tin kho-*tehl*	евтин хотел
good hotel	*khu*-bahf kho-*tehl*	хубав хотел
nearby hotel	kho-*tehl* bnah-*bli*-zo	хотел наблизо
clean hotel	chis kho-*tehl*	чист хотел

BULGARIAN

SIGNS

КЪМПИНГ	CAMPING GROUND
ПАНСИОН	GUESTHOUSE
МОТЕЛ	MOTEL
ОБЩЕЖИТИЕ	YOUTH HOSTEL
СВОБОДНИ СТАИ	ROOMS AVAILABLE
ХОТЕЛ	HOTEL

What's the address?
    kah-*kaf* eh ah-*dreh*-sat?   Какъв е адресът?
Could you write the address, please?
    bikh-teh li mo-*ghli*,   Бихте ли могли
    dah mi nah-*pi*-sheh-teh   да ми напишете
    ah-*dreh*-sah?   адреса?

At the Hotel

Do you have any rooms available?
    i-mah-teh li   Имате ли
    svo-*bo*-dni *stah*-i?   свободни стаи?

I'd like ...	bikh zheh-*lahl* ...	Бих желал ...
a single room	*stah*-ya s eh-*dno* leh-*ghlo*	стая с едно легло
a double room	*stah*-ya s dveh leh-*ghlah*	стая с две легла
a room with a bathroom	*stah*-ya z *bah*-nya	стая с баня
to share a dorm	leh-*ghlo* f op-shtah *spahl*-nya	легло в обща спалня
a bed	leh-*ghlo*	легло

I want a room with a ...	is-kahm *stah*-ya sas ...	Искам стая с ...
bathroom	*bah*-nya	баня
shower	dush	душ
window	pro-*zo*-rehts	прозорец

How much is it per night/person?
    kol-ko eh nah *veh*-chehr/   Колко е на вечер/
    cho-*vehk*?   човек?
Can I see it?
    mo-ghah li dah ya *vi*-dya?   Мога ли да видя?
Are there any others?
    i-mah-li *dru*-ghi?   Има ли други?
Can I see the bathroom?
    mo-ghah li dah *vi*-dya   Мога ли да видя
    bah-nya-tah?   банята?

Is there a reduction for students/children?

    i-mah li nah-mah-*leh*-
    nieh zah stu-*dehn*-ti/deh-*tsah*?

Има ли намаление
за студенти/деца?

It's fine, I'll take it.

    do-*breh*, shteh ya *vzeh*-mah

Добре, ще я взема.

I'm not sure how long I'm staying.

    neh znahm *kol*-ko
    vreh-meh shteh o *stah*-nah

Не знам колко
време ще остана.

Is there hot water all day?

    i-mah-li *to*-plah vo-*dah*
    prehs *tseh*-li-ya dehn?

Има ли топла вода
през целия ден?

I'm/We're leaving now.

    zah-mi-*nah*-vahm si/
    zah-mi-*nah*-vah-mehsi seh-*ghah*

Заминавам си/
Заминаваме си сега.

I'd like to pay the bill.

    bikh *is*-kahl dah plah-*ta*
    smeht-kah-tah

Бих искал да
платя сметката.

Requests & Complaints

Can I use the telephone?

    mo-ghah li dah
    pol-zvahm teh-leh-*fo*-nah?

Мога ли да
ползувам телефона?

The room needs to be cleaned.

    stah-ya-tah *tryab*-vah
    dah seh po-*chis*-ti

Стаята трябва
да се почисти.

I can't open/close the window.

    neh *mo*-ghah dah
    zah-*tvo*-rya/ot-*vo*-rya
    pro-*zo*-reh-tsah

Не мога да отворя/
затворя прозореца.

I've locked myself out of my room.

    vrah-*tah*-tah nah
    stah-ya-tah mi
    seh-czah-*klyu*hi i neh
    mo-ghah dah *flya*-zah

Вратата на
стаята ми
се заключи и не.
мога да вляза.

The toilet won't flush.

    vo-*dah*-tah f to-ah-*leh*-
    tnah-tah neh seh *pus*-ka

Водата в тоалетната
не се пуска.

BULGARIAN

AROUND TOWN

I'm looking
for a/the ...   tar-*sya* ...   Търся ...

art gallery	khu-*do*-nah-tah zheh-stveh ghah-*leh*-ri-ya	художествената галерия
bank	*bahn*-kah	банка
church	*tsar*-kvah-tah	църквата
city centre	*tsehn*-ta -rah nah grah-*dah*	центъра на града
... embassy	po-*sol*-stvo-to nah ...	посолството на ...
market	pah-*zah*-rah	пазара
museum	mu-*zeh*-ya	музея
police	po-*li*-tsi-ya-tah	полицията
post office	*po*-shtah-tah	пощата
public toilet	*ghraht*-skah to-ah-*leh*-tnah	градска тоалетна
telephone centre	teh-leh-*fon*-nah-tah tsehn-*trah*-lah	телефонната централа
tourist information office	byu-*ro*-to zah tu-ri-*sti*-chehs-kah in-for-*mah*-tsi-ya	бюрото за туристическа информация

What time does it open/close?
   f *kol*-ko chah-*sa* gho   В колко часа го
   ot-*vah*-ryat/zaht-*vah*-ryat?   отварят/затварят?

For directions, see the Getting Around section, pages 66-67.

BULGARIAN

At the Post Office

I'd like some stamps.
dahy-teh mi *po*-shtehn-
ski *mahr*-ki, *mo*-lya

Дайте ми пощенски
марки, моля.

How much is the postage?
kol-ko *stru*-vah
praht-kah-tah?

Колко струва
пратката?

I'd like to send a/an ...	is-kahm dah is-*prah*-tya ...	Искам да изпратя ...
aerogram	pi-*smo* z vaz-*du*-shnah *po*-shtah	писмо с въздушна поща
letter	pis-*mo*	писмо
parcel	ko-*leht*	колет
postcard	*po*-shtehn-skah *kahr*-tich-kah	пощенска картичка
telegram	teh-leh-*ghrah*-mah	телеграма
air mail	vaz-*du*-shnah *po*-shtah	въздушна поща
envelope	plik zah pi-*smo*	плик за писмо
mail box	*po*-shtehn-skah ku-*ti*-ya	пощенска кутия
parcel	ko-*leht*	колет
registered mail	preh-po-*ra*-chah-nah *po*-shtah	препоръчана поща
surface mail	o-bil-no-*veh*-nah *po*-shtah	обикновена поща

Telephone

I want to ring ...
zheh-*lah*-ya dah se
o-*bah*-dya nah ...

Желая да се
обадя на ...

The number is ...
no-meh-rat eh ...

Номерът е ...

I want to speak for (three) minutes.
    is-kahm dah gho-*vo*-rya
    (tri) mi-*nu*-ti

Искам да говоря
(три) минути.

How much does a three-
minute call cost?
    kol-ko stru-vahtri-*minu*-
    tehn *rahz*-gho-vor?

Колко струва
триминутен разговор?

I'd like to speak to (Mr Perez).
    bikh *is*-kahl dah
    gho-*vo*-rya z (ghos-po-*din*
    peh-rehs)

Бих искал да
говоря с (господин
Перес).

I want to make a reverse-
charges phone call.
    is-kahm dah seh
    o-*bah*-dya zah *tya*-khnah
    smeht-kah

Искам да се
обадя за тяхна
сметка.

It's engaged.
    dah-vah zah-*eh*-to

Дава заето.

I've been cut off.
    preh-*ka*-snah-khah meh

Прекъснаха ме.

Internet

Where can I get Internet access?
    ka-*deh mo*-gha dah
    po-*lu*-cha *dos*-tap do
    in-tar-neht

Къде мога да получа
достъп до интернет?

How much is it per hour?
    kol-ko seh *plah*-shta
    na chahs

Колко се плаща
на час?

I want to check my email.
    is-kam dah pro-veh-*rya*
    eh-lehk-*tron*-ata si *po*-shta

Искам да проверя
електронната си поща.

At the Bank

I want to exchange some ...	*is*-kahm dah ...	Искам да ...
money	o-bmeh-*nya* pah-*ri*	обменя пари
travellers	*pa*-tni-chehs-ki	пътнически
cheques	*cheh*-ko-veh	чекове

What's the exchange rate?
    kah-*kaf* eh o-*bmehn*-
    ni-ya kurs?

Какъв е обменният
курс?

How many leva per dollar?
    kol-ko *leh*-vah zah *do*-lah?

Колко лева за долар?

Can I have money transferred
here from my bank?
    ot *mo*-ya-tah *bahn*-kah
    mo-ghaht li dah mi preh-
    veh-*da*t pah-*ri* tuk?

От моята банка
могат ли да ми
преведат пари тук?

How long will it take to arrive?
    zah *kol*-ko *vreh*-meh
    shteh pri-*sti*-ghneh
    preh-vo-da t?

За колко време
ще пристигне
преводът?

Has my money arrived yet?
    pah-*ri*-teh mi pri-*sti*-
    ghnah-khah li *veh*-cheh?

Парите ми присти-
гнаха ли вече?

bankdraft	*bahn*-kov *preh*-vod*zah*-pis	банков превод запис
banknotes	bahn-*kno*-ti	банкноти
cashier	kah-si-*her*/ kah-si-*ehr*-kah	касиер (m) касиерка (f)
coins	mo-*neh*-ti	монети
credit card	*kreh*-di-tnah *kahr*-tah	кредитна карта
exchange	vah-*lu*-tnah o-*bmya*-nah	валутна обмяна
loose change	pah-*ri* nah *dreh*-bno	пари на дребно
signature	*pod*-pis	подпис

BULGARIAN

INTERESTS & ENTERTAINMENT
Sightseeing

Do you have a ...?   *i*-mah-teh li ...?   Имате ли ...?
  guidebook   tu-ris-*ti*-cheh-ski   туристическ
    pa-teh-vo-*di*-tehl   пътеводител
  local map   *kahr*-tah   карта

What are the main attractions?
  ko-*i* sah *ghlah*-vni-the   Кои са главните
  zah-beh-leh-*zhi*-tehl-nos-ti?   забележителности?
What's that?
  kahk-*vo* eh o-no-*vah*?   Какво е онова?
How old is it?
  ot *kol*-ko gho-*di*-ni eh?   От колко години е?
Can I take photographs?
  mo-ghah li dah *prah*-vya   Мога ли да правя
  snim-ki?   снимки?

ancient	*dreh*-vehn	древен
archaeological	ahr-kheh-o-lo-*gi*-chehs-ki	археологически
beach	*mor*-ski bryak plahsh	морски бряг/плаж
building	*zghrah*-dah	сграда
castle	*zah*-mak	замък
cathedral	kah-teh-*drah*-lah	катедрала
church	*tsark*-vah	църква
concert hall	kon-*tsehr*-tnah *zah*-lah	концертна зала
library	bi-bli-o-*teh*-kah	библиотека
main square	tsehn-*trah*-lehn plo-*shtaht*	централен площад
market	pah-*zahr*	пазар
monastery	mah-nahs-*tir*	манастир
monument	*pah*-meh-tnik	паметник
mosque	dzhah-*mi*-ya	джамия
old city	*stah*-ri-ya ghraht	старият град
opera house	*o*-peh-rah	опера

palace	dvo-*rehts* pah-*laht*	дворец/палат
ruins	rahz-vah-li-*ni*	развалини
	o-stahn-ki	останки
stadium	stah-di-*on*	стадион
statues	*stah*-tu-i	статуи
synagogue	si-nah-*gho*-ghah	синагога
temple	khrahm	храм
university	du-ni-vahr-si-*taht*	университет

Going Out

What's there to do in the evenings?
kahk-*vi* rahz-vleh-*cheh*-ni-ya *i*-mah *veh*-chehr?
Какви развлечения има вечер?

Are there any nightclubs?
i-mah li dis-ko-*teh*-ki?
Има ли дискотеки?

Are there places where you can hear local folk music?
mo-zheh li *nya*-ka-deh dah seh *slu*-shah *bal*-gahr-skah nah-*rod*-nah nah-*rod*-nah *mu*-zi-kah?
Може ли някъде да се слуша българска народна музика?

How much does it cost to get in?
kol-ko *stru*-vah *vkho*-dah?
Колко струва входът?

cinema	*ki*-no	кино
concert	kon-*tsehrt*	концерт
nightclub	dis-ko-*teh*-kah	дискотека
theatre	teh-*ah*-tar	театър

BULGARIAN

Sports & Interests

What sports do you play?

s *kahk*-vi *spor*-to-veh seh
zah-ni-*mah*-vahsh?

С какви спортове се
занимавш?

What are your interests?

kahk-vi sah *vah*-shi-the
in-the-*reh*-si?

Какви са вашите
интереси?

art	is-*kus*-tvo	изкуство
basketball	*bahs*-keht-bol	баскетбол
chess	shahkh	шах
collecting things	ko-*lehk*-tsi-o-ni-rahm neh-*shtah*	колекционирам неща
dancing	*tahn*-tsi	танци
food	khrah-*nah*	храна
football	*fut*-bol	футбол
hiking	tu-*ri*-zam	туризъм
martial arts	*boy*-ni is-*kust*-vah	бойни изкуства
meeting friends	dah seh *sreh*-stahm s pri-*ya*-teh-li	да се срещам с приятели
movies	*ki*-no	кино
music	*mu*-zi-kah	музика
nightclubs	*nosht*-ni zah-veh-*deh*-ni-ya	нощни заведения
photography	fo-to-*grah*-fi-ya	фотография
reading	dah cheh-*tah*	да чета
shopping	dah pa-zah-*ru*-vahm	да пазарувам
skiing	dah *kah*-ram ski	да карам ски
swimming	dah *plu*-vahm	да плувам
tennis	*teh*-nis	тенис
travelling	dah pa-*tu*-vahm	да пътувам
TV/videos	the-leh-*vi*-zi-ya/ *vi*-deh-o	телевизия/видео
visiting friends	dah *ho*-dya nah *gos*-ti u pri-*ya*-teh-li	да хода на гости у приятели
walking	dah seh ras-*hozh*-dahm	да се разхождам

BULGARIAN

Festivals & Public Holidays

1 January – New Year's Day
no-*vah* gho-*di*-na
Нова година

3 March – Liberation Day
o-svo-bozh-*deh*-ni-eh nah bal *ghah*-ri-ya
Освобождение на България

April/Easter
vas-kreh-*seh*-ni-eh khri-*sto*-vo/veh-*lik*-dehn
Възкресение Христово/Великден

1 May – International Labour Day
mehzh-du-na-*ro*-dehn dehn nah tru-*dah*
Международен ден на труда

24 May – Day of the Slavonic script and of Bulgarian education
and culture
dehn nah *bal*-ghar-skah-ta pros-veh-ta i kul-*tu*-rah i nah
sla-*vyan*-ska-tah *pis*-meh-nost
Ден на българската просвета и на
славянската писменост

25–26 December – Christmas
rozh-*dehs*-tvo khri-*sto*-vo/*ko*-leh-da
Рождество Христово/Коледа

Festival traditions in Bulgaria are connected also with a number
of important Bulgarian Orthodox Church festivals, such as:

St Nicholas' Day (December 6)
St Jordan's Day/Epiphany (January 6)
Candlemas (February 2)
The Annunciation (March 25)
St George's Day (May 6)
Ascension Day (June 9)
Whitsuntide (June 20)
The Assumption (August 15)

BULGARIAN

IN THE COUNTRY
Weather

What's the weather like?
kahk-*vo* eh *vreh*-meh-to?   Какво е времето?

The weather's	*vreh*-meh-to	Времето
... today.	dnehs eh ...	днес е ...
Will it be ...	shteh *ba*-deh li	Ще бъде ли
tomorrow?	... u-treh?	... утре?
cloudy	*o*-blah-chno	облачно
cold	stu-*deh*-no	студено
foggy	ma -*ghli*-vo	мъгливо
frosty	mrah-zo-*vi*-to	мразовито
hot	gho-*reh*-shto	горещо
raining	da zh-do-*vi*-to	дъждовно
snowing	sneh-gho-*vi*-to	снеговито
sunny	*slan*-cheh-vo	слънчево
windy	veh-tro-*vi*-to	ветровито

Camping

Am I allowed to camp here?
mo-ghah li dah
lah-gheh-*ru*-vahm tuk?   Мога ли да
лагерувам тук?

Is there a campsite nearby?
i-mah li *kam*-pink
nah-*bli*-zo?   Има ли къмпинг
наблизо?

backpack	tu-ris-*ti*-chehs-kah	туристическа
	rah-ni-tsah	раница
can opener	ot-vah-*rahch*-kah	отварачка
	zah kon-*sehr*-vi	за консерви
compass	kom-*pas*	компас
crampons	*kot*-ki	котки
firewood	dar-*vah* zah *o*-gan-ya	дърва за огъня
gas cartridge	pa l-*ni*-tehl z ghas	пълнител с газ

hammock	khah-*mahk*	хамак
ice axe	*pi*-kehl	пикел
mattress	dyu-*shehk*	дюшек
penknife	*nosh*-cheh	ножче
rope	va-*zheh*	въже
tent	pah-*laht*-kah	палатка
tent pegs	*kol*-cheh-tah zah	колчета за
	pah-*laht*-kah	палатка
torch	feh-*nehr*-cheh	фенерче
(flashlight)		
sleeping bag	*spah*-lehn chu-*vahl*	спален чувал
stove	*pehch*-kah	печка
water bottle	mah-*nehr*-kah	манерка

FOOD

In summer, Bulgarians consume a lot of refreshing meals and drinks, canned foods and cold cuts. Autumn is the season of plenty in Bulgaria – fruits and vegetables, fresh veal, beef or mutton. In winter, Bulgarians traditionally eat more hearty, nutritious foods and pickled vegetables, while in spring Bulgarians eat a lot of readily available leaf vegetables.

breakfast	zah-*kus*-kah	закуска
lunch	*o*-beht	обед
dinner	veh-*cheh*-rya	вечеря

Vegetarian Meals

I'm a vegetarian.

ahs sam veh-gheh-
tah-ri-*ah*-nehts
veh-gheh-tah-ri-*ahn*-kah

Аз съм
вегетарианец/
вегетарианка. (m/f)

I don't eat meat.

neh yam meh-*so*

Не ям месо.

I don't eat chicken, fish or ham.

neh yam *pi*-leh *ri*-bah i
shun-kah

Не ям пиле, риба и
шунка.

BULGARIAN

BULGARIAN

MENU DECODER

Vegetarian Specialities

Баница
bah-ni-tsah
thin, flaky pastry rolls stuffed with white cheese, yogurt and eggs, baked in the oven

Бъркани яйца с печени чушки
bar-kah-ni yay-*tsah* s peh-cheh-ni *chush*-ki
scrambled eggs with diced roasted peppers and grated white cheese. Served with finely chopped parsley.

Градинарска чорба
grah-di-*nahr*-skah chor-*bah*
soup of celery, carrots, parsley, cabbage, potatoes with white cheese and milk, seasoned with ground black pepper

гювеч
gyu-*vehch*
peppers, tomatoes, eggplant, vegetable marrow, okra, onions, potatoes, green peas, parsley, etc, cooked in the oven. It can also be prepared with meat pieces.

Зрял фасул
zryal fah-*sul*
boiled kidney beans with onions, carrots, celery, dried red pepper (hot or sweet) and mint. Served sprinkled with parsley.

Кьопоолу
kyop-o-o-lu
eggplant puree with crushed garlic, salt, vinegar and chopped parsley; garnished with slices of tomato or hardboiled egg and parsley

Спанак Загора
spah-*nahk* zah-*go*-rah
spinach cooked, drained and baked on a buttered baking dish with garlic, sour cream, coarsely chopped walnuts, parmesan cheese, chopped onion, pepper and salt to taste

Таратор
tah-rah-*tor*
finely chopped cucumber, crushed walnuts, garlic, oil, dill and salt, mixed thoroughly in yogurt. Served with finely chopped parsley and dill.

MENU DECODER

Чорба от зрял фасул
chor-bah ot zryal fah-*sul*
boiled haricot beans with tomato puree, paprika, mint, salt to taste, oil and lightly fried flour added. Served with chopped parsley, small hot peppers and vinegar to taste.

Шопска салата
shop-skah sah-*lah*-tah
salad of fresh tomatoes, cucumbers, sweet peppers and grated white cheese

Main Meals

Агнешка курбан-чорба
ah-ghneh-shkah kur-*bahn* chor-*bah*
boiled lamb, cut into cubes with chopped onion, paprika, rice, salt to taste, parsley, and eggs

Дроб-сарма
drop-sar-mah
boiled lamb's liver and intestines with rice and onions wrapped in fat and baked in the oven. Served with a thick egg sauce.

Кебапчета на скара
keh-*bahp*-cheh-tah nah *skah*-rah
rissoles prepared with lamb and veal, mixed together with finely chopped onion, cinnamon and salt to taste, then grilled at a high temperature until a thin crust is formed, sealing in the meat's juices

Мусака от телешко месо
mu-sah-*kah* ot *teh*-lehsh-ko meh-*so*
minced beef, sliced eggplant and tomatoes, finely chopped onion and parsley, black peppercorns and salt to taste, covered with a sauce made of flour, lard, eggs, milk and salt to taste, and baked in the oven

Печено пиле с домати
peh-cheh-no *pi*-leh z do-*mah*-ti
chicken rubbed with salt and oil and roasted in the oven with halved tomatoes arranged around it. Seasoned with salt and plenty of black pepper and served with rice.

BULGARIAN

BULGARIAN

MENU DECODER

Пълнена риба на фурна
pal-neh-nah *ri*-bah nah *fur*-nah
carp, sea bass or pike is stuffed with rice, sauteed onion, coarsely
ground hazelnuts, basil and rosemary, then baked in olive oil
and lemon. Served cold.

Риба-плакия
ri-bah plah-ki-ya
one of the best known Bulgarian fish dishes, usually made with
carp, baked with slices of lemon and sauteed onion in oil, garlic,
salt and pepper, with paprika, sugar, water and tomato paste

Сърми с лозови листа
sar-*mi* s *lo*-zo-vi li-*stah*
vine leaves stuffed with a mixture of minced lean lamb or veal,
white bread, finely chopped onion, rice, chopped herbs, salt
and pepper, and cooked in a sauce of tomatoes or tomato puree,
with sour cream or yogurt. Served with red cabbage and salad.

Чорба от пиле
chor-*bah* ot *pi*-leh
soup made by cooking rice in chicken stock with yogurt, flour
and beaten egg yolks. Seasoned with pepper and salt to taste
and garnished with fresh mint and butter.

Desserts

Баклава
bah-klah-*vah*
thin, flaky pastry, butter, walnuts, cinnamon and sugar syrup;
baked in the oven

Бисквити с орехи
bi-*skvi*-ti s o-reh-khi
biscuit shapes cut out of soft dough (well-kneaded flour with
melted butter, sugar, ground walnuts and grated lemon rind),
dipped one side only into beaten egg white and crushed
walnuts and sugar, then baked on a lightly buttered baking tray

Халва
khahl-*vah*
dessert usually made of melted butter, sugar and water. Served
with crushed walnut kernels and cinnamon.

Non-Alcoholic Drinks

buttermilk	ahy-*ryan*	айрян
fruit juice	*plo*-dof sok	плодов сок
mineral water	mi-neh-*rahl*-nah	минерална
nectar	nehk-*tahr*	нектар
soda water	ghah-*zi*-rah-nah	газирана вода
soft drink	li-mo-*nah*-dah	лимонада
water	vo-*dah*	вода
coffee	kah-*feh*	кафе
espresso	kah-*feh* eks-*preh*-so	кафе-експресо
instant coffee	nehs	нес
tea	chahy	чай
Turkish coffee	*tur*-sko	турско
with milk	s *mlya*-ko	с мляко
with lemon	s li-*mon*	с лимон

Alcoholic Drinks

beer	*bi*-rah	бира
bottled	bu-ti-*li*-rah-nah	бутилирана
on tap	nah-*liy*-nah	наливна
brandy	rah-*ki*-ya	ракия
fruit brandy	plo-*do*-vah	плодова
grape brandy	*ghroz*-do-vah	гроздова
plum brandy	*sli*-vo-vah	сливова
wine	*vi*-no	вино
bottled wine	bu-ti-li-*rah*-no	бутилирано
dry	*su*-kho	сухо
red/white	chehr-*veh*-no/*bya*-lo	червено/бяло
sparkling	shu-*myash*-to	шумящо
boza; millet ale	bo-*zah*	боза
champagne	shahm-*pahn*-sko	шампанско
cognac	ko-*nyak*	коняк
vodka	*vot*-kah	водка
whisky	*uy*-ski	уйски

BULGARIAN

AT THE MARKET

Basics

bread	khlyap	хляб
butter	*krah*-veh *mahs*-lo	краве масло
cereal	*zar*-neh-ni khra-ni	зърнени храни
cheese	*si*-reh-neh	сирене
chocolate	sho-ko-*laht*	шоколад
eggs	yay-*tsah*	яйца
flour	brash-*no*	брашно
honey	meht	мед
margarine	mar-ga-*rin*	маргарин
milk	*mlya*-ko	мляко
olive oil	zehkh-*tin*	зехтин
pasta	spa-*gheh*-ti i	спагети и
	ma-ka-*ro*-ni	макарони
pepper	*pi*-pehr	пипер
rice	o-*ris*	ориз
salt	sol	сол
sugar	*zah*-khar	захар
table salt	ghot-*vahr*-ska sol	готварска сол
yogurt	*ki*-seh-lo *mlya*-ko	кисело мляко

Meat & Fish

beef	go-*vehzh*-do meh-*so*	говеждо месо
chicken	*pi*-lehsh-ko meh-*so*	пилешко месо
crayfish	*rah*-tsi	раци
ham	*shun*-ka	шунка
hamburger	*khahm*-bur-gehr	хамбургер
lamb	*ahgh*-nehsh-ko meh-*so*	агнешко месо
mussels	*mi*-di	миди
oysters	*stri*-di	стриди
pork	*svin*-sko meh-*so*	свинско месо
sausage	*nah*-deh-ni-tsa	наденица
shrimp	ska-*ri*-di	скариди
snails	*okh*-lyu-vi	охлюви
turkey	*pu*-ehsh-ko meh-*so*	пуешко месо
veal	*teh*-lehsh-ko meh-*so*	телешко месо

AT THE MARKET

Vegetables

beetroot	tsvehk-*lo*	цвекло
(green) beans	(zeh-*lehn*) bop	(зелен) боб
cabbage	*zeh*-leh	зеле
(red/green) capsicum	(*cheh*-rehn/ zeh-*lehn*) pi-*pehr*	(червен/ зелен) пипер
carrot	*mor*-kof	морков
cauliflower	kar-fi-*ol*	карфиол
celery	*tseh*-li-na	целина
cucumber	*krahs*-ta-vi-tsa	краставица
dock	*lah*-pad	лапад
eggplant	sin do-*maht*	син домат
hot peppers	lyu-*ti*-vi pi-*pehr*-ki	лютиви пиперки
leeks	prahs	праз
lettuce	ma-*ru*-lya	маруля
mountain spinach	*lo*-bo-da	лобода
mushrooms	*ga*-bi	гъби
nettles	ko-*pri*-va	коприва
onions	kro-*mit*	кромид
peas	ghrahkh	грах
pepper	pi-*pehr*	пипер
potato	kar-*tof*	картоф
sorrel	*ki*-seh-lehts	киселец
tomato	do-*maht*	домат

Fruit

apple	*ya*-bal-ka	ябълка
apricot	kay-*si*-ya	кайсия
banana	ba-*nahn*	банан
fig	smo-*ki*-nya	смокиня
grapes	*ghroz*-deh	грозде
kiwifruit	*ki*-vi	киви
lemon	li-*mon*	лимон
orange	por-to-*kahl*	портокал
peach	*prahs*-ko-va	праскова
pear	*kru*-sha	круша
plum	*sli*-va	слива
strawberry	*ya*-gho-da	ягода

BULGARIAN

BULGARIAN

SHOPPING

Where's the nearest ...?	ka-*deh* eh nay *blis*-ki-yat ...?	Къде е най-близкият ...?
bookshop	kni-*zhahr*-ni-tsah	книжарница
camera shop	mah-ghah-*zin* zah fo-to-ah-pah-*rah*-ti	магазин за фотоапарати
chemist	ahp-*teh*-kah	аптека
clothing store	mah-ghah-*zin* zah o-bleh-*klo*	магазин за облекло
delicatessen	deh-li-kah-*teh*-sehn mah-ghah-*zin*	деликатесен магазин
greengrocer	mah-ghah-*zin* zah plo-do-veh i zeh-lehn-*chu*-tsi	магазин за плодове и зеленчуци
laundry	op-*shtehst*-veh-nah peh-*rahl*-nah	обществена перална
market	pah-*zahr*	пазар
newsagency	rehp	РП
souvenir shop	mah-ghah-*zin* zah su-veh-ni-ri	магазин за сувенири
supermarket	su-pehr-*mahr*-keht	супермаркет

How much is it?
kol-ko *stru*-vah?   Колко струва?

Do you accept credit cards?
pri-*eh*-mah-teh li
kreh-di-tni *kahr*-ti?   Приемате ли кредитни карти?

Souvenirs

earrings	o-beh-*tsi*	обеци
handicraft	*rach*-no iz-rah-*bo*-teh-ni iz-*deh*-li-ya	ръчно изработени изделия
necklace	ghehr-*dahn*	гердан
pottery	keh-*rah*-mi-kah	керамика
ring	*pra*-stehn	пръстен
rug	ki-*lim*	килим

Clothing

clothing	o-bleh-*klo*	облекло
coat	pahla-*o*	палто
dress	*ro*-klya	рокля
jacket	*ya*-keh/sah-*ko*	яке/сако
jumper (sweater)	pu-*lo*-vehr	пуловер
shirt	*ri*-zah	риза
shoes	o-*buf*-ki	обувки
skirt	po-*lah*	пола
trousers	pahn-tah-*lo*-ni	панталони
underwear	*dol*-ni *dreh*-khi/	долни дрехи/
	beh-*lyo*	бельо

Essential Groceries

I'd like ...	*mo*-lya *dahy*-teh	Моля, дайте
	mi ...	ми ...
bread	khlyap	хляб
butter	*krah*-veh *mahs*-lo	краве масло
cheese	*si*-reh-neh	сирене
chocolate	sho-ko-*laht*	шоколад
eggs	yay-*tsah*	яйца
ham	*shun*-ka	шунка
honey	meht	мед
margarine	mar-ga-*rin*	маргарин
marmalade	mar-ma-*laht*	мармалад
matches	*ki*-brit	кибрит
milk	*mlya*-ko	мляко
shampoo	shahm-po-*ahn*	шампоан
soap	sa-*pun*	сапун
sugar	*zah*-khar	захар
toilet paper	to-a-*leht*-na	тоалетна
	khar-*ti*-ya	хартия
toothpaste	*pahs*-ta za *za*-bi	паста за
		зъби
washing	*prahkh* za pra-*neh*	прах за
powder		пране

BULGARIAN

Materials

What is it made of?

ot ka-*kaf* ma-teh-ri-*ahl*
eh na-*prah*-vehn?

От какъв материал
е направен?

cotton	pah-*muk*	памук
handmade	*rach*-nah iz-rah-*bot*-kah	ръчна изработка
leather	*ko*-zhah	кожа
of brass	ot *meh*-sink	от месинг
of gold	ot *zlah*-to	от злато
of silver	ot sreh-*bro*	от сребро
silk	ko-*pri*-nah	коприна
wool	*val*-nah	вълна

Colours

black	*cheh*-rehn	черен
blue	sin	син
brown	ka-*fyaf*	кафяв
green	zeh-*lehn*	зелен
orange	o-*rahm*-zhehf	оранжев
red	chehr-*vehn*	червен
white	byal	бял
yellow	zhalt/	жълт

Toiletries

comb	*ghreh*-behn	гребен
condoms	preh-zehr-vah-*ti*-vi	презервативи
deodorant	deh-zo-do-*rahnt*	дезодорант
hairbrush	*cheht*-kah zah ko-*sah*	четка за коса
moisturiser	khi-drahn-*tehn* krehm	хидрантен крем
shaving razor	*nosh*-cheh zah	ножче за
	bra-sneh-neh	бръснене
sanitary	*dahm*-ski	дамски
napkins	preh-vras-ki	превръзки
shaving cream	krehm zah	крем за
	bra-sneh-neh	бръснене
soap	*sah*-pun	сапун
sunscreen	krehm *pro*-tif	крем против
	slan-cheh-vo	слънчево
	iz-*ghah*-rya-neh	изгаряне
tampons	tahm-*po*-ni	тампони
tissues	knij-ni *kar*-pi-chki	книжни
		кърпички
toothbrush	*cheht*-kah zah *za*-bi	четка за зъби

Stationery & Publications

map	*kahr*-tah	карта
paper	khahr-*ti*-ya	хартия
pen (ballpoint)	pi-*sahl*-kah	писалка
	khi-mi-*khahl*-kah	химикалка
scissors	*no*-zhi-tsi	ножици
English-language	... nah ahn-*ghliy*-ski	... наанглийски
newspaper	*veh*-snik	вестник
novels	ro-*mah*-ni nah	романи

Photography

How much is it to process this film?

kol-ko *stru*-vah	Колко струва
pro-ya-*vya*-vah-neh-to	проявяването
nah *to*-zi film?	на този филм?

When will it be ready?

    ko-*ghah* shteh *ba* -deh gho-*tof*? Кога ще бъде готов?

I'd like a film for this camera.

    zheh-*lah*-ya film zah   Желая филм за

    to-zi ah-pah-*raht*   този апарат.

B&W (film)	cher-no-byal	черно-бял
camera	fo-to-ah-pah-*raht*	фотоапарат
colour (film)	*tsveh*-tehn film	цветен филм
film	film	филм
flash	sveht-*kah*-vi-tsah	светкавица
lens	o-behk-*tif*	обектив
light meter	sveh-tlo-*mehr*	светломер

Smoking

Do you smoke?

    pu-shi-teh li   Пушите ли?

Please don't smoke.

    mo-lya neh pu-*sheh*-teh   Моля, не пушете.

A packet of cigarettes, please.

    pah-*keht* tsi-*ghah*-ri, *mo*-lya Пакет цигари, моля.

Are these cigarettes mild?

    teh-zi tsi-*ghah*-ri   Тези цигари

    meh-ki li sah?   меки ли са?

Do you have a light?

    i-mah-teh li o-ghan-cheh?   Имате ли огънче?

cigarette papers	khahr-*tiy*-ki zah	хартийки за
	tsi-*ghah*-ri	цигари
cigarettes	tsi-*ghah*-ri	цигари
filtered	s *fil*-ta r	с филтър
lighter	zah-*pahl*-kah	запалка
matches	ki-*brit*	кибрит
menthol	mehn-*tol*	ментол
pipe	lu-*lah*	лула
tobacco (pipe)	tyu-*tyun* za lu-*lah*	тютюн за лула

Sizes & Comparisons

small	*mah*-lak	малък
big	gho-*lyam*	голям
heavy	*teh*-zhak	тежък
light	lehk	лек
more	*po*-veh-cheh	повече
less	po *mahl*-ko	по-малко
too much/many	*tvar*-deh *mno*-gho	твърде много

HEALTH

Where is	ka-*deh* seh	Къде се
the ...?	*nah*-mi-*rah* ...?	намира ...?
chemist	ahp-*teh*-kah	аптека
dentist	za-bo-*leh*- kahr-yat	зъболекарят (m)
	za-bo-*leh*-kahr-kah-tah	зъболекарката (f)
doctor	*leh*-kahr-yat	лекарят (m)
	leh-kahr-kah-tah	лекарката (f)
hospital	*bol*-ni-tsah-tah	болницата

I'm sick.	
bo-lehn sam	Болен съм. (m)
bol-nah sam	болна съм. (f)
My friend is sick.	
pri-*ya*-teh-lyat	Приятелят
mi eh *bo*-lehn	ми е болен. (m)
pri-*ya*-tehl-kah-tah	Приятелката
mi eh *bol*-nah	ми е болна. (f)
It hurts here.	
tuk meh bo-*li*	Тук ме боли.

Ailments

I have (a/an) ...	*i*-mahm ...	Имам ...
allergy	ah-*lehr*-ghi-ya	алергия
anaemia	ah-*neh*-mi-ya	анемия
burn	iz-*ghah*-rya-neh	изгаряне
constipation	*zah*-pehk	запек
cough	d*kah*-shli-tsah	кашлица
diarrhoea	di-*ah*-ri-ya	диария
fever	tehm-peh-rah-*tu*-rah *trehs*-kah	температура треска
headache	ghlah-vo-*bo*-li-eh	главоболие
hepatitis	kheh-pah-*tit*	хепатит
indigestion	sto-*mah*-shno rahs-*stroy*-stvo	стомашно разстройство
infection	in-*fehk*-tsi-ya	инфекция
influenza	ghrip	грип
lice	*vash*-ki	въшки
low/high blood pressure	*nis*-ko/vi-*so*-ko *kra*-vno nah-*lya*-ghah-neh	ниско/високо кръвно-налягане
pain	*bol*-kah	болка
sore throat	vas-pah-*leh*-no *ghar*-lo	възпалено гърло
sprain	nah-*vyakh*-vah-neh	навяхване
sunburn	*slan*-cheh-vo iz-*ghah*-rya-neh	слънчево изгаряне
venereal disease	veh-neh-*ri*-chnah *bo*-les	венерична болест
worms	*ghli*-sti	глисти

I have a cold.

| pros-tu-*dil*/ pros-tu-*di*-lah sam she | Простудил/ Простудила съм се. (m/f) |

Parts of the Body

My ... hurts.	bo-*li* meh ...	Боли ме ...
ankle	*ghleh*-zeh-nat	глезенът
arm	ra-*kah*-tah	ръката
back	ghar-*bay*	гърбът
chest	*ghra*-dni-yat kosh	гръдният кош
ear	u-*kho*-to	ухото
eye	o-*ko*-to	окото
finger	*pras*-tat	пръстът
foot	sta-*pah*-lo-to	стъпалото
hand	ra-*kah*-tah	ръката
head	ghlah-*vah*-tah	главата
heart	sar-*tseh*-to	сърцето
leg	krah-*kat*	кракът
mouth	u-*stah*-tah	устата
nose	no-*sat*	носът
skin	*ko*-zhah-tah	кожата
spine	ghra-*bnah*-kat	гръбнакът
stomach	sto-*mah*-khat	стомахът
throat	*ghar*-lo-to	гърлото

At the Chemist

I need medication for ...		
	nuzh-*dah*-ya seh ot	Нуждая се от
	leh-*kahr*-stveh-no	лекарствено
	leh-*cheh*-ni-eh zah ...	лечение за ...
I have a prescription.		
	i-mahm reh-*tsehp*-tah	Имам рецепта.

antibiotics	ahn-ti-bi-*o*-ti-tsi	антибиотици
antiseptic	ahn-ti-sehp-*ti*-chno	антисептично
	srehd-stvo	средство
aspirin	ahs-pi-*rin*	аспирин
bandage	bint	бинт

At the Dentist

I have a toothache.
  bo-*li* meh zap Боли ме зъб.

I've lost a filling.
  pah-dnah mi plom-bah Падна ми пломба.

I've broken a tooth.
  schu-pikh si zap Счупих си зъб.

My gums hurt.
  bo-*lyat* meh vehn-tsi-the Болят ме венците.

I don't want it extracted.
  neh *is*-kahm dah gho Не искам да го
  vah-di-teh вадите.

Please give me an anaesthetic.
  mo-lya *dahy*-teh mi Моля, дайте ми
  o-behz-bo-*lya*-vah-shto обезболяващо.

TIME & DATES

What time is it?
  kol ko eh chah-*sat*? Колко е часът?

It's ... am/pm.
  chah-*sat* eh ... preh-*di* Часът е ... преди
  o-beht/sleht o-beht обед/след обед.

What date is it today?
  ko-*ya dah*-tah eh dnehs? Коя дата е днес?

in the morning	*su*-trin	сутрин
in the afternoon	sleh-*do*-beht	следобед
in the evening	*veh*-chehr	вечер

Days

Monday	po-neh-*dehl*-nik	понеделник
Tuesday	*ftor*-nik	вторник
Wednesday	*srya*-dah	сряда
Thursday	cheht-*var*-tak	четвъртък
Friday	*peh*-tak	петък
Saturday	*sa*-bo-tah	събота
Sunday	neh-*deh*-lya	неделя

BULGARIAN

Months

January	ya-nu-*ah*-ri	януари
February	feh-vru-*ah*-ri	февруари
March	mart	март
April	ah-*pril*	алрил
May	mahy	май
June	*yu*-ni	юни
July	*yu*-li	юли
August	ahv-*ghus*	август
September	sehp-*tehm*-vri	септември
October	ok-*tom*-vri	октомври
November	no-*ehm*-vri	ноември
December	deh-*kehm*-vri	декември

Seasons

summer	*lya*-to	лято
autumn	*eh*-sehn	есен
winter	*zi*-mah	зима
spring	*pro*-leht	пролет

Present

today	dnehs	днес
this morning	*tah*-zi *su*-trin	тази сутрин
tonight	do-*veh*-cheh-rah	довечера
this week/year	*tah*-zi *seh*-dmi-tsah	тази седмина

Past

yesterday	*fcheh*-rah	вчера
(morning)	(su-trin-*tah*)	(сутринта)
last ...	*mi*-nah-lah-tah ...	миналата ...
night	nosh *veh*-chehr-nah-lah-tah	нощ вечер
week	gho-*di*-nah	година

Future

tomorrow	utreh	утре
day after tomorrow	vdru-ghi dehn	другиден
next year	*slehd*-vah-shtah-tah	ледвашата
	gho-*di*-nah	година

BULGARIAN

During the Day

afternoon	slehd-*o*-beht	следобед
dawn; early morning	*u*-tro	утро
day	dehn	ден
early	*rah*-no	рано
midday	*o*-beht	обед
midnight	sreh-*dnosh*	среднощ
morning	*su*-trin	сутрин
night	nosh	нощ
sunset	*zah*-lehs	залез
sunrise	*iz*-ghrehf	изгрев

NUMBERS & AMOUNTS

0	*nu*-lah	нула
1	eh-*din*	един
2	dvah	два
3	tri	три
4	*cheh*-ti-ri	четири
5	peht	пет
6	shehs	шест
7	*seh*-dehm	седем
8	*o*-sehm	осем
9	*deh*-veht	девет
10	*deh*-seht	десет
20	*dvahy*-seht	двайсет
30	*triy*-seht	трийсет
40	cheh-*ti*-riy-seht	четирийсет
50	pehd-deh-*seht*	петдесет
60	shehz-deh-*seht*	шестдесет
70	seh-dehm-deh-*seht*	седемдесет
80	o-sehm-deh-*seht*	осемдесет
90	deh-vehd-deh-*seht*	деветдесет
100	sto	сто
1000	khi-*lya*-dah	хиляда
one million	eh-*din* mi-li-*on*	един милион

BULGARIAN

Useful Words

Enough!	do-*stah*-ta-chno!	Достатъчно!
a little (amount)	*mahl*-ko ko-*li*-cheh-stvo	малко количество
double	*dvoy*-no	двойно
dozen	du-*zi*-nah	дузина
few	*mahl*-ko *nya*-kol-ko	малко/няколко
less	po *mahl*-ko	по-малко
many	*mno*-gho	много
more	*po*-veh-cheh	повече
once	veh-*dnash*/eh-*din* pat	веднъж/ един път
pair	chif	чифт
per cent	pro-tsehnt	процент
some	*nya*-kol-ko/*mahl*-ko	няколко/малко
too much	*tvar*-deh *mno*-gho	твърде много
twice	dvah *pa*-ti	два пъти

ABBREVIATIONS

БДЖ	Bulgarian Railways
БТА	Bulgarian Telegraph Agency
г-н/г-жа/г-ца	Mr/Mrs/Ms
СОС	SOS
ЕИО	European Economic Community
д-р	Dr
и т.н.	etcetera
КАТ	Traffic Police
от н.е./от ст.е.	AD/BC
ООН	United Nations
ул/бул/пл	street/road/square
ч/мин/сек	hours/minutes/seconds

EMERGENCIES

Help!
   po-mosh!   Помощ!

It's an emergency.
   i-mah *speh*-shehn   Има спешен случай.
   slu-chahy

There's been an accident.
   stah-nah-lah eh   Станала е
   kah-tah-*stro*-fah   катастрофа.

Call ...	po-*vi*-kahy-teh ...!	Повикайте ...!
a doctor	*leh*-kahr	лекар
an ambulance	*bar*-zah *po*-mosh	Бърза помощ
the police!	po-*li*-tsi-ya	полиция

I've been raped.
   iz-nah-*si*-li-khah meh   Изнасилиха ме.

I've been robbed.
   o-*ghrah*-bi-khah meh   Ограбиха ме.

Where's the police station?
   ka-*deh* seh nah-*mi*-rah   Къде се намира
   po-li-*tsehy*-sko-to   полицейското
   u-prah-*vleh*-ni-eh?   управление?

Go away!
   mah-khahy-teh seh!   Махайте се!

I'll call the police.
   shteh iz-*vi*-kahm   Ще извикам полиция.
   po-*li*-tsi-ya

Thief!
   krah-*dehts*!   Крадец!

I'm ill.
   zleh sam/neh *seh*   Зле съм/Не се
   chuf-stvahm do-*breh*   чувствувам добре.

I'm lost.
   zah-*ghu*-bikh seh   Загубих се.

BULGARIAN

Where are the toilets?
　　ka-*deh* i-mah
　　to-ah-*leh*-tni?　　　　　　Къде има тоалетни?

Could you help me please?
　　bikh-teh li mi
　　po-*mo*-ghnah li?　　　　　Бихте ли ми
　　　　　　　　　　　　　　　помогнали?

Could I please use the
telephone?
　　iz-vi-*neh*-teh *mo*-ghah li　Извинете, мога ли
　　dah *pol*-zvahm　　　　　　да ползувам
　　teh-leh-*fo*-nah?　　　　　　телефона?

I'm sorry. (I apologise)
　　pro-*shtah*-vahy-teh　　　　Прощавайте.

I didn't realise I was doing
anything wrong.
　　neh *znah*-ehkh cheh　　　　Не знаех, че
　　var-shah *neh*-shto　　　　върша нещо
　　neh-*reh*-dno　　　　　　　нередно.

I didn't do it.
　　neh *gho* nah-*prah*-vikh　　Не го направих аз.
　　ahs

I want to contact my
embassy/consulate.
　　zheh-*lah*-ya dah seh　　　　Желая да се свържа
　　svar-zhah s *nahsh*-to　　　с нашето посолство/
　　po-*sol*-stvo/*kon*-sul-stvo　консулство.

I have medical insurance.
　　i-mahm *zdrah*-vnah　　　　Имам здравна
　　zah-strah-*khof*-kah　　　　застраховка.

My possessions are insured.
　　veh-shti-teh mi sah　　　　Вещите ми са
　　zah-strah-*kho*-vah-ni　　　застраховани.

My ... was stolen.
　　ot-*krah*-dnah-khah mi ...　Откраднаха ми ...

I've lost my ...	iz-*ghu*-bikh si ...	Изгубих си ...
bags	*chahn*-ti-teh	чантите
handbag	*rach*-nah-tah	ръчната
	chahn-tah	чанта
money	pah-*ri*-teh	парите
travellers	*pat*-ni-chehs-ki-the	пътническите
cheques	*cheh*-ko-veh	чекове
passport	pahs-*por*-tah	паспорта
wallet	port-*fehl*	портофел

CROATIAN

QUICK REFERENCE

Hello.	zdr-avo	Zdravo.
Goodbye.	do vi-dje-nya	*Do viđenja.*
Yes./No.	da/ne	Da./Ne.
Excuse me.	o-pros-ti-te	Oprostite.
May I?	mo-gu li?	Mogu li?
Do you mind?	sme-ta li vam?	Smeta li vam?
Sorry.	par-don	Pardon.
(excuse/forgive me)		
Please.	mo-lim	Molim.
Thank you.	hva-la	Hvala.
You're welcome.	ne-ma na che-mu	Nema na čemu.
Where are the toilets?	gdye su za-ho-di?	Gdje su zahodi?
What time is it?	ko-li-ko ye sa-ti?	Koliko je sati?
How much is it?	ko-li-ko kosh-ta?	Koliko košta?
Where's ...?	gdye ye ...?	Gdje je ...?

Turn left/right	skre-ni-te li-ye-vo/	Skrenite lijevo/
at the ...	des-no ...	desno ...
next corner	na slye-de-tchem ug-lu	na sljedećem uglu
traffic lights	kod se-ma-fo-ra	kod semafora

I'd like a...	zhe-lim ...	Želim ...
single room	yed-no-kre-vet-nu so-bu	jednokrevetnu sobu
one-way ticket	kar-tu u yed-nom prav-cu	kartu u jednom pravcu
return ticket	po-vrat-nu kar-tu	povratnu kartu

I (don't) understand.
    (ne) ra-zu-mi-yem   (Ne) razumijem.
Do you speak English?
    go-vo-ri-te li en-gles-ki?   Govorite li engleski?

1	ye-dan	*jedan*	6	shest	*šest*
2	dva	*dva*	7	se-dam	*sedam*
3	tri	*tri*	8	o-sam	*osam*
4	che-ti-ri	*četiri*	9	de-vet	*devet*
5	pet	*pet*	10	de-set	*deset*

CROATIAN

Croatian belongs to the South Slavic branch of the Slavic group of languages, together with Slovenian, Serbian, Macedonian and Bulgarian. There are close to 5 million speakers of Croation in Croatia.

The earliest Serbian literature dates from the 9th century when Cyril and Methodius, two monks who were familiar with the Slav dialect of Macedonia, were sent to Moravia by the Byzantine Emperor to preach Christianity to the inhabitants. The two missionaries set about translating the Scriptures and prayer books, but first they needed a script to reproduce the sounds of the Slav dialect. Thus, the Glagolitic alphabet came about .

Two of Cyril's students from Ohrid, Kliment and Naum, replaced the Glagolitic script with the far more commonly used Cyrillic script, named in honour of their master. The Cyrillic alphabet was adopted wherever Christian Slav-Orthodox rites were followed. The Catholics forbade the use of the national language in their Slav churches, but the Croats, who by this time had created their own independent kingdom, continued to use Glagolitic characters in various parishes. With the splitting of the Roman Empire into the Catholic West under the aegis of Rome and the Orthodox East under Byzantium, came the major division of the alphabet: the Cyrillic was adopted by those belonging to the Orthodox church, and the Roman alphabet by the Roman Catholics.

Standard written Croatian, which uses the Roman alphabet, began developing in the 11th century from a number of Croatian dialects. It was one of the first languages to emerge from the common Slavic substratum. Since the early Middle Ages Croatian has developed under influences of western culture and civilization, both in its Latin-Mediterranean and Pannonian-Central European forms. However, there has been an unyielding desire by the Croat people to preserve their cultural, political and linguistic authenticity. In the 14th and 15th centuries people in the Croat inhabited regions called their language Slavic, Illyrian or Croatian, which encompassed the Shtokavian, Chakavian and Kajkavian dialects.

In the 16th century, Croats started publishing grammars and dictionaries of their language. In the 17th and 18th centuries, Shtokavian, Chakavian and Kajkavian authors were keenly aware that they wrote in the same language, although they called it by different names. Due to the highly developed language of Dubrovnik authors who wrote in the Jekavian variant of the Shtokavian dialect, the language of Dubrovnik became the standard official language in all Croat populated areas in the mid-19th century.

PRONUNCIATION

The spelling of Croatian is phonetic, that is, most words are written exactly as they are pronounced. Every letter is pronounced. There are 30 letters in the Croatian alphabet.

QUESTION WORDS		
How?	ka-ko?	Kako?
When?	ka-da?	Kada?
Where?	gdye?	Gdje?
Which?	ko-yi?	Koji?
Who?	tko?	Tko?
Why?	zash-to?	Zašto?

Vowels		Transliteration
a	a	as the 'a' in 'rather'
e	e	as the 'ea' in 'bear'
i	i	as the 'i' in 'machine'
o	o	as the 'o' in 'shore'
u	u	as the 'u' in 'flute'

CROATIAN

Consonants

Consonants not mentioned here are pronounced as they are in English.

c	ts	as the 'ts' in 'cats'
ć	tch	as the 'tu' in 'future'
č	ch	as the 'ch' in 'chop'
đ	dj	as the 'du' in 'verdure'
dž	j	as the 'j' in 'just'
g	g	as the 'g' in 'got'
j	y	as the 'y' in 'young'
lj	ly	as the 'lli' in 'million'
nj	ny	as the 'ny' in 'canyon'
r	r	as the 'r' in 'rock'
s	s	as the 's' in 'sin'
š	sh	as the 'sh' in 'hush'
z	z	as the 'z' in 'zero'
ž	zh	as the 's' in 'treasure'

Stress

Only one rule can be given with regards to stress – the last syllable of a word is never stressed.

SUBJECT PRONOUNS		
SG		
I	ya	ja
you (inf)	ti	ti
he/she/it	on/o-na/o-no	on/ona/ono
PL		
we	mi	mi
you	vi	vi
they (m/f/ neut)	o-ni	oni
	o-ne	one
	o-na	ona

CROATIAN

GREETINGS & CIVILITIES
Top Useful Phrases

Hello.	zdra-vo	*Zdravo.*
Goodbye.	do vi-dje-nya	*Do viđenja.*
Yes./No.	da/ne	*Da./Ne.*
Excuse me.	o-pros-ti-te	*Oprostite.*
Please.	mo-lim	*Molim.*
Thank you.	hva-la	*Hvala.*
Many thanks.	pu-no hva-la	*Puno hvala.*

May I? Do you mind?
   mo-gu li? sme-ta li vam?   *Mogu li? Smeta li vam?*
Sorry. (excuse me, forgive me)
   par-don   *Pardon.*
That's fine. You're welcome.
   u re-du ye. ne-ma   *U redu je. Nema*
   na che-mu   *na čemu.*

Greetings

Good morning.	do-bro yu-tro	*Dobro jutro.*
Good afternoon.	do-bar dan	*Dobar dan.*
Good evening/	do-bro ve-che;	*Dobro veče;*
night.	la-ku notch	*Laku noć.*
How are you?	ka-ko ste?	*Kako ste?*
Well, thanks.	do-bro, hva-la	*Dobro, hvala.*

Forms of Address

Madam/Mrs	gos-po-dja	*Gospođa*
Sir/Mr	gos-po-din	*Gospodin*
Miss	gos-po-dji-tsa	*Gospođica*
companion	pri-druzh-nik	*pridružnik*
friend	pri-ya-tely	*prijatelj* (m)
	pri-ya-te-lyi-tsa	*prijateljica* (f)

CROATIAN

SMALL TALK
Meeting People

What's your name?
ka-ko se zo-ve-te? *Kako se zovete?*

My name's ...
zo-vem se *Zovem se ...*

I'd like to introduce you to ...
zhe-lim vas u-poz-na-ti sa ... *Želim vas upoznati sa ...*

Pleased to meet you.
dra-go mi ye *Drago mi je.*

Nationalities

Where are you from?
o-dak-le ste? *Odakle ste?*

I'm from ...	ya sam iz ...	*Ja sam iz ...*
Australia	au-stra-li-ye	*Australije*
Canada	ka-na-de	*Kanade*
England	en-gles-ke	*Engleske*
Ireland	irs-ke	*Irske*
New Zealand	no-vog ze-lan-da	*Novog Zelanda*
Scotland	shkot-ske	*Škotske*
USA	a-me-ri-ke	*Amerike*
Wales	vel-sa	*Velsa*

Religion

What's your religion?
ko-ye ste vye-re? *Koje ste vjere?*

I'm not religious.
ya ni-sam re-li-gi-o-zan *Ja nisam religiozan.*

I'm ...	ya sam ...	*Ja sam ...*
Buddhist	bu-dist	*budist*
Catholic	ka-to-lik	*katolik*
Christian	krsh-tcha-nin	*kršćanin*
Hindu	hin-dus	*hindus*
Jewish	zhi-dov	*židov*
Muslim	mus-li-man	*musliman*
Orthodox	pra-vo-sla-van	*pravoslavan*

CROATIAN

Occupations

What do you do?
shta ste po za-ni-ma-nyu? *Šta ste po zanimanju?*

I'm unemployed.
ni-sam za-pos-len *Nisam zaposlen.*

I'm a/an ...	ya sam ...	*Ja sam ...*
artist	u-myet-nik	*umjetnik*
businessperson	u biz-ni-su	*u biznisu*
computer	pro-gra-mer	*programer*
programmer	ra-chu-na-la	*računala*
doctor	li-yech-nik	*liječnik*
engineer	in-zhe-nyer	*inženjer*
farmer	far-mer	*farmer*
journalist	no-vi-nar	*novinar*
lawyer	od-vyet-nik	*odvjetnik*
manual worker	rad-nik	*radnik*
mechanic	me-ha-ni-char	*mehaničar*
nurse	bol-ni-char	*bolničar (m)*
	me-di-tsin-ska	*medicinska*
	ses-tra	*sestra (f)*
office worker	sluzh-be-nik	*službenik*
scientist	znan-stve-nik	*znanstvenik*
student	stu-dent	*student*
teacher	u-chi-tely	*učitelj (m)*
	u-chi-tely-itsa	*učiteljica (f)*
waiter	kel-ner	*kelner (m)*
	kel-ne-ri-tsa	*kelnerica (f)*
writer	spi-sa-tely	*spisatelj*

Family

Are you married?
da li ste o-zhe-nye-ni/u-da-ti? *Da li ste oženjeni/udati?* (m/f)

I'm single.
ya sam sa-mats/sa-mi-tsa *Ja sam samac/samica.* (m/f)

I'm married.
ya sam o-zhe-nyen/u-da-ta *Ja sam oženjen/udata.* (m/f)

How many children do you have?
  ko-li-ko dye-tse i-ma-te?   *Koliko djece imate?*
I don't have any children.
  ne-mam dye-tse   *Nemam djece.*
I have a daughter/a son.
  i-mam ktcher-ku/si-na   *Imam kćerku/sina.*
Do you have a boyfriend/girlfriend?
  i-ma-te li dech-ka/dye-voy-ku? *Imate li dečka/djevojku?*

brother	bra-ta	*brata*
children	dye-ce	*djece*
daughter	ktcher-ku	*kćerku*
family	o-bi-tely	*obitelj*
father	o-tsa	*oca*
grandfather	dye-da	*djeda*
grandmother	ba-bu	*babu*
husband	su-pru-ga/mu-zha	*supruga/muža*
mother	may-ku	*majku*
sister	ses-tru	*sestru*
son	si-na	*sina*
wife	su-pru-gu/zhe-nu	*suprugu/ženu*

Feelings

I (don't) like ...   (ne) vo-lim ...   *(Ne) volim ...*

I'm ...	me-ni ...	*Meni ...*
cold	ye hlad-no	*je hladno*
hot	ye vru-tche	*je vruće*
right	ye do-bro	*je dobro*
sleepy	se spa-va	*se spava*

I'm ...	ya sam ...	*Ja sam ...*
angry	**lyut/lyu-ta**	*ljut/ljuta* (m/f)
happy	**sre-tan/sret-na**	*sretan/sretna* (m/f)
hungry	**gla-dan/glad-na**	*gladan/gladna* (m/f)
in a hurry	**u zhur-bi**	*u žurbi*
sad	**tu-zhan/tuzh-na**	*tužan/tužna* (m/f)
thirsty	**zhe-dan/zhed-na**	*žedan/žedna* (m/f)
tired	**u-mo-ran/u-mor-na**	*umoran/umorna* (m/f)
well	**dob-ro**	*dobro*
worried	**za-bri-nut**	*zabrinut/*
	za-bri-nu-ta	*zabrinuta* (m/f)

I'm sorry.	**zhao mi ye**	*Žao mi je.*
I'm grateful.	**za-hva-lan/**	*Zahvalan/*
	za-hval-na sam	*Zahvalna sam.* (m/f)

BREAKING THE LANGUAGE BARRIER

Do you speak English?
go-vo-ri-te li en-gles-ki?   *Govorite li engleski?*
Does anyone speak English?
go-vo-ri li net-ko en-gles-ki?   *Govori li netko engleski?*
I speak a little ...
ya go-vo-rim ma-lo ...   *Ja govorim malo ...*
I (don't) understand.
(ne) ra-zu-mi-yem   *(Ne) razumijem.*
Could you speak more slowly,
please?
go-vo-ri-te po-la-ko, mo-lim   *Govorite polako, molim.*
Could you repeat that?
po-no-vi-te mo-lim   *Ponovite, molim.*
Please write that down.
na-pi-shi-te mi mo-lim vas   *Napišite mi, molim vas.*
How do you say ...?
ka-ko se ka-zhe ...?   *Kako se kaže ...?*
What does ... mean?
shta zna-chi ...?   *Šta znači ...?*

BODY LANGUAGE

When a Croat shakes their head from left to right, it means that they don't agree with something or that they respond negatively to your question. Nodding the head usually indicates an affirmative response. A person wagging an outstretched index finger or touching it to their temple probably wants to tell you that you've angered them or that you've made an error. Patting on the back or shoulder means approval, shrugging of the shoulders is done when someone does not know the answer to a question.

PAPERWORK

address	a-dre-sa	*adresa*
age	uz-rast	*uzrast*
birth certificate	krs-ni list	*krsni list*
border	gra-ni-tsa	*granica*
customs	tsa-ri-na	*carina*
date of birth	da-tum ro-dje-nya	*datum rođenja*
driver's licence	vo-zach-ka doz-vo-la	*vozačka dozvola*
identification	i-den-ti-fi-ka-tsi-ya	*identifikacija*
immigration	pa-sosh-ka kon-tro-la	*pasoška kontrola*
marital status	brach-no sta-nye	*bračno stanje*
name	i-me	*ime*
nationality	na-tsi-o-nal-nost	*nacionalnost*
passport	pu-tov-ni-tsa	*putovnica*
passport number	broy pu-tov-ni-tse	*broj putovnice*
place of birth	myes-to ro-dje-nya	*mjesto rođenja*
profession	za-ni-ma-nye	*zanimanje*
reason for travel	raz-log pu-to-va-nya	*razlog putovanja*
religion	vye-ra	*vjera*
sex	spol	*spol*
tourist card	tu-ris-tich-ka kar-ta (le-gi-ti-ma-tsi-ya)	*turistička karta (legitimacija)*
visa	vi-za	*viza*

CROATIAN

GETTING AROUND

What time does	ka-da po-la-zi/	*Kada polazi/*
the ... leave/arrive?	do-la-zi ...?	*dolazi ...?*
aeroplane	zra-ko-plov	*zrakoplov*
boat	brod	*brod*
bus (city)	a-u-to-bus (grad-ski)	*autobus (gradski)*
bus (intercity)	a-u-to-bus	*autobus*
	(me-dju-grad-ski)	*(međugradski)*
train	vlak	*vlak*
tram	tram-vay	*tramvaj*

Directions

How do I get to ...?
  ka-ko da stig-nem do ...?   *Kako da stignem do ...?*

Is it far from/near here?
  ye li da-le-ko/bli-zu od-av-de?   *Je li daleko/blizu odavde?*

Can you show me (on the map)?
  mo-zhe-te li mi   *Možete li mi*
  po-ka-za-ti (na kar-ti)?   *pokazati (na karti)?*

I want to go to ...
  zhe-lim o-ti-tchi u ...   *Želim otići u ...*

Go straight ahead.
  i-di-te pra-vo na-pri-yed   *Idite pravo naprijed.*

Where's ...?	gdye ye ...?	*Gdje je ...?*

Turn left/right	skre-ni-te li-ye-vo/	*Skrenite lijevo/*
at the ...	des-no ...	*desno ...*
next corner	na slye-de-tchem ug-lu	*na sljedećem uglu*
traffic lights	kod se-ma-fo-ra	*kod semafora*

behind	iza	*iza*
far	da-le-ko	*daleko*
in front of	is-pri-yed	*isprijed*
near	bli-zu	*blizu*
opposite	pre-ko	*preko*

north	sye-ver	*sjever*
south	yug	*jug*
east	is-tok	*istok*
west	za-pad	*zapad*

Booking Tickets

Excuse me, where's the ticket office?
    o-pros-ti-te, gdye   *Oprostite, gdje*
    ye bla-gay-na?   *je blagajna?*
Where can I buy a ticket?
    gdye mo-gu ku-pi-ti kar-tu?   *Gdje mogu kupiti kartu?*
I want to go to ...
    zhe-lim o-ti-tchi u ...   *Želim otići u ...*
Do I need to book?
    da li mi ye po-treb-na   *Da li mi je potrebna*
    re-zer-va-tsi-ya?   *rezervacija?*
I'd like to book a seat to ...
    zhe-lim da re-zer-vi-shem   *Želim da rezervišem*
    myes-to do ...   *mjesto do ...*
Is it completely full?
    da li ye sas-vim pu-no?   *Da li je sasvim puno?*

SIGNS

HLADNO	COLD
INFORMACIJE	INFORMATION
IZLAZ	EXIT
IZLAZ ZA SLUČAJ OPASNOSTI	EMERGENCY EXIT
OTVORENO	OPEN
REZERVISANO	RESERVED
TELEFON	TELEPHONE
ULAZ	ENTRANCE
ULAZ SLOBODAN	FREE ADMISSION
ULAZ ZABRANJEN	NO ENTRY
VRUĆE	HOT
ZABRANJENO	PROHIBITED
ZABRANJENO PUŠENJE	NO SMOKING
ZAHODI	TOILETS
ZATVORENO	CLOSED

CROATIAN

THEY MAY SAY ...

pu-no ye	It's full.
po-treb-na vam ye re-zer-va-tsi-ya	You need to book.

I'd like ...	zhe-lim ...	*Želim ...*
a one-way ticket	kar-tu u yed-nom prav-cu	*kartu u jednom pravcu*
a return ticket	po-vrat-nu kar-tu	*povratnu kartu*
two tickets	dve kar-te	*dvije karte*
tickets for all of us	kar-te za sve nas	*karte za sve nas*
a student's fare	stu-dent-sku tsi-ye-nu	*studentsku cijenu*
a child's fare	dyech-yu tsi-ye-nu	*dječju cijenu*
a pensioner's fare	u-mi-ro-vlye-nich-ku tsye-nu	*umirovljeničku cijenu*
1st class	pr-vu kla-su	*prvu klasu*
2nd class	dru-gu kla-su	*drugu klasu*

Bus

Where's the bus stop?
gdye ye a-u-to-bus-ka pos-ta-ya?   *Gdje je autobuska postaja?*

Which bus goes to ...?
ko-yi a-u-to-bus i-de za ...?   *Koji autobus ide za ...?*

Does this bus go to ...?
i-de li o-vay a-u-to-bus za ...?   *Ide li ovaj autobus za ...?*

How often do buses pass by?
ka-ko ches-to pro-la-ze a-u-to-bu-si?   *Kako često prolaze autobusi?*

What time's the ... bus?	ka-da po-la-zi ... a-u-to-bus?	*Kada polazi ... autobus?*
first	pr-vi	*prvi*
last	zad-nyi	*zadnji*
next	slye-de-tchi	*sljedeći*

Could you let me know
when we get to ...?

mo-zhe-te li mi re-tchi
kad sti-zhe-mo u ...?

Možete li mi reći kad stižemo u ...?

I want to get off!

zhe-lim da si-djem!

Želim da siđem!

Train & Metro

Is this the right
platform for ...?

da li ye o-vo pe-ron za ...?

Da li je ovo peron za ...?

Which line takes me to ...?

ko-ya li-ni-ya i-de za ...?

Koja linija ide za ...?

What's the
next station?

ko-ya ye slye-de-tcha pos-ta-ya?

Koja je sljedeća postaja?

Is that seat taken?

da li ye o-vo sye-da-lo
za-u-ze-to?

Da li je ovo sjedalo zauzeto?

I want to get off at ...

zhe-lim da si-djem u ...

Želim da siđem u ...

change trains	pro-mye-ni-ti vlak	*promjeniti vlak*
change platforms	pro-mye-ni-ti pe-ron	*promjeniti peron*
dining car	ko-la za ru-cha-va-nye	*kola za ručavanje*
express	eks-pres	*ekspres*
local	lo-kal-ni	*lokalni*
sleeping car	ko-la za spa-va-nye	*kola za spavanje*

Taxi

Can you take me to ...?
mo-zhe-te li me od-ves-ti do ...? *Možete li me odvesti do ...?*

Please take me to ...
mo-lim vas od-ve-zi-te me do ... *Molim vas odvezite me do ...*

How much does it cost to go to ...?
ko-li-ko kosh-ta *Koliko košta*
vozh-nya do ...? *vožnja do ...?*

Here's fine, thank you.
ov-dye iz-la-zim, hva-la *Ovdje izlazim, hvala.*

The next corner, please.
na slye-de-tchem ug-lu,mo-lim *Na sljedećem uglu, molim.*

Continue!
Pro-du-zhi-te! *Produžite!*

The next street to the left/right.
slye-de-tcha u-li-tsa *Sljedeća ulica*
li-ye-vo/des-no *lijevo/desno.*

Stop here!
sta-ni-te ov-dye! *Stanite ovdje!*

Please slow down.
us-po-ri-te mo-lim *Usporite molim.*

Please wait here.
sa-che-kay-te ov-dye, mo-lim *Sačekajete ovdje, molim.*

Car

Where can I rent a car?
gdye mo-gu da na-djem *Gdje mogu da nađem*
rent-a-kar? *rent-a-car?*

How much is it daily/weekly?
ko-li-ko kosh-ta dnev-no/ *Koliko košta dnevno/*
tyed-no? *tjedno?*

Does that include
insurance/mileage?
da li to u-klyu-chu-ye *Da li to uključuje*
o-si-gu-ra-nye/ *osiguranje/*
ki-lo-me-tra-zhu? *kilometražu?*

CROATIAN

What make is it?
   ko-ya mar-ka ye to?   *Koja marka je to?*

Where's the next petrol station?
   gdye ye slye-de-tcha   *Gdje je sljedeća*
   ben-zin-ska sta-ni-tsa?   *benzinska stanica?*

Please fill the tank.
   mo-lim vas na-pu-ni-te   *Molim vas napunite*
   re-zer-vo-ar   *rezervoar.*

I want ... litres of petrol (gas).
   zhe-lim ... lit-re ben-zi-na   *Želim ... litre benzina.*

Please check the oil and water.
   mo-lim vas pro-vye-ri-te   *Molim vas provjerite*
   u-lye i vo-du   *ulje i vodu.*

How long can I park here?
   ka-ko du-go mo-gu   *Kako dugo mogu*
   ov-dye par-ki-ra-ti?   *ovdje parkirati?*

Does this road lead to ...?
   da li o-vay put vo-di do ...?   *Da li ovaj put vodi do ...?*

I need a mechanic.
   tre-ba mi   *Treba mi*

air (for tyres)	zrak	*zrak*
battery	a-ku-mu-la-tor	*akumulator*
brakes	koch-ni-tse	*kočnice*
clutch	kva-chi-lo	*kvačilo*
driver's licence	vo-zach-ka doz-vo-la	*vozačka dozvola*
engine	ma-shi-na	*mašina*
lights	svi-yet-la	*svijetla*
oil	u-lye	*ulje*
petrol	ben-zi-n	*benzin*
puncture	pro-bu-she-na	*probušena*
radiator	ra-di-ya-tor	*radijator*
road map	au-to-kar-ta	*auto-karta*
tyres	gu-me	*gume*
windscreen	vyet-ro-bran	*vjetrobran*

ACCOMMODATION

Where's a ... hotel?	gdye i-ma ... ho-tel?	*Gdje ima ... hotel?*
cheap	yef-tin	*jeftin*
good	do-bar	*dobar*
clean	chist	*čist*

I'm looking for a nearby hotel.
tra-zhim ho-tel u bli-zi-ni	*Tražim hotel u blizini.*

What's the address?
ko-ya ye a-dre-sa?	*Koja je adresa?*

Could you please write down
the address?
mo-zhe-te li mi na-pi-sa-ti	*Možete li mi napisati*
a-dre-su mo-lim?	*adresu molim?*

At the Hotel

Do you have any rooms available?
i-ma-te li slo-bod-nu so-bu?	*Imate li slobodnu sobu?*

I'd like ...	zhe-lim ...	*Želim ...*
a single room	yed-no-kre-vet-nu so-bu	*jednokrevetnu sobu*
a double room	dvo-kre-vet-nu so-bu	*dvokrevetnu sobu*
a room with	so-bu sa	*sobu sa*
a bathroom	ku-pa-o-ni-tsom	*kupaonicom*
to share a dorm	kre-vet u stu-dent-skom do-mu	*krevet u studentskom domu*
a bed	kre-vet	*krevet*

I want a room with a ...	zhe-lim so-bu sa ...	*Želim sobu sa ...*
bathroom	ku-pa-o-ni-tsom	*kupaonicom*
shower	tu-shem	*tušem*
television	te-le-vi-zo-rom	*televizorom*
window	pro-zo-rom	*prozorom*

CROATIAN

I'm going to stay for ...	os-tat tchu ...	*Ostat ću ...*
one day	ye-dan dan	*jedan dan*
two days	dva da-na	*dva dana*
one week	ye-dan tye-dan	*jedan tjedan*

How much is it per night/per person?
 ko-li-ko kosh-ta za
 yed-nu notch/po o-so-bi? — *Koliko košta za jednu noć/ po osobi?*

Can I see it?
 mo-gu li vi-dye-ti? — *Mogu li vidjeti?*

Are there any others?
 i-ma-te li dru-ge so-be? — *Imate li druge sobe?*

Can I see the bathroom?
 mo-gu li da vi-dim
 ku-pa-o-ni-tsu? — *Mogu li da vidim kupaonicu?*

Is there a reduction for students/children?
 i-ma li po-pust za
 stu-den-te/dye-tsu? — *Ima li popust za studente/djecu?*

Is there hot water all day?
 i-ma li vru-tche vo-de
 pre-ko tsye-log da-na? — *Ima li vruće vode preko cjelog dana?*

It's fine, I'll take it.
 dob-ra ye, u-zet tchu ye — *Dobra je, uzet ću je.*

Requests & Complaints

Do you have a safe where I
can leave my valuables?
    i-ma-te li ka-su gdye   *Imate li kasu gdje*
    mo-gu chu-va-ti   *mogu čuvati*
    mo-ye vri-yed-ne stva-ri   *moje vrijedne stvari?*
Is there somewhere to wash clothes?
    mo-gu li neg-dye   *Mogu li negdje da*
    da o-pe-rem svoy vesh   *operem svoj veš?*
Can I use the telephone?
    mo-gu li te-le-fo-ni-ra-ti?   *Mogu li telefonirati?*
The room needs to be cleaned.
    so-bu tre-ba o-tchis-ti-ti   *Sobu treba očistiti.*

I can't open/close the window.
    ne mo-gu da ot-vo-rim/   *Ne mogu da otvorim/*
    zat-vo-rim pro-zor   *zatvorim prozor.*
I've locked myself out of my room.
    zak-lyu-tcha-o/zak-lyu-tcha-la   *Zaključao/Zaključala*
    sam se spo-lya   *sam se spolja.* (m/f)
The toilet won't flush.
    to-a-let ne push-ta vo-du   *Toalet ne pušta vodu.*
I'd like to pay the bill.
    zhe-lim da pla-tim ra-chun   *Želim da platim račun.*

CROATIAN

AROUND TOWN
At the Post Office

I'd like some stamps.

zhe-lim posh-tan-ske mar-ke   *Želim poštanske marke.*

How much is the postage?

ko-li-ko kosh-ta posh-ta-ri-na?   *Koliko košta poštarina?*

I'd like to send a/an ...	zhe-lim pos-la-ti ...	*Želim poslati ...*
aerogram	a-e-ro-gram	*aerogram*
letter	pis-mo	*pismo*
postcard	raz-gled-ni-tsu	*razglednicu*
parcel	pa-ket	*paket*
telegram	br-zo-yav	*brzojav*
airmail	a-vi-on-ski	*avionski*
envelope	ko-ve-rat	*koverat*
mailbox	posh-tan-sko san-du-che	*poštansko sanduče*
parcel	pa-ket	*paket*
registered mail	pre-po-ru-che-no pis-mo	*preporučeno pismo*
surface mail	o-bich-no pis-mo	*obično pismo*

Telephone

I want to ring ...

zhe-lim da te-le-fo-ni-ram ...   *Želim da telefoniram ...*

The number is ...

broy ye ...   *Broj je ...*

I want to speak for three minutes.

zhe-lim da go-vo-rim   *Želim da govorim*
ri mi-nu-ta   *tri minuta.*

How much does a three-minute call cost?

ko-li-ko kosh-ta   *Koliko košta*
raz-go-vor od tri mi-nu-ta?   *razgovor od tri minuta?*

CROATIAN

I'd like to speak to (Mr Perez).

zhe-lim go-vo-ri-ti sa
(gos-po-di-nom pe-re-zom)

*Želim govoriti sa
(gospodinom Perezom).*

I want to make a reverse-charges
phone call.

zhe-lim da te-le-fo-ni-ram
na nyi-hov ra-chun

*Želim da telefoniram
na njihov račun.*

It's engaged.

za-u-ze-to ye

Zauzeto je.

I've been cut off.

pre-ki-nu-li su me

Prekinuli su me.

Internet

Where can I get Internet access?

gdye mo-gu do-bi-ti
pris-tup na in-ter-net?

*Gdje mogu dobiti
pristup na internet?*

How much is it per hour?

ko-li-ko kosh-ta na sat?

Koliko košta na sat?

I want to check my email.

zhe-lim pro-vye-ri-ti svo-yu
e-lek-tron-sku posh-tu

*Želim provjeriti svoju
elektronsku poštu.*

At the Bank

I want to exchange some
(money/travellers cheques).

zhe-lim da raz-mye-nim
(no-vats/put-nich-ke che-ko-ve)

*Želim da razmjenim
(novac/putničke čekove).*

What's the exchange rate?

ko-yi ye kurs raz-mye-ne?

Koji je kurs razmjene?

How many ... per kuna?

ko-li-ko ... za ye-dan ku-na?

Koliko ... za jedan kuna?

Can I have money transferred
here from my bank?

mo-gu li da pre-ba-tsim no-vats
iz mo-ye u o-vu ban-ku?

*Mogu li da prebacim novac
iz moje u ovu banku?*

CROATIAN

How long will it take to arrive?
   ko-li-ko tche vre-me-na   *Koliko će vremena*
   tre-ba-ti da stig-ne?   *trebati da stigne?*
Has my money arrived yet?
   da li ye sti-ga-o moy no-vats?   *Da li je stigao moj novac?*

bankdraft	ban-kov-ni chek	*bankovni ček*
banknotes	nov-cha-ni-tsa	*novčanica*
cashier	bla-gay-nik	*blagajnik*
coins	me-tal-ni no-vats	*metalni novac*
credit card	kre-dit-na kar-ti-tsa	*kreditna kartica*
exchange	raz-mye-na	*razmjena*
loose change	si-tan no-vac	*sitan novac*
signature	pot-pis	*potpis*

INTERESTS & ENTERTAINMENT
Sightseeing

Do you have a guidebook/local map?
   da li i-ma-te tu-ris-tich-ki   *Da li imate turistički*
   vo-dich/lo-kal-nu kar-tu?   *vodič/lokalnu kartu?*
What are the main attractions?
   ko-ye su glav-ne   *Koje su glavne*
   za-nim-lyi-vos-ti?   *zanimljivosti?*
How old is it?
   ko-li-ko ye sta-ro?   *Koliko je staro?*
Can I take photographs?
   mo-gu li fo-to-gra-fi-ra-ti?   *Mogu li fotografirati?*
What time does it open/close?
   ka-da se ot-va-ra/zat-va-ra?   *Kada se otvara/zatvara?*

CROATIAN

ancient	sta-ro	*staro*
archaeological	ar-he-o-losh-ko	*arheološko*
beach	pla-zha	*plaža*
building	zgra-da	*zgrada*
castle	za-mak	*zamak*
cathedral	ka-te-dra-la	*katedrala*
church	tsrk-va	*crkva*
concert hall	kon-cert-na dvo-ra-na	*koncertna dvorana*
library	knjizh-ni-tsa	*knjižnica*
main square	glav-ni trg	*glavni trg*
market	pi-ya-tsa	*pijaca*
monastery	ma-nas-tir	*manastir*
monument	spo-me-nik	*spomenik*
mosque	dja-mi-ya	*džamija*
old city	sta-ri grad	*stari grad*
palace	pa-la-cha	*palača*
opera house	o-per-ska ku-tcha	*operska kuća*
ruins	ru-she-vi-ne	*ruševine*
stadium	sta-di-on	*stadion*
statues	sta-tu-e	*statue*
synagogue	si-na-go-ga	*sinagoga*
temple	hram	*hram*
university	sve-u-chi-lish-te	*sveučilište*

Going Out

What's there to do in the evenings?

| gdye se mo-zhe i-za-tchi u-ve-che? | *Gdje se može izaći uveče?* |

Are there any nightclubs?

| i-ma li ov-dye dis-ko? | *Ima li ovdje disko?* |

Are there places where you can hear local folk music?

| i-ma li gdye da se slu-sha lo-kal-na na-rod-na mu-zi-ka? | *Ima li gdje da se sluša lokalna narodna muzika?* |

How much does it cost to get in?

| ko-li-ko kosh-ta u-laz-ni-tsa? | *Koliko košta ulaznica?* |

cinema	ki-no	*kino*
concert	kon-tsert	*koncert*
nightclub	dis-ko-te-ka	*diskoteka*
theatre	ka-za-lish-te	*kazalište*

Sports & Interests

What sports do you play?
    ko-yim se spor-tom ba-vi-te?   *Kojim se sportom bavite?*
What are your interests?
    shto vas za-ni-ma?   *Što vas zanima?*

art	u-myet-nost	*umjetnost*
basketball	ko-shar-ka	*košarka*
chess	shah	*šah*
collecting things	ko-lek-tsi-o-nar-stvo	*kolekcionarstvo*
dancing	ples	*ples*
food	ye-lo	*jelo*
football	no-go-myet	*nogomjet*
hiking	pye-sha-che-nye	*pješačenje*
martial arts	bo-ri-lach-ke vyesh-ti-ne	*borilačke vještine*
meeting friends	dru-zhe-nye s	*druženje s*
	pri-ya-te-lyi-ma	*prijateljima*
movies	fil-mo-vi	*filmovi*
music	glaz-ba	*glazba*
nightclubs	notch-ni klu-bo-vi	*noćni klubovi*
photography	fo-to-gra-fi-ra-nye	*fotografiranje*
reading	chi-ta-nye	*čitanje*
shopping	ku-po-vi-na	*kupovina*
skiing	ski-ya-nye	*skijanje*
swimming	pli-va-nye	*plivanje*
tennis	te-nis	*tenis*
travelling	pu-to-va-nya	*putovanja*
TV/videos	TV/vi-de-o	*TV/video*
visiting friends	po-sye-ti	*posjeti*
	pri-ya-te-lyi-ma	*prijateljima*
walking	shet-nye	*šetnje*

CROATIAN

Festivals

Dubrovačke Ljetnje Igre dub-ro-vach-ke lyet-nye ig-re
Dubrovnik Summer Festival held from mid-July to mid-August, this is a major cultural event with over 100 performances at different venues in the old city

Fešta Svetog Blaža fesh-ta sve-tog bla-zha
feast of Saint Blaise celebrated on 3 February

Fešta Svetog Duje fesh-ta sve-tog du-ye
feast of St Dujo held every year on 7 May

Festival Narodne Glazbe fes-ti-val na-rod-ne glaz-be
festival of Popular Music held around the end of June, this is a four-day festival of music

Splitsko Ljeto split-sko lye-to
Split Summer Festival held from mid-July to mid-August, this festival features opera, drama, ballet and concerts on open-air stages

Zagrebački Bienale Savremene Muzike (*Zagreb*)
zag-re-bach-ki bi-e-na-le sav-re-me-ne mu-zi-ke
biennial of Contemporary Music held in April during odd numbered years, this is Croatia's most important music event

Zagrebačko Ljeto zag-re-bach-ko lye-to
Zagreb Summer Festival during July and August you can see concerts and theatre performances on open stages in the upper town

IN THE COUNTRY
Weather

What's the weather like?
   kak-vo ye vri-ye-me?   *Kakvo je vrijeme?*
Will it be ... tomorrow?
   da li tche sut-ra bi-ti ...?   *Da li će sutra biti ...?*

The weather's ... today.	vri-ye-me ye da-nas ...	*Vrijeme je danas ...*
cloudy	ob-lach-no	*oblačno*
cold	hlad-no	*hladno*
foggy	mag-lo-vi-to	*maglovito*
frosty	mra-zo-vi-to	*mrazovito*
hot	vru-tche	*vruće*
raining	kish-no	*kišno*
snowing	sni-ye-go-vi-to	*snijegovito*
sunny	sun-cha-no	*sunčano*
windy	vyet-ro-vi-to	*vjetrovito*

Camping

Am I allowed to camp here?
mo-gu li da kam-pi-ram
ov-dye?

*Mogu li da kampiram
ovdje?*

Is there a campsite nearby?
da li i-ma kam-ping
u bli-zi-ni?

*Da li ima kamping
u blizini?*

backpack	ruk-sak	*ruksak*
can opener	ot-va-rach za kon-zer-ve	*otvarač za konzerve*
compass	kom-pas	*kompas*
crampons	zhe-lyez-na ku-ka	*željezna kuka*
firewood	dr-va za o-grev	*drva za ogrev*
gas cartridge	bo-tsa s pli-nom	*boca s plinom*
hammock	mre-zha za le-zha-nye	*mreža za ležanje*
ice axe	sye-ki-ri-tsa	*sjekirica*
mattress	mad-rats	*madrac*
penknife	pe-ro-rez	*perorez*
rope	uzhe	*uže*
tent	sha-tor	*šator*
tent pegs	ko-chi-tchi za sha-tor	*kočići za šator*
torch (flashlight)	ruch-na svye-tily-ka	*ručna svjetiljka*
sleeping bag	vre-tcha za spa-va-nye	*vreća za spavanje*
stove	petch	*peć*
water bottle	bo-tsa za vo-du	*boca za vodu*

CROATIAN

FOOD

Croatian cuisine reflects the cultures that have influenced the country over the course of its history. Thus, there's a sharp divide between the Italian-style cuisine on the coast and the Hungarian, Viennese and Turkish-style cuisine in the interior of the country.

Each region has its own speciality, but wherever you go, you'll be delighted by the generally good quality food, made from fresh, seasonal ingredients.

breakfast	do-ru-chak	*doručak*
lunch	ru-chak	*ručak*
dinner	ve-che-ra	*večera*

Vegetarian Meals

I'm a vegetarian.
  ya sam ve-ge-ta-ri-ya-nats/
  ve-ge-ta-ri-yan-ka
       Ja sam vegetarijanac/
       vegetarijanka. (m/f)
I don't eat meat.
  ne ye-dem me-so
       Ne jedem meso.
I don't eat chicken, fish or ham.
  ne ye-dem pi-le-ti-nu,
  ni ri-bu, ni shun-ku
       Ne jedem piletinu,
       ni ribu, ni šunku.

CROATIAN

MENU DECODER

Starters & Snacks

ajvar	ay-var spicy mixture of grilled peppers, eggplant and carrots blended together. Try this spread on bread.
Dalmatinski pršut	dal-ma-tin-ski pr-shut lightly smoked ham
salama gavrilović	sa-la-ma gav-ri-lo-vitch as good as the very best Hungarian or Italian salami
pogačice sa čvarcima	po-ga-chi-tse sa chvar-tsi-ma oven-browned savoury rolls with small chunks of fried pork

Main Dishes

pljeskavica	plyes-ka-vi-tsa minced pork, beef or lamb shaped as a hamburger
pljeskavica sa kajmakom	plyes-ka-vi-tsa sa kay-ma-kom as the dish above, except with cream
ražnjići	razh-nyi-tchi small chunks of pork grilled on a skewer
ćevapčići	tche-vap-chi-tchi minced pork, beef or lamb shaped into small sausages
punjene paprike	pu-nye-ne pap-ri-ke peppers stuffed with minced beef or pork and rice in a fresh tomato sauce

Desserts

The style of cakes in Croatia is familiar to Western eyes and palates.

doboš	do-bosh this cake is of Hungarian origin and is garnished with coffee and caramel
štrukle	shtruk-le a fantastic blend of pastry and fruit: *sa jabukama* sa ya-bu-ka-ma is with apples, *sa trešnjama* sa tresh-nya-ma is with cherries.
baklava	bak-la-va a flaky pastry with nuts, soaked in sugar syrup

CROATIAN

Non-Alcoholic Drinks

coffee	**ka-va**	*kava*
tea	**chay**	*čaj*
with milk	**sa mli-ye-kom**	*sa mlijekom*
with sugar	**sa she-tche-rom**	*sa šećerom*
fruit juice	**votch-ni sok**	*voćni sok*
hot chocolate	**top-la cho-ko-la-da**	*topla čokolada*
mineral water	**mi-ne-ral-na vo-da**	*mineralna voda*
(boiled) water	**(vre-la) vo-da**	*(vrela) voda*

Alcoholic Drinks

This is great vine-growing country, and virtually every region produces its own wine. Popular wines include:

WHITE		RED	
Smederevka	**sme-de-rev-ka**	*Teran*	**te-ran**
Žilavka	**zhi-lav-ka**	*Dingač*	**din-gach**
		Negotin	**ne-go-tin**

dark red	**tsr-no**	*crno*
rosé	**ru-zhi-tsa**	*ružica*
white	**bye-lo**	*bjelo*

All local spirits are extremely strong. Most distilled drinks are simply known as 'brandy', though you'll most often encounter plum brandy.

brandy	**ra-ki-ya**	*rakija*
plum brandy	**shlyi-vo-vi-tsa**	*šljivovica*

At the Market

How much is it?	ko-li-ko kosh-ta?	*Koliko košta?*
Could you lower the price?	mo-zhe-te li sma-nyi-ti tsi-ye-nu?	*Možete li smanjiti cijenu?*
I don't have much money.	ne-mam mno-go nov-tsa	*Nemam mnogo novca.*

I'd like ... grams/kilos.		
zhe-lim ... gra-ma/ki-la		*Želim .... grama/kila.*

Staple Foods

bread	kru-ha	*kruha*
butter	mas-la-tsa	*maslaca*
cereal	zhi-ta-ri-tse	*žitarice*
cheese	si-ra	*sira*
chocolate	cho-ko-la-du	*čokoladu*
eggs	ya-ya	*jaja*
flour	brash-no	*brašno*
honey	me-da	*meda*
margarine	mar-ga-ri-na	*margarina*
marmalade	mar-me-la-du	*marmeladu*
milk	mli-ye-ka	*mlijeka*
olive oil	mas-li-no-vo u-lye	*maslinovo ulje*
pasta	tyes-te-ni-ne	*tjestenine*
pepper	pa-par	*papar*
rice	ri-zha	*riža*
salt	so	*so*
sugar	she-tcher	*šećer*
yogurt	yo-gurt	*jogurt*

CROATIAN

Meat & Fish

beef	go-ve-di-na	*govedina*
chicken	pi-le-ti-na	*piletina*
fish	ri-ba	*riba*
ham	shun-ke	*šunke*
hamburger	ham-bur-ger	*hamburger*
lamb	ja-nye-ti-na	*janjetina*
lobster	yas-tog	*jastog*
mackerel	sku-sha	*skuša*
meat	me-so	*meso*
mussels	shkoly-ke	*školjke*
oysters	os-tri-ge	*ostrige*
pork	svi-nye-ti-na	*svinjetina*
red mullet	bar-bu-ni	*barbuni*
sausage	ko-ba-si-tsa	*kobasica*
shrimp	shkam-pe	*škampe*
squid	lig-nye	*lignje*
turkey	pu-re-ti-na	*puretina*
veal	yu-ne-ti-na	*junetina*

Fruit

apple	ya-bu-ka	*jabuka*
apricot	kay-si-ya	*kajsija*
banana	ba-na-na	*banana*
fig	smok-va	*smokva*
grapes	grozh-dje	*grožde*
kiwifruit	ki-vi	*kivi*
lemon	li-mun	*limun*
orange	na-ran-cha	*naranča*
peach	bres-kva	*breskva*
pear	krush-ka	*kruška*
plum	shlyi-va	*šljiva*
strawberry	ya-go-da	*jagoda*

CROATIAN

Vegetables

aubergine/eggplant	pat-li-jan	*patlidžan*
(green) beans	bo-ran-ya	*boranja*
beetroot	tsik-la	*cikla*
broad beans	bo-ran-ya	*boranja*
cabbage	ku-pus	*kupus*
carrot	mrk-va	*mrkva*
red/green	tsr-ve-na/	*crvena/zelena*
capsicum	ze-le-na ba-bu-ra	*babura*
cauliflower	tsvi-ye-ta-cha	*cvijetača*
celery	tse-ler	*celer*
chickpeas	leb-le-bi-ya	*leblebija*
chillies	fe-fe-ro-ne	*feferone*
courgette/zucchini	tik-vi-tsa	*tikvica*
cucumber	kras-ta-vats	*krastavac*
garlic	bi-ye-li luk	*bijeli luk*
ginger	gjum-bir	*đumbir*
kidney beans	grah	*grah*
lentils	so-chi-vo	*sočivo*
lettuce	ze-le-na sa-la-ta	*zelena salata*
mushrooms	glyi-ve	*gljive*
onion	tsr-ni luk	*crni luk*
peas	gra-shak	*grašak*
potato	krum-pir	*krumpir*
spinach	shpi-nat	*špinat*
tomato	ray-chi-tsa	*rajčica*
vegetables	po-vr-tche	*povrće*

ISTRIAN FEAST

Istria, the largest Peninsula in the Adriatic, is the most cosmopolitan region in Croatia. Its cuisine closely resembles that of its Italian neighbour, but with a few distinctive touches. The recipes below use typically Istrian ingredients or combine flavours in a way that Italians normally would not, such as wrapping shellfish in meat. Risotto and polenta are Istrian staples that are becoming widely available either in original or instant versions. Here are some simple recipes that serve four people.

Antipasto
On a large platter arrange eight slices of Istrian prosciutto and eight thinly sliced wedges of formaggio pecorino or Istrian sheep cheese around a pile of black olives.

Brodetto all'istriana
Istrian-style fish stew
Choose about one kilo of mixed shellfish such as shrimp, crab, mussels and clams and one whole white fish such as snapper, sea bass, halibut or groper. Cut 150g (one-third of a pound) of squid into small bite-size rounds. (Unless the squid is young it may need to be beaten with a hammer first to tenderise it.) Clean and wash the fish. Heat ¼ cup of olive oil in a large pot and saute the fish until brown. Add the shellfish and squid, 250g (½ lb) of sliced onion, four peeled garlic cloves, 300g (two-thirds of a pound) fresh tomatoes cut into quarters, two tablespoons of chopped parsley, two bay leaves and salt and pepper to taste. Add water to cover and bring to a boil. When it reaches a boil add ½ cup wine. Cook for 30 minutes, stirring from time to time. Serve with polenta or large chunks of bread.

CROATIAN

ISTRIAN FEAST

Involtini di Prosciutto Agli Scampi
Shrimp wrapped in prosciutto

Take 12 prawns and drop them into boiling water. Cook for up to five minutes, depending on the size of the prawn. Remove, peel and cut off the heads and tails. Wrap each prawn in a slice of prosciutto. Heat a third of a cup of good olive oil in a skillet. Brown the prawns quickly over medium-high heat until the prosciutto colours slightly, turning frequently. Add ½ cup of wine and reduce heat to low. Sprinkle with freshly ground pepper and salt to taste. Simmer for eight minutes and serve on top of risotto.

Frittelle istriane
Istrian pancakes

Beat three egg yolks with 120g (¼ cup) sugar until thick. Add ¼ teaspoon each of grated orange and lemon peel and one tablespoon of grappa. Beat egg whites until stiff and fold into the yolk mixture along with 400g (¾ lb) cream cheese or ricotta. Mix until thick and creamy. In another bowl blend three eggs with a pinch of salt. Add 250g (½ lb) flour, one cup milk and one cup mineral water. Ladle onto a hot skillet and fry the pancakes. Add the filling to the fried pancakes on one end only and roll them. Place on a buttered, ovenproof dish and top with a dollop of sour cream. Place under a hot grill until piping hot and serve immediately.

CROATIAN

SHOPPING

How much is it?
ko-li-ko kosh-ta?   *Koliko košta?*

Where's the nearest ...	gdye ye nay-bli-zhi ...?	*Gdje je najbliži ...?*
bookshop	knyizh-ni-tsa	*knjižnica*
camera shop	rad-nja za fo-to-a-pa-ra-te	*radnja za foto-aparate*
clothing store	rad-nya za o-dye-tchu	*radnja za odjeću*
delicatessen	de-li-ka-tes-na rad-nya	*delikatesna radnja*
general store	rad-nya sa raz-no-vrs-nom ro-bom	*radnja sa raz novrsnom robom*
laundry	pe-ri-o-ni-tsa	*perionica*
market	pi-ya-tsa	*pijaca*
newsagency	ki-osk za no-vi-ne	*kiosk za novine*
stationers	knyizh-ni-tsa	*knjižnica*
pharmacy	lye-kar-na	*ljekarna*
shoeshop	rad-nya za tsi-pe-le	*radnja za cipele*
souvenir shop	rad-nya za su-ve-ni-re	*radnja za suvenire*
supermarket	su-per-mar-ket	*supermarket*
green grocer	pi-lyar-ni-tsa	*piljarnica*

Do you accept credit cards?
mo-gu li pla-ti-ti
kre-dit-nom kar-ti-tsom?   *Mogu li platiti*
                                     kreditnom karticom?

Essential Groceries

I'd like ...	zhe-lim ku-pi-ti ...	*Želim kupiti ...*
batteries	ba-te-ri-ye	*baterije*
bread	kru-ha	*kruha*
butter	mas-la-tsa	*maslaca*
cheese	si-ra	*sira*
chocolate	cho-ko-la-du	*čokoladu*
honey	me-da	*meda*
margarine	mar-ga-ri-na	*margarina*
marmalade	mar-me-la-du	*marmeladu*
matches	shi-bi-tse	*šibice*
milk	mli-ye-ka	*mlijeka*
shampoo	sham-pon	*šampon*
soap	sa-pun	*sapun*
toilet paper	to-a-let-ni pa-pir	*toaletni papir*
toothpaste	pas-tu za zu-be	*pastu za zube*
washing powder	de-ter-jent za	*deterdžent za*
	pra-nye rub-lya	*pranje rublja*

Souvenirs

earrings	min-dju-she	*minđuše*
handicraft	ruch-ni rad	*ručni rad*
necklace	o-gr-li-tsa	*ogrlica*
pottery	grn-cha-ri-ya	*grnčarija*
ring	prs-ten	*prsten*
rug	tchi-lim	*ćilim*

Clothing

clothing	o-dye-tcha	*odjeća*
coat	ka-put	*kaput*
dress	ha-lyi-na	*haljina*
jacket	sa-ko	*sako*
jumper (sweater)	jem-per	*džemper*
shirt	ko-shu-lya	*košulja*
shoes	ci-pe-le	*cipele*
skirt	suk-nya	*suknja*
trousers	pan-ta-lo-ne	*pantalone*
underwear	do-nye rub-lye	*donje rublje*

CROATIAN

Materials

What's it made of?
od che-ga ye iz-ra-gje-no? *Od čega je izrađeno?*

cotton	pa-muk	*pamuk*
handmade	ruch-ni rad	*ručni rad*
leather	ko-zha	*koža*
of brass	od bak-ra	*od bakra*
of gold	od zla-ta	*od zlata*
of silver	od sreb-ra	*od srebra*
silk	svi-la	*svila*
wool	vu-na	*vuna*

Colours

black	tsr-na	*crna*
blue	pla-va	*plava*
brown	sme-dja	*smeđa*
green	ze-le-na	*zelena*
orange	na-ran-djas-ta	*narandžasta*
pink	ru-zhi-chas-ta	*ružičasta*
purple	lyu-bi-tchas-ta	*ljubičasta*
red	tsr-ve-na	*crvena*
white	bi-ye-la	*bijela*
yellow	zhu-ta	*žuta*

Toiletries

comb	che-shaly	*češalj*
condoms	kon-do-mi	*kondomi*
deodorant	de-zo-do-rans	*dezodorans*
hairbrush	chet-ka za ko-su	*četka za kosu*
moisturising cream	na-vlazh-u-yu-tcha kre-ma	*navlažujuća krema*
razor	bri-yach	*brijač*
sanitary napkins	hi-gi-yen-ske u-losh-ke	*higijenske uloške*
shampoo	sham-pon	*šampon*
shaving cream	kre-ma za bri-ya-nye	*krema za brijanje*

soap	sa-pun	*sapun*
sunscreen	kre-ma za zash-ti-tu od sun-ca	*krema za zaštitu od sunca*
tampons	tam-po-ni	*tamponi*
tissues	pa-pir-ne ma-ra-mi-tse	*papirne maramice*
toilet paper	to-a-let-ni pa-pir	*toaletni papir*
toothbrush	chet-ki-tsa za zu-be	*četkica za zube*
toothpaste	pas-ta za zu-be	*pasta za zube*

Stationery & Publications

map	kar-ta	*karta*
(English-language)...	... na en-gles-kom	*... na engleskom*
newspaper	no-vi-ne	*novine*
novels	knyi-ge	*knjige*
paper	pa-pir	*papir*
pen (ballpoint)	ke-miy-ska o-lov-ka	*kemijska olovka*
scissors	ma-ka-ze	*makaze*

Photography

How much is it to process this film?
ko-li-ko kosh-ta da se raz-vi-ye o-vay film?	*Koliko košta da se razvije ovaj film?*

When will it be ready?
ka-da tche bi-ti go-tov?	*Kada će biti gotov?*

I'd like a film for this camera.
zhe-lim film za o-vay fo-to-a-pa-rat	*Želim film za ovaj foto-aparat.*

B&W (film)	tsr-no-bi-ye-li	*crno-bijeli*
camera	fo-to-a-pa-rat	*foto-aparat*
colour (film)	u bo-yi (film)	*u boji (film)*
film	film	*film*
flash	blits	*blic*
lens	so-chi-vo	*sočivo*

Smoking

Do you smoke?
da li pu-shi-te? *Da li pušite?*

Please don't smoke.
mo-lim vas ne-moy-te *Molim vas nemojte*
pu-shi-ti *pušiti.*

A packet of cigarettes, please.
pak-lo tsi-ga-re-ta, mo-lim *Paklo cigareta, molim.*

Are these cigarettes strong/mild?
da li su o-ve tsi-ga-re-te *Da li su ove cigarete*
ya-ke/sla-be? *jake/slabe?*

Do you have a light?
i-ma-te li u-pa-lyach? *Imate li upaljač?*

cigarette papers	pa-pir za tsi-ga-re-te	*papir za cigarete*
cigarettes	tsi-ga-re-te	*cigarete*
filtered	sa fil-te-rom	*sa filterom*
lighter	u-pa-lyach	*upaljač*
matches	shi-bi-tse	*šibice*
menthol	men-tol	*mentol*
pipe	lu-la	*lula*
tobacco (pipe)	du-han (za lu-lu)	*duhan (za lulu)*

Sizes & Comparisons

small	ma-li	*mali*
big	ve-li-ki	*veliki*
heavy	te-zhak	*težak*
light	la-gan	*lagan*
more	vi-she	*više*
less	ma-nye	*manje*
too much/many	pre-vi-she	*previše*

HEALTH

Where's the ...?	gdye ye ...?	*Gdje je ...?*
chemist	lye-kar-na	*ljekarna*
dentist	zu-bar	*zubar*
doctor	li-yech-nik	*liječnik*
hospital	bol-ni-tsa	*bolnica*

Where does it hurt?	gdye vas bo-li?	*Gdje vas boli?*
It hurts here.	bo-li me ov-dye	*Boli me ovdje.*

I'm sick
    bo-les-tan/bo-les-na sam   *Bolestan/Bolesna sam.* (m/f)
My friend is sick.
    moy pri-ya-tely ye bo-les-tan   *Moj prijatelj je bolestan.* (m)
    mo-ya pri-ya-te-lyi-tsa   *Moja prijateljica je*
    ye bo-les-na   *bolesna.* (f)
What's the matter?
    u che-mu ye pro-blem?   *U čemu je problem?*

Parts of the Body

My ... hurts.	bo-li me ...	*Boli me ...*
ankle	chla-nak	*članak*
arm	ru-ka	*ruka*
back	le-dja	*leđa*
chest	gru-di	*grudi*
ear	u-ho	*uho*
eye	o-ko	*oko*
finger	prst	*prst*
foot	sto-pa-lo	*stopalo*
hand	ru-ka	*ruka*
head	gla-va	*glava*
heart	sr-tse	*srce*
leg	no-ga	*noga*
mouth	us-ta	*usta*
nose	nos	*nos*
spine	kich-ma	*kičma*
stomach	sto-mak	*stomak*
teeth	zu-bi	*zubi*
throat	gr-lo	*grlo*

CROATIAN

Ailments

I have (a/an) ...	i-mam ...	*Imam ...*
allergy	a-ler-gi-yu	*alergiju*
anaemia	a-ne-mi-yu	*anemiju*
bite	u-yed	*ujed*
blister	mye-hu-ritch	*mjehurić*
burn	o-pek-li-nu	*opeklinu*
cold	na-zeb	*nazeb*
constipation	zat-vor	*zatvor*
cough	ka-shaly	*kašalj*
diarrhoea	pro-lyev	*proljev*
fever	groz-ni-tsu	*groznicu*
headache	gla-vo-bo-lyu	*glavobolju*
hepatitis	he-pa-ti-tis,	*hepatitis,*
	zhu-ti-tsu	*žuticu*
indigestion	lo-shu	*lošu*
	pro-ba-vu	*probavu*
infection	in-fek-tsi-yu	*infekciju*
influenza	grip	*grip*
itch	svrab	*svrab*
lice	vash-ke	*vaške*
low/high	ni-zak/vi-sok	*nizak/visok*
blood pressure	krv-ni tlak	*krvni tlak*
nausea	much-ni-na	*mučnina*
pain	bol	*bol*
sore throat	u-pa-lu gr-la	*upalu grla*
sprain	u-ga-nu-tche	*uganuće*
stomachache	bo-lo-ve u	*bolove u*
	sto-ma-ku	*stomaku*
sunburn	o-pek-li-ne od	*opekline od*
	sun-tsa	*sunca*
temperature	tem-pe-ra-tu-ru	*temperaturu*
toothache	zu-bo-bo-lyu	*zubobolju*
venereal disease	ve-ne-rich-nu	*veneričnu*
	(spol-nu) bo-lest	*(spolnu) bolest*
worms	glis-te	*gliste*

At the Chemist
I need medication for ...
   tre-ba mi li-yek za ...   *Treba mi lijek za ...*
I have a prescription.
   i-mam re-tsept   *Imam recept.*

antibiotics	an-ti-bi-o-ti-tsi	*antibiotici*
antiseptic	an-ti-sep-tik	*antiseptik*
bandage	za-voy	*zavoj*
contraceptive	sred-stva za	*sredstva za*
	kon-tra-tsep-tsi-yu	*kotracepciju*
medicine	li-yek	*lijek*
vitamins	vi-ta-mi-ni	*vitamini*

At the Dentist
I have a toothache.
   i-mam zu-bo-bo-lyu   *Imam zubobolju.*
I've lost a filling.
   iz-gu-bi-o/iz-gu-bi-la   *Izgubio/Izgubila*
   sam plom-bu   *sam plombu.* (m/f)
I've broken a tooth.
   slo-mi-o mi se zub   *Slomio mi se zub.*
My gums hurt.
   bo-le me des-ni   *Bole me desni.*
I don't want it extracted.
   ne zhe-lim da se va-di   *Ne želim da se vadi.*
Please give me an anaesthetic.
   mo-lim vas day-te   *Molim vas dajte*
   mi a-nes-te-zi-yu   *mi anesteziju.*

CROATIAN

TIME & DATES

What date is it today?

ko-yi ye da-nas da-tum?		*Koji je danas datum?*

What time is it?	ko-li-ko ye sa-ti?	*Koliko je sati?*
It's ... am/pm.	sa-da ye ... sa-ti	*Sada je ... sati.*
in the morning	u-yut-ro	*ujutro*
in the afternoon	po-pod-ne	*popodne*
in the evening	u-ve-cher	*uveče*

Days

Monday	po-ne-de-lyak	*ponedjeljak*
Tuesday	u-to-rak	*utorak*
Wednesday	sri-ye-da	*srijeda*
Thursday	tchet-vr-tak	*četvrtak*
Friday	pe-tak	*petak*
Saturday	su-bo-ta	*subota*
Sunday	ne-dye-lya	*nedjelja*

Months

January	sye-chany	*sječanj*
February	ve-lya-cha	*veljača*
March	o-zhu-yak	*ožujak*
April	tra-vany	*travanj*
May	svi-bany	*svibanj*
June	li-pany	*lipanj*
July	sr-pany	*srpanj*
August	ko-lo-voz	*kolovoz*
September	ru-yan	*rujan*
October	lis-to-pad	*listopad*
November	stu-de-ni	*studeni*
December	pro-si-nats	*prosinac*

Seasons

summer	lye-to	*ljeto*
autumn	ye-sen	*jesen*
winter	zi-ma	*zima*
spring	pro-lye-tche	*proljeće*

CROATIAN

Present

today	da-nas	*danas*
this morning	yut-ros	*jutros*
tonight	ve-che-ras	*večeras*
this week	o-vay tye-dan	*ovaj tjedan*
this year	o-ve go-di-ne	*ove godine*
now	sa-da	*sada*

Past

yesterday	yu-cher	*jučer*
day before yesterday	prek-yu-cher	*prekjučer*
yesterday morning	yu-cher u-yut-ro	*jučer ujutro*
last night	si-notch	*sinoć*
last week	prosh-li tye-dan	*prošli tjedan*
last year	prosh-la go-di-na	*prošle godine*

Future

tomorrow	sut-ra	*sutra*
day after tomorrow	pre-ko-sut-ra	*prekosutra*
tomorrow morning	sut-ra u-yut-ro	*sutra ujutro*
tomorrow afternoon/ evening	sut-ra po-pod-ne/ u-ve-cher	*sutra popodne/ uvečer*
next week	i-du-tchi tye-dan	*idući tjedan*
next year	i-du-tche go-di-ne	*iduće godine*

During the Day

afternoon	po-pod-ne	*popodne*
dawn/early morning	zo-ra/ra-no yut-ro	*zora/rano jutro*
day	dan	*dan*
early	ra-no	*rano*
midnight	po-notch	*ponoć*
morning	yut-ro	*jutro*
night	notch	*noć*
noon/midday	pod-ne	*podne*
sunset	za-la-zak sun-tsa	*zalazak sunca*
sunrise	iz-la-zak sun-tsa	*izlazak sunca*

CROATIAN

NUMBERS & AMOUNTS

0	nu-la	*nula*
1	ye-dan	*jedan*
2	dva	*dva*
3	tri	*tri*
4	che-ti-ri	*četiri*
5	pet	*pet*
6	shest	*šest*
7	se-dam	*sedam*
8	o-sam	*osam*
9	de-vet	*devet*
10	de-set	*deset*
11	je-da-na-est	*jedanaest*
12	dva-na-est	*dvanaest*
13	tri-na-est	*trinaest*
14	che-tr-na-est	*četrnaest*
15	pet-na-est	*petnaest*
16	shes-na-est	*šesnaest*
17	se-dam-na-est	*sedamnaest*
18	o-sam-na-est	*osamnaest*
19	de-vet-na-est	*devetnaest*
20	dva-de-set	*dvadeset*
21	dva-de-set i ye-dan	*dvadeset i jedan*
22	dva-de-set i dva	*dvadestet i dva*
30	tri-de-set	*trideset*
40	che-tr-de-set	*četrdeset*
50	pe-de-set	*pedeset*
60	shez-de-set	*šezdeset*
70	se-dam-de-set	*sedamdeset*
80	o-sam-de-set	*osamdeset*
90	de-ve-de-set	*devedeset*
100	sto	*sto*
1000	ti-su-tchu	*tisuću*
one million	ye-dan mi-li-yun	*jedan milijun*

1st	pr-vi	*prvi*
2nd	dru-gi	*drugi*
3rd	tre-tchi	*treći*
last	zad-nyi/zad-nya/ zad-nye	*zadnji* (m)/*zadnja* (f)/ *zadnje* (neut)
1/4	yed-na chet-vr-ti-na	*jedna četvrtina*
1/3	yed-na tre-tchi-na	*jedna trećina*
1/2	yed-na po-lo-vi-na	*jedna polovina*
3/4	tri chet-vr-ti-ne	*tri četvrtine*

Useful Words

a little (amount)	ma-lo	*malo*
double	dup-lo	*duplo*
a dozen	tu-tset	*tucet*
Enough!	do-voly-no!	*Dovoljno!*
few	ne-ko-li-ko	*nekoliko*
less	ma-nye	*manje*
many	mno-go	*mnogo*
more	vi-she	*više*
once	yed-nom	*jednom*
a pair	par	*par*
per cent	po-sto-tak	*postotak*
some	nesh-to	*nešto*
too much	pre-vi-she	*previše*
twice	dva-put	*dvaput*

CROATIAN

ABBREVIATIONS

SIDA	AIDS
Odd.	Dept/HQ
EZ	EC
OI	ID
G-din	Mr
G-dja	Mrs
G-dica	Miss or Ms
S/J	Nth/Sth
Ul	St
VB	UK
UN	UN
SAD	USA

CULTURAL EVENTS!

The arts were heavily subsidised by the communists, and admission to operas, operettas and concerts is still reasonable. In the interior, winter is the best time to enjoy the theatre and concerts – the main season at the opera houses of Rijeka, Split and Zagreb runs from October to May.

In summer the cultural scene shifts to the many summer festivals. Pula's impressive Roman ampitheatre attracts first-rate international musicians and opera companies all year round.

'Terrace dancing' is a summer tradition all along the coast. At least one hotel in every coastal resort hires a couple of musicians to play on their terrace. The play list usually includes a smattering of local tunes along with international favourites.

CROATIAN

EMERGENCIES

Help!	u-po-motch!	*Upomoć!*
It's an emergency.	hit-no ye	*Hitno je.*
Go away!	i-di-te!	*Idite!*
Thief!	lo-pov!	*Lopov!*
I'm ill.	bo-les-tan/	*Bolestan/Bolesna*
	bo-les-na sam	*sam.* (m/f)
I'm lost.	iz-gub-lyen/iz-gub-	*Izgubljen/Izgubljena*
	lye-na sam	*sam.* (m/f)

I'll call the police.
  zva-tchu po-li-tsi-yu   *Zvaću policiju.*

There's been an accident.
  do-go-di-la se ne-sre-tcha   *Dogodila se nesreća.*

Call a doctor!
  po-zo-vi-te li-yech-ni-ka!   *Pozovite liječnika!*

Call the police!
  po-zo-vi-te po-li-tsi-yu!   *Pozovite policiju!*

Call an ambulance!
  po-zo-vi-te hit-nu po-motch!   *Pozovite hitnu pomoć!*

I've been raped.
  si-lo-va-na sam   *Silovana sam.*

I've been robbed.
  po-kra-den/po-kra-de-na sam   *Pokraden/Pokradena sam.* (m/f)

Where's the police station?
  gdye ye sta-ni-tsa po-li-tsi-ye?   *Gdje je stanica policije?*

Where are the toilets?
  gdye su za-ho-di?   *Gdje su zahodi?*

Could you help me, please?
  mo-zhe-te li mi po-mo-tchi?   *Možete li mi pomoći?*

Could I please use the telephone?
  mo-gu li da te-le-fo-ni-ram?   *Mogu li da telefoniram?*

I'm sorry. I apologise.
  zhao mi ye; iz-vi-nya-vam se   *Žao mi je. Izvinjavam se.*

I didn't realise I was doing
anything wrong.
  ni-sam mis-li-o/   *Nisam mislio/*
  mi-sli-la da ra-dim   *mislila da radim*
  nesh-to po-gresh-no   *nešto pogrešno.* (m/f)

I didn't do it.
ya ni-sam to u-ra-di-o/
u-ra-di-la
Ja nisam to uradio/
uradila. (m/f)

I wish to contact my
embassy/consulate.
zhe-lim da
kon-tak-ti-ram mo-yu
am-ba-sa-du/moy kon-zu-lat
Želim da
kontaktiram moju
ambasadu/moj konzulat.

I speak English.
ya go-vo-rim en-gles-ki
Ja govorim engleski.

I have medical insurance.
i-mam zdrav-stve-no
o-si-gu-ra-nye
Imam zdravstveno
osiguranje.

My possessions are insured.
mo-ye stva-ri su o-si-gu-ra-ne
Moje stvari su osigurane.

My ... was stolen.
moy ... ye u-kra-den/
u-kra-den a
Moj ... je ukraden/
ukradena. (m/f)

I've lost my ...	iz-gu-bi-o/ iz-gu-bi-la sam ...	*Izgubio/ Izgubila sam ... (m/f)*
bags	mo-ye tor-be	*moje torbe*
handbag	ruch-nu tor-bu	*ručnu torbu*
money	moy no-vats	*moj novac*
travellers cheques	mo-ye put-nich-ke che-ko-ve	*moje putničke čekove*
passport	mo-ya pu-tov-ni-tsa	*moja putovnica*
wallet	lis-ni-tsa	*lisnica*

CZECH

QUICK REFERENCE

CZECH

Hello	*dob*-ree-dehn	Dobrý den.
Goodbye.	*nah*-skhleh-dah-noh	Na shledanou.
Yes./No.	*ah*-no/neh	Ano./Ne.
Excuse me.	*zdo*-vo-leh-nyeem	S dovolením.
May I?	*do*-vol-teh-mi?	Dovolte mi?
Sorry.	*pro*-miny-teh	Promiňte.
Please.	*pro*-seem	Prosím.
Thank you.	*dyeh*-ku-yi	Děkuji.
That's fine.	*neh*-nyee zahch.	Není zač.
You're welcome.	*pro*-seem	Prosím.
What time is it?	*ko*-lik-yeh *ho*-dyin?	Kolik je hodin?
Where's ...?	*gdeh*-yeh ...?	Kde je ...?
Go straight ahead.	*ydyeh*-teh *przhee*-mo	Jděte přímo

Turn left/right ...	*zah*-to-chteh *vleh*-vo/*prah*-vo ...	Zatočte vlevo/vpravo ...
at the next corner	nah *przhee*-shtyeem *ro*-hu	na příštím rohu

I'd like a ...	*przhaal*/*przhaa*-lah bikh-si ...	Přál/Přála bych si ... (m/f)
single room	*yeh*-dno-loozh-ko-vee *po*-koy	jednolůžkový pokoj
one-way ticket	*yeh*-dno-smyehr-noh *yeez*-dehn-ku	jednosměrnou jízdenku
return ticket	*spaa*-teh-chnyee *yeez*-dehn-ku	zpáteční jízdenku

I don't understand.	*neh*-roh-zu-meem	Nerozumím.
Do you speak English?	*mlu*-vee-teh *ahn*-glits-ki?	Mluvíte anglicky?
Where are the toilets?	*gdeh*-ysoh *zaa*-kho-di?	Kde jsou záchody?
How do I get to ...?	*yahk*-seh *do*-stah-nu k ...?	Jak se dostanu k ...?

1	*yeh*-dna	jedna	6	shehst	šest
2	dvah	dva	7	se*h*-dum	sedm
3	trzhi	tři	8	o-sum	osm
4	*chti*-rzhi	čtyř	9	de*h*-vyeht	devět
5	pyeht	pět	10	*deh*-seht	deset

The Czech language belongs to the Slavonic group of Indo-European languages, which is subdivided into East, West and South Slavonic groups. Czech, together with Slovak, Polish and Lusatian, is part of the West Slavonic group. It is the main language of the Czech Republic and is spoken by 10 million people.

Although Czech has several dialects, this phrasebook uses a standardised form of the language, literary Czech (*spisovná čeština*), which is based on the central Bohemian dialect. However, this is no longer associated with a particular social group or territory, and functions as a common language understood by all Czechs. Therefore, you won't have trouble communicating wherever you are in the country.

Some Czech sentences will be phrased differently depending on whether you are male or female, so both forms are given when applicable.

PRONUNCIATION
Czech is spelled as it's pronounced, and once you become familiar with the sounds, it can be read easily.

Vowels
An accent over a vowel indicates that it is lengthened.

Short Vowels

a	ah	as the 'u' in 'cut'
e	eh	as the 'e' in 'bet'
ě	yeh	as the 'ye' in 'yet'
i/y	i	as the 'i' in 'bit'
o	o	as the 'o' in 'pot'
u	u	as the 'u' in 'pull'

CZECH

Long Vowels

á	aa	as the 'a' in 'father'
é	air	as the 'ai' in 'air'
í/ý	ee	as the 'ee' in 'see'
ó	aw	as the 'aw' in 'saw'
ú/ů	oo	as the 'oo' in 'zoo'

Vowel Combinations

aj	ahy	as the 'i' in 'ice'
áj	aay	as 'eye'
au	ow	an 'ow' as in 'clown'
ej	ehy	as the 'ey' in 'hey'
ij, yj	iy	as the 'ee' in 'see' followed by the 'y' in 'year'
íj, ýj	eey	as the 'ee' in 'see' followed by the 'y' in 'year'; pronounced longer than ij and yj
oj	oi/oy	as the 'oy' in 'boy'
ou	ou/ouh	as the 'o' in 'note' followed by the 'u' in 'pull'
uj	uy	as the 'u' in 'pull', followed by the 'y' in 'year'
ůj	ooi/ooy	ad the 'oo' in 'zoo', followed by the 'y' in 'year'

Consonants

Consonants not described here are pronounced as in English, except *k*, *p* and *t*, which are pronounced without a puff of breath.

c	ts	as the 'ts' in 'lets'
č	ch	as the 'ch' in 'chew'
ch	kh	as the 'ch' in Scottish 'loch'
g	g	as the 'g' in 'get'
j	y	as the 'y' in 'year'
r	r	a rolled 'r', made with the tip of the tongue
ř	rzh	a rolled 'r' followed by the 's' in 'treasure'
s	s	as the 's' in 'sit', never as in 'rose'
š	sh	as the 'sh' in 'ship'
ž	zh	as the 's' in 'treasure'
ď, ň, ť	dy, ny, ty	pronounced with the tongue touching the roof of the mouth, adding a 'y' sound
d, n, t	dy, ny, ty	when followed by *i*, *í* and *ě*, pronounced as *ď*, *ň*, *ť*

Stress

In Czech the first syllable is usually stressed. Vowels are pronounced the same whether they are stressed or not.

SUBJECT PRONOUNS		
SG		
I	jaah	já
you (inf)	tih	ty
(pol)	vih	Vy
he/she/it	ohn/oh-nah/oh-noh	on/ona/ono
PL		
we	mih	my
you	vih	vy
they (m)	oh-nyih	oni
(f)	oh-nih	ony
(neut)	oh-nah	ona

CZECH

GREETINGS & CIVILITIES
Top Useful Phrases

Hello./Goodbye.	*dob*-ree-dehn/	*Dobrý den./*
	nah-skhleh-dah-noh	*Na shledanou.*
Yes./No.	*ah*-no/neh	*Ano./Ne.*
Yes. (col)	yo	*Jo.*
Excuse me.	*zdo*-vo-leh-nyeem	*S dovolením.*
May I?	*do*-vol-teh-mi?	*Dovolte mi?*
Do you mind?		
Sorry.	*pro*-miny-teh	*Promiňte.*
(excuse/forgive me)		
Please.	*pro*-seem	*Prosím.*
Thank you.	*dyeh*-ku-yi	*Děkuji.*

Many thanks.		
mots-kraat *dyeh*-ku-yi		*Mockrát děkuji.*
That's fine. You're welcome.		
neh-nyee zahch *pro*-seem		*Není zač. Prosím.*

CZECH

Greetings

Good morning.
dob-rair *yit*-ro/ *raa*-no   *Dobré jitro/ráno.*

Good afternoon.
dob-rair *ot*-po-lehd-neh   *Dobré odpoledne.*

Good evening.
dob-ree *veh*-chehr   *Dobrý večer.*

Good night.
dob-roh nots   *Dobrou noc.*

How are you?
yahk-seh *maa*-teh?   *Jak se máte?*

Well, thanks.
dyeh-ku-yi, *dob*-rzheh   *Děkuji, dobře.*

Forms of Address

Madam/Mrs	*pah*-nyee	*Paní*
Sir/Mr	pahn	*Pan*
Miss	*slehch*-nah	*Slečna*
companion/friend	*przhee*-tehl	*přítel* (m)
	przhee-tehl-ki-nyeh	*přítelkyně* (f)

QUESTION WORDS		
How?	yahk?	Jak?
When?	gdi?	Kdy?
Where?	gde?	Kde?
Which?	kteh-ree?	Který?
Who?	gdo?	Kdo?
Why?	proch?	Proč?

CZECH

SMALL TALK
Meeting People

What's your name?
   yahk-seh *ymeh*-nu-yeh-teh?   *Jak se jmenujete?*
My name's ...
   ymeh-nu-yi-seh ...   *Jmenuji se ...*
I'd like to introduce you to ...
   mo-hu vaas przheht-   *Mohu vás představit ...*
   stah-vit ...
Pleased to meet you.
   tye-shee mnyeh, zheh   *Těší mě, že vás*
   vaas *po*-znaa-vaam   *poznávám.*
How old are you?
   ko-lik yeh vaam leht?   *Kolik je vám let?*
I'm ... years old.
   yeh mi ... let   *Je mi ... let.*

Nationalities

Where are you from?
   od-kud *po*-khaa-zee-teh?   *Odkud pocházíte?*

I'm from ...	ysehm ...	Jsem ...
Australia	*sow*-straa-li-yeh	z Austrálie
Canada	*skah*-nah-di	z Kanady
England	*sahn*-gli-yeh	z Anglie
Ireland	sir-skah	z Irska
New Zealand	*sno*-vair-ho	z Nového
	zair-lahn-du	Zélandu
Scotland	zeh *skot*-skah	ze Skotska
the USA	zeh *spo*-yeh-neekh	ze Spojených
	staa-too	států
Wales	*zvah*-leh-su	z Walesu

CZECH

Occupations

I'm a/an ...	ysehm ...	Jsem ...
artist	u-myeh-lehts	umělec (m)
	u-myehl-ki-nyeh	umělkyně (f)
business	op-kho-dnyeek	obchodník (m)
person	op-kho-dnyi-tseh	obchodnice (f)
computer	proh-grah-maa-tor	programátor (m)
programmer	proh-grah-maa-tor-kah	programátorka (f)
doctor	lair-kahrzh	lékař (m)
	lair-kahrzh-kah	lékařka (f)
engineer	in-zheh-neer	inženýr (m)
	in-zheh-neer-kah	inženýrka (f)
lawyer	praa-vnyeek	právník (m)
	praa-vnyi-chkah	právnička (f)
manual worker	dyehl-nyeek	dělník (m)
	dyehl-nyi-tseh	dělnice (f)
mechanic	ow-to-meh-khah-nik	automechanik (m)
	ow-to-meh-khah-nich-kah	automechanička (f)
nurse	o-sheh-trzho-vah-tehl	ošetřovatel (m)
	o-sheh-trzho-vah-tehl-kah	ošetřovatelka (f)
office worker	oo-rzheh-dnyeek	úředník (m)
	oo-rzheh-dnyi-tseh	úřednice (f)
scientist	vyeh-dehts	vědec (m)
	vyeht-ki-nyeh	vědkyně (f)
student	stu-dehnt	student (m)
	stu-dehnt-kah	studentka (f)
teacher	u-chi-tehl	učitel (m)
	u-chi-tehl-kah	učitelka (f)
waiter	chee-shnyeek	číšník (m)
	chee-shnyi-tseh	číšnice (f)
	(sehr-veer-kah)	(servírka) (f)
writer	spi-so-vah-tehl	spisovatel (m)
	spi-so-vah-tehl-kah	spisovatelka (f)

What do you do?
tso *dyeh*-laa-teh?   *Co děláte?*
I'm unemployed.
ysehm neh-zah-myest-nah-nee/   *Jsem nezaměstnaný/*
neh-zah-myest-nah-naa   *nezaměstnaná.* (m/f)

Religion
What's your religion?
yah-kair-ho ysteh   *Jakého jste náboženského*
naa-bo-zhehn-skair-ho   *vyznání?*
vi-znaa-nyee
I'm not religious.
ysehm behz *vi*-znaa-nyee   *Jsem bez vyznání.*

I'm ...   ysehm ...   *Jsem ...*
  Buddhist   *bu*-dhi-stah   *buddhista* (m)
              bu-dhist-kah   *buddhistka* (f)
  Catholic   *kah*-to-leek   *katolík* (m)
              kah-to-li-chkah   *katolička* (f)
  Christian   *krzheh*-styahny   *křestan* (m)
              krzheh-styahny-kah *křestanka* (f)
  Hindu   *hin*-du   *hindu* (m/f)
  Jewish   zhid   *žid* (m)
              zhi-dof-kah   *židovka* (f)
  Muslim   *mu*-slim   *muslim* (m)
              mu-slim-kah   *muslimka* (f)

Family
Are you married?
ysteh *zheh*-nah-tee?/   *Jste ženatý/vdaná?* (m/f)
vdah-naa?
I'm single.
ysehm *svo*-bo-dnee/   *Jsem svobodný/*
svo-bo-dnaa   *svobodná.* (m/f)
I'm married.
ysehm *zheh*-nah-tee/   *Jsem ženatý/*
fdah-naa   *vdaná.* (m/f)

CZECH

How many children do you have?
    ko-lik maa-teh dyeh-tyee?   *Kolik máte dětí?*
I don't have any children.
    neh-maam dyeh-tyi   *Nemám děti.*
I have a daughter/son.
    maam si-nah/tseh-ru   *Mám syna/dceru.*

brother	*brah-tr*	*bratr*
children	*dyeh-tyi*	*děti*
daughter	*tseh-rah*	*dcera*
family	*ro-dyi-nah*	*rodina*
father	*o-tehts*	*otec*
grandfather	*dyeh-deh-chehk*	*dědeček*
grandmother	*bah-bi-chkah*	*babička*
husband	*mahn-zhehl*	*manžel*
mother	*maht-kah*	*matka*
sister	*sehs-trah*	*sestra*
son	*sin*	*syn*
wife	*mahn-zhehl-kah*	*manželka*

Feelings

I'm ...

angry	hnyeh-vaam seh	*Hněvám se.*
cold	yeh mi *zi*-mah	*Je mi zima.*
happy	ysehm *shtyahst*-nee/	*Jsem štastný/*
	shtyahst-naa	*štastná.* (m/f)
hot	yeh mi *hor*-ko	*Je mi horko.*
hungry	maam hlaht	*Mám hlad.*
in a hurry	*spyeh*-khaam	*Spěchám.*
right	maam *prahf*-du	*Mám pravdu.*
sad	ysehm *smut*-nee/	*Jsem smutný/*
	smut-naa	*smutná.* (m/f)
thirsty	maam *zhee*-zehny	*Mám žízeň.*
tired	ysehm *u*-nah-veh-nee/	*Jsem unavený/*
	u-nah-veh-naa	*unavená.* (m/f)
well	*mnyeh*-yeh *dob*-rzheh	*Mně je dobře.*
worried	maahm *stah*-rost	*Mám starost.*

I (don't) like ...
    mnyeh *seh*-to *(neh-)*lee-bee ...   *Mně se to (ne)líbí ...*
I'm sorry. (condolence)
    u-przhee-mnoh *soh*-strahst   *Upřímnou soustrast.*
I'm grateful.
    ysehm vaam *vdyehch-* nee/   *Jsem vám vděčný/*
    vdyehch-naa   *vděčná.* (m/f)

BREAKING THE LANGUAGE BARRIER

Do you speak English?
    mlu-vee-teh *ahn*-glits-ki?   *Mluvíte anglicky?*
Does anyone speak English?
    mlu-vee *nyeh*-gdo   *Mluví někdo anglicky?*
    ahn-glits-ki?
I speak a little ...
    mlu-veem *tro*-khu ...   *Mluvím trochu ...*
I understand.
    ro-zu-meem   *Rozumím.*
I don't understand.
    neh-roh-zu-meem   *Nerozumím.*
Could you speak more
slowly, please?
    moo-zheh-teh *mlu*-vit   *Můžete mluvit pomaleji?*
    po-mah-leh-yi?
Could you repeat that?
    moo-zheh-teh to   *Můžete to opakovat?*
    o-pah-ko-vaht?
How do you say ...?
    yahk-seh *rzheh*-kneh ...?   *Jak se řekne ...?*
What does ... mean?
    tso *znah*-meh-naa ...?   *Co znamená ...?*

CZECH

BODY LANGUAGE

Czech speakers are friendly and knowledgeable about a number of subjects. They have a marvellous sense of humour that can be fully appreciated only in their own language. This might be a good reason for you to try and break the language barrier – it will be worthwhile. Their body language doesn't have any typical gestures which distinguish them from other Eastern Europeans.

PAPERWORK

address	*ah*-dreh-sah	*adresa*
age	vyehk	*věk*
date of birth	*dah*-tum *nah*-ro-zeh-nyee	*datum narození*
driver's licence	*rzhi*-dyich-skee *proo*-kahz	*řidičský průkaz*
identification	*leh*-gi-ti-mah-tseh	*legitimace*
marital status	*mahn*-zhehl-skee stahf	*manželský stav*
name	*ymair*-no	*jméno*
nationality	*staa*-tynyee	*státní*
	przhee-slush-nost	*příslušnost*
passport	pahs	*pas*
passport number	*pah*-su (*chee*-slo)	*pas č. (číslo)*
place of birth	*mees*-to *nah*-ro-zeh-nyee	*místo narození*
profession	*po*-vo-laa-nyee	*povolání*
reason for travel	*oo*-chehl *tsehs*-ti	*účel cesty*
business	*ob*-khod-nyee	*obchodní*
	yed-naa-nyeeh	*jednání*
holiday	*doh*-voh-leh-naa	*dovolená*
religion	*naa*-bo-zhehn-stvee	*náboženství*
sex	*po*-hlah-vee	*pohlaví*
surname	*przheey*-meh-nyee	*příjmení*
visa	*vee*-zum	*vízum*

GETTING AROUND

What time does	gdi *ot*-yee-zhdyee/	*Kdy odjíždí/*
the ... leave/arrive?	*przhi*-yee-zhdyee ...?	*přijíždí ...?*
boat	lody	*loď*
(inter)city bus	(*meh*-zi-)myehst-skee	(*mezi*)*městský*
	ow-to-bus	*autobus*
train	vlahk	*vlak*
tram	*trahm*-vahy	*tramvaj*

CZECH

SIGNS

INFORMACE	INFORMATION
NOUZOVÝ VÝCHOD	EMERGENCY EXIT
OTEVŘENO/ZAVŘENO	OPEN/CLOSED
TELEFON	TELEPHONE
TEPLÁ/STUDENÁ	HOT/COLD
VCHOD	ENTRANCE
VSTUP VOLNÝ	FREE ADMISSION
VSTUP ZAKÁZÁN	NO ENTRY
VÝCHOD	EXIT
ZÁCHODY/WC/TOALETY	TOILETS
ZADÁNO/RESERVOVÁNO	RESERVED
ZAKÁZÁNO	PROHIBITED
ZÁKAZ KOUŘENÍ	NO SMOKING

Directions

Where's ...?	*gdeh*-yeh ...?	*Kde je ...?*

How do I get to ...?
    yahk-seh *do*-stáh-nu k ...?   *Jak se dostanu k ...?*
Is it far/closeby?
    yeh to *dah*-leh-ko/*blees*-ko?   *Je to daleko/blízko?*
Can I walk there?
    do-stah-nu-seh tahm *pyehsh*-ki?   *Dostanu se tam pěšky?*

CZECH

Can you show me (on the map)?		
moo-zheh-teh mi-to		*Můžete mi to ukázat*
u-kaa-zaht (nah mah-pyeh)?		*(na mapě)?*
I want to go to ...		
khtsi yeet ...		*Chci jít ...*
Go straight ahead.		
ydyeh-teh przhee-mo		*Jděte přímo.*
It's two blocks down.		
o dvyeh u-li-tseh daal		*O dvě ulice dál.*

Turn left/right	*zah-to-chteh*	*Zatočte*
at the ...	*vleh-vo/prah-vo ...*	*vlevo/vpravo ...*
next corner	*nah przhee-shtyeem ro-hu*	*na příštím rohu*
traffic lights	*u seh-mah-for-ru*	*u semaforu*

behind	**zah**	*za*
in front of	**przhehd**	*před*
far	*dah-leh-ko*	*daleko*
near	*blees-ko*	*blízko*
opposite	*nah-pro-tyi*	*naproti*

Booking Tickets

I'd like ...	raad/*raa*-dah	*Rád/Ráda*
	bikh ...	*bych ... (m/f)*
a one-way ticket	*yeh-*dno-smyehr-noh *yeez*-dehn-ku	*jednosměrnou jízdenku*
a return ticket	*spaa*-teh-chnyee *yeez*-dehn-ku	*zpáteční jízdenku*
two tickets	dvyeh *yee*-zdehn-ki	*dvě jízdenky*
tickets for all of us	*yeez*-dehn-ki pro *vshehkh*-ni	*jízdenky pro všechny*
a student's fare	*stu*-dehnts-koh *yeez*-dehn-ku	*studentskou jízdenku*
a child's fare	dyets-koh *yeez*-dehn-ku	*dětskou jízdenku*

Where can I buy a ticket?
gdeh-seh *pro*-daa-vah-yee
yeez-dehn-ki?

Where can I buy a ticket? — *Kde se prodávají jízdenky?*

I want to go to ...
khtsi yeht *do* ...

Chci jet do ...

Do I need to book?
po-trzheh-bu-yi
mees-tehn-ku?

Potřebuji místenku?

1st class	pr-vnyee trzhee-du	*první třídu*
2nd class	dru-hoh trzhee-du	*druhou třídu*

Bus

Where's the bus/tram stop?
gdeh-yeh *stah*-nyi-tseh
ow-to-bu-soo/*trahm*-vah-yee?

Kde je stanice autobusů/tramvají?

Which bus goes to ...?
kteh-ree *ow*-to-bus yeh-deh *do* ...?

Který autobus jede do ...?

Does this bus go to ...?
yeh-deh *tehm*-hleh *ow*-to-bus *do* ...?

Jede tenhle autobus do ...?

How often do buses pass by?
yahk *chahs*-to *tu*-di
yehz-dyee *ow*-to-bus?

Jak často tudy jezdí autobus?

Could you let me know when
we get to ...?
mohl/*moh*-lah *bi*-steh-mi
pro-seem *rzhe*-tsi, gdi
przhi-yeh-deh-meh *do* ...?

Mohl/Mohla byste mi prosím říci, kdy přijedeme do ...? (m/f)

I want to get off!
khtsi *vi*-stow-pit!

Chci vystoupit!

What time's the	gdi *yeh*-deh ...	*Kdy jede ...*
... bus?	*ow*-to-bus?	*autobus?*
first	pr-vnyee	*první*
last	*po*-sleh-dnyee	*poslední*
next	*przheesh*-tyee	*příští*

CZECH

Taxi

Can you take me to ...?
moo-zheh-teh mnyeh
do-vairst *do* ...?

*Můžete mě
dovést do ...?*

Please take me to ...
pro-seem, *od*-vehs-teh
mnyeh *do* ...?

Prosím, odvezte mě do ...?

How much does it cost to go to ...?
ko-lik sto-yee tsehs-tah do ...?

Kolik stojí cesta do ...?

Here's fine, thank you.
zahs-tahf-teh zdeh, *pro*-seem

Zastavte zde, prosím.

The next corner, please.
nah *przheesh*-tyeem *ro*-hu,
pro-seem

*Na příštím rohu,
prosím.*

The next street to the left/right.
przhee-shtyee *u*-li-tsi
vleh-vo/*fprah*-vo

Příští ulici vlevo/vpravo.

Stop here!
zah-stahf-teh zdeh!

Zastavte zde!

Please wait here.
poch-kehy-teh zdeh, *pro*-seem

Počkejte zde, prosím.

Train & Metro

Which line takes me to ...?
kteh-raa *trah*-sah
veh-deh *do* ...?

Která trasa vede do ...?

What's the next station?
yahk-seh *ymeh*-nu-yeh
przhee-shtyee stah- nyi-tseh?

Jak se jmenuje příští stanice?

Is this the right platform for ...?
yeh-deh vlahk *do* ...
sto-ho-to *naa*-stu-pi-shtyeh?

*Jede vlak do ...
z tohoto nástupiště?*

dining car	*yee*-dehl-nyee vooz	*jídelní vůz*
express	*ri*-khleek	*rychlík*
local	*mees*-tnyee	*místní*
sleeping car	*spah*-tsee vooz	*spací vůz*
1st/2nd class	*prv*-nyeeh/*druh*-haa *trzhee*-dah	*1./2. třída*

Car

Where can I rent a car?
    gdeh-si *mo*-hu *pro*-nahy-moht *ow*-to?   *Kde si mohu pronajmout auto?*

How much is it daily/weekly?
    ko-lik *sto*-yee *deh*-nyeh/*tee*-dnyeh?   *Kolik stojí denně/týdně?*

Does that include (insurance/mileage)?
    yeh *zah*-hr-nu-tah *ftseh*-nyeh *po*-yist-kah/*po*-plah-tehk zah *nah*-yeh-tair *ki*-lo-meh-tri)?   *Je zahrnuta v ceně (pojistka/poplatek za najeté kilometry)?*

ON THE ROAD

AUTOMECHANIK	MECHANIC
AUTOOPRAVNA	REPAIRS
BENZÍNOVÁ PUMPA	GARAGE
DÁLNICE	FREEWAY
DEJ PŘEDNOST V JÍZDĚ	GIVE WAY
JEDNOSMĚRNÝ PROVOZ	ONE WAY
OBJÍŽĎKA	DETOUR
PRO INVALIDY	DISABLED
SAMOOBSLUHA	SELF SERVICE
STANDART	UNLEADED
SUPER	SUPER
ZÁKAZ PARKOVÁNÍ NO	NO PARKING
ZÁKAZ VJEZDU	NO ENTRY
ZASTAVTE/STOP	STOP

CZECH

Where's the next petrol station?
gdeh-yeh *przheesh*-tyee
behm-zee-no-vaa *pum*-pah?

Kde je příští benzínová pumpa?

How long can I park here?
yahk *dloh-ho* zdeh
mo-hu *pahr*-ko-vaht?

Jak dlouho zde mohu parkovat?

Does this road lead to ...?
veh-deh *tah*-to *tsehs*-tah *do* ...?

Vede tato cesta do ...?

I need a mechanic.
po-trzheh-bu-yi
ow-to-meh-khah-ni-kah

Potřebuji automechanika.

air (for tyres)	vzdukh	vzduch
battery	*bah*-teh-ri-yeh	baterie
brakes	brz-di	brzdy
clutch	spoy-kah	spojka
driver's licence	rzhi-dyich-skee	řidičský
	proo-kahz	průkaz
engine	mo-tor	motor
lights	svyeh-tlah	světla
oil	o-lehy	olej
petrol	behn-zee-nu	benzínu
puncture	pee-khlaa	píchlá
	pneh-u-mah-ti-kah	pneumatika
radiator	khlah-dyich	chladič
road map	ow-to-mah-pah	automapa
tyres	pneh-u-mah-ti-ki	pneumatiky
windscreen	przheh-dnyee sklo	přední sklo

ACCOMMODATION

I'm looking for ...	*hleh*-daam ...	*Hledám* ...
Where's a ... hotel?	*gdeh*-yeh ... *ho*-tehl?	*Kde je ... hotel?*
cheap	*leh*-vnee	*levný*
good	*do*-bree	*dobrý*
nearby	*bleez*-kee	*blízký*

At the Hotel

Do you have any rooms available?
   maa-teh *vol*-nair *po*-ko-yeh?   *Máte volné pokoje?*

I'd like a ...	*przhaal/przhaa*-lah bikh-si ...	*Přál/Přála bych si ... (m/f)*
single room	*yeh*-dno-loozh-ko-vee *po*-koy	*jednolůžkový pokoj*
double room	*dvoh*-loozh-ko-vee *po*-koy	*dvoulůžkový pokoj*

I want a room with a ...	*mo*-hu meet *po*-koy ...	*Mohu mít pokoj ...*
bathroom	*skoh*-pehl-noh	*s koupelnou*
shower	*seh*-spr-khoh	*se sprchou*
television	*steh*-leh-vi-zee	*s televizí*
window	*so*-knehm	*s oknem*

I'm going to stay for ...	*zoo*-stah-nu ...	*Zůstanu ...*
one day	*yeh*-dehn dehn	*jeden den*
two days	dvah dni	*dva dny*
one week	*yeh*-dehn *tee*-dehn	*jeden týden*

How much is it per night?
   ko-lik *sto*-yee *yeh*-dnah *nots*?   *Kolik stojí jedna noc?*
How much is it per person?
   ko-lik to *sto*-yee *zah* o-so-bu?   *Kolik to stojí za osobu?*
Can I see it?
   mo-hu-seh *nah*-nyey *po*-dyee-vaht?   *Mohu se na něj podívat?*

CZECH

Are there any others?
> *neh*-maa-teh *yi*-nee *po*-koj?   *Nemáte jiný pokoj?*

Is there a reduction for students/
children?
> *maa*-teh *sleh*-vu pro
> *stu*-dehn-ti/*dyeh*-tyi?   *Máte slevu pro studenty/ děti?*

It's fine, I'll take it.
> *to*-yeh *fpo*-rzhaat-ku,
> yaa toh *vehz*-mu   *To je v pořádku, já to vezmu.*

I'm/We're leaving now.
> *od*-yeezh-dyeem/
> *od*-yeezh-dyee-meh *tehdy*   *Odjíždím/Odjíždíme teď.*

Requests & Complaints

Do you have a safe where I can
leave my valuables?
> *maa*-teh-tu *treh*-zor *gde*-si
> *mo*-hu *u*-lo-zhit *tseh*-no-styi?   *Máte tu trezor kde si mohu uložit cennosti?*

Can I use the telephone?
> *mo*-hu-si *zah*-teh-leh-
> fo-no-vaht?   *Mohu si zatelefonovat?*

I've locked myself out of my room.
> *zah*-klahp-nul/
> *zah*-klahp-nu-lah
> ysehm-si *klee*-cheh
> fmairm *po*-ko-yi   *Zaklapnul/Zaklapnula jsem si klíče v mém pokoji. (m/f)*

AROUND TOWN

I'm looking for a/the ...	*hleh*-daam ...	*Hledám ...*
art gallery	*u*-myeh-lehts-koh	*uměleckou*
	gah-lair-ri-i	*galérii*
bank	*bahn*-ku	*banku*
church	*ko*-stehl	*kostel*
city (centre)	strzhehd *myehs*-tah	*střed města*
	(*tsehn*-trum)	*(centrum)*
... embassy	*vehl*-vi-slah-nehts-vee ...	*velvyslanectví ...*
... hotel	... *ho*-tehl	*... hotel*
market	*tr*-zhi-shtyeh	*tržiště*
museum	*mu*-seh-um	*museum*
police	*po*-li-tsi-yi	*policii*
post office	*posh*-tu	*poštu*
public toilet	*veh*-rzhehy-nair	*veřejné*
	zaa-kho-di	*záchody*
telephone	*teh*-leh-fo-nyee	*telefonní*
centre	*oo*-strzheh-dnu	*ústřednu*
tourist	*in*-for-mah-chnyee	*informační*
information	*kahn*-tse-laarzh	*kancelářpro*
office	pro *tu*-ri-sti	*turisty*

What time does it open/close?
fko-lik *ho*-dyin
o-teh-vee-rah-yee/
zah-vee-rah-yee?

*V kolik hodin otevírají/
zavírají?*

For directions, see the Getting Around section, pages 169-70.

At the Post Office

I'd like some stamps.
raad/*raa*-dah bikh
nyeh-yah-kair *znaam*-ki

*Rád/Ráda bych nějaké
námky.* (m/f)

How much is the postage?
ko-lik *sto*-yee *posh*-to-vnair?

Kolik stojí poštovné?

CZECH

I'd like to send a/an ...	khtyehl/khtyeh-lah bikh pos-laht ...	Chtěl/Chtěla bych poslat ... (m/f)
aerogram	ah-eh-ro-grahm	aerogram
letter	do-pis	dopis
postcard	po-hlehd	pohled
telegram	teh-leh-grahm	telegram
air mail	leh-teh-tski	letecky
envelope	o-baal-kah	obálka
mail box	po-shto-vnye skhraan-kah	poštovní schránka
parcel	bah-leek	balík
registered mail	do-po-ru-cheh-nyeh	doporučeně
surface mail	o-bi-chehy-noh posh-toh	obyčejnou poštou

Telephone

I want to ring ...	raad bikh-si zah-teh-leh-fo-no-vahl ... raa-dah bikh-si zah-teh-leh-fo-no-vah-lah ...	Rád bych si zatelefonoval ... (m) Ráda bych si zatelefonovala ... (f)
The number is ...	chees-lo yeh ...	Číslo je ...

How much does a three-minute call cost?	ko-lik sto-yee trzhee-mi-nu-to-vee ho-vor?	Kolik stojí tříminutový hovor?
I want to make a reverse-charges call.	raad bikh zah-vo-lal nah oo-cheht vo-lah-nair-ho raa-dah bikh zah-vo-la-lah nah oo-cheht vo-lah-nair-ho	Rád bych zavolal na účet volaného. (m) Ráda bych zavolala na účet volaného. (f)
I've been cut off.	bil ysehm przheh-ru-shehn bi-lah ysehm przheh-ru-sheh-nah	Byl jsem přerušen. (m) Byla jsem přerušena. (f)

I'd like to speak to Mr Perez.
    khtyehl bikh *mlu*-vit   *Chtěl bych mluvit s panem*
    spah-nehm *Peh*-rehz   *Perez.* (m)
    khtyeh-lah bikh *mlu*-vit   *Chtěla bych mluvit*
    spah-nehm *Peh*-rehz   *s panem Perez.* (f)

It's engaged.
    yeh *op*-sah-zeh-no   *Je obsazeno.*

CZECH

At the Bank

I want to exchange some
(money/travellers cheques).
    khtyehl/*khtyeh*-lah bikh   *Chtěl/Chtěla bych*
    vi-mnyeh-nyit *(peh-nyee-zeh/*   *vyměnit (peníze/*
    tsehs-tov-nyee *sheh*-ki)   *cestovní šeky).* (m/f)

What's the exchange rate?
    yah-kee yeh *vee*-mnyeh-   *Jaký je výměnný kurs?*
    nee *kurs*?

How many crowns per US dollar?
    ko-lik *ko*-run *do*-stah-nu   *Kolik korun dostanu za*
    zah *yeh*-dehn *ah*-meh-   *jeden americký dolar?*
    ri-tskee *do*-lahr?

bankdraft	*bahm*-ko-vnyee *smnyehn*-kah	*bankovní směnka*
banknotes	*bahn*-kof-ki	*bankovky*
cashier	*po*-klah-dnyeek	*pokladník*
coins	*min*-tseh	*mince*
credit card	*oo*-vyeh-ro-vaa *kahr*-tah	*úvěrová karta*
exchange	*smyeh*-naar-nah	*směnárna*
signature	*pot*-pis	*podpis*

CZECH

Internet

Where can I get Internet access?
    gdeh yeh zdeh   *Kde je zde*
    kdis-poh-zih-tsi *inter*-net?   *k dispozici internet?*
How much is it per hour?
    koh-lick toh stoh-yee   *Kolik to*
    nah *hoh*-dyi-nuh?   *stojí na hodinu?*
I want to check my email.
    khtyehl/*khtyeh*-lah bikh sih   *Chtěl/Chtěla bych si*
    zkon-troh-loh-vat *e*-mail   *zkontrolovat e-mail.* (m/f)

INTERESTS & ENTERTAINMENT
Sightseeing

Do you have a guidebook/local map?
    maa-teh *proo*-vot-tseh/   *Máte průvodce/*
    mah-pu o-ko-lee?   *mapu okolí?*
What are the main attractions?
    yah-kair ysoh *zdehy*-shee   *Jaké jsou zdejší*
    po-zo-ru-ho-dno-styi?   *pozoruhodnosti?*
What's that?
    tso-yeh to?   *Co je to?*
How old is it?
    yahk-yeh to *stah*-rair?   *Jak je to staré?*
Can I take photographs?
    yeh zdeh *po*-vo-leh-no   *Je zde povoleno*
    fo-to-grah-fo-vaht?   *fotografovat?*

ancient	*stah*-ro-vyeh-kee	*starověký*
archaeological	*ahr*-kheh-o-lo-gits-kair	*archeologické*
beach	plaazh	*pláž*
castle	hrahd/*zaa*-mehk	*hrad/zámek*
cathedral	*kah*-teh-draa-lah	*katedrála*
church	*ko*-stehl	*kostel*
concert hall	*kon*-tsehrt-nyee seeny	*koncertní síň*
library	*knyi*-ho-vnah	*knihovna*
main square	*hla*-vnyee *naa*- myeh-styee	*hlavní náměstí*
market	trh	*trh*

monastery	*klaash*-tehr	*klášter*
monument	*pah*-maa-tyneek/	*památník/*
	po-mnyeek	*pomník*
old city	*stah*-rair *myehs*-to	*staré město*
palace	*pah*-laats	*palác*
opera house	*o*-peh-rah	*opera*
ruins	*zrzhee*-tseh-nyi-ni	*zříceniny*
stadium	*stah*-di-awn	*stadión*
statues	*so*-khi	*sochy*
temple	khraam	*chrám*
university	*u*-ni-vehr-si-tah	*universita*

CZECH

Going Out

What's there to do in the evenings?
    kahm-seh-tu daa *veh*-
    chehr yeet?
    Kam se tu dá večer jít?

Are there any nightclubs?
    ysoh zdeh *dis*-ko-tair-ki?
    Jsou zde diskotéky?

Are there places where you can
hear local folk music?
    hrah-yee *nyeh*-gdeh
    li-do-voh *hud*-bu?
    Hrají někde
    lidovou hudbu?

cinema	*ki*-no	*kino*
concert	*kon*-tsehrt	*koncert*
nightclub	*dis*-ko-tair-kah	*diskotéka*
theatre	*dyi*-vah-dlo	*divadlo*

CZECH

Sports & Interests

What sports do you play?
    yakeeh spohrt *dyieh*-laah-the?   *Jaký sport děláte?*
What are your interests?
    yakeh maateh *zaay*-mih?   *Jaké máte zájmy?*

art	*uh*-mnyeh-nyeeh	*umění*
basketball	*bas*-ket-bahl	*basketbal*
chess	shah-khih	*šachy*
collecting things	*zbyeh*-rah-tel-stveeh	*sběratelství*
dancing	*tah*-netz	*tanec*
food	*yeed*-loh	*jídlo*
football	*fot*-bahl/*koh*-pah-no	*fotbal/kopanou*
hiking	*pyeh*-sheeh *tuh*-ris-tickuh	*pěší turistiku*
martial arts	*boh*-yo-vaah	*bojová*
	uh-myeh-nyeeh	*umění*
movies	*phil*-mih	*filmy*
music	*hood*-buh	*hudbu*
nightclubs	*bah*-rih/*notch*-nyeeh	*bary/noční*
	pod-nyi-kih	*podniky*
photography	*phoh*-toh-graph-yee	*fotografii*
reading	*chteh*-nyeeh	*čtení*
shopping	*nah*-kuh-poh-vaa-nyeeh	*nakupování*
skiing	*lih*-zho-vaa-nyeeh	*lyžování*
swimming	*plah*-vaa-nyeeh	*plavání*
tennis	tennis	*tenis*
travelling	*tses*-toh-vaa-nyeeh	*cestování*
TV/videos	*teh*-leh-vih-zee/*vih*-deh-ah	*televizi/videa*
visiting friends	*nah*-fshtyeh-voh-vaa-nyeeh przhaa-tell	*navštěvování přátel*
walking	*proh*-khaaz-kih	*procházky*

CZECH

Festivals & Public Holidays

1 January	New Year's Day	*Nový rok*
	Easter Friday	*Velikonoční pátek*
	Easter Monday	*Velikonoční pondělí*
1 May	Labour Day	*Svátek práce*
8 May	Liberation Day (1945)	*Den osvobození*
5 July	Cyril & Methodius Memorial Day	*od fašizmu* *Cyril a Metoděj*
6 July	Jan Hus Memorial Day	*Mistr Jan Hus*
28 October	Czechoslovak Independence Day (1918)	*Den vzniku Československa*
24 December	Christmas Eve	*Štědrý den*
25 December	Christmas Day	*1. svátek Vánoční*
26 December	Boxing Day	*2. svátek Vánoční*

IN THE COUNTRY
Weather

What's the weather like?
  yah-kair yeh *po*-chah-see? — *Jaké je počasí?*

Will it be ...	*bu*-deh	*Bude*
tomorrow?	*zee*-trah ...?	*zítra ...?*
cloudy	*zah*-tah-zheh-no	*zataženo*
cold	*khlah*-dno	*chladno*
foggy	*ml*-hah-vo	*mlhavo*
frosty	mraaz	*mráz*
hot	*hor*-ko	*horko*
sunny	*slu*-neh-chno	*slunečno*
windy	vyeh-tr-no	*větrno*

| It's raining. | *pr*-shee | *Prší.* |
| It's snowing. | *snyeh*-zhee | *Sněží.* |

Camping

Am I allowed to camp here?
  mo-hu zdeh *stah*-no-vaht? — *Mohu zde stanovat?*
Is there a campsite nearby?
  yeh *fo*-ko-lee *taa*-bo-rzhi-shtyeh? — *Je v okolí tábořiště?*

CZECH

backpack	*bah*-tyoh	bat'oh
can opener	*o*-tvee-rahch kon-zehrf	otvírač konzerv
compass	*kom*-pahs	kompas
crampons	*mah*-chki	mačky
firewood	*drzheh*-vo	dřevo
gas cartridge	*pli*-no-vaa *bom*-bi-chkah	plynová bombička
hammock	*ha*-mahk	hamak
ice axe	*tseh*-peen	cepín
mattress	*mah*-trah-tseh	matrace
penknife	*kah*-peh-snyee noozh	kapesní nůž
rope	*pro*-vahz	provaz
tent	stahn	stan
tent pegs	*stah*-no-vair *ko*-lee-kih	stanové kolíky
torch (flashlight)	*bah*-tehr-kah	baterka
sleeping bag	*spah*-tsee *pi*-tehl	spací pytel
stove	*vah*-rzhich	vařič
water bottle	*pol*-nyee *laa*-hehf	polní láhev

FOOD

Czechs are big lovers of food and take great pride in the culinary experience that their country has to offer. Excellent smoked goods, beer and desserts are all worth experiencing as is the traditional fare of dumplings.

breakfast	*snyee*-dah-nyeh	snídaně
lunch	*o*-byehd	oběd
dinner	*veh*-cheh-rzheh	večeře

Vegetarian Meals

Vegetarian dishes aren't all that common on Czech menus, so vegetarians may have some problems ordering certain dishes.

I'm a vegetarian.
    ysehm *veh*-geh-tah-ri-aan/   Jsem vegetarián/
    veh-geh-tah-ri-aan-kah   vegetariánka. (m/f)
I don't eat meat.
    neh-yeem *mah*-so   Nejím maso.
I don't eat chicken/fish/ham.
    neh-yeem *ku*-rzheh/*ri*-bu/*shun*-ku Nejím kuře/rybu/šunku.

Breakfast

bacon and eggs	*vei*-tseh seh *sla*-nyih-no	*vejcese slaninou*
ham and eggs	*vei*-tseh seh *shun*-kough	*vejce se šunkou*
omelette	*oh*-meh-leh-tah	*omeleta*
soft/hard-boiled eggs	*vei*-tseh nah *mnyeh*-koh/*tvr*-doh	*vejce na měkko/tvrdo*
jam	jam/*mar*-meh-laa-dah	*džem/marmeláda*
type of croissant	*low*-paah-check	*loupáček*
... eggs	... *vei*-tseh	... *vejce*
boiled	*vah*-rzheh-naah	*vařená*
fried	*sma*-zheh-naah	*smažená*
scrambled	*mee*-kha-naah	*míchaná*

Soup

beef	*hoh*-vyeh-zee	*hovězí*
beef chunks with spices	*guh*-laah-sho-vaah	*gulášová*
broth with egg	*buh*-yohn	*bujón*
mushroom	*ho*-boh-vaah	*houbová*
pea	*hrah*-khoh-vaah	*hrachová*
potato	*bram*-boh-roh-vaah	*bramborová*
tomato with a little rice	*rai*-skaah	*rajská*
vegetable	*zeh*-leh-nyih-noh-vaah	*zeleninová*

Desserts

apple strudel	*yah*-bl-koh-veeh *zaah*-vin	*jablkový závin*
preserved and canned fruit	*kohm*-pot	*kompot*
poppy-seed cake	*mah*-koh-veeh *koh*-laach	*makový koláč*
fruit slices	*oh*-vots-neh *koh*-laacheh	*ovocné koláče*
pancakes	*pah*-lah-chin-kih	*palačinky*
meringue with whipped cream	*rah*-qvich-kih	*rakvičky*
ice cream	zmrz-lih-nah	*zmrzlina*

CZECH

MENU DECODER

Starters & Buffet Meals

klobásy	*kloh*-baa-sih	sausages – can be mild or spicy
langoše	*lan*-goh-sheh	a snack made of fried pastry coated in garlic, cheese, butter or jam
obložené chlebíčky	*ob*-loh-zheh-neh *khleh*-beach-kih	open sandwiches
párky	*paar*-kih	frankfurt or wiener-type sausages
uherský salám s okurkou	*ooh*-her-skeeh *sah*-laam s *oh*-khur-kough	Hungarian salami with gherkin
sýrový nářez	*see*-roh-veeh *naah*-rzhez	a serve of two or three cheeses
tlačenka s octem a cibulí	*tlah*-chen-kah s *ots*-tem ah *tzih*-buh-leeh	seasoned jellied meat loaf with vinegar and fresh onion
zavináče	*zah*-vih-naa-tcheh	rollmops – herring fillets rolled around onion and/or gherkin, and pickled
houskové/ bramborové knedlíky	*hough*-skoh-veh/ *bram*-boh-roh-veh *kned*-lee-kih	potato/bread dumplings

Main Meals

dušená roštěnka	*duh*-shehnaa *rosh*-tyien-kah	braised slices of beef in sauce
hovězí guláš	*hoh*-vyeh-zee *guh*-laash	beef chunks in a brown sauce
hovězí karbanátky	*hoh*-vyeh-zee *kar*-bah-naat-kih	a type of beef burger with breadcrumbs, egg and onion

CZECH

pečená ...	*peh*-tcheh-naah ...	roasted ...
husa	*hooh*-sah	goose
kachna	*kakh*-nah	duck
kuře	*kuh*-rzheh	chicken
plněné	*pl*-nyeh-neh	capsicum stuffed with a
papriky	*pah*-prickih	mixture of minced meat and rice, served with tomato sauce
řízek ...	*rzhee*-zeck ...	... schnitzel
telecí	*teh*-le-tseeh	veal
vepřový	*vep*-rzhoh-veeh	pork
segedínský	*seh*-geh-dean-skih	a goulash with three
guláš	*guh*-laash	types of meat, and sauerkraut
svíčková	*sveetch*-koh-vaah	roast beef served with a sour cream sauce and spices
vepřová	*vep*-rzhoh-vaah	roast pork with caraway
pečeně	*peh*-cheh-nyeh	seed
zajíc na	*zah*-yeets nah	hare in a cream sauce
smetaně	*smeh*-tah-nyeh	
znojemská	*znoh*-yem-skaah	slices of roast beef in a
pečeně	*peh*-cheh-nyeh	gherkin sauce

Desserts

meruňkové	*meh*-runyi-koh-veh	apricots wrapped in pastry
knedlíky	*kned*-lee-kih	and topped with cottage cheese, melted butter and sugar
švestkové	*shvest*-koh-veh	plums wrapped in pastry
knedlíky	*kned*-lee-kih	and topped with crushed poppy seeds, melted butter and sugar

CZECH

Non-Alcoholic Drinks

... coffee	*kaah*-vah	*káva*
black	*chair*-naah	*černá*
white	*bee*-laah	*bílá*
espresso	*es*-press-soh	*espreso*
hot chocolate	*kah*-kah-oh	*kakao*
Vienna coffee	vee-dyen-skaah *kaah*-vah	*vídeňská káva*
tea ...	*chai* ...	*čaj* ...
with sugar	s *tsuk*-rehm	s *cukrem*
with milk	s *mleh*-kehm	s *mlékem*
fruit juice	*oh*-vots-naah *sh*-tyaah-vah	*ovocná šťáva*
ice	led	*led*
mineral water	*mih*-neh-raal-kah	*minerálka*
milk	*mleh*-koh	*mléko*
soft drink	*lih*-moh-naah-dah	*limonáda*

Alcoholic Drinks

beer	*pih*-voh	*pivo*
spirits	*lih*-hoh-vih-nih	*lihoviny*
whisky	*viskih*	*whisky*
(red/white) wine	(*cher*-veh-nair/ *bee*-lair) *vee*-noh	(*červené/bílé*) *víno*

BEAUTIFUL BEER GUTS

The Czechs drink the largest volume of *pivo*, 'beer' per capita of any country in the world. Beer culture is centuries old, and is celebrated at hundreds of festivals, where competitions include speed drinking and the largest beer gut to name but a few.

A favourite Czech saying is:

Pivo dělá pěkná těkla.

'Beer makes beautiful bodies.'

SHOPPING

Where's the nearest ...?	*Gdeh* yeh zdeh *nei*-blizh-shee ...?	*Kde je zde nejbližší ...?*
bookshop	*knyih*-ku-pets-tvee	*knihkupectví*
camera shop	*fo*-to *po*-trzheh-bi	*foto potřeby*
chemist (pharmacy)	*lair*-kaar-nah	*lékárna*
clothing store	*o*-dyeh-vi	*oděvy*
delicatessen	*lah*-hoot-ki	*lahůdky*
general store	*smee*-sheh-nair zbo-zhee/ *po*-trah-vi-ni; *o*-pkhod	*smíšené zboží/ potraviny; obchod*
greengrocer	*zeh*-leh-nyi-nah ah *oh*-vo-tseh	*zelenina a ovoce*
laundry	*praa*-dehl-nah	*prádelna*
market	trh	*trh*
newsagency	*no*-vi-no-vee *staa*-nehk/ *tah*-baak	*novinový stánek/tabák*
shoeshop	*oh*-buv	*obuv*
souvenir shop	*su*-veh-nee-ri	*suvenýry*
stationers	*pah*-peer-nyits-tvee	*papírnictví*
supermarket	*sah*-mo-op-slu-hah	*samoobsluha*

CZECH

How much is it?	*ko*-lik-to *sto*-yee?	*Kolik to stojí?*
Do you accept credit cards?	*przhi*-yee-maa-teh *oo*-vyeh-ro-vair *kahr*-ti?	*Přijímáte úvěrové karty?*

CZECH

AT THE MARKET

Basics

bread	khleehb	chléb
butter	*maas*-loh	máslo
cereal	*oh-bil*-nyih-noh-vee	obilninové
	kah-sheh	kaše
cheese	seer	sýr
chocolate	*choh*-koh-laa-duh	čokoládu
eggs	*vei*-tseh	vejce
flour	*mow*-kuh	mouku
honey	med	med
margarine	*mar*-gah-reen	margarín
marmalade	jam/*mar*-meh-laa-duh	džem/marmeládu
milk	*mleh*-koh	mléko
(olive) oil	(*oh*-lih-vo-vee) *oh*-ley	(olivový) olej
pasta	*tyes*-toh-vih-nih	těstoviny
pepper	pep-rzh	pepř
rice	*reeh*-zheh	rýže
salt	sool	sůl
sugar	*tsuh*-kr	cukr
yogurt	*yo*g-oort	jogurt

Meat & Poultry

beef	*hoh*-vyeh-zee *mah*-soh	hovězí maso
chicken	*kuh*-rzheh	kuře
ham	*shoon*-kah	šunka
hamburger	*hahm*-buhr-gr/	hamburger/
	kahr-bah-naa-teck	karbanátek
kidneys	*led*-vin-kih	ledvinky
lamb	yeh-hnyeh-chee *mah*-soh	jehněčí maso
liver	*yaah*-trah	játra
pork	*veh*-przhoh-vee *mah*-soh	vepřové maso
sausage	*kloh*-baa-sah/*uh*-zen-kah	klobása/uzenka
turkey	*kroh*-tsan	krocan
veal	*teh*-leh-tsee *mah*-soh	telecí maso

Seafood

lobster	*mohrzh*-skee rahk	mořský rak
mussels	*muhsh*-leh	mušle
oysters	*ooh*-strzhi-tseh	ústřice
shrimp (prawns)	*kreh*-veh-tah/*gar*-naaht	kreveta/garnát

AT THE MARKET

Vegetables

beans	*fah*-zol-kih	fazolky
beetroot	*cher*-veh-naa *rzheh*-pah	červená řepa
cabbage	*zeh*-lee	zelí
capsicum	*pah*-prih-kah	paprika
carrot	*mrh*-kev	mrkev
cauliflower	*kvyeh*-taak	květák
celery	*tseh*-lehr	celer
cucumber	*oh*-kuhr-kah	okurka
eggplant (aubergine)	*bah*-klah-zhaan/*lih*-leck	baklažán/lilek
lettuce	*hlaav*-koh-vee *sah*-laat	hlávkový salát
mushrooms	*hough*-bih	houby
onion	*tsih*-buh-leh	cibule
peas	*hraa*-sheck	hrášek
potatoes	*bram*-boh-rih	brambory
spinach	*shpeh*-naat	špenát
tomato	*rai*-cheh	rajče

Fruit

apple	*yah*-bl-koh	jablko
apricots	*meh*-roony-kih	meruňky
banana	*bah*-naan	banán
grapes	*vih*n-nair *hroz*-nih	vinné hrozny
kiwi fruit	kih-vih	kivi
lemon	*tsih*-rawn	citrón
orange	*poh*-meh-ranch	pomeranč
peach	*bros*-kev	broskev
pears	hrooh-shkih	hrušky
plums	*shv*est-kih	švestky
strawberries	*yah*-hoh-dih	jahody

Spices & Condiments

chillies	*paa*-lih-vair *pap*-rich-kih	pálivé papričky
garlic	*ches*-neck	česnek
ginger	*zaaz*-vor	zázvor
horseradish	krzhehn	křen
mustard	*horzh*-chi-tseh	hořčice
pickled cabbage/ vegetables	*steh*-rih-lih-zoh-vah-neh *zeh*-lee/*zeh*-leh-nyih-nah	sterilizované zelí/zelenina

CZECH

Essential Groceries

I'd like ...	mohl/*moh*-lah bikh ... *doh*-staht?	*Mohl/Mohla bych ... dostat?* (m/f)
batteries	*bah*-ter-kih	*baterky*
bread	kh-lehb	*chléb*
butter	*maah*-sloh	*máslo*
cheese	seer	*sýr*
chocolate	*choh*-koh-laa-duh	*čokoládu*
eggs	*vei*-tseh	*vejce*
honey	med	*med*
margarine	*mar*-gah-reen	*margarín*
matches	*sir*-kih/*zaah*-pal-kih	*sirky/zápalky*
milk	*mleh*-koh	*mléko*
shampoo	*sham*-pohn	*šampon*
soap	*meed*-loh	*mýdlo*
toilet paper	*toah*-let-nyeeh *pah*-peer	*toaletní papír*
toothpaste	*zub*-nyeeh *pass*-tuh	*zubní pastu*
washing powder	*prah*-tseeh *praa*-shek	*prací prášek*

Souvenirs

Glass and crystal, herb liqueurs and jewellery made with garnets are all popular souvenirs to be found in the Czech Republic.

earrings	*naah*-ooh-shnyi-tseh	*náušnice*
handicraft	*li*-do-vair *ooh*-myeh-nyee	*lidové umění*
necklace	*naa*-hr-dehl-nyeek	*náhrdelník*
pottery	*keh*-rah-mi-kah	*keramika*
ring	*pr*-stehn	*prsten*
rug	*ko*-beh-rehts	*koberec*

Clothing

clothing	*oh*-dyehv	*oděv*
coat	*kah*-baat	*kabát*
dress	*shah*-ti	*šaty*
jacket	*sah*-ko	*sako*
jumper (sweater)	*sveh*-tr	*svetr*
shirt	*ko*-shi-leh	*košile*
shoes	*bo*-tih	*boty*
skirt	*su*-knyeh	*sukně*
trousers	*kahl*-ho-tih	*kalhoty*
underwear	*spod*-nyee *praa*-dloh	*spodní prádlo*

Materials

brass	*mo*-sahz	*mosaz*
cotton	*bah*-vl-nah	*bavlna*
gold	*zlah*-to	*zlato*
handmade	*ru*-chnyeh *vi*-ro-beh-nair	*ručně vyrobené*
leather	*koo*-zheh	*kůže*
silk	*hehd*-vaa-bee	*hedvábí*
silver	*strzhree*-bro	*stříbro*
wool	*vl*-nah	*vlna*

Toiletries

comb	*hrzheh*-behn	*hřeben*
condoms	*preh*-zehr-vah-ti-vi	*prezervativy*
deodorant	*deh*-oh-do-rant	*deodorant*
hairbrush	*kahr*-taach *nah*-vlah-si	*kartáč na vlasy*
moisturising cream	*pleh*-tyo-vee krairm	*pletový krém*
razor	*brzhi*-tvah	*břitva*
shaving cream	*ho*-li-tsee krairm	*holící krém*
sunscreen	krairm nah	*krém na*
	oh-pah-lo-vaa-nyee	*opalování*
tampons	*tahm*-paw-ni	*tampóny*
tissues	*pah*-pee-ro-vair	*papírové*
	kah-pehs-nyee-ki	*kapesníky*
toothbrush	*kahr*-taa-check nah *zu*-bi	*kartáček na zuby*

CZECH

Colours

black	*chehr*-nee	černý
blue	*mo*-dree	modrý
brown	*hnyeh*-dee	hnědý
green	*zeh*-leh-nee	zelený
orange	*oh*-rahn-zho-vee	oranžový
pink	*roo*-zho-vee	růžový
red	*chehr*-veh-nee	červený
white	*bee*-lee	bílý
yellow	*zhloo*-tee	žlutý

Photography

How much is it to process this film?
   ko-lik *sto*-yee   *Kolik stojí vyvolání filmu?*
   vi-vo-laa-nyee *fil*-mu?
When will it be ready?
   gdi *bu*-deh *ho*-to-vee?   *Kdy bude hotový?*
I'd like a film for this camera.
   maa-teh film do *to*-ho-to   *Máte film do tohoto*
   fo-to-ah-pah-raa-tu   *fotoaparátu.*

B&W (film)	*chehr*-no-bee-lee	černobílý
camera	*fo*-to-ah-pah-raat	fotoaparát
colour (film)	*bah*-reh-vnee	barevný
film	film	film
flash	blehsk	blesk
lens	*ob*-yehk-tiv	objektiv
light meter	*ehks*-po-zi-meh-tr	exposimetr

Sizes & Comparisons

small	*mah*-lair	malé
big	*veh*-li-kair	veliké
heavy	*tyezh*-kair	těžké
light	*leh*-kair	lehké
more	*vee*-tseh	více
less	*mair*-nyeh	méně
too much/	*przhee*-lish ho-	příliš hodně/
many	dnyeh/*mno*-ho	mnoho

Smoking

Do you smoke?
khou-rzheesh? khou-rzhee-teh? *Kouříš?*(inf)/*Kouříte?* (pol)

Please don't smoke.
neh-kow-rzhit proh-seem *Nekouřit prosím.*

A packet of cigarettes, please.
pro-sil/pro-si-lah bikh *Prosil/Prosila bych*
kra-bich-ku tsi-gah-reht *krabičkucigaret.* (m/f)

Are these cigarettes strong/mild?
ysoh-ti tsi-gah-reh-ti *Jsou ty cigarety příliš silné/*
przhee-lish sil-nair/yehm-nair? *jemné?*

Do you have a light?
maa-teh zaa-pahl-ki/ *Máte zápalky/zapalovač?*
zah-pah-lo-vahch?

cigarette papers	tsi-gah-reh-to-vair pah-peer-ki	cigaretové papírky
cigarettes	tsi-gah-reh-ti	cigarety
filtered	sfil-trehm	sfiltrem
lighter	zah-pah-lo-vahch	apalovač
matches	zaa-pahl-ki/sir-ki	zápalky/sirky
menthol	mehn-tol-ki	mentolky
pipe	deem-kah	dýmka
tobacco	tah-baak	tabák
(pipe)	(pro deem-ku)	(pro dýmku)

Stationery & Publications

map	mah-pah	mapa
newspaper	no-vi-ni	noviny
paper	pah-peer	papír
pen (ballpoint)	pro-pi-so-vach-ka	propisovačka
scissors	noozh-ki	nůžky
English-language ...	... v-ahm-glich-tyi-nyeh	... vangličtině
newspaper	no-vi-ni	noviny
novels	knyi-hi	knihy

CZECH

HEALTH

Where's the ...?	gde-yeh ...?	Kde je ...?
chemist	lair-kaar-nah	lékárna
dentist	zub-nyee lair-kahrzh/	zubní lékař/
	zu-bahrzh	zubař
doctor	dok-tor	doktor
hospital	neh-mo-tsnyi-tseh	nemocnice

It hurts here.   bo-lee-myeh zdeh   *Bolí mě zde.*

I'm sick.
  ysehm *neh*-mo-tsnee/   *Jsem nemocný/*
  neh-mo-tsnaa   *nemocná.* (m/f)

My friend is sick.
  mooy *przhee*-tehl yeh   *Můj přítel je nemocný.* (m)
  neh-mo-tsnee
  mo-yeh *przhee*-tehl-ki-   *Moje přítelkyně je nemocná.* (f)
  nyeh yeh *neh*-mots-naa

Parts of the Body

My ... hurts.	bo-lee-myeh ...	Bolí mě ...
ankle	kot-nyeek	kotník
arm	pah-zheh	paže
back	zaa-dah	záda
chest	hroohdy/hrood-nyeek	hrud'/hrudník
ear	u-kho	ucho
eye	o-ko	oko
finger	prst	prst
foot	kho-dyi-dlo	chodidlo
hand	ru-kah	ruka
head	hlah-vah	hlava
leg	no-hah	noha

At the Chemist

I need medication for ...
  po-trzheh-bu-yi *lair*-ki ...   *Potřebuji léky ...*
I have a prescription.
  maam *przhehd*-pis   *Mám předpis.*

CZECH

Women's Health

Could I see a female doctor?
   przhaa-la *bikh*-si
   nahf-shtyee-vit *dok*-tor-ku?

*Přála bych
si navštívit doktorku?*

I'm pregnant.
   ysehm *tyeh*-ho-tnaa

Jsem těhotná.

I'm on the Pill.
   u-zhee-vaam *ahn*-ti-
   kon-tsehp-chnyee *praash*-ki

*Užívám antikoncepční
prášky.*

I haven't had my period for
... months.
   neh-mnyieh-lah ysehm
   mehn-stru-ah-tsi
   uzh ... *myeh*-see-tseh

*Neměla jsem menstruaci
už ... měsíců.*

Useful Phrases

I'm ...	maam ...	*Mám ...*
asthmatic	*ahst*-muh	*astmu*
diabetic	*tsu*-krof-ku	*cukrovku*
epileptic	*eh*-pi-leh-psi-i	*epilepsii*

I'm allergic to antibiotics/penicillin.
   ysehm *ah*-lehr-gits-kee
   nah *ahn*-ti-bio-ti-kah/
   peh-ni-tsi-lean

*Jsem alergický
na antibiotika/
penicilín.*

I've been vaccinated.
   bil ysehm *o*-chko-vah-nee
   bi-lah ysehm *o*-chko-vah-naa

Byl jsem očkovaný. (m)
Byla jsem očkovaná. (f)

I have my own syringe.
   maam *svough vlast*-nyee
   i-nyeh-kchnyee *strzhe*-kahch-ku

*Mám svou vlastní
injekčnístříkačku.*

CZECH

At the Dentist

I have a toothache.
bo-lee-myeh zub — *Bolí mě zub.*

I've lost a filling.
vi-pah-dlah-mi *plom*-bah — *Vypadla mi plomba.*

I've broken a tooth.
maam *zlo*-meh-nee zub — *Mám zlomený zub.*

My gums hurt.
bo-lee-myeh *daa*-snyeh — *Bolí mě dásně.*

I don't want it extracted.
neh-tr-hehy-teh-mi *tehn*-to zub — *Netrhejte mi tento zub.*

Please give me an anaesthetic.
pro-seem *umr*-tvyeh-teh *mi*-to — *Prosím, umrtvěte mi to.*

Ailments

I have a(n) ...	maam ...	Mám ...
(low/high)	(*nyeez*-kee/*vi*-so-kee)	(*nízký/vysoký*)
blood pressure	*kreh*-vnyee tlak	*krevní tlak*
constipation	*zaats*-pu	*zácpu*
cough	*kah*-shehl	*kašel*
diarrhoea	*proo*-yehm	*průjem*
fever	*ho*-rehch-ku	*horečku*
hepatitis	*zhloh*-tehn-ku	*žloutenku*
infection	*in*-fehk-tsi	*infekci*
influenza	*khrzhip*-ku	*chřipku*
lice	fshi	*vši*
sprain	*pod*-vr-tnu-tyee	*podvrtnutí*
venereal disease	*po*-hlah-vnyee	*pohlavní*
	neh-mots	*nemoc*
worms	*chehr*-vi	*červy*

I have a ...	*bo*-lee-myeh ...	Bolí mě ...
headache	*hlah*-vah	*hlava*
sore throat	*fkr*-ku	*v krku*
stomachache	*brzhi*-kho	*břicho*

TIME & DATES

Telling the time in Czech is difficult to explain in the short space of this chapter. Ask for specific times to be written down.

What time is it?
  ko-lik-yeh *ho*-dyin?   *Kolik je hodin?*
Please write that down.
  nah-pi-shteh mi-to pro-seem.   *Napište mi to, prosím.*
What date is it today?
  ko-li-kaa-tair-ho yeh dnehs?   *Kolikátého je dnes?*

in the morning	*raa*-no	*ráno*
in the afternoon	*ot*-po-leh-dneh	*odpoledne*
in the evening	*veh*-chehr	*večer*

CZECH

Days

Monday	*pon*-dyeh-lee	*pondělí*
Tuesday	*oo*-teh-ree	*úterý*
Wednesday	*strzheh*-dah	*středa*
Thursday	*chtvr*-tehk	*čtvrtek*
Friday	*paa*-tehk	*pátek*
Saturday	*so*-bo-tah	*sobota*
Sunday	*neh*-dyeh-leh	*neděle*

HELICOPTER HALOS

Many people wonder why so many Czech statues have golden-looking helicopter blades on their heads – they're actually halos which indicate that the statue is of a saint.

The one exception is the statue of St Jan Nepomucký, who has no blades, but a circle of stars. No, he didn't get hit on the head like in a cartoon – Jan Nepomucký was thrown off Charles' Bridge in Prague and drowned. According to legend, the stars appeared above the water indicating where his body lay.

CZECH

Months

January	*leh*-dehn	*leden*
February	*oo*-nor	*únor*
March	*brzheh*-zehn	*březen*
April	*du*-behn	*duben*
May	*kvyeh*-tehn	*květen*
June	*chehr*-vehn	*červen*
July	*chehr*-veh-nehts	*červenec*
August	*sr*-pehn	*srpen*
September	*zaa*-rzhee	*září*
October	*rzhee*-yehn	*říjen*
November	*lis*-to-pahd	*listopad*
December	*pro*-si-nehtz	*prosinec*

Seasons

summer	*lair*-to	*léto*
autumn	*pod*-zim	*podzim*
winter	*zi*-mah	*zima*
spring	*yah*-ro	*jaro*

Present

today	dnehs	*dnes*
this morning	dnehs *raa*-no	*dnes ráno*
tonight	dnehs *veh*-chehr/	*dnes večer/*
	dnehs *vno*-tsi	*dnes v noci*
this week	*tehn*-to *tee*-dehn	*tento týden*
this year	*leh*-tos/*vleh*-	*letos/*
	tosh-nyeem *ro*-tseh	*v letošním roce*
now	teh-dyi	*ted'*

Past

yesterday	*fcheh*-rah	*včera*
day before	*przheh*-dehf-	*předevčírem*
yesterday	chee-rehm	
last night	*fcheh*-rah *veh*-chehr	*včera večer*
last week/year	*mi*-nu-lee *tee*-dehn/rok	*minulý týden/rok*

CZECH

Future

tomorrow	*zee*-trah	*zítra*
day after tomorrow	*po-*zee-trzhee	*pozítří*
tomorrow afternoon	*zee*-trah *ot*-po-leh-dneh/ *veh*-chehr	*zítra odpoledne/ večer*
next week	*przheesh*-tyee *tee*-dehn	*příští týden*
next year	*przheesh*-tyee rok	*příští rok*

During the Day

afternoon	*ot*-po-leh-dneh	*odpoledne*
dawn	*svee*-taa-nyee	*svítání*
day	dehn	*den*
early	*br*-zo	*brzo*
midday	*po*-leh-dneh	*poledne*
midnight	*pool*-nots	*půlnoc*
morning (9 am – midday)	*raa*-no/ *do*-po-leh-dneh	*ráno/ dopoledne*
night	nots	*noc*
sunrise	*vee*-khod *slun*-tseh	*východ slunce*
sunset	*zaa*-pahd *slun*-tseh	*západ slunce*

CZECH

NUMBERS & AMOUNTS

0	*nu*-lah	nula
1	*yeh*-dna	jedna
2	dvah	dva
3	trzhi	tři
4	*chti*-rzhi	čtyři
5	pyeht	pět
6	shehst	šest
7	*seh*-dum	sedm
8	*o*-sum	osm
9	*deh*-vyeht	devět
10	*deh*-seht	deset
11	*yeh*-deh-naatst	jedenáct
12	*dvah*-naatst	dvanáct
13	*trzhi*-naatst	třináct
14	*chtr*-naatst	čtrnáct
15	*pah*-tnaatst	patnáct
16	*shehst*-naatst	šestnáct
17	*seh*-dum-naatst	sedmnáct
18	*o*-sum-naatst	osmnáct
19	*deh*-vah-teh-naatst	devatenáct
20	*dvah*-tseht	dvacet
21	*dva*-tseht *yeh*-dnah/	dvacet jedna/
	yeh-dna-dvah-tseht	jednadvacet
30	*trzhi*-tseht	třicet
40	*chti*-rzhi-tseht	čtyřicet
50	*pah*-deh-saat	padesát
60	*sheh*-deh-saat	šedesát
70	*seh*-dum-deh-saat	sedmdesát
80	*o*-sum-deh-saat	osmdesát
90	*deh*-vah-deh-saat	devadesát
100	stoh	sto
1000	*tyi*-seets	tisíc
10 000	*deh*-seht *tyi*-seets	deset tisíc
100 000	stoh *tyi*-seets	sto tisíc
one million	*mi*-li-yawn	milión

Useful Words

Enough!	dost!	*Dost!*
a little (amount)	*tro*-khu	*trochu*
double	*dvoh*-yi-tee	*dvojitý*
dozen	*tu*-tseht	*tucet*
few	*nyeh*-ko-lik	*několik*
less	*mair*-nyeh	*méně*
many	*mno*-ho	*mnoho*
more	*vee*-tseh	*více*
once	*yeh*-dnoh	*jednou*
pair	paar	*pár*
per cent	*pro*-tsehn-to	*procento*
some	*nyeh*-kteh-ree	*některý*
too much	*przhee*-lish *ho*-dnyeh	*příliš hodně*
twice	*dvah*-kraat	*dvakrát*

ABBREVIATIONS

cm/m/km	cm/m/km
č./čís.	number/s
ČAD	Czech Coachline
ČČK	Czech Red Cross
ČD	Czech Railway
ČEDOK	Czech Travel Agency
ČR	Czech Republic
ČSA	Czechoslovak Airlines
ČTK	Czech Press Agency
h/hod	hour, or halíř (h), small unit of currency
hl. m.	capital city
Kč	Czech crown
nám.	town square
OSN	United Nations
p./sl.	Mr/Miss
pí.	Mrs/Ms
SBČ	Czech State Bank
ul.	street

CZECH

EMERGENCIES

Help!
po-mots!   *Pomoc!*

It's an emergency.
to-yeh *nah*-lair-hah-vee   *To je naléhavý případ.*
przhee-paht

There's been an accident.
do-shlo kneh-ho-dyeh   *Došlo k nehodě.*

Call ...!	*zah*-vo-lehy-teh ...!	*Zavolejte ...!*
a doctor	*do*-kto-rah	*doktora*
an ambulance	*sah*-nit-ku	*sanitku*
the police	*po*-li-tsi-yi	*policii*

Where's the police station?
gdeh-yeh *po*-li-tsehy-nyee   *Kde je policejní stanice?*
stah-nyi-tseh?

I've been raped.
bi-lah ysehm *znaa*-sil-   *Byla jsem znásilněna.*
nyeh-nah

I've been robbed.
bil ysehm *o*-krah-dehn   *Byl jsem okraden.* (m)
bi-lah ysehm *o*-krah-deh-nah   *Byla jsem okradena.* (f)

Go away!
dyih-teh *prich*!/*byezh*-teh   *Jděte pryč!/Běžte pryč!*
prich!

I'll call the police.
zah-vo-laam *po*-li-tsi-yi   *Zavolám policii.*

Thief!
zlo-dyehy!   *Zloděj!*

I'm ill.
ysehm *neh*-mo-tsnee/   *Jsem nemocný/*
neh-mo-tsnaa   *nemocná.* (m/f)

I'm lost.
zah-bloh-dyil-sem/   *Zabloudil/*
zah-bloh-dyi-lah-sem   *Zabloudila jsem.* (m/f)

Where are the toilets?
  gdeh-ysoh *zaa*-kho-di?   *Kde jsou záchody?*
Could you help me, please?
  pro-seem *moo*-zheh-teh   *Prosím, můžete mi*
  mi *po*-mo-tsi?   *pomoci?*
Could I please use the telephone?
  do-vo-lee-teh, ah-bikh-si   *Dovolíte, abych si*
  zah-teh-leh-fo-no-vahl/   *zatelefonoval/*
  zah-teh-leh-fo-no-vah-lah?   *zatelefonovala?* (m/f)
I'm sorry. I apologise.
  pro-miny-teh.   *Promiňte.*
  o-mloh-vaam-seh.   *Omlouvám se.*
I didn't realise I was doing
anything wrong.
  neh-u-vyeh-do-mil   *Neuvědomil jsem si,*
  ysehm-si zheh ysehm   *že jsem udělal něco*
  u-dyeh-lahl *nyeh*-tso   *špatného.* (m)
  shpaht-nair-ho
  neh-u-vyeh-do-mi-lah   *Neuvědomila jsem si,*
  ysehm-si zheh ysehm   *že jsem udělala něco*
  u-dyeh-lah-lah *nyeh*-tso   *špatného.* (f)
  shpaht-nair-ho
I didn't do it.
  neh-u-dye-lahl/*neh*-u-dye-   *Neudělal/Neudělala*
  lahl-lah ysehm-to   *jsem to.* (m/f)
I wish to contact my
embassy/consulate.
  przheh-yi-si *mlu*-vit   *Přeji si mluvit s*
  zmeem *vehl*-vi-slah-   *mým velvyslanectvím/*
  nehts-tveem/*kon*-zu-laa-tehm   *konzulátem.*
I have medical insurance.
  maam *neh*-mo-tsehns-koh   *Mám nemocenskou*
  po-yist-ku   *pojistku.*
My possessions are insured.
  mo-yeh *zah*-vah-zah-dlah   *Moje zavazadla*
  y-sow poh-yish-tyieh-nah   *jsou pojištěna.*

CZECH

My ... was stolen.	u-krah-dli mnyieh ...	*Ukradli mně ...*
I've lost my ...	strah-tyil/strah-tyi-lah ysehm ...	*Ztratil/Ztratila jsem ... (m/f)*
bags	mo-yeh zah-vah-zah-dlah	*moje zavazadla*
handbag	mo-yi kah-behl-kuh	*moji kabelku*
money	mo-yeh peh-nyee-zeh	*moje peníze*
passport	mooy pahs	*můj pas*
travellers cheques	mo-yeh tsehs-to-vnyee sheh-kih	*moje cestovní šeky*
wallet	peh-nyeh-zhen-kah	*peněženka*

HUNGARIAN

HUNGARIAN

QUICK REFERENCE

Hello.	yoh nah-pot	Jó napot
	kee-vaa-nok si-ah	kívánok. (pol) Szia. (inf)
Goodbye.	vi-sont-laa-taash-rah	Viszontlátásra. (pol)
	si-ah!	Szia! (inf)
Yes./No.	i-ghen/nem	Igen./Nem.
Excuse me.	bo-chaa-naht	Bocsánat.
May I?	le-het?	Lehet?
Sorry.	bo-chaa-naht	Bocsánat.
Please.	keh-rem	Kérem.
Thank you.	ker-ser-nerm	Köszönöm.
You're welcome.	see-ve-shen	Szívesen.
What time is it?	haany oh-rah?	Hány óra?
Where's the ...?	hol vahn ah/ahz ...?	Hol van a/az ...?

Turn left/right.
  for-dul-yon bahl-rah/   Forduljon balra/
  yobb-rah.   jobbra.
Go straight ahead.
  men-yen e-dje-ne-shen e-loere   Menjen egyenesen előre.
I (don't) understand.
  (nem) ehr-tem   (Nem) értem.
Do you speak English?
  be-sehl ahn-gho-lul?   Beszél angolul?
Where are the toilets?
  hol vahn ah veh-tseh?   Hol van a WC?
How much is it?
  meny-nyi-be ke-rül?   Mennyibe kerül?

I'd like a ...	se-ret-nehk ...	Szeretnék ...
room	so-baat	szobát
ticket to ...	edj he-yet	egy helyet
	fogh-lahl-ni ...	foglalni ...

| one-way | edj ye-djet chahk odah | egy jegyet csak oda |
| return | edj re-toor-ye-djet | egy retúrjegyet |

1	edj	egy	6	haht	hat
2	ket-toer	kettő	7	heht	hét
3	haa-rom	három	8	nyolts	nyolc
4	nehdj	négy	9	ki-lents	kilenc
5	ert	öt	10	teez	tíz

HUNGARIAN

Hungarian, or Magyar as it is known to the Magyars (who constitute 95 percent of the population in Hungary), is a unique language in Europe. The roots of this Finno-Ugric tongue and its people lie in the lands east of the Ural mountain chain, from where, in around 2000 BC, there was a major migration west. In the process, the group split, some moving north to Finland and Estonia, and the others, the Ugric people, moving through to Hungary. Their language was also split into two groups. While it picked up certain Persian, Turkish and Bulgar words along the way, it developed into modern Hungarian which is now only spoken in Hungary. Finnish is the nearest European relative, bearing some resemblances in form and structure, but the two languages are mutually incomprehensible.

There is a Hungarian-speaking population of 10.3 million in Hungary, and a sizable ethnic Hungarian-speaking community around the borders: nearly two million in Romania, mostly in Transylvania, some 600,000 in the Slovak Republic, half a million in Vojvodina and Croatia, and 200,000 in the Ukraine.

However daunting it may appear at first sight, there is a regularity and code to the language. Word formation is agglutinative, meaning that you start with a 'root' and build on it. There's a complicated set of rules governing prepositions, which in Hungarian are actually word endings. In order to simplify the language guide, we've generally omitted the wide variety of endings that could be used. Although this makes for some grammatically incorrect sentences, such as 'Which bus goes Buda?', there should be no problems in being understood. Just for your information, some of the common endings you may see or hear are: -ba, -be, -ra, -re, -hoz, -hez, -höz, -nal, -nál and -nél. The definite article ('the' in English) has two forms in Hungarian: az before a word starting with a vowel, and a before a consonant.

For beginners, good pronunciation will get you further than good grammar, and Hungarians are delighted to hear any of their tongue emerge from a non-Magyar.

HUNGARIAN

PRONUNCIATION
The rules are simple, and the actual pronunciation just takes a little practice. There are no diphthongs (vowel combinations) – each vowel is pronounced.

Short Vowels

a	ah	between the 'o' in 'hot' and the 'a' in 'was'
e	e	as the 'e' in 'set'
i	i	as the 'i' in 'pit'
o	o	as the 'o' in 'solitude'
ö	er	as the 'o' in 'worse'
u	u	as the 'oo' in 'hoop'
ü	ü	as the 'ew' in 'few'

Long Vowels
Long vowels are indicated with an accent (*á, ő, ű*).

á	aa	as the 'a' in 'father'
é	eh	as the 'a' in 'make'
í	ee	as the 'ee' in 'flee'
ó	oh	as the 'o' in 'note'
ő	oer	as the 'o' in 'world'
ő	oer	as the 'o' in 'world'
ú	oo	as the 'u' in 'flute'
ű	üü	as the 'ew' in 'few'

QUESTION WORDS		
How?	hodj?	*Hogy?*
When?	mi-kor?	*Mikor?*
Where?	hol?	*Hol?*
Which?	me-yik?	*Melyik?*
Who?	ki?	*Ki?*
Why?	mi-ehrt?	*Miért?*

Consonants

Most double consonants should be lengthened to the point where you can just distinguish the two letters. Consonants not described here are pronounced as they are in English.

c	ts	as the 'ts' in 'hats'
cs	ch	as the 'ch' in 'church'
g	gh	as in 'ghost', slightly softer than the 'g' in 'got'
gy	dj	as the 'j' in 'jury'
j	y	as the 'y' in 'yellow'
ly	y	as the 'y' in 'yellow'
ny	ny	as in 'new'
r	r	as in 'red', but harder and sharper
s	sh	as the 'sh' in 'shower'
sz	s	as the 's' in 'sin'
ty	ty	a 'tch' sound, as the 'tu' in 'statue'
zs	zh	as the 's' in 'pleasure'

Stress

In the vast majority of words, there's a slight stress on the first syllable. Each syllable after the first is given equal weight, even in the longest words.

SUBJECT PRONOUNS		
SG		
I	ehn	*én*
you (inf)	te	*te*
you (pol)	ern-erk	*önök*
he/she/it	oer	*o*
PL		
we	mi	*mi*
you	ern-erk	*önök*
they	oerk	*ok*

HUNGARIAN

GREETINGS & CIVILITIES
Top Useful Phrases

Hello.

    yoh nah-pot kee-vaa-nok   *Jó napot kívánok.* (pol)

    si-ah   *Szia.* (inf)

Goodbye.

    vi-sont-laa-taash-rah   *Viszontlátásra.* (pol)

    si-ah!   *Szia!* (inf)

Yes./No.	i-ghen/nem	*Igen./Nem.*
Excuse me.	bo-chaa-naht	*Bocsánat.*
Please.	keh-rem	*Kérem.*
Thank you.	ker-ser-nerm	*Köszönöm.*

Many thanks.

    nah-djon ker-ser-nerm   *Nagyon köszönöm.*

May I? Do you mind?

    le-het?   *Lehet?*

Sorry. (excuse/forgive me)

    bo-chaa-naht   *Bocsánat.*

That's fine. You're welcome.

    rend-ben see-ve-shen   *Rendben. Szívesen.*

Greetings

Good morning.

    yoh regh-ghelt   *Jó reggelt.*

Good afternoon.

    yoh nah-pot   *Jó napot.*

Good evening/night.

    yoh esh-teht/ehy-sah-kaat   *Jó estét/éjszakát.*

How are you?

    hodj vahn/vahdj?   *Hogy van/vagy?* (pol/inf)

Well, thanks.

    ker-ser-nerm, yohl   *Köszönöm, jól.*

HUNGARIAN

Forms of Address

Madam/Mrs	herldj/as-sony	*Hölgy/Asszony*
Sir/Mr	oor	*Úr*
Miss	kish-as-sony	*Kisasszony*
companion	taarsh	*társ*
friend	bah-raat	*barát*

HUNGARIAN

SMALL TALK
Meeting People

What's your name?
   hodj heev-yaak?   *Hogy hívják?*

My name is ...
   ah ne-vem ...   *A nevem ...*

I'd like to introduce you to ...
   se-ret-nehm ernt   *Szeretném Önt*
   be-mu-taht-ni ...   *bemutatni ...*

Pleased to meet you.
   er-rü-lerk hodj megh-ish-   *Örülök, hogy*
   mer-he-tem   *megismerhetem.*

How old are you?
   ern haany eh-vesh?   *Ön hány éves?*

I'm ... years old.
   ... eh-vesh vah-djok   *... éves vagyok.*

HUNGARIAN

Occupations

What do you do?
mi ah fogh-lahl-ko-zaa-shah? *Mi a foglalkozása?*

I'm unemployed.
mun-kah-nehl-kü-li vah-djok *Munkanélküli vagyok.*

I'm a/an ...	... vah-djok	... vagyok
artist	müü-vehs	*művész*
businessperson	üz-let-em-ber	*üzletember* (m)
	üz-let-as-sony	*üzletasszony* (f)
computer	saa-mee-toh-ghehp	*számítógép*
programmer	progh-rah-mo-zoh	*programozó*
doctor	or-vosh	*orvos*
engineer	mehr-nerk	*mérnök*
farmer	ghahz-dah	*gazda*
journalist	ooy-shaagh-ee-roh	*újságíró*
lawyer	yo-ghaas	*jogász*
manual worker	fi-zi-kahi mun-kaash	*fizikai munkás*
mechanic	se-re-loer	*szerelő*
nurse	aa-po-loh	*ápoló* (m)
	aa-po-loh-noer	*ápolónő* (f)
office worker	iro-dah-i dol-gho-zoh	*irodai dolgozó*
scientist	tu-dohsh	*tudós*
student	di-aak	*diák*
teacher	tah-naar	*tanár* (m)
	tah-naar-noer	*tanárnő* (f)
waiter	pin-tsehr	*pincér* (m)
	pin-tsehr-noer	*pincérnő* (f)
writer	ee-roh	*író*

Family

Are you married?
noers? *Nős?* (m)
fehry-nehl vahn? *Férjnél van?* (f)

I'm single.
noert-len/hah-yah-don *Nőtlen/Hajadon*
vah-djok *vagyok.* (m/f)

I'm married.
　　noersh/fehry-nehl
　　vah-djok

Nős/Férjnél
vagyok. (m/f)

I'm widowed.
　　erz-vedj-ahs-sony/
　　erz-vedj-em-ber vah-djok

Özvegyasszony/
Özvegyember vagyok. (m/f)

I'm divorced.
　　el-vaal-tahm

Elváltam.

How many children do you have?
　　haany djer-me-ke vahn?

Hány gyermeke van?

I don't have any children.
　　ninch djer-me-kem

Nincs gyermekem.

I have a daughter/son.
　　edj laa-nyom/fi-ahm vahn

Egy lányom/fiam van.

brother	fioo-tesht-vehr	*fiútestvér*
children	dje-re-kek	*gyerekek*
daughter	laany	*lány*
family	chah-laad	*család*
father	ah-pah	*apa*
grandfather	nahdj-pah-pah	*nagypapa*
grandmother	nahdj-mah-mah	*nagymama*
husband	fehry	*férj*
mother	ah-nyah	*anya*
sister	le-aany-tesht-vehr	*leánytestvér*
son	fioo	*fiú*
wife	fe-le-shehgh	*feleség*

Religion

I'm ...	... vah-djok	... *vagyok*
Buddhist	bud-hish-tah	*buddhista*
Catholic	kah-to-li-kush	*katolikus*
Christian	ke-res-tehny	*keresztény*
Hindu	hin-du	*hindu*
Jewish	zhi-doh	*zsidó*
Muslim	mu-zul-maan	*muzulmán*

HUNGARIAN

HUNGARIAN

What's your religion?
mi-yen vahl-laa-shoo? — *Milyen vallású?*
I'm not religious.
nem vah-djok vahl-laa-shosh — *Nem vagyok vallásos.*

Nationalities

Where are you from?
ern hon-nahn yertt? — *Ön honnan jött?*

I'm from ...	... bohl yert-tem	... ból jöttem.
Australia	ah-ust-raa-li-ah	*Ausztrália*
Canada	kah-nah-dah	*Kanada*
England	ahn-ghli-ah	*Anglia*
Ireland	eer-or-saagh	*Írország*
New Zealand	ooy zeh-lahnd	*Új-Zéland*
Scotland	shkoh-tsi-ah	*Skócia*
the USA	ahz e-dje-shült	*Az Egyesült*
	aal-lah-mok	*Államok*
Wales	vels	*Wales*

Feelings

I'm ...		
angry	mehr-ghesh vah-djok	*Mérges vagyok.*
cold	faa-zom	*Fázom.*
hot	me-le-ghem vahn	*Melegem van.*
happy	bol-dogh vah-djok	*Boldog vagyok.*
hungry	eh-hesh vah-djok	*Éhes vagyok.*
thirsty	som-yahsh vah-djok	*Szomjas vagyok.*
in a hurry	shi-e-tek	*Sietek.*
right	yohl vah-djok	*Jól vagyok.*
sad	so-mo-roo vah-djok	*Szomorú vagyok.*
sleepy	aal-mosh vah-djok	*Álmos vagyok.*
tired	faa-rahdt vah-djok	*Fáradt vagyok.*
well	yohl vah-djok	*Jól vagyok.*
worried	ahgh-ghoh-dom	*Aggódom.*

I (don't) like ...
   ne-kem (nem) tet-sik ...   *Nekem (nem) tetszik ...*
I'm sorry. (condolence)
   shahy-naa-lom   *Sajnálom.*
I'm grateful.
   haa-laash vah-djok   *Hálás vagyok.*

BREAKING THE LANGUAGE BARRIER

Do you speak English?
   be-sehl ahn-gho-lul?   *Beszél angolul?*
Does anyone speak English?
   be-sehl vah-lah-ki ahn-gho-lul?   *Beszél valaki angolul?*
I speak a little ...
   ehn be-seh-lek edj ki-chit   *Én beszélek egy kicsit*
   ... ul/ül   *... ul/ül.*
I don't speak ...
   nem be-seh-lek ... ul/ül   *Nem beszélek ... ul/ül.*
I (don't) understand.
   (nem) ehr-tem   *(Nem) értem.*
Could you speak more slowly, please?
   keh-rem tud-nah lahsh-shahb-   *Kérem, tudna lassabban*
   ban be-sehl-ni?   *beszélni?*
Could you repeat that?
   megh-ish-meh-tel-neh?   *Megismételné?*
How do you say ...?
   hodj kell mon-dah-ni ...?   *Hogy kell mondani ...?*

BODY LANGUAGE

Waving the hands about, gesticulating wildly, nodding the head, curious signals with fingers, rolling of the eyes – the Hungarians don't do any of it. However, that's not to say that you shouldn't. At the very least, it will get you noticed.

HUNGARIAN

HUNGARIAN

PAPERWORK

address	tseem	*cím*
age	kor	*kor*
date of birth	sü-le-teh-shi	*születési*
	daa-tum	*dátum*
driver's licence	yo-gho-sheet-vaany	*jogosítvány*
identification	se-mehy-ah-	*személya-*
	zo-nosh-shaagh	*zonosság*
marital status	chah-laa-di	*családi*
	aal-lah-pot	*állapot*
name	nehv	*név*
nationality	nem-ze-ti-shehgh	*nemzetiség*
passport	oot-le-vehl	*útlevél*
passport number	oot-le-vehl-saam	*útlevélszám*
place of birth	sü-le-teh-shi hey	*születési hely*
profession	fogh-lahl-ko-zaa- shah	*foglalkozása*
reason for travel	ahz u-tah-zaash	*az utazás*
	tsehl-yah	*célja*
religion	vahl-laash	*vallás*
sex	nem	*nem*
tourist card	tu-rish-tah	*turista*
	kaar-tyah	*kártya*
visa	vee-zum	*vízum*

GETTING AROUND

What time does the ... leave/arrive?	mi-kor in-dul/ ehr-ke-zik ah ...?	*Mikor indul/ érkezik a ...?*
aeroplane	re-pü-loer-ghehp	*repülőgép*
boat	hah-yoh	*hajó*
bus (city)	he-yi ah-u-toh-bus	*helyi autóbusz*
bus (intercity)	taa-vol-shaa-ghi ah-u-toh-bus	*távolsági autóbusz*
train	vo-naht	*vonat*
tram	vil-lah-mosh	*villamos*

Directions

Where's ...?
   hol vahn ah/ahz ...? · *Hol van a/az ...?*
How do I get to ...?
   hodj yu-tok ah/ahz ...? · *Hogy jutok a/az ...?*
Is it far away?
   mes-se vahn in-nen? · *Messze van innen?*
Is it near here?
   ker-zel vahn ide? · *Közel van ide?*
Can you show me (on the map)?
   megh tud-naa ne-kem · *Meg tudná nekem*
   mu-taht-ni (ah tehr-keh-pen)? · *mutatni (a térképen)?*
I want to go to ...
   se-ret-nehk ... men-ni · *Szeretnék ... menni.*
Go straight ahead.
   men-yen e-dje-ne-shen e-loere · *Menjen egyenesen előre.*
It's two blocks down.
   keht shah-rok-rah vahn in-nen · *Két sarokra van innen.*

Turn left ...	for-dul-yon bahl-rah ...	*Forduljon balra ...*
Turn right ...	for-dul-yon yobb-rah ...	*Forduljon jobbra ...*
at the next corner	ah ker-vet-ke-zoer shah-rok-naal	*a következő saroknál*
at the traffic lights	ah kerz-le-ke-deh-shi laam-paa-naal	*a közlekedési lámpánál*

behind	mer-ghertt	*mögött*
in front of	e-loertt	*előtt*
far	mes-se	*messze*
near	ker-zel	*közel*
opposite	sem-ben	*szemben*

HUNGARIAN

THEY MAY SAY ...	
te-le vahn	It's full.

HUNGARIAN

Booking Tickets

Where can I buy a ticket?
   hol ve-he-tem megh ah   *Hol vehetem meg a*
   ye-djet?   *jegyet?*
I want to go to ...
   se-ret-nehk ... men-ni   *Szeretnék ... menni.*
Do I need to book?
   sük-sheh-ghesh he-yet   *Szükséges helyet*
   fogh-lahl-nom?   *foglalnom?*
Can I get a stand-by ticket?
   kahp-hah-tok edj stand-by   *Kaphatok egy stand-by*
   ye-djet?   *jegyet?*

I'd like ...	se-ret-nehk ...	*Szeretnék ...*
a one-way ticket	edj ye-djet	*egy jegyet*
	chahk odah	*csak oda*
a return ticket	edj	*egy*
	re-toor-ye-djet	*retúr-jegyet*
two tickets	keht ye-djet	*két jegyet*
a student's fare	edj di-aak-ye-djet	*egy diákjegyet*
a child's/	edj dje-rek-ye-djet/	*egy*
pensioner's fare	ye-djet	*gyerekjegyet/*
	nyugh-dee-yash-	*nyugdíjasjegyet*
1st class	el-shoer os-taay	*első osztály*
2nd class	maa-shod-os-taay	*másodosztály*

Bus

Where's the bus/tram stop?
   hol vahn ahz ah-u-toh-bus/   *Hol van az autóbusz/*
   ah vil-lah-mosh megh-aal-loh? *a villamos megálló?*
How often do buses pass by?
   mi-yen djahk-rahn yaar-   *Milyen gyakran járnak*
   nahk ahz ah-u-toh-busok   *az autóbuszok?*
Which bus goes to ...?
   me-yik ah-u-toh-bus medj ...? *Melyik autóbusz megy ...?*
Does this bus go to ...?
   ez ahz ah-u-toh-bus medj ...? *Ez az autóbusz megy ...?*

Could you let me know when we get to ...?
    sohl-nah keh-rem ah-mi-kor   *Szólna kérem, amikor*
    megh-ehr-ke-zünk ...?   *megérkezünk ...?*
I want to get off!
    se-ret-nehk le-saall-ni!   *Szeretnék leszállni!*

What time's the	mi-kor in-dul ah/ahz	*Mikor indul a/az*
... bus?	... ah-u-toh-bus?	*... autóbusz?*
first	el-shoer	*első*
last	u-tol-shoh	*utolsó*
next	ker-vet-ke-zoer	*következő*

Train & Metro

Which line takes me to ...?
    me-yik vo-nahl medj ...?   *Melyik vonal megy...?*
What's the next station?
    mi ah ker-vet-ke-zoer   *Mi a következő*
    aal-lo-maash?   *állomás?*
Is this the right platform for ...?
    er-roerl ah vaa-ghaany-rohl   *Erről a vágányról*
    in-dul ah vo-naht ...?   *indul a vonat ...?*

dining car	eht-ke-zoer-ko-chi	*étkezőkocsi*
express	ex-press	*expressz*
local	he-yi	*helyi*
sleeping car	haa-loh-ko-chi	*hálókocsi*

Taxi

Can you take me to ...?
    el tud-nah vin-ni ...?   *El tudna vinni ...?*
Please take me to ...
    keh-rem vi-djen el ...   *Kérem, vigyen el ...?*
How much does it cost to go to ...?
    meny-nyi-be ke-rül ... igh?   *Mennyibe kerül ... ig?*

HUNGARIAN

Here's fine, thank you.
    itt joh les, ker-ser-nerm   *Itt jó lesz, köszönöm.*

The next corner, please.
    ah ker-vet-ke-zoer shah-   *A következő saroknál,*
    rok-naal, le-djen see-vesh   *legyen szíves.*

The next street to the left/right.
    ah ker-vet-ke-zoer ut-tsaa-naal   *A következő utcánál*
    bahl-rah/yobb-rah   *balra/jobbra.*

Stop here!
    aall-yon megh itt!   *Álljon meg itt!*

Please slow down.
    keh-rem, lash-sheet-shon le   *Kérem, lassítson le.*

Please wait here.
    keh-rem, vaar-yon itt   *Kérem, várjon itt.*

Car

Where can I rent a car?
    hol beh-rel-he-tek   *Hol bérelhetek egy autót?*
    edj ah-u-toht?

How much is it daily/weekly?
    meny-nyi-be ke-rül   *Mennyibe kerül*
    nah-pon-tah/he-ten-te?   *naponta/hetente?*

Does that include insurance/mileage?
    ahz aar tahr-tahl-mahz-   *Az ár tartalmazza a*
    zah ah biz-to-shee-taasht/   *biztosítást/kilómétert?*
    ki-loh-meh-tert?

Where's the next petrol station?
    hol vahn ah legh-ker-ze-   *Hol van a legközelebbi*
    leb-bi ben-zin-koot?   *benzinkút?*

How long can I park here?
    med-digh pahr-kol-hah-tok itt?   *Meddig parkolhatok itt?*

I need a mechanic.
    sük-sheh-ghem vahn edj   *Szükségem van egy*
    se-re-loer-re   *szerelőre.*

air (for tyres)	le-ve-ghoer	*levegő*
battery	ahk-ku-mu-laa-tor	*akkumulátor*
brakes	fehk	*fék*
clutch	kup-lungh	*kuplung*
driver's licence	yo-gho-sheet-vaany	*jogosítvány*
engine	mo-tor	*motor*
lights	vi-laa-ghee-taash	*világítás*
oil	o-lahy	*olaj*
petrol	ben-zint	*benzint*
puncture	de-fekt	*defekt*
radiator	hüü-toer	*hűtő*
road map	ah-u-tohsh tehr-kehp	*autós térkép*
tyres	ke-rehk-ghu-mi	*kerékgumi*
windscreen	sehl-veh-doer	*szélvédő*

HUNGARIAN

ON THE ROAD

AUTÓPÁLYA	FREEWAY
EGYIRÁNYÚ	ONE WAY
GARÁZS	GARAGE
JAVÍTÁSOK	REPAIRS
KERÜLŐÚT	DETOUR
NEM BEJÁRAT	NO ENTRY
NORMÁL	NORMAL
ÓLOMMENTES	UNLEADED
SZERELŐ	MECHANIC
SZUPER	SUPER
TILOS A PARKOLÁS	NO PARKING

ACCOMMODATION

Where's a ...	hol vahn edj ...	*Hol van egy ...*
hotel?	saal-lo-dah?	*szálloda?*
cheap	ol-choh	*olcsó*
clean	tis-tah	*tiszta*
good	yoh	*jó*
nearby	ker-ze-li	*közeli*

HUNGARIAN

At the Hotel

Do you have any rooms available?
vahn sah-bahd so-baa-yuk? *Van szabad szobájuk?*

I'd like ...	se-ret-nehk edj ...	*Szeretnék egy ...*
a single room	edj-aa-djahsh so-baat	*egyágyas szobát*
a double room	keht-aa-djahsh so-baat	*kétágyas szobát*
a room with a bathroom	für-doer-so-baash so-baat	*fürdőszobás szobát*
to share a dorm	aa-djaht edj haa-loh-te-rem-ben	*ágyat egy hálóteremben*

I want a room with a ...	se-ret-nehk edj so-baat ...	*Szeretnék egy szobát ...*
bathroom	für-doer-so-baa-vahl	*fürdőszobával*
shower	zu-hah-nyo-zoh-vahl	*zuhanyozóval*
window	ahb-lahk-kahl	*ablakkal*

I'm staying for ...	... mah-rah-dok	*... maradok*
one day	edj nah-pig	*Egy napig*
two days	keht nah-pig	*Két napig*
one week	edj heh-tig	*Egy hétig*

SIGNS

BEJÁRAT	ENTRANCE
ÉSZKIJÁRAT	EMERGENCY EXIT
FOGLALT	RESERVED
INFORMÁCIÓ	INFORMATION
KIJÁRAT	EXIT
MELEG/HIDEG	HOT/COLD
NYITVA/ZÁRVA	OPEN/CLOSED
SZABAD BELÉPÉS	FREE ADMISSION
TILOS BELÉPNI	NO ENTRY
TILOS A DOHÁNYZÁS	NO SMOKING
TILOS	PROHIBITED
TELEFON	TELEPHONE
WC/TOALETT	TOILETS

How much is it per night/person?
    meny-nyi-be ke-rül
    ehy-sah-kaan-kehnt/
    se-meh-yen-kehnt?

*Mennyibe kerül
éjszakánként/
személyenként?*

Can I see it?
    megh-neh-he-tem ah so-baat?

Megnézhetem a szobát?

Are there any others?
    vahn edj maa-shik so-bah?

Van egy másik szoba?

Is there hot water all day?
    e-ghehs nahp vahn
    me-legh veez?

*Egész nap van meleg
víz?*

Is there a reduction for
students/children?
    vahn ked-vez-mehny
    di-aa-kok-nahk/dje-re-kek-nek?

*Van kedvezmény
diákoknak/ gyerekeknek?*

It's fine, I'll take it.
    ez yoh les

Ez jó lesz.

I'm leaving now/tomorrow.
    mosht/hol-nahp me-djek el

Most/holnap megyek el.

Requests & Complaints

Do you have a safe where I
can leave my valuables?
    vahn er-nerk-nehl sehf,
    ah-hol ahz ehr-teh-ke-
    i-met-hahdj-hah-tom?

*Van önöknél széf, ahol az
értékeimet hagyhatom?*

Is there somewhere to wash clothes?
    vahn vah-lah-hol edj hey,
    ah-hol mosh-hah-tok?

*Van valahol egy hely,
ahol moshatok?*

Can I use the telephone?
    hahs-naal-hah-tom ah

Használhatom a telefont?

I've locked myself out of my room.

ki-zaar-tahm mah-ghahm	*Kizártam magam a*
ah so-baam-bohl	*szobámból.*

The room needs to be cleaned.

ah so-baat ki kell	*A szobát ki kell takarítani.*

AROUND TOWN

I'm looking for a/the ...	ke-re-shem ...	*Keresem ...*
art gallery	ah gah-leh-ri-aat	*a galériát*
bank	ah bahn-kot	*a bankot*
city centre	ah vaa-rosh-kerz-pon-tot	*a városköz-pontot*
... embassy	ah/ahz ... ker-vet-sheh-ghet	*a/az ... követséget*
hotel	ah saal-lo-daa-maht	*a szállodámat*
market	ah pi-ah-tsot	*a piacot*
museum	ah moo-ze-u-mot	*a múzeumot*
police	ah ren-doer-sheh-ghet	*a rendőrséget*
post office	ah posh-taat	*a postát*
public toilet	ah nyil-vaa-nosh veh tseht	*a nyilvános WCt*
telephone centre	ah te-le-fon-kerz-pon-tot	*a telefon-központot*
tourist information office	ah tu-rish-tah in-for-maa-tsi-ohsh i-ro-daat	*a turista információs irodát*

What time does it open?

mi-kor nyit ki?	*Mikor nyit ki?*

What time does it close?

mi-kor zaar be?	*Mikor zár be?*

What street/suburb is this?

me-yik ut-tsah/ke-rü-let ez?	*Melyik utca/kerület ez?*

For directions, see the Getting Around section, page 219.

HUNGARIAN

At the Post Office

I'd like some stamps.
    beh-ye-ghet se-ret-nehk ven-ni   *Bélyeget szeretnék venni.*
How much is the postage?
    meny-nyi-be ke-rül ah beh-yegh?   *Mennyibe kerül a bélyeg?*

I'd like to	se-ret-nehk	*Szeretnék*
send a/an ...	el-kül-de-ni ...	*elküldeni ...*
letter	edj le-ve-let	*egy levelet*
postcard	edj keh-pesh-lah-pot	*egy képeslapot*
parcel	edj cho-mah-ghot	*egy csomagot*
telegram	edj taa-vi-rah-tot	*egy táviratot*

air mail	leh-ghi-posh-tah	*légiposta*
envelope	bo-ree-tehk	*boríték*
mail box	posh-tah-laa-dah	*postaláda*
registered mail	ah-yaan-lott	*ajánlott*
	kül-de-mehny	*küldemény*
surface mail	shi-mah posh-tah	*síma posta*

Internet

Where can I get Internet access?
    hol hahs-naal-hah-tom ahz   *Hol használhatom az*
    in-ter-ne-tet?   *Internetet?*
How much is it per hour?
    meny-nyibe ke-rül edj   *Mennyibe kerül egy órára?*
    oh-raa-rah?
I want to check my email.
    se-ret-nehm meg-nehz-ni,   *Szeretném megnézni,*
    hodj ehr-ke-zett-e i-meh-lem   *hogy érkezett-e emailem.*

HUNGARIAN

Telephone

I want to ring ...
se-ret-nehm fel-heev-ni ... *Szeretném felhívni ...*
The number's ...
ah saam ... *A szám ...*
How much does a three-minute
call cost?
meny-nyi-be ke-rül edj *Mennyibe kerül egy*
haa-rom-per-tsesh hee-vaash? *három perces hívás?*
I want to make a reverse-charges
phone call.
er be-sehl-ghe-tehsht se-ret-nehk *R beszélgetést szeretnék.*
I'd like to speak to (Mr Perez).
(pe-rez oor-rahl) *(Perez úrral) szeretnék*
se-ret-nehk be-sehl-ni *beszélni.*
It's engaged.
fog-lahlt *Foglalt.*
I've been cut off.
meg-sah-kahdt ah vo-nahl *Megszakadt a vonal.*

At the Bank

I want to exchange some
(money/travellers cheques).
se-ret-nehk (pehnzt/utah- *Szeretnék (pénzt/utazási*
zaa-shi chek-ket) vaal-tah-ni *csekket) váltani.*
What's the exchange rate?
meny-nyi ahz aar-fo-yahm? *Mennyi az árfolyam?*
How many forints per dollar?
haany fo-rint edj dol-laar? *Hány forint egy dollár?*

bankdraft	bahnk-in-tehz-vehny	*bankintézvény*
banknotes	bahnk-ye-djek	*bankjegyek*
cashier	pehnz-taar	*pénztár*
coins	ehr-mehk	*érmék*
credit card	hi-tel-kaar-tyah	*hitelkártya*
exchange	vaal-taash	*váltás*
signature	ah-laa-ee-raash	*aláírás*

INTERESTS & ENTERTAINMENT
Going Out

What's there to do in the evenings?

| mit le-het chi-naal-ni esh-tehn-kehnt? | *Mit lehet csinálni esténként?* |

Are there any danceclubs?

| vahn-nahk dis-kohk? | *Vannak diszkók?* |

Are there places where you can hear local folk music?

| vah-nahk o-yahn he-yek, ah-hol he-yi nehp-ze-neht le-het hahll-ghaht-ni? | *Vannak olyan helyek, ahol helyi népzenét lehet hallgatni?* |

How much does it cost to get in?

| meny-nyi-be ke-rül ah be-leh-poer? | *Mennyibe kerül a belépő?* |

cinema	mo-zi	*mozi*
concert	kon-tsert	*koncert*
danceclub	dis-koh	*diszkó*
theatre	seen-haaz	*színház*

Sightseeing

Do you have a guidebook/local map?

| vahn ooti-kerny-vük/ tehr-keh-pük? | *Van útikönyvük/ térképük?* |

What are the main attractions?

| me-yek ah foerbb laat-ni-vah-lohk? | *Melyek a főbb látnivalók?* |

What's that?

| mi ahz? | *Mi az?* |

How old is it?

| mi-yen reh-ghi? | *Milyen régi?* |

Can I take photographs?

| fehny-keh-pez-he-tek? | *Fényképezhetek?* |

What time does it open/close?

| mi-kor nyit ki/zaar be? | *Mikor nyit ki/zár be?* |

HUNGARIAN

Festivals

BudaFest Nyári Opera és Balett Fesztivál
BudaFest Summer Opera and Ballet Festival
staged in the Budapest Opera House to packed houses every
August, this festival attracts outstanding guest performers

Budapesti Őszszi Fesztivál
Budapest Autumn Festival
festival of contemporary art held the second half of October

Budapesti Tavaszi Fesztivál (BTF)
Budapest Spring Festival
this festival of festivals covers a vast range of artistic fields and
attracts many international artists. It's held during the second
half of March.

Budapesti Nemzetközi Borfesztivál
Budapest International Wine Festival
everything about wine – Hungarian and international (early
September)

Gyulai Várszínház
Gyula Castle Theatre
held during July and August, this festival covers spectacular
historical dramas, opera, operetta, ballet, medieval music, jazz
and folk music

Mindenszentek
All Saints' Day
November 1

Pepsi Sziget
Pepsi Island
Hungary's very own weeklong pop festival on Shipyard Island
in Budapest is held in early August. Bring a tent and ear plugs.

Soproni Ünnepi Hetek
Festive Weeks in Sopron
held June-July, this celebrates early music, street theatre, children's progammes and jazz

Szegedi Szabadtéri Játékok
Summer Festival Szeged
popular theatrical productions, opera, folklore, musicals and
rock operas (July and August)

HUNGARIAN

IN THE COUNTRY
Weather

What's the weather like?
mi-yen ahz i-doer?   *Milyen az idő?*

The weather's ...	ahz i-doer ...	*Az idő ...*
today.	mah	*ma.*
Will it be ...	... les	*... lesz*
tomorrow?	hol-nahp?	*holnap?*
cloudy	fel-hoersh	*felhős*
cold	hi-degh	*hideg*
foggy	ker-dersh	*ködös*
frosty	hüü-versh	*hűvös*
hot	me-legh	*meleg*
raining	e-shoer	*eső*
snowing	hah-vah-zaash	*havazás*
sunny	nah-posh	*napos*
windy	se-lesh	*szeles*

Camping

Am I allowed to camp here?
itt le-het kem-pin-ghez-ni?   *Itt lehet kempingezni?*

Is there a campsite nearby?
vahn itt vah-lah-hol ah   *Van itt valahol a*
ker-zel-ben edj kem-pingh?   *közelben egy kemping?*

backpack	haa-ti-zhaak	*hátizsák*
can opener	kon-zerv-nyi-toh	*konzervnyitó*
compass	i-raany-tüü	*iránytű*
crampons	yehgh-segh	*jégszeg*
firewood	tüü-zi-fah	*tűzifa*
gas cartridge	gaaz-paht-ron	*gázpatron*
hammock	fügh-ghoer-aadj	*függőágy*
ice axe	yehgh-chaa-kaany	*jégcsákány*
mattress	maht-rats	*matrac*
penknife	zheb-kehsh	*zsebkés*
rope	ker-tehl	*kötél*

HUNGARIAN

tent	shaa-tor	*sátor*
tent pegs	shaa-tor tser-ler-perk	*sátor cölöpök*
torch (flashlight)	zheb-laam-pah	*zseblámpa*
sleeping bag	haa-loh-zhaak	*hálózsák*
stove	kem-pingh-foer-zoer	*kempingfőző*
water bottle	vi-zesh-pah-lahtsk	*vizespalack*

FOOD

As befits a country that has been at the crossroads of history for centuries, Hungarian cuisine is a special mixture of foods from many cultures, such as Balkan, Czech, German and Austrian. Add to this traditional regional specialities and the visitor won't be disappointed in the wide range of spicy, sweet, sour and smoky flavours.

breakfast	regh-ghe-li	*reggeli*
lunch	e-behd	*ebéd*
dinner	vah-cho-rah	*vacsora*

Vegetarian Meals

It's still not a great country for vegetarians who wish to eat out, although things are changing fast in the cities. In summer, vegetables and fruit are plentiful and cheap.

I'm a vegetarian.
    ve-ghe-taa-ri-aa-nush vah-djok   *Vegetáriánus vagyok.*
I don't eat meat.
    nem e-sem hoosht   *Nem eszem húst.*
I don't eat chicken, fish or ham.
    nem e-sem chir-keht,   *Nem eszem csirkét,*
    hah-laht, shon-kaat   *halat, sonkát.*

Staple Foods & Condiments

bread	ke-nye-ret	*kenyeret*
butter	vah-yaht	*vajat*
cereal	ghah-bonah-eh-te-lek	*gabonaételek*
	regh-ghe-li-re	*reggelire*
cheese	shahy-tot	*sajtot*
chocolate	cho-ko-laa-deht	*csokoládét*
eggs	to-yaasht	*tojást*
flour	lis-tet	*lisztet*
margarine	mahr-ghah-rint	*margarint*
marmalade	lek-vaart	*lekvárt*
milk	te-yet	*tejet*
olive oil	o-li-vah-o-lah-yaht	*olivaolajat*
pepper	bor-shot	*borsot*
rice	ri-zh	*rizs*
salt	shoht	*sót*
sugar	tsuk-rot	*cukrot*
yogurt	yogh-hur-tot	*joghurtot*

HUNGARIAN

Breakfast Menu

On the whole, Hungarians aren't big breakfast eaters, preferring a cup of tea or coffee with an unadorned bread roll.

bread	ke-nye-ret	*kenyeret*
butter	vah-yaht	*vajat*
cereal	ghah-bonah-eh-te-lek	*gabonaételek*
	regh-ghe-li-re	*reggelire*
eggs	to-yaasht	*tojást*
fruit juice	djü-merlch-leh	*gyümölcslé*
margarine	mahr-ghah-rint	*margarint*
marmalade	lek-vaart	*lekvárt*
coffee	kaa-veh	*kávé*
tea	te-ah	*tea*
with milk	tey-yel	*tejjel*
with sugar	tsu-kor-rahl	*cukorral*

HUNGARIAN

MENU DECODER

Starters & Snacks

hortobágyi húsos palacsinta
> hor-to-baa-dji hoo-shosh pah-lah-chin-tah pancake stuffed with stewed and minced meat and herbs, covered with a sauce of gravy and sour cream

libamáj
> li-bah-maay goose liver; a particular delicacy in Hungary. May be cooked in several ways, either in a light meat stock, with onion and water, in milk, or fried. Often served cold with bread as a starter.

rántott gomba
> raan-tott ghom-bah fried mushrooms in breadcrumbs, generally served with rice and tartar sauce or mayonnaise

rántott sajt
> raan-tott shahyt fried cheese in breadcrumbs, served like *rántott gomba*

Soups

bableves
> bahb-le-vesh bean soup with turnip, carrot and sour cream

gombaleves
> ghom-bah-le-vesh a delicious mushroom soup with seasoning, onion, sour cream and parsley

gulyásleves
> ghu-yaash-le-vesh goulash soup, chopped meat fried in onions and paprika, and added to water or stock, with potatoes and a dash of white wine

halászlé
> hah-laas-leh a strong and rich broth of usually several kinds of fish (but always containing carp) in large pieces, with tomatoes, green paprika and red paprika. Beware, this soup has a bite to it! Usually brought to the table in a small cauldron called a *bogrács*, which is placed on a tripod.

hideg gyümölcsleves
> hi-degh djü-merlch-le-vesh cold fruit soup, often cherry, prepared with cream, lemon peel, cinnamon and red wine

káposzta leves
    kaa-pos-tah le-vesh cabbage soup; comes in several
    variations. A popular one is 'hangover' soup, *korhelyleves*
    (kor-hey-le-vesh), made with sauerkraut, smoked sausage,
    onion, paprika and sour cream.

újházy tyúkhúsleves
    ooy-haa-zi tyook-hoosh-le-vesh chicken-and-meat broth
    with root vegetables and vermicelli

Main Meals

lecsó
    le-choh a delicious thick stew of onions, tomatoes, green
    peppers and lard. Can be served either as a vegetarian
    dish with rice, or with smoked sausage.

pörkölt
    perr-kerlt beef (*marha*), pork (*sertés*), veal (*borjú*) and game
    (*vad*) stew cooked in lard with onions, bacon and paprika,
    plus the obligatory sour cream

töltött paprika
    terl-tertt pahp-ri-kah green peppers stuffed with a mix-
    ture of minced meat, bacon, egg, onion and rice, and baked
    in a sauce of sour cream

aprópecsenye
    ahp-roh-pe-che-nye braised cutlets of pork with paprika,
    onion and sour cream. Served with vinegar or lemon juice.

sült csülök
    shült chü-lerk knuckle of pork boiled then coated in flour
    and fried. Served with horseradish.

gombás fogas
    ghom-baash fo-ghahsh pike-perch, sometimes known as
    süllő, braised with mushrooms and a sauce of white wine,
    butter, lemon juice, eggs and bone stock

HUNGARIAN

HUNGARIAN

rántott hal
  raan-tott hahl fish fried in breadcrumbs; may be carp *(ponty)* or catfish *(harcsa)*
becsinált csirke
  be-chi-naalt chir-ke chicken fricassee fried with cauliflower, kohlrabi, celery root, carrot, turnip and mushrooms then braised in stock with lemon juice. Flavoured with egg yolks.
pirított libamáj
  pi-ree-tott li-bah-maay fried goose liver, first boiled in milk and then fried without seasoning
fácán narancsos mártással
  faa-tsaan nah-rahn-chosh maar-taash-shahl pheasant in orange sauce, cooked with carrots, onions, mushrooms, lemon peel and smoked meat. Before serving, it is boiled in stock with sugar and orange peel.
nyúl vörös borban
  nyool ver-rersh bor-bahn hare braised in red wine, with butter, pork cubes and an onion
lángos
  laan-ghosh an institution in Hungary; light dough mixed with pureed potato, quick-fried in deep fat and served with cheese or sour cream. Also known as a 'heart attack special'.
túrós csusza
  too-rohsh chu-sah fine white noodles mixed with cottage cheese or curds, and lashings of sour cream. Can be savoury with bacon pieces, or sweet with powdered sugar.

Desserts
dobostorta
  do-bosh-tor-tah a sponge cake with layers of buttered cocoa, topped with a hard brown caramel coating
gesztenyepüré
  ghes-te-nye-pü-reh mashed sweet chestnuts cooked in milk with vanilla and served with cream and/or rum
rétes
  reh-tesh strudel filled with a variety of fruits such as sour-cherry *(meggy)*, apple *(alma)*, walnut *(dió)*, poppy seed *(mák)*, or a particular Hungarian favourite, cottage cheese *(túró)*

marmalade	lek-vaart	*lekvárt*
coffee	kaa-veh	*kávé*
tea	te-ah	*tea*
with milk	tey-yel	*tejjel*
with sugar	tsu-kor-rahl	*cukorral*

Alcoholic Drinks

brandy	paa-lin-kah	*pálinka*
champagne	pezh-ghoer	*pezsgő*
spirits	rer-vid i-tah-lok	*rövid italok*
spritzer	frertsch	*fröccs*
... beer	... sherr	*... sör*
bottled	ü-ve-ghesh	*üveges*
dark	bahr-nah	*barna*
draught	chah-polt	*csapolt*
lager	vi-laa-ghosh	*világos*

HUNGARIAN

BOOZE BOX

Hungary has around 20 winegrowing areas, concentrated in Transdanubia, the Northern Uplands and the Great Plain. Distinctive reds come from Villány and Szekszárd in Southern Transdanubia, while some of the best whites are from around Lake Balaton and the Mátra Hills.

When choosing wine, look for the words:

minőség bor   'quality wine'

These are the closest thing Hungary has to *appellation controlée*. The quality of a label can vary widely from bottle to bottle. On the label, the first word indicates where the wine comes from. The second word is the grape variety.

HUNGARIAN

Non-Alcoholic Drinks

drinks	i-tah-lok	*italok*
fruit juice	djü-merlch-leh	*gyümölcslé*
ice	yehgh	*jég*
mineral water	aash-vaany-veez	*ásványvíz*
soft drinks	ü-dee-toerk	*üdítők*
(boiled) water	(for-rahlt) veez	*(forralt) víz*
coffee	kaa-veh	*kávé*
tea	te-ah	*tea*
with milk	tey-yel	*tejjel*
with sugar	tsu-kor-rahl	*cukorral*

SHOPPING

Where's the	hol vahn ah	*Hol van a*
nearest ...?	leg-ker-ze-leb-bi ...?	*legközelebbi...?*
bookshop	kerny-vesh-bolt	*könyvesbolt*
camera shop	fo-toh-üz-let	*fotóüzlet*
chemist	djohdj-ser-taar	*gyógyszertár*
delicatessen	de-li-kaat-üz-let	*delikátüzlet*
green grocer	zerld-sheh-ghesh	*zöldséges*
laundry	pah-tyo-laht	*patyolat*
market	pi-ats	*piac*
newsagency	ooy-shaa-ghosh	*újságos*
stationer's	pah-peer-üz-let	*papírüzlet*
supermarket	eh-lel-mi-ser-aa-ru-haaz	*élelmiszeráruház*

Colours

black	fe-ke-te	*fekete*
blue	kehk	*kék*
brown	bahr-nah	*barna*
green	zerld	*zöld*
orange	nah-rahnch-shaar-ghah	*narancssárga*
pink	roh-zhah-seen	*rózsaszín*
red	pi-rosh	*piros*
white	fe-hehr	*fehér*
yellow	shaar-ghah	*sárga*

Essential Groceries

I'd like ...	keh-rek ...	*Kérek ...*
batteries	e-le-met	*elemet*
bread	ke-nye-ret	*kenyeret*
butter	vah-yaht	*vajat*
cheese	shahy-tot	*sajtot*
chocolate	cho-ko-laa-deht	*csokoládét*
eggs	to-yaasht	*tojást*
ham	shon-kaat	*sonkát*
honey	meh-zet	*mézet*
margarine	mahr-ghah-rint	*margarint*
marmalade	lek-vaart	*lekvárt*
matches	dju-faat	*gyufát*
milk	te-yet	*tejet*
shampoo	shahm-pont	*sampont*
soap	sahp-pahnt	*szappant*
toilet paper	veh tseh pah-peert	*WC papírt*
toothpaste	fogh-kreh-met	*fogkrémet*
washing powder	mo-shoh-port	*mosóport*

How much is it?
    meny-nyi-be ke-rül?   *Mennyibe kerül?*
Do you accept credit cards?
    el-fo-ghahd-nahk   *Elfogadnak*
    hi-tel-kaar-tyaat?   *hitelkártyát?*

HUNGARIAN

HUNGARIAN

AT THE MARKET

Basics

bread	ke-nye-ret	*kenyeret*
butter	vah-yaht	*vajat*
cereal	ghah-bonah-eh-te-lek	*gabonaételek*
	regh-ghe-li-re	*reggelire*
cheese	shahy-tot	*sajtot*
chocolate	cho-ko-laa-deht	*csokoládét*
eggs	to-yaasht	*tojást*
flour	lis-tet	*lisztet*
margarine	mahr-ghah-rint	*margarint*
marmalade	lek-vaart	*lekvárt*
milk	te-yet	*tejet*
olive oil	o-li-vah-o-lah-yaht	*olivaolajat*
pepper	bor-shot	*borsot*
rice	ri-zh	*rizs*
salt	shoht	*sót*
sugar	tsuk-rot	*cukrot*
yogurt	yogh-hur-tot	*joghurtot*

Meat & Poultry

ham	shon-kaat	*sonkát*
hamburger	hahm-bur-gher	*hamburger*
lamb	baa-raany	*bárány*
sausage	kol-baas	*kolbász*
turkey	puy-kahv	*pulyka*
veal	bor-yoo	*borjú*

Vegetables

beetroot	tsehk-lah	*cékla*
broad beans	bahb	*bab*
cabbage	kaa-pos-tah	*káposzta*
green beans	zerld-bahb	*zöldbab*
(red/green)	(pi-rosh/zerld)	*(piros/zöld)*
capsicum	pahp-ri-kah	*paprika*
cauliflower	kahr-fi-ol	*karfiol*
carrot	shaar-gha h-reh-pah	*sárgarépa*
celery	zel-ler	*zeller*

AT THE MARKET

chickpeas	chi-che-ri-bor-shoh	csicseriborsó
chillies	e-roersh pi-rosh	erős piros
	pahp-ri-kah	paprika
cucumber	u-bor-kah	uborka
eggplant (aubergine)	pahd-li-zhaan	padlizsán
garlic	fok-hadj-mah	fokhagyma
gherkin	u-bor-kah	uborka
ginger	djerm-behr	gyömbér
kidney beans	shpah-nyol-bahb	spanyolbab
lentils	len-che	lencse
lettuce	fe-yesh shah-laa-tah	fejes saláta
onion	hahdj-mah	hagyma
peas	bor-shoh	borsó
potato	bur-gho-nyah/krump-li	burgonya/krumpli
spinach	pah-rahy/shpe-noht	paraj/spenót
tomato	pah-rah-di-chom	paradicsom
zucchini	tsuk-ki-ni	cukkini

Seafood

lobster	ho-maar	homár
mussels	kahdj-loh	kagyló
oysters	ost-ri-gha	hosztriga
shrimp	ahp-roh ten-ghe-ri raak	apró tengeri rák

Fruit

apricot	shaar-ghah-bah-ratsk	sárabarack
banana	bah-naan	banán
fig	fu-ghe	füge
grapes	soer-loer	szőlő
kiwifruit	ki-vi	kivi
lemon	tsit-rom	citrom
orange	nah-rahnch	narancs
peach	oersi-bah-rahtsk	őszibarack
pear	kerr-te	körte
plum	sil-vah	szilva
strawberry	ferl-di-e-per	földieper

HUNGARIAN

HUNGARIAN

Clothing

clothing	ru-haa-zaht	*ruházat*
coat	kah-baat	*kabát*
dress	ru-hah	*ruha*
jacket	zah-koh	*zakó*
jumper (sweater)	pu-loh-ver	*pulóver*
shirt	ingh	*ing*
shoes	tsi-poer	*cipő*
skirt	sok-nyah	*szoknya*
trousers	nahd-raagh	*nadrág*
underwear	fe-hehr-ne-müü	*fehérnemű*

Materials

What's it made of?

   mi-boerl keh-sült?   *Miből készült?*

brass	rehz	*réz*
cotton	pah-mut	*pamut*
gold	ah-rahny	*arany*
handmade	keh-zi-mun-kah	*kézimunka*
leather	boer	*bőr*
pure alpaca	tis-tah ahl-pah-kah	*tiszta alpaka*
silk	she-yem	*selyem*
silver	e-züsht	*ezüst*
wool	djahp-yoo	*gyapjú*

Stationery & Publications

map	tehr-kehp	*térkép*
paper	pah-peer	*papír*
pen (ballpoint)	go-yohsh-toll	*golyóstoll*
scissors	ol-loh	*olló*
(English-language) ...	ahn-ghol nyel-vüü ...	*angol nyelvű ...*
newspaper	ooy-shaagh	*újság*
novels	re-gheh-nyek	*regények*

Souvenirs

earrings	fül-be-vah-loh	*fülbevaló*
handicraft	keh-zi-mun-kah	*kézimunka*
necklace	nyahk-laants	*nyaklánc*
pottery	ah-djagh-aa-ru	*agyagáru*
ring	djüü-rüü	*gyűrű*
rug	ki-shebb soer-nyegh	*kisebb szőnyeg*

HUNGARIAN

Toiletries

comb	feh-shüü	*fésű*
condoms	ko-ton	*koton*
deodorant	de-zo-dor	*dezodor*
hairbrush	hahy-ke-fe	*hajkefe*
moisturiser	krehm saa-rahz boer-re	*krém száraz bőrre*
razor	bo-rot-vah	*borotva*
sanitary napkins	e-ghehs-shehgh-üdji be-teht	*egészségügyi betét*
shampoo	shahm-pont	*sampont*
shaving cream	bo-rot-vaal-ko-zoh krehm	*borotválkozó krém*
soap	sahp-pahnt	*szappant*
sunscreen	nahp-o-lahy	*napolaj*
tampons	tahm-pon	*tampon*
tissues	pah-peer-zheb-ken-doer	*papírzsebkendő*
toothbrush	fogh-ke-fe	*fogkefe*

HUNGARIAN

Smoking

A packet of cigarettes, please.

edj cho-mahgh tsi-ghah-ret-taat keh-rek	*Egy csomag cigarettát kérek.*

Are these cigarettes strong/mild?

ez ah tsi-ghah-ret-tah e-roersh/djen-ghe?	*Ez a cigaretta erős/gyenge?*

Do you have a light?

vahn tü-ze?	*Van tüze?*

Do you smoke?

ern do-haany-zik?	*Ön dohányzik?*

Please don't smoke.

keh-rem ne do-haa-nyoz-zon!	*Kérem, ne dohányozzon.*

cigarette papers	tsi-ghah-ret-tah pah-peer	*cigaretta papír*
cigarettes	tsi-ghah-ret-tah	*cigaretta*
filtered	füsht-süü-roersh	*füstszűrős*
lighter	ern-djooy-toh	*öngyújtó*
matches	dju-fah	*gyufa*
menthol	men-to-losh	*mentolos*
pipe	pi-pah	*pipa*
tobacco (pipe)	pi-pah-do-haany	*pipadohány*

Photography

How much is it to process this film?

meny-nyi-be ke-rül eloer-heev-ni ezt ah fil-met?	*Mennyibe kerül előhívni ezt a filmet?*

When will it be ready?

mi-kor les kehs?	*Mikor lesz kész?*

I'd like a film for this camera.

edj fil-met se-ret-nehk eb-be ah fehny-keh-pe-zoer-ghehp-be	*Egy filmet szeretnék ebbe a fényképezőgépbe.*

B&W (film)	fe-ke-te fe-hehr-film	*fekete-fehér film*
camera	fehny-keh-pe-zoer-ghehp	*fényképezőgép*
colour (film)	see-nesh-film	*színesfilm*
film	film	*film*
lash	vah-ku	*vaku*
lens	len-che	*lencse*
light meter	fehny-meh-roer	*fénymérő*

Sizes & Comparisons

small	ki-chi	*kicsi*
big	nahdj	*nagy*
heavy	ne-hehz	*nehéz*
light	kerny-nyüü	*könnyű*
more	terbb	*több*
less	ke-ve-shebb	*kevesebb*
too much/many	tool shok	*túl sok*

HUNGARIAN

HEALTH

Where's the ...?	hol vahn ...?	*Hol van ...?*
chemist	ah djohdj-ser-taar	*a gyógyszertár*
dentist	ah fogh-or-vosh	*a fogorvos*
doctor	ahz or-vosh	*az orvos*
hospital	ah kohr-haaz	*a kórház*

| I'm sick. | ros-sul vah-djok | *Rosszul vagyok.* |
| It hurts here. | itt faay | *Itt fáj.* |

My friend is sick.
ah bah-raa-tom ros-sul vahn   *A barátom rosszul van.*

LONG TAILED ONE!

The ancient Magyars were strong believers in magic, and the *táltos*, 'shaman', enjoyed an elevated position in their society. Animals such as bears, stags and wolves were totemic, and it was taboo to mention them directly by name. Thus, the wolf was the 'long-tailed one'.

Parts of the Body

ankle	bo-kaam	*bokám*
arm	kah-rom	*karom*
back	haa-tahm	*hátam*
chest	mell-kah-shom	*mellkasom*
ear	fü-lem	*fülem*
eye	se-mem	*szemem*
finger	uy-yahm	*ujjam*
foot	laab-fe-yem	*lábfejem*
hand	ke-zem	*kezem*
head	fe-yem	*fejem*
heart	see-vem	*szívem*
leg	laa-bahm	*lábam*
mouth	saam	*szám*
nose	or-rom	*orrom*
ribs	bor-daam	*bordám*
skin	boer-rerm	*bőröm*
stomach	djom-rom	*gyomrom*
teeth	fo-ghahm	*fogam*
throat	tor-kom	*torkom*

At the Dentist

I have a toothache.
    faay ah fo-ghahm   *Fáj a fogam.*
I've lost a filling.
    ki-e-shett ah ter-mehsh   *Kiesett a tömés.*
I've broken a tooth.
    el-tert edj fo-ghahm   *Eltört egy fogam.*
My gums hurt.
    faay ahz ee-nyem   *Fáj az ínyem.*
I don't want it extracted.
    nem ah-kah-rom ki-hoo-zaht-ni *Nem akarom kihúzatni.*
Please give me an anaesthetic.
    keh-rem ahd-yon   *Kérem adjon*
    ehr-zehsh-te-le-nee-toert   *érzéstelenítőt.*

Ailments

I have (a/an) ...

allergy	ahl-ler-ghi-aash vah-djok	*Allergiás vagyok.*
blister	hoh-yahgh vahn rahy-tahm	*Hólyag van rajtam.*
burn	megh-eh-ghet-tem mah-ghahm	*Megégettem magam.*
cold	megh-faaz-tahm	*Megfáztam.*
constipation	sehk-re-ke-deh-shem vahn	*Székrekedésem van.*
cough	ker-her-gherk	*Köhögök.*
diarrhoea	hahsh-me-neh-shem vahn	*Hasmenésem van.*
fever	laa-zahm vahn	*Lázam van.*

HUNGARIAN

headache	faay ah fe-yem	*Fáj a fejem.*
hepatitis	maay-djul-lah-daa-shom-vahn	*Májgyulladásomvan.*
(low/high) blood pressure	(ah-lah-chony/ mah-ghahsh) ah vehr-nyo-maa-shom	*(Alacsony/ Magas) a vérnyomásom.*
pain	faay-dahl-mahm vahn	*Fájdalmam van.*
sore throat	faay ah tor-kom	*Fáj a torkom.*
sprain	fi-tsah-mom vahn	*Ficamom van.*
stomachache	faay ah djom-rom	*Fáj a gyomrom.*
venereal disease	ne-mi be-tegh-sheh-ghem vahn	*Nemi betegségem van.*
worms	ghi-lis-taam vahn	*Gilisztám van.*

HUNGARIAN

At the Chemist

I need medication for ...
djohdj-ser-re vahn sük-sheh-ghem ...   *Gyógyszerre van szükségem ...*

I have a prescription.
vahn edj re-tsep-tem   *Van egy receptem.*

antibiotics	**ahn-ti-bi-o-ti-kum**	*antibiotikum*
antiseptic	**fer-toer-zehsh-ghaat-loh**	*fertőzésgátló*
aspirin	**as-pi-rin**	*aszpirin*
bandage	**ker-tehsh**	*kötés*
contraceptive	**fo-ghahm-zaash-ghaat-loh**	*fogamzásgátló*
vitamins	**vi-tah-mi-nok**	*vitaminok*

TIME & DATES

What time is it?
haany oh-rah?   *Hány óra?*

What date is it today?
haa-nyah-di-kah vahn mah?   *Hányadika van ma?*

It's ... o'clock.
... oh-rah vahn   *... óra van.*

in the morning	**regh-ghel**	*reggel*
in the afternoon	**deh-lu-taan**	*délután*
in the evening	**esh-te**	*este*

Days

Monday	**heht-foer**	*hétfő*
Tuesday	**kedd**	*kedd*
Wednesday	**ser-dah**	*szerda*
Thursday	**chü-ter-terk**	*csütörtök*
Friday	**pehn-tek**	*péntek*
Saturday	**som-baht**	*szombat*
Sunday	**vah-shaar-nahp**	*vasárnap*

Months

January	yah-nu-aar	*január*
February	feb-ru-aar	*február*
March	maar-tsi-ush	*március*
April	aap-ri-lish	*április*
May	maa-yush	*május*
June	yoo-ni-ush	*június*
July	yoo-li-ush	*július*
August	ah-u-ghus-tush	*augusztus*
September	sep-tem-ber	*szeptember*
October	ok-toh-ber	*október*
November	no-vem-ber	*november*
December	de-tsem-ber	*december*

HUNGARIAN

During the Day

afternoon	deh-lu-taan	*délután*
dawn; very early morning	hahy-nahl	*hajnal*
day	nahp	*nap*
early	ko-raan	*korán*
midday	dehl	*dél*
midnight	ehy-fehl	*éjfél*
morning	regh-ghel	*reggel*
night	ehy-yel	*éjjel*
sunrise	nahp-fel-kel-te	*napfelkelte*
sunset	nahp-le-men-te	*naplemente*

HUNGARIAN

Seasons

summer	nyaar	*nyár*
autumn	oers	*ősz*
winter	tehl	*tél*
spring	tah-vahs	*tavasz*

Present

now	mosht	*most*
this morning	mah regh-ghel	*ma reggel*
today	mah	*ma*
tonight	mah esh-te	*ma este*
this week	e-zen ah heh-ten	*ezen a héten*
this year	eb-ben ahz ehv-ben	*ebben az évben*

Past

last night	tegh-nahp esh-te	*tegnap este*
yesterday	tegh-nahp	*tegnap*
day before yesterday	tegh-nahp-e-loertt	*tegnapelőtt*
last week/year	moolt heh-ten/ ehv-ben	*múlt héten/ évben*

Future

tomorrow	hol-nahp	*holnap*
tomorrow evening	hol-nahp esh-te	*holnap este*
day after tomorrow	hol-nahp-u-taan	*holnapután*
next week	yer-voer heh-ten	*jövő héten*
next year	yer-voer-re	*jövőre*

Useful Words

Enough!	e-lehgh!	*Elég!*
a little (amount)	edj ke-vehsh	*egy kevés*
double	dup-lah	*dupla*
dozen	edj tu-tsaht	*egy tucat*
few	neh-haany	*néhány*
less	ke-ve-shebb	*kevesebb*
many	shok	*sok*
more	terbb	*több*
once	edj-ser	*egyszer*
some	vah-lah-meny-nyi	*valamennyi*
too much	tool shok	*túl sok*

NUMBERS & AMOUNTS

0	nul-lah	*nulla*
1	edj	*egy*
2	ket-toer	*kettő*
3	haa-rom	*három*
4	nehdj	*négy*
5	ert	*öt*
6	haht	*hat*
7	heht	*hét*
8	nyolts	*nyolc*
9	ki-lents	*kilenc*
10	teez	*tíz*
20	hoos	*húsz*
30	hahr-mints	*harminc*
40	nedj-ven	*negyven*
50	ert-ven	*ötven*
60	haht-vahn	*hatvan*
70	het-ven	*hetven*
80	nyolts-vahn	*nyolcvan*
90	ki-lents-ven	*kilencven*
100	saaz	*száz*
1000	e-zer	*ezer*
one million	edj mil-li-oh	*egy millió*

ABBREVIATIONS

db	piece
de./du.	am/pm
É/D	Nth/Sth
EK	UK
EU	EU
ENSZ	UN
Ft/HUF	Hungarian Forint (currency)
gr/kg	gm/kg
id.	snr
ifj.	jnr
i.sz./i.e.	AD/BC
kb.	approx.
MALÉV	Hungarian Airlines
MÁV	Hungarian State Railways
n/fßhn	quarter past/half past/quarter to (time)
Oszt./Közp.	Dept/HQ
OTP	National Savings Bank
p/mp	minute/second
stb.	etc
u.i./ford.	ps/pto
u/ú/krt/k	St/Rd/Blvd/Lane
I.Vh/II.Vh	WWI/WWII

HUNGARIAN

EMERGENCIES

Help!	she-gheet-shehgh!	*Segítség!*
Go away!	men-yen el!	*Menjen el!*
Thief!	tol-vahy!	*Tolvaj!*
I'm ill.	be-tegh vah-djok	*Beteg vagyok.*
I'm lost.	el-teh-ved-tem	*Eltévedtem.*
I've been robbed!	ki-rah-bol-tahk!	*Kiraboltak!*
I'll call the police!	hee-vom ah ren-doert!	*Hívom a rendőrt!*
It's an emergency!	shüür-ghoersh!	*Sürgős!*
Call a doctor!	heev-yon edj or-vosht!	*Hívjon egy orvost!*
I've been raped.	megh-eroer-sah-kol-tahk	*Megerőszakoltak.*
My friend is ill.	ah bah-raa-tom be-tegh	*A barátom beteg.*

There's been an accident!
    bah-le-shet ter-tehnt! — *Baleset történt!*

Call an ambulance!
    heev-yah ah men-toer-ket! — *Hívja a mentőket!*

Call the police!
    heev-yah ah ren-doer-sheh-ghet! — *Hívja a rendőrséget!*

Where's the police station?
    hol ah ren-doer-shehgh? — *Hol a rendőrség?*

Where are the toilets?
    hol vahn ah veh-tseh? — *Hol van a WC?*

Could you help me, please?
    tud-nah she-ghee-te-ni keh-rem? — *Tudna segíteni kérem?*

Could I please use the telephone?
    keh-rem hahs-naal-haht naam ah te-le-font? — *Kérem, használhatnám a telefont?*

I'm sorry. I apologise.
    shahy-naa-lom. — *Sajnálom.*
    el-neh-zehsht keh-rek — *Elnézést kérek.*

I didn't do it.
    nem ehn chi-naal-tahm — *Nem én csináltam.*

I didn't realise I was doing
anything wrong.

    nem tud-tahm hodj vah-
    lah-mi ros-saht tet-tem   *Nem tudtam, hogy valami*
                                           rosszat tettem.

I want to contact my
embassy/consulate.

    se-ret-nehk ah ker-vet-
    shehgh-ghel/kon-zu-laa-   *Szeretnék a követséggel/*
    tush-shahl be-sehl-ni   *konzulátussal beszélni.*

I speak English.

    be-seh-lek (ahn-gho-lul)   *Beszélek (angolul).*

I have medical insurance.

    vahn be-tegh-biz-to-shee-   *Van betegbiztosításom.*
    taa-shom

My possessions are insured.

    vahn vah-djon-biz-to-   *Van vagyonbiztosításom.*
    shee-taa-shom

I've lost my ...	el-ves-tet-tem ...	*Elvesztettem ...*
My ... was stolen.	el-lop-taak ...	*Ellopták ...*
bags	ah taash-kaa-i-maht	*a táskáimat*
handbag	ah keh-zi-taash-kaa-maht	*a kézitáskámat*
money	ah pehn-ze-met	*a pénzemet*
travellers cheques	ahz u-tah-zaa-shi chekk-ye-i-met	*az utazási csekkjeimet*
passport	ahz oot-le-ve-le-met	*az útlevelemet*
wallet	pehnz-taar-tsah	*pénztárca*

MACEDONIAN

QUICK REFERENCE

Hello.	zdra-vo	Здраво.
Goodbye.	do gle-da-nye	До гледање.
Yes./No.	da/ne	Да./Не.
Excuse me.	pros-te-te	Простете.
May I?	mo-zham li?	Модам ли?
Sorry.	pros-te-te ve mo-lam	Простете, ве молам.
Please.	mo-lam	Молам.
Thank you.	bla-go-da-ram	Благодарам.
That's fine.	ne-ma za shto	Нема за што.
You're welcome.	mo-lam	Молам.
Where's ...?	ka-de e ...?	Каде е ...?
What time is it?	kol-ku e cha-sot?	Колку е часот?
Go straight ahead.	o-de-te pra-vo nap-red	Одете право напред.

Turn left/right	svr-te-te le-vo/des-no ...	Свртете лево/десно ...
at the ...		
next corner	na sled-ni-ot a-gol	на следниот агол
traffic lights	na se-ma-fo-ri-te	на семафорите

I'd like a ...	yas sa-kam ...	Јас сакам ...
single room	ed-no-kre-vet-na so-ba	еднокреветна соба
one-way ticket	bi-let vo e-den pra-vec	билет во еден правец
return ticket	po-vra-ten bi-let	повратен билет

I (don't) understand.	
yas (ne) raz-bi-ram	Јас (не) разбирам.
Do you speak English?	
zbo-ru-va-te li an-glis-ki?	Зборувате ли англиски?
How much is it?	
kol-ku chi-ni to-a?	Колку чини тоа?
Where are the toilets?	
ka-de se to-a-le-ti-te?	Каде се тоалетите?
How do I get to ...?	
ka-ko da stig-nam do ...?	Како да стигнам до ...?

1	e-den	еден	6	shest	шест
2	dva	два	7	se-dum	седум
3	tri	три	8	o-sum	осум
4	che-ti-ri	четири	9	de-vet	девет
5	pet	пет	10	de-set	десет

MACEDONIAN

MACEDONIAN

Macedonian, written in the Cyrillic alphabet (with several modifications and extra letters), is the official language of Macedonia. For the Macedonian people the language is of extreme significance as it offers confirmation of their history and identity. Macedonian is also spoken and cherished in many other European countries, as well as the Balkans, the USA, Canada and Australia – wherever Macedonians live.

Macedonian is an Indo-European language and belongs to the South-Slavic group. The historical development of the Macedonian language dates back to the 9th century AD and the foundation of the well-known Ohrid Literary School, when Slavonic literacy began with a standard Macedonian language. It was written in the Glagolitic script until the 11th century after which it was written in the Cyrillic script.

From the 1860s, attempts were made to create a Macedonian literary standard. The modern codification of the Macedonian literary language was done in 1944. The period since 1944 has led to a swift development and comprehensive affirmation of the Macedonian literary language within the country and abroad.

The first grammar was published in 1946. A detailed grammar in two volumes by Blazhe Koneski followed in 1952, along with the first Macedonian grammar by a foreign scholar (H. Lunt). A comprehensive Dictionary of the Macedonian Language and many bilingual dictionaries have been prepared and there is now abundant literature in Macedonian covering all fields. A large number of works, from classical literature up to the contemporary literature of many peoples, have been translated into Macedonian.

Macedonian is taught as a subject in universities around the world and is being taught in all universities of the former Yugoslavia.

PRONUNCIATION

Macedonian has 31 sounds. Spelling does not present any difficulties because there is one symbol for each sound. Pronunciation of the Cyrillic letter and its Roman equivalent is given here:

Roman	Cyrillic		Transliteration
A	А	а	a
B	Б	б	b
V	В	в	v
G	Г	г	g
D	Д	д	d
GJ	Ѓ	ѓ	dj/gy
E	Е	е	e
Ž	Ж	ж	zh
Z	З	з	z
DZ	Ѕ	ѕ	dz
I	И	и	i
J	Ј	ј	y
K	К	к	k
L	Л	л	l
LJ	Љ	љ	ly
M	М	м	m
N	Н	н	n
NJ	Њ	њ	ny
O	О	о	o
P	П	п	p
R	Р	р	r
S	С	с	s
T	Т	т	t
KJ	Ќ	ќ	ky
U	У	у	u
F	Ф	ф	f
H	Х	х	h
C	Ц	ц	ts
Č	Ч	ч	ch
DŽ	Џ	џ	j
Š	Ш	ш	sh

Vowels

a	as the 'a' in 'rather'
e	as the 'ea' in 'bear'
i	as the 'i' in 'machine'
o	as the 'o' in 'shore'
u	as the 'u' in 'flute'

Consonants

Consonants not described here are pronounced as they are in English.

ch	as the 'ch' in 'chop'
dj	as the 'du' in 'verdure';
dz	as the 'dz' sound, similar to 'z'
g	as the 'g' in 'goat'
gy	as the 'gu' in 'Guatemala'
j	as the 'j' in 'just'
ky	as the 'cu' in 'cure'
ly	as the 'lli' in 'million'
ny	as the 'ny' in 'canyon'
r	as the 'r' in 'rock'
s	as the 's' in 'sin'
ts	as 'ts' in 'cats'
y	as 'y' in 'young'
zh	as the 's' in 'pleasure'

MACEDONIAN

SUBJECT PRONOUNS		
SG		
I	yas	јас
you	ti	ти
he/she/it	toy/ta-a/to-a	тој/таа/тоа
PL		
we	ni-e	ние
you	vi-e	вие
they	ti-e	тие

Stress

A characteristic feature of the Macedonian literary standard is the three-syllable accent, meaning the accent always falls on the third syllable from the end in words of three syllables or more. If the word has only two syllables, the first is stressed.

GREETINGS & CIVILITIES
Top Useful Phrases

Hello.	zdra-vo	Здраво.
Goodbye.	do gle-da-nye	До гледање.
Yes.	da	Да.
No.	ne	Не.
Excuse me.	pros-te-te	Простете.
May I?	mo-zham li? vi	Можам ли?
Do you mind?	pre-chi li?	Ви пречи ли?
Sorry. (excuse me, forgive me)	pros-te-te ve mo-lam	Простете, ве молам.
Please.	mo-lam	Молам.
Thank you.	bla-go-da-ram	Благодарам.
That's fine.	ne-ma za shto.	Нема за што.
You're welcome.	mo-lam	Молам.

Greetings

Good morning.	do-bro ut-ro	Добро утро.
Good afternoon.	do-bar den	Добар ден.
Good evening/night.	do-bro-ve-cher/ do-bra noky	Добровечер/ Добра ноќ.
How are you?	ka-ko ste?	Како сте?
Well, thanks.	do-bro bla-go-da-ram	Добро, благодарам.

Forms of Address

Madam/Mrs	gos-po-gya	госпоѓа
Sir/Mr	gos-po-din	господин
Miss	gos-po-gyi-tsa	госпоѓица
companion	pri-druzh-nik	придружник
friend	pri-ya-tel	пријател (m)
	pri-ya-tel-ka	пријателка (f)

SMALL TALK
Meeting People

What's your name?
ka-ko se vi-ka-te?　　　　　Како се викате?

My name's ...
yas se vi-kam ...　　　　　Јас се викам ...

I'd like to introduce you to ...
da ve pret-sta-vam ...　　　　Да ве претставам ...

Pleased to meet you.
dra-go mi e shto ve　　　　Драго ми е што ве
za-poz-nav　　　　　　　запознав

How old are you?
kol-ku go-di-ni i-ma-te?　　　Колку години имате?

I'm ... years old.
yas i-mam ... go-di-ni　　　Јас имам ... години.

Nationalities

Where are you from?　od ka-de ste?　　　Од каде сте?

I'm from ...　　　yas sum od ...　　　Јас сум од ...
　　Australia　　　av-stra-li-ya　　　Австралија
　　Canada　　　ka-na-da　　　Канада
　　England　　　an-gli-ya　　　Англија
　　Ireland　　　ir-ska　　　Ирска
　　New Zealand　　nov ze-land　　　Нов Зеланд
　　Scotland　　　shkot-ska　　　Шкотска
　　America　　　a-me-ri-ka　　　Америка
　　Wales　　　vels　　　Велс

MACEDONIAN

QUESTION WORDS		
How?	ka-ko?	Како?
When?	ko-ga?	Кога?
Where?	ka-de?	Каде?
Which?	koy?	Кој?
Who?	koy?	Кој?
Why?	zosh-to?	Зошто?

Occupations

What do you do?	shto ra-bo-ti-te?	Што работите?
I'm unemployed.	ne sum vra-bo-ten	Не сум вработен

I'm (a/an) ...	yas sum ...	Jac сум ...
artist	u-met-nik	уметник
businessman/ woman	biz-nis-men	бизнисмен
computer programmer	kom-pyu-ter-ski pro-gra-mer	компјутерски програмер
doctor	le-kar	лекар
engineer	in-zhe-ner	инженер
farmer	far-mer	фармер
journalist	no-vi-nar	новинар
lawyer	prav-nik	правник
manual worker	ra-bot-nik ra-bot-nich-ka	работник (m) работничка (f)
mechanic	me-ha-ni-char	механичар
nurse	me-di-tsin-ska ses-tra bol-ni-char	болничар (m) медицинска сестра (f)
office worker	sluzh-be-nik	службеник
scientist	na-uch-nik	научник
secretary	se-kre-tar sek-re-tar-ka	секретар (m) секретарка (f)
student	stu-dent	студент
teacher	u-chi-tel u-chi-tel-ka	учител (m) учителка (f)
waiter	kel-ner kel-ner-ka	келнер (m) келнерка (f)
writer	pi-sa-tel pi-sa-tel-ka	писател (m) писателка (f)

Religion

What's your religion?
ko-ya ve-ra ste? — Која вера сте?

I'm not religious.
ne sum re-li-gi-oz-en/ — Не сум религиозен/
re-li-gi-oz-na — религиозна. (m/f)

I'm ...	yas sum ...	Јас сум ...
Buddhist	bu-dist	будист
Catholic	ka-to-lik	католик
Christian	hris-ti-ya-nin	христијанин
Hindu	hin-du	хинду
Jewish	ev-re-in	Евреин
Muslim	mus-li-man	муслиман
Ortodox	pra-vo-sla-ven	православен

Family

Are you married?
da-li ste zhe-net/ma-zhe-na? — Дали стеженет/мажена?(m/f)

I'm single.
yas sum sa-mets/sa-mi-tsa — Јас сум самец/самица. (m/f)

I'm married.
yas sum zhe-net/ma-zhe-na — Јас сум женет/мажена. (m/f)

I'm ...	yas sum ...	Јас сум ...
a widow	vdo-vi-tsa	вдовица
a widower	vdo-vets	вдовец
divorced	raz-ve-den	разведен (m)
	raz-ve-de-na	разведена (f)
separated	raz-de-len	разделен (m)
	raz-de-le-na	разделена (f)

How many children do you have?
kol-ku de-tsa i-ma-te? — Колку деца имате?

I don't have any children.
ne-mam de-tsa — Немам деца.

I have a daughter/son.
i-mam kyer-ka/sin — Имам ќерка/син.

brother	brat	брат
children	de-tsa	деца
daughter	kyer-ka	ќерка
family	se-mey-stvo	семејство
father	tat-ko	татко
grandfather	de-do	дедо
grandmother	ba-ba	баба
husband	so-prug	сопруг
mother	may-ka	мајка
sister	ses-tra	сестра
son	sin	син
wife	so-pru-ga	сопруга

Feelings

I (don't) like ...	(ne) mi se do-pa-gya ...	(Не) ми се допаѓа ...

I'm ...	me-ne mi e ...	Мене ми е ...
cold	stu-de-no	студено
hot	top-lo	топло
right	dob-ro	добро

I'm ...	yas sum ...	Jac сум ...
hungry	gla-den/glad-na	гладен/гладна (m/f)
thirsty	zhe-den/zhed-na	жеден/жедна (m/f)
angry	lut/lu-ta	лут/лута (m/f)
happy	sre-kyen/sreky-na	среќен/среќна (m/f)
sad	ta-zhen/tazh-na	тажен/тажна (m/f)
tired	u-mo-ren/u-mor-na	уморен/уморна (m/f)
well	do-bro	добро
worried	za-gri-zhen	загрижен

I'm sleepy.	me-ne mi se spi-e	Мене ми се спие.
I'm in a hurry.	me-ne mi se br-za	Мене ми се брза.

I'm sorry. (condolence)
  **zhal mi e/mo-e-to
  so-chuv-stvo**

Жал ми е./Моето
сочувство.

I'm grateful.
  **bla-go-da-ren/
  bla-go-dar-na sum**

Благодарен/
Благодарна сум. (m/f)

BREAKING THE LANGUAGE BARRIER

Do you speak English?
  zbo-ru-va-te li an-glis-ki?   Зборувате ли англиски?

Does anyone speak English?
  zbo-ru-va li ne-koy an-glis-ki? Зборува ли некој англиски?

I speak a little ...
  yas zbo-ru-vam mal-ku ...   Јас зборувам малку ...

I (don't) understand.
  yas (ne) raz-bi-ram   Јас (не) разбирам.

Could you speak more
slowly, please?
  **zbo-ru-vay-te po-le-ka
  ve mo-lam?**

Зборувјте полека,
ве молам!

Could you repeat that?
  **mo-zhe li da go
  pov-to-ri-te to-a?**

Може ли да го
повторите тоа?

How do you say ...?
  ka-ko se ve-li ...?   Како се вели ...?

What does ... mean?
  shto zna-chi ...?   Што значи ...?

MACEDONIAN

BODY LANGUAGE

As far as body language goes in Macedonia, don't be afraid of being misunderstood because of some improper gesture – Macedonian body language doesn't differ greatly from that of other European countries.

Macedonians shake their head to mean 'No', and nod to mean 'Yes'. When they're angry or being demonstrative, they wag their index finger, and with that same finger bent, they beckon. If they're pleased with you, they'll pat you on the shoulder, and when they don't know the answer to a question, they'll usually shrug their shoulders.

PAPERWORK

address	ad-re-sa	адреса
age	voz-rast	возраст
date of birth	da-tum na ra-gya-nye	датум на раѓање
driver's licence	vo-zach-ka doz-vo-la	возачка дозвола
identification	i-den-ti-fi-ka-tsi-ja	идентифи-кација
marital status	brach-na sos-toy-ba	брачна состојба
nationality	na-tsi-o-nal-nost	националност
passport	pa-sosh	пасош
passport number	broy na pa-so-shot	број на пасошот
place of birth	mes-to na ra-gya-nye	место на раѓање
profession	za-ni-ma-nye	занимање
reason for the travel	pri-chi-na za pa-tu-va-nye-to	причина за патувањето
sex	pol	пол
tourist card	tu-ri-stich-ka kar-ta	туристичка карта
visa	vi-za	виза

GETTING AROUND

What time does the ... leave/arrive?	ko-ga po-a-gya/ do-a-gya ... ?	Кога поаѓа/ доаѓа ...?
aeroplane	a-vi-o-not	авионот
boat	bro-dot	бродот
bus (city)	av-to-bu-sot (grad-ski)	автобусот (градски)
bus (intercity)	av-to-bu-sot (me-gyu-grad-ski)	автобусот (меѓуградски)
train	vo-zot	возот
tram	tram-va-yot	трамвајот

Directions

Where's ...?
ka-de e ...? Каде е ...?

How do I get to ...?
ka-ko da stig-nam do ...? Како да стигнам до ...?

Is it far/close by?
da-le-ku/blis-ku li e? Далеку/блиску ли е?

Can I walk there?
mo-zham li da pe-sha-cham do ta-mu? Можам ли да пешачам до таму?

Can you show me (on the map)?
mo-zhe-te li da mi po-ka-zhe-te (na kar-ta-va)? Можете ли да ми покажете (на картава)?

Go straight ahead.
o-de-te pra-vo nap-red Одете право напред.

It's two blocks down.
to-a e dva blo-ka po-do-lu Тоа е два блока подолу.

Turn left/ right at the ...	svr-te-te le-vo/ des-no na ...	Свртете лево/ десно на ...
next corner	sled-ni-ot a-gol	следниот агол
traffic lights	se-ma-fo-ri-te	семафорите

MACEDONIAN

behind	**zad**	зад
in front of	**pred**	пред
far	**da-le-ku**	далеку
near	**blis-ku**	блиску
opposite	**spro-ti**	спроти
north	**se-ver**	север
south	**yug**	југ
east	**is-tok**	исток
west	**za-pad**	запад

Booking Tickets

Where can I buy a ticket?
> **ka-de mo-zham da**
> **ku-pam bi-let?**

Каде можам да
купам билет?

I want to go to ...
> **sa-kam da o-dam vo ...**

Сакам да одам во ...

I'd like to book a seat to ...
> **sa-kam da re-zer-vi-ram**
> **ed-no se-dish-te do ...**

Сакам дарезервирам
едно седиште до ...

Do I need to book?
> **mi tre-ba li**
> **re-zer-va-tsi-ya?**

Ми треба ли
резервација?

Is it completely full?
> **da-li e so-sem pol-no?**

Дали е сосем полно?

I'd like ...	**sa-kam ...**	Сакам ...
a one-way ticket	**bi-let vo e-den pra-vec**	билет во еден правец
a return	**po-vra-ten bi-let**	повратен билет
two tickets	**dva bi-leta**	два билета
tickets for all of us	**bi-le-ti za si-te nas**	билети за сите нас
a student's fare	**stu-dent-ska tse-na**	студентска цена

MACEDONIAN

| a child's fare | det-ska tse-na | детска цена |
| a pensioner's fare | pen-zi-o-ner-ska tse-na | пензионерска цена |

| 1st class | pr-va kla-sa | прва класа |
| 2nd class | vto-ra kla-sa | втора класа |

Bus

Where's the bus/tram stop?
 ka-de e av-to-bus-ka-ta/ tram-vay-ska-ta sta-ni-ca? Каде е автобуската/ трамвајската станица?

Which bus goes to ...?
 koy av-to-bus o-di za ...? Кој автобус оди за ...?

Does this bus go to ...?
 da-li o-voy av-to-bus o-di za ...? Дали овој автобус оди за ...?

How often do buses pass by?
 kol-ku ches-to i-ma av-to-bu-si? Колку често има автобуси?

What time's the ... bus?	ko-ga po-a-gya ... av-to-bus?	Кога поаѓа ... автобус?
first	pr-v-iot	првиот
last	pos-led-ni-ot	последниот
next	sled-ni-ot	следниот

Could you let me know when we get to ...?
 mo-zhe-te li da mi ka-zhe-te ko-ga kye stig-ne-me vo ...? Можете ли да ми кажете кога ќе стигнеме во ...?

I want to get off!
 sa-kam da sle-zam! Сакам да слезам!

Train

Is this the right platform for ...?
    da-li e o-va pe-ron za ...?   Дали е ова перон за ...?
Is that seat taken?
    da-li se-dish-te-to e
    za-fa-te-no?   Дали седиштето е
                                         зафатено?

dining car	va-gon res-to-ran	вагон ресторан
express	eks-pres	експрес
local	lo-ka-len	локален
sleeping car	ko-la za spi-e-nye	кола за спиење

THEY MAY SAY ...

vo-zot trg-nu-va od   The train leaves from
    pe-ron broy ...   platform ...

pat-ni-tsi-te mo-ra ...   Passengers must ...
    da go pro-me-nat   change trains
    vo-zot
    da go pro-me-nat   change platforms
    pe-ro-not

vo-zot dots-ni/   The train is delayed/
    e u-ki-nat   cancelled.
dots-ni ... cha-sa   There's a delay of ... hours.

Taxi

Can you take me to ...?
    mo-zhe li da me   Може ли да ме
    od-ve-ze-te do ...?   одвезете до ...?
Please take me to ...
    ve mo-lam   Ве молам
    od-ve-ze-te me do ...   одвезете ме до ...
How much does it cost to go to ...?
    kol-ku kye chi-ni da   Колку ќе чини да
    me od-ve-ze-te do ...?   ме одвезете до ...?

MACEDONIAN

Here's fine, thank you.
    os-ta-ve-te me ov-de
    bla-go-da-ram

Оставете ме овде,
благодарам.

The next corner, please.
    na sled-ni-ot
    a-gol ve mo-lam

На следниот
агол, ве молам.

Continue!
    Pro-dol-zhe-te!

Продолжете!

The next street to the left/right.
    sled-na-ta u-li-tsa
    le-vo/des-no

Следната улица
лево/десно.

Stop here!
    zas-ta-ne-te ov-de!

Застанете овде!

Please wait here.
    pri-che-kay-te
    ov-de ve mo-lam

Причекајте овде,
ве молам.

Please slow down.
    vo-ze-te po-bav-no
    ve mo-lam

Возете побавно,
ве молам.

Car

Where can I rent a car?
    ka-de mo-zhe da nay-dam
    rent-a-kar?

Каде може да најдам
рент-а-кар?

How much is it daily/weekly?
    kol-ku chi-ni dnev-no/
    ne-del-no?

Колку чини дневно/
неделно?

Does that include insurance/mileage?
    da-li vo to-a e vklu-che-no
    o-si-gu-ru-va-nye-to/
    vklu-che-na
    ki-lo-me-tra-zha-ta?

Дали во тоа е вклучено
осигурувањето/
вклучена
километражата?

Where's the next petrol station?
    ka-de e sled-na-ta
    ben-zin-ska pum-pa?

Каде е следната
бензинска пумпа?

How long can I park here?
kol-ku dol-go mo-zham da   Колку долго можам да
par-ki-ram ov-de?   паркирам овде?

Does this road lead to ...?
da-li o-voy pat vo-di do ...?   Дали овој пат води до ...?

I need a mechanic.
mi tre-ba me-ha-ni-char   Ми треба механичар.

air (for tyres)	**voz-duh**	воздух
battery	**a-ku-mu-la-tor**	акумулатор
brakes	**koch-ni-tsi**	кочници
clutch	**kum-plung**	кумплунг
driver's licence	**vo-zach-ka**	возачка
	doz-vo-la	дозвола
engine	**mo-tor**	мотор
lights	**svet-la**	светла
oil	**mas-lo**	масло
petrol	**ben-zin**	бензин
puncture	**dup-na-ta**	дупната
radiator	**ra-di-ya-tor**	радијатор
road map	**av-to-kar-ta**	авто-карта
tyres	**gu-mi**	гуми
windscreen	**vet-ro-bran**	ветробран

ACCOMMODATION

I'm looking for a ...
ba-ram ...   Барам ...

Where's a ...?	**ka-de i-ma ...?**	Каде има ...?
cheap hotel	**ev-tin ho-tel**	евтин хотел
good hotel	**do-bar ho-tel**	добар хотел
nearby hotel	**ho-tel vo**	хотел во
	bli-zi-na-ta	близината
clean hotel	**chist ho-tel**	чист хотел

What's the address?
ko-ya e ad-re-sa-ta?   Која е адресата?
Could you write down
the address, please?
na-pi-she-te mi ya   Напишете ми ја
ad-re-sa-ta ve mo-lam   адресата, ве молам.

At the Hotel

Do you have any
rooms available?
da-li i-ma-te   Дали имате
slo-bod-ni so-bi?   слободни соби?

I'd like ...	**yas sa-kam ...**	Јас сакам ...
a single room	**ed-no-kre-vet-na**	еднокреветна
	so-ba	соба
a double room	**dvo-kre-vet-na**	двокреветна
	so-ba	соба
a room with a	**so-ba so ba-nya**	соба со бања
bathroom		
to share a dorm	**kre-vet vo**	кревет во
	stu-dent-ski	студентски
	dom	дом
a bed	**kre-vet**	кревет

I want a room with a ...	sa-kam so-ba so ...	Сакам соба со ...
bathroom	ba-nya	бања
shower	tush	туш
television	te-le-vi-zor	телевизор
window	pro-zo-rets	прозорец

Can I see it?
mo-zhe li da ya vi-dam?   Може ли да ја видам?

Are there any others?
i-ma-te li dru-gi?   Имате ли други?

Can I see the bathroom?
mo-zhe li da ya
vi-dam ba-nya-ta?   Може ли да ја
видам бањата?

Is there hot water all day?
da-li i-ma top-la
vo-da tsel den?   Дали има топла вода
цел ден?

How much is it per night/
per person?
ko-ya e tse-na-ta za noky/
po cho-vek?   Која е цената за ноќ/
по човек?

Is there a reduction for
students/children?
i-ma li po-pust za
stu-den-ti/de-tsa?   Има ли попуст за
студенти/деца?

It's fine, I'll take it.
dob-ra e kye ya ze-mam   Добра е, ќе ја земам.

I'm leaving now.	yas si o-dam se-ga	Јас си одам сега.
We're leaving now.	nie si o-di-me se-ga	Ние си одиме сега.
I'd like to pay the bill.	sa-kam da ya pla-tam smet-ka-ta	Сакам да ја платам сметката.

Requests & Complaints

Do you have a safe where
I can leave my valuables?

da-li i-ma-te sef ka-de shto   Дали имате сеф каде што
mo-zham da gi sta-vam   можам да ги ставам моите
mo-i-te vre-dni pred-me-ti?   вредни предмети?

Is there somewhere
to wash clothes?

ka-de mo-zham da   Каде можам да исперам
is-pe-ram ob-le-ka?   облека?

Can I use the telephone?

mo-zhe li da   Може ли да
te-le-fo-ni-ram?   телефонирам?

The room needs to be cleaned.

so-ba-ta tre-ba da se   Собата треба да се
is-chis-ti   исчисти.

I can't open/close the window.

ne mo-zham da go   Не можам да го
ot-vo-ram/   отворам/
zat-vo-ram pro-zo-re-tsot.   затворам прозорецот.

I've locked myself
out of my room.

se za-klu-chiv od-nad-vor   Се заклучив однадвор.

The toilet won't flush.

to-a-le-tot ne push-ta vo-da   Тоалетот не пушта вода.

MACEDONIAN

AROUND TOWN
At the Post Office

I'd like to send a/an ...	sa-kam da i s-pra-tam ...	Сакам да испратам ...
aerogram	a-e-ro-gram	аерограм
letter	pis-mo	писмо
parcel	pa-ket	пакет
postcard	raz-gled-ni-tsa	разгледница
telegram	te-le-gra-ma	телеграма

I'd like some stamps.
	sa-kam da ku-pam posh-ten-ski mar-ki	Сакам да купам поштенски марки.

How much is the postage?
	kol-ku chi-ni posh-ta-ri-na-ta?	Колку чини поштарината?

air mail	a-vi-on-ski	авионски
envelope	plik	плик
mailbox	posh-ten-sko san-da-che	поштенско сандаче
registered mail	pre-po-ra-cha-no	препорачано
surface mail	o-bich-no	обично

Telephone

I want to ring ...
sa-kam da te-le-fo-ni-ram ...	Сакам да телефонирам ...

The number is ...
broy-ot e ...	Бројот е ...

I want to speak for three minutes.
sa-kam da zbo-ru-vam tri mi-nu-ti	Сакам да зборувам три минути.

How much does a three-minute call cost?
kol-ku chi-ni raz-go-vor od tri mi-nu-ti?	Колку чини разговор од три минути?

I'd like to speak to Mr ...
    sa-kam da zbo-ru-vam so   Сакам да зборувам со
    gos-po-din ...   господин ...
I want to make a reverse-charges
phone call.
    sa-kam da te-le-fo-ni-ram   Сакам да телефонирам
    na niv-na smet-ka   на нивна сметка.
It's engaged.
    za-fa-te-no e   Зафатено е.
I've been cut off.
    li-ni-ya-ta se pre-ki-na   Линијата се прекина.

At the Bank

I want to exchange some
money/travellers cheques.
    sa-kam da raz-me-nam   Сакам да разменам
    pa-ri/pat-nich-ki che-ko-vi пари/патнички чекови.
What's the exchange rate?
    ka-kov e kur-sot?   Каков е курсот?
How many ... per dollar?
    kol-ku ... za e-den do-lar? Колку ... за еден долар?

banknotes	**bank-no-ti**	банкноти
cashier	**bla-gay-nik**	благајник
coins	**me-tal-ni pa-ri**	метални пари
credit card	**kre-dit-na**	кредитна
	kar-tich-ka	картичка
exchange	**raz-me-na**	размена
signature	**potpis**	потпис

MACEDONIAN

MACEDONIAN

Internet

Where can I get Internet access?
ka-de mo-zhe da do-bi-yam Каде може да добијам
pri-stap na in-ter-net пристап на интернет?

How much is it per hour?
kol-ku chi-ni na chas Колку чини на час?

I want to check my email.
sa-kam da si ya pro-ve-ram Сакам да си ја проверам
e-lek-tron-ska-ta posh-ta електронската пошта.

INTERESTS & ENTERTAINMENT
Sightseeing

Do you have a ...? i-ma-te li kni-ga ...? Имате ли книга ...?
  guidebook vo-dach водач
  local map lo-kal-na kar-ta локална карта

What are the main attractions?
ko-i se glav-ni-te Кои се главните
zna-me-ni-tos-ti? знаменитости?

How old is it?
kol-ku e sta-ro o-va? Колку е старо ова?

Can I take photographs?
mo-zhe li da sli-kam? Може ли да сликам?

What time does it open/close?
ko-ga ot-vo-ra/zat-vo-ra? Кога отвора/затвора?

ancient	star	стар
archaeological	ar-he-o-losh-ki	археолошки
beach	pla-zha	плажа
building	zgra-da	зграда
castle	za-mok	замок
cathedral	ka-te-dra-la	катедрала
church	tsrk-va	црква
concert hall	kon-tsert-na	концертна
	sa-la	сала
library	bi-bli-o-te-ka	библиотека
main square	gla-ven	главен
	plosh-tad	плоштад
market	pa-zar	пазар
monastery	ma-nas-tir	манастир
monument	spo-me-nik	споменик
mosque	ja-mi-ya	џамија
museum	mu-zey-ot	музејот
old city	star grad	стар град
palace	pa-la-ta	палата
opera house	o-per-ska ku-kya	оперска куќа
ruins	ur-na-ti-ni	урнатини
stadium	sta-di-on	стадион
statues	sta-tu-i	статуи
synagogue	si-na-go-ga	синагога
temple	hram	храм
university	u-ni-ver-zi-tet	универзитет

MACEDONIAN

Going Out

What's there to do in the
evenings?

   ka-de mo-zhe da se iz-le-ze   Каде може да се излезе
   na-ve-cher?   навечер?

Are there any nightclubs?

   i-ma li dis-ka?   Има ли диска?

Where can I hear local folk music?
   ka-de mo-zham da slu-sham
   lo-kal-na na-rod-na mu-zi-ka?   Каде можам да слушам
                                локална народна музика?
How much does it cost to get in?
   kol-ku chi-ni vle-zot?   Колку чини влезот?

cinema	**ki-no**	кино
concert	**kon-tsert**	концерт
nightclub	**dis-ko-te-ka**	дискотека
theatre	**te-a-tar**	театар

Sports & Interests

What sports do you play?
   so ko-i spor-to-vi
   se za-ni-ma-va-te?   Со кои спортови
                              се занимавате?
What are your interests?
   shto ve in-te-re-si-ra?   Што ве интересира?

art	**u-met-nost**	уметност
basketball	**ko-shar-ka**	кошарка
chess	**shah**	шах
collecting things	**ko-lek-tsi-o-ner-stvo**	колекци онерство
dancing	**tan-tsu-va-nye**	танцување
food	**ya-de-nye**	јадење
football	**fud-bal**	фудбал
hiking	**pro-shet-ki**	прошетки
martial arts	**bo-rech-ki vesh-ti-ni**	боречки вештини
meeting friends	**dru-zhe-nye so pri-ya-te-li**	дружење со пријатели
movies	**fil-mo-vi**	филмови
music	**mu-zi-ka**	музика
nightclubs	**noky-ni klu-bo-vi**	ноќни клубови
photography	**fo-to-gra-fi-ra-nye**	фотографирање

reading	chi-ta-nye	читање
shopping	ku-pu-va-nye	купување
skiing	ski-ya-nye	скијање
swimming	pli-va-nye	пливање
tennis	te-nis	тенис
travelling	pa-tu-va-nya	патувања
TV/videos	TV/vi-de-o	ТВ/видео
visiting friends	po-se-ti na	посети
	pri-ya-te-li	на пријатели
walking	pe-sha-che-nye	пешачење

Festivals

Скопско лето   skop-sko le-to
  Skopje Summer Festival
  (July-August) features concerts, theatre and art performances,
  as well as many other events at different venues in the city

Мајски оперски вечери   may-ski o-per-ski ve-che-ri
  May Opera Evenings
  (May) international opera festival

Меѓународен џез фестивал   me-dju-na-ro-den jez fes-ti-val
  international Jazz Festival
  (October)

Млад отворен театар   mlad ot-vo-ren te-a-tar
  Open Youth Theatre Festival
  (September)

Охридско лето   oh-rid-sko le-to
  Ohrid Summer Festival
  (mid-July to mid-August) features classical concerts and theatre
  performances in the magnificient ambience of the cathedral
  church of Sveta Sofija

Балкански фестивал на   bal-kan-ski fes-ti-val
народни игри и песни   na na-rod-ni ig-ri i pes-ni
  Balkan Festival of Folk Dances & Songs
  (early July) brings together folkloric groups from around the
  Balkans to Ohrid

MACEDONIAN

Струшки вечери на strush-ki ve-che-ri na
поезијата po-e-zi-ya-ta
 Struga Poetry Evenings
 (August) some 200 poets from about 50 countries come to
 celebrate poetry at the banks of the river Drim in Struga

Меѓународен фестивал me-dju-na-ro-den fes-ti-val
на народни носии na na-rod-ni no-si-i
 International Festival of National Costumes (August)

Меѓународен фестивал на me-dju-na-ro-den fes-ti-val na
филмска камера film-ska ka-me-ra
"Браќа Манаки" bra-kya ma-na-ki
 International Film Camera Festival 'Manaki Brothers'
 (September) held in honour of the brothers Milton and
 Janaki Manaki who, in 1905, shot the first filmed material
 in the Balkans in their native town of Bitola and thus laid
 the foundations of 'the seventh art' in this region

Галичка свадба ga-lich-ka svad-ba
 (mid-July) each year in the village of Galičnik a traditional
 wedding celebration takes place

IN THE COUNTRY
Weather

What's the weather like?
 kak-vo e vre-me-to? Какво е времето?

The weather's	vre-me-to	Времето
... today.	de-nes e ...	денес е ...
Will it be ...	da-li ut-re	Дали утре
tomorrow?	kye bi-de ...?	ќе биде ...?
cloudy	ob-lach-no	облачно
cold	stu-de-no	студено
foggy	mag-lo-vi-to	магловито
frosty	sla-no-vi-to	слановито
hot	zhesh-ko	жешко
raining	vr-nezh-li-vo	врнежливо
snowing	snezh-no	снежно
sunny	son-che-vo	сончево
windy	vet-ro-vi-to	ветровито

MACEDONIAN

Camping

Am I allowed to camp here?
mo-zhe li da
kam-pu-vam ov-de?

Може ли да
кампувам овде?

Is there a campsite nearby?
da-li vo bli-zi-na-ta
i-ma kamp?

Дали во близината
има камп?

backpack	ra-nets	ранец
can opener	ot-vo-rach	отворач
	za kon-zer-vi	за конзерви
compass	kom-pas	компас
crampons	zhe-lez-ni ku-ki	железни куки
firewood	dr-va za o-grev	дрва за огрев
gas cartridge	tsi-lin-dar so gas	цилиндар со гас
ice axe	pla-ni-nar-ski	планинарски
	ko-pach	копач
mattress	du-shek	душек
penknife	no-zhe	ноже
rope	ya-zhe	јаже
tent	sha-tor	шатор
tent pegs	kol-chi-nya	колчиња за
	za sha-tor	шатор
torch (flashlight)	rach-na sve-til-ka	рачна светилка
sleeping bag	vre-kya za	вреќа за
	spi-e-nye	спиење
stove	re-sho	решо
water bottle	shi-she za vo-da	шише за вода

MACEDONIAN

FOOD

As this country was long under Turkish rule, some of the dishes have been influenced by Turkish cuisine. Lunches tend to be more interesting than dinners, as Macedonians generally take their main meal at midday or early afternoon.

Large towns have many attractive restaurants, some privately run, where you can eat well at any time. Many restaurants provide a lunchtime set menu which includes a soup and a main course.

breakfast	po-ya-dok	појадок
lunch	ru-chek	ручек
dinner	ve-che-ra	вечера

Soups & Starters

clear chicken soup	pi-lesh-ka su-pa	пилешка супа
clear beef soup	go-ved-ska su-pa	говедска супа
clear fish soup	rib-ya chor-ba	рибја чорба

Vegetarian Meals

Although you won't find many vegetarian restaurants in Macedonia, there are plenty of vegetarian dishes on most restaurant menus.

I'm a vegetarian.
    yas sum ve-ge-ta-ri-ya-nets/   Јас сум вегетаријанец/
    ve-ge-ta-ri-yan-ka   вегетаријанка. (m/f)
I don't eat meat.
    ne ya-dam me-so   Не јадам месо.
I don't eat chicken, fish or ham.
    ne ya-dam pi-lesh-ko,   Не јадам пилешко,
    ni ri-ba,   ни риба,
    ni-tu svin-sko   ниту свинско.

Desserts & Sweets

Desserts tend to be very rich. The following are all recommended to those with a very sweet tooth:

кадаиф	ka-da-if
гурабии	gu-ra-bi-i
шампити	sham-pi-ti
тулумби	tu-lum-bi

баклава	bak-la-va	a flaky pastry with nuts, soaked in sugar syrup
алва	al-va	made with egg whites, sugar and nuts
црна алва	tsr-na al-va	sesame seeds crushed in honey

Non-Alcoholic Drinks

Be sure to try боза **bo-za**, a fresh drink made from fermented corn flour.

coffee	ka-fe	кафе
Turkish coffee	tur-sko ka-fe	турско кафе
fruit juice	o-vo-shen sok	овошен сок
hot chocolate	top-la cho-ko-la-da	топла чоколада
mineral water	mi-ne-ral-na vo-da	минерална вода
tea	chay	чај
with milk	so mle-ko	со млеко
with sugar	so she-kyer	со шеќер
(boiled) water	(vre-la) vo-da	(врела) вода

Alcoholic Drinks

The Тиквеш (**tik-vesh**) area produces excellent wines. Two very good ones are:

| тжга за југ | t-ga za yug | a full-bodied red |
| темјаника | tem-ya-ni-ka | a dry white |

All Macedonian spirits are strong. The generic name for most distilled drinks is brandy. Brandy lovers should try aniseed brandy.

brandy	lo-zo-va/sli-vo-va	лозова/сливова
spirit	ra-ki-ya	ракија
aniseed brandy	mas-ti-ka	мастика

MACEDONIAN

MACEDONIAN

MENU DECODER

Hors d'Oeuvres
Called мезе, meze, these are served hot or cold:

Ајвар	ay-var	a spicy mixture of grilled sweet or hot peppers, eggplant and carrots, blended together. Try this spread on bread.
Качамак	ka-cha-mak	a paste-like entree, made of ground maize cooked in salt water, and served with feta cheese
Погачки/ Погачки со џимиринки	po-gach-ki/ po-gach-ki so dzhi-mi-rin-ki	oven-browned savory rolls with small chunks of fried pork
Бурек	bu-rek	flaky pastry with layers of cheese, spinach or minced meat and onion. Try it with yogurt – it's delicious.
Пита/баница	pi-ta/ba-ni-tsa	flaky pastry filled with spinach and cheese, cheese and eggs, or pumpkin

Main Dishes
Many restaurants offer grilled meat as the main course. The first three dishes described below are served with finely chopped raw onion or salads.

Ќебапчиња	kye-bap-chi-nya	grilled minced pork, beef or lamb, shaped into small sausages
Плескавица	ples-ka-vi-tsa	burger of minced pork, beef or lamb
Раденчиња	ra-zhen-chi-nya	small chunks of pork, grilled on a skewer

MENU DECODER

шопска салата	shop-ska sa-la-ta	a salad of peppers, cucumber, tomatoes, onions and feta cheese
Полнети пиперки	pol-ne-ti pi-per-ki	peppers stuffed with minced beef or pork and rice
Полнети тиквички	pol-ne-ti tik-vich-ki	similar to the dish above but zucchini is used instead of peppers
Мусака	mu-sa-ka	made of alternate layers of minced meat and potato or eggplant
Пилав	pi-lav	a rice dish where the meat is cut into small pieces and mixed with seasoned rice before being grilled
Подварок	pod-va-rok	finely shredded sour cabbage roasted with slices of meat
Сарма	sar-ma	minced meat rolled in sour cabbage leaves
Тавче гравче	tav-che grav-che	baked beans with herbs, served plain or with pork sausages
Пастрмка	pas-trm-ka	a special variety of salmon-trout found nowhere else in the world. It is prepared in a variety of ways.

MACEDONIAN

MACEDONIAN

At the Market
Staples

bread	leb	леб
butter	pu-ter	путер
cereal	zhi-to	жито
cheese	si-re-nye	сирење
chocolate	cho-ko-la-da	чоколада
eggs	yay-tsa	јајца
flour	brash-no	брашно
honey	med	мед
margarine	mar-ga-rin	маргарин
marmalade	mar-ma-lad	мармалад
milk	mle-ko	млеко
olive oil	mas-li-no-vo	маслиново
	mas-lo	масло
pasta	tes-te-ni-ni	тестенини
pepper	tsrn pi-per	црн пипер
rice	o-riz	ориз
salt	sol	сол
sugar	she-kyer	шеќер
yogurt	yo-gurt	јогурт

Meat & Fish

beef	go-ved-sko	говедско
chicken	pi-lesh-ko	пилешко
ham	shun-ka	шунка
hamburger	ham-bur-ger	хамбург
lamb	jag-nesh-ko	јагнешко
meat	me-so	месо
pork	svin-sko	свинско
sausage	kol-bas	колбас
turkey	mi-sir-ka	мисирка
veal	ju-nesh-ko	јунешко
fish	ri-ba	риба
lobster	yas-tog	јастог
mussels	shkol-ki	школки
oysters	os-tri-gi	остриги
shrimp	shkam-pi	шкампи

Vegetables

(green) beans	bo-ra-ni-ya	боранија
beetroot	tsvek-lo	цвекло
cabbage	zel-ka	зелка
carrot	mor-kov	морков
red/green capsicum	tsr-ve-na/ze-le-na ba-bu-ra	црвена/ зелена бабура
cauliflower	kar-fi-ol	карфиол
celery	tse-ler	целер
chillies	fe-fe-ro-ni	феферони
cucumber	kras-ta-vi-tsa	краставица
eggplant	mo-dar do-mat	модар домат
garlic	luk	лук
ginger	gyum-bir	ѓумбир
lettuce	ze-le-na sa-la-ta	зелена салата
mushrooms	pe-chur-ki	печурки
onion	kro-mid	кромид
peas	gra-shok	грашок
potato	kom-pir	компир
spinach	spa-naky	спанаќ
tomato	do-mat	домат
vegetables	ze-len-chuk	зеленчук
zucchini	tik-vich-ka	тиквичка

MACEDONIAN

Pulses

broad beans	bo-ra-ni-ya	боранија
chickpeas	leb-le-bi-ya	леблебија
kidney beans	grav	грав
lentils	le-kya	леќа

Fruit

apple	ya-bol-ko	јаболко
apricot	kay-si-ya	кајсија
banana	ba-na-na	банана
fig	smok-va	смоква
grapes	groz-ye	грозје
kiwifruit	ki-vi	киви
lemon	li-mon	лимон
orange	por-to-kal	портокал
peach	pras-ka	праска
pear	kru-sha	круша
plum	sli-va	слива
strawberry	ya-go-da	јагода

SHOPPING

Where's the	ka-de e	Каде е
nearest ...?	nay-blis-ki-ot ...?	најблискиот ...?
bookshop	kni-zhar-ni-tsa	книжарница
camera shop	pro-dav-ni-tsa za	продавница за
	fo-to-a-pa-ra-ti	фото-апарати
chemist	ap-te-ka	аптека
clothing store	pro-dav-ni-tsa za	продавница за
	ob-le-ka	облека
delicatessen	de-li-ka-tes-na	деликатесна
	pro-dav-ni-tsa	продавница
general store	pro-dav-ni-tsa	продавница
greengrocer	pro-dav-ni-tsa za	продавница за
laundry	pe-ral-na	перална
market	pa-zar	пазар
newsagency	ki-osk za	киоск за
	ves-ni-tsi	весници
shoeshop	pro-dav-ni-tsa	продавница за
	za chev-li	чевли
souvenir shop	pro-dav-ni-tsa	продавница за
	za su-ve-ni-ri	сувенири
stationers	kni-zhar-ni-tsa	книжарница
supermarket	su-per-mar-ket	супермаркет
	ze-len-chuk	зеленчук

How much is it?
  kol-ku chi-ni to-a?   Колку чини тоа?
Do you accept credit cards?
  pri-ma-te li kre-dit-ni   Примате ли кредитни
  kar-tich-ki?   картички?

Essential Groceries

I'd like ...	sa-kam ...	Сакам ...
batteries	ba-te-ri-i	батерии
bread	leb	леб
butter	pu-ter	путер
cheese	si-re-nye	сирење
chocolate	cho-ko-la-da	чоколада
eggs	yay-tsa	јајца
honey	med	мед
margarine	mar-ga-rin	маргарин
marmalade	mar-ma-lad	мармалад
matches	kyib-rit	ќибрит
milk	mle-ko	млеко
shampoo	sham-pon	шампон
soap	sa-pun	сапун
toilet paper	to-a-let-na har-ti-ya	тоалетна хартија
toothpaste	pas-ta za za-bi	паста за заби
washing powder	pra-shak za pe-re-nye	прашак за перење

MACEDONIAN

Souvenirs

earrings	o-bet-ki	обетки
handicraft	ra-ko-tvor-bi	ракотворби
necklace	djer-dan	ѓердан
Ohrid pearl	oh-rid-ski bi-ser	охридски бисер
pottery	grn-cha-ri-ya	грнчарија
ring	prs-ten	прстен
rug	kyi-lim	ќилим

Clothing

clothing	ob-le-ka	облека
coat	ka-put	капут
dress	fus-tan	фустан
jacket	sa-ko	сако
jumper (sweater)	jem-per	џемпер
shirt	ko-shu-la	кошула
shoes	chev-li	чевли
skirt	zdol-nish-te	здолниште
trousers	pan-ta-lo-ni	панталони
underwear	dol-na ob-le-ka	долна облека

Materials

What is it made of?

od shto e na-pra-ve-no?   Од што е направено?

cotton	pa-muk	памук
handmade	rach-na ra-bo-ta	рачна работа
leather	ko-zha	кожа
of brass	od ba-kar	од бакар
of gold	od zla-to	од злато
of silver	od sreb-ro	од сребро
silk	svi-la	свила
wool	vol-na	волна

Colours

black	tsr-na	црна
blue	si-na	сина
brown	ka-fe-a-va	кафеава
green	ze-le-na	зелена
orange	por-to-ka-lo-va	портокалова
pink	ro-zo-va	розова
purple	vi-o-le-to-va	виолетова
red	tsr-ve-na	црвена
white	be-la	бела
yellow	zhol-ta	жолта

Toiletries

comb	che-shel	чешел
condoms	kon-do-mi	кондоми
deodorant	de-zo-do-rans	дезодоранс
hairbrush	chet-ka za ko-sa	четка за коса
moisturising cream	krem za	крем за
	nav-lazh-nu-va-nje	авлажнување
	na ko-zha-ta	нна кожата
razor	zhi-let	жилет
sanitary napkins	hi-gi-en-ski	хигиенски
	vlosh-ki	влошки
shampoo	sham-pon	шампон
shaving cream	krem za	крем за
	bri-che-nye	бричење
sunblock cream/	krem za	крем за
sunscreen	zash-ti-ta	заштита
	od son-ce	од сонце
tampons	tam-po-ni	тампони
tissues	har-ti-e-ni	хартиени
	sha-mi-chi-nya	шамичиња
toothbrush	chet-ka za za-bi	четка за заби

MACEDONIAN

Stationery & Publications

map	kar-ta	карта
newspaper	ves-nik	весник
paper	har-ti-ya	хартија
pen (ballpoint)	pen-ka-lo	пенкало
scissors	no-zhi-tsi	ножици
English-language ...	... an-glis-ki	... на англиски
newspaper	ves-nik na	весник
novels	kni-gi na	книги на

Photography

How much is it to process
this film?

    kol-ku chi-ni da se raz-vi-e Колку чини да се развие
o-voy film? овој филм?

When will it be ready?

    ko-ga kye bi-de go-tov? Кога ќе биде готов?

I'd like a film for this camera.

    sa-kam film za o-voy Сакам филм за овој
fo-to-a-pa-rat фото-апарат.

B&W (film)	tsr-no-bel (film)	црно-бел (филм)
camera	fo-to-a-pa-rat	фото-апарат
colour (film)	(film) vo bo-ya	(филм) во боја
film	film	филм
flash	blits	блиц
lens	ob-yek-tiv	објектив
light meter	me-rach na svet-li-na	мерач на светлина

Smoking

Do you smoke?

    da-li pu-shi-te Дали пушите?

Please don't smoke.

    ve mo-lam ne pu-she-te Ве молам не пушете.

A packet of cigarettes, please.

    ku-ti-ya tsi-ga-ri Кутија цигари,
ve mo-lam ве молам.

Are these cigarettes
strong/mild?

    da-li se o-vi-e Дали се овие
tsi-ga-ri ya-ki/sla-bi? цигари јаки/слаби?

Do you have a light?

    i-ma-te li za-pal-ka? Имате ли запалка?

cigarette papers	har-ti-ya za tsi-ga-ri	хартија за цигари
cigarettes	tsi-ga-ri	цигари
filtered	so fil-ter	со филтер
lighter	za-pal-ka	запалка
matches	kyib-rit	ќибрит
menthol	men-tol	ментол
pipe	lu-le	луле
tobacco (pipe)	tu-tun (za lu-le)	тутун (за луле)

Sizes & Comparisons

small	mal	мал
big	go-lem	голем
heavy	te-zhok	тежок
light	le-sen	лесен
more	po-ve-kye	повеќе
less	po-mal-ku	помалку
too much/many	pre-mno-gu	премногу

MACEDONIAN

SIGNS

ВЛЕЗ	ENTRANCE
ВЛЕЗ СЛОБОДЕН	FREE ADMISSION
ЗАБРАНЕТ ВЛЕЗ	NO ENTRY
ЗАБРАНЕТО	PROHIBITED
ЗАБРАНЕТО ПУШЕЊЕ	NO SMOKING
ИЗЛЕЗ ВО СЛУЧАЈ НА ОПАСНОСТ	EMERGENCY EXIT
ИЗЛЕЗ	EXIT
ИНФОРМАЦИИ	INFORMATION
ОТВОРЕНО/ЗАТВОРЕНО	OPEN/CLOSED
ПАСОШКА КОНТРОЛА	IMMIGRATION
РЕЗЕРВИРАНО	RESERVED
ТЕЛЕФОН	TELEPHONE
ТОАЛЕТИ	TOILETS
ТОПЛО/ЛАДНО	HOT/COLD

HEALTH

Where's the ...?	ka-de i-ma ...?	Каде има ...?
chemist	ap-te-ka	аптека
dentist	za-bo-le-kar	заболекар
doctor	le-kar	лекар
hospital	bol-ni-tsa	болница

I'm sick.
    yas sum bo-len/bol-na   Jac сум болен/болна. (m/f)
My friend is sick.
    mo-yot pri-ya-tel e bo-len   Мојот пријател е болен/
    mo-ya-ta pri-ya-tel-ka e   Мојата пријателка е
    bol-na   болна. (m/f)
It hurts here.
    ov-de me bo-li   Овде ме боли.

Parts of the Body

My ... hurts.	me bo-li ...	Ме боли ...
ankle	zglob	зглоб
arm	ra-ka	рака
back	grb	грб
chest	gra-di	гради
ear	u-vo	уво
eye	o-ko	око
finger	prst	прст
foot	sta-pa-lo	стапало
hand	ra-ka	рака
head	gla-va	глава
heart	sr-tse	срце
leg	no-ga	нога
mouth	us-ta	уста
nose	nos	нос
ribs	reb-ra	ребра
skin	ko-zha	кожа
spine	r-bet	жрбет
stomach	sto-mak	стомак
teeth	za-bi	заби
throat	gr-lo	грло

MACEDONIAN

Ailments

I have (a/an) ...	i-mam ...	Имам ...
allergy	a-ler-gi-ya	алергија
anaemia	a-ne-mi-ya	анемија
burn	iz-go-re-ni-tsa	изгореница
cold	nas-tin-ka	настинка
constipation	kon-sti-pa-tsi-ya/	констипација/
	za-pek	запек
cough	kash-li-tsa	кашлица
diarrhoea	pro-liv	пролив
fever	tres-ka	треска
headache	gla-vo-bol-ka	главоболка
indigestion	lo-sho va-re-nye	лошо варење
an infection	in-fek-tsi-ya	инфекција
influenza	grip	грип
lice	vosh-ki	вошки
itch	ja-dezh	јадеж
low/high blood	ni-zok/vi-sok	низок/висок
pressure	kr-ven pri-ti-sok	крвен
		притисок
pain	bol-ka	болка
sore throat	vos-pa-le-ni-e na	воспаление на
	gr-lo-to	грлото
sprain	is-cha-shu-va-nye	исчашување
stomachache	bol-ki vo	болки во
	sto-ma-kot	стомакот
venereal	ve-ne-rich-na	венерична
disease	bo-lest	болест
worms	glis-ti	глисти
temperature	tem-pe-ra-tu-ra	температура

At the Chemist

I need medication for ...
    mi tre-ba lek za ...   Ми треба лек за ...
I have a prescription.
    i-mam re-tsept   Имам рецепт.

antibiotics	an-ti-bi-o-ti-tsi	антибиотици
antiseptic	an-ti-sep-tik	антисептик
bandage	za-voy	завој
contraceptive	sred-stva za	средства за
	kon-tra-tsep-tsi-ya	котрацепција
medicine	lek	лек
vitamins	vi-ta-mi-ni	витамини

MACEDONIAN

At the Dentist

I have a toothache.
    me bo-li zab   Ме боли заб.
I've lost a filling.
    mi pad-na plom-ba   Ми падна пломба.
I've broken a tooth.
    mi se skr-shi za-bot   Ми се скрши забот.
My gums hurt.
    me bo-lat ven-tsi-te   Ме болат венците.
I don't want it extracted.
    ne sa-kam da se va-di   Не сакам да се вади.
Please give me an anaesthetic.
    ve mo-lam day-te   Ве молам дајте
    mi o-poj-ka   ми опојка.

TIME & DATES

What date is it today?
   koy da-tum e de-nes?   Кој датум е денес?
What time is it?
   kol-ku e cha-sot?   Колку е часот?
It's ... am/pm.
   se-ga e ... cha-sot   Сега е ... часот
   pret-plad-ne/po-plad-ne   претпладне/попладне.

in the morning	pret-plad-ne	претпладне
in the afternoon	po-plad-ne	попладне
in the evening	na-ve-cher	навечер

Days

Monday	po-ne-del-nik	понеделник
Tuesday	vtor-nik	вторник
Wednesday	sre-da	среда
Thursday	chet-vr-tok	четврток
Friday	pe-tok	петок
Saturday	sa-bo-ta	сабота
Sunday	ne-de-la	недела

Months

January	ya-nu-a-ri	јануари
February	fev-ru-a-ri	февруари
March	mart	март
April	ap-ril	април
May	may	мај
June	yu-ni	јуни
July	yu-li	јули
August	av-gust	август
September	sep-tem-vri	септември
October	ok-tom-vri	октомври
November	no-em-vri	ноември
December	de-kem-vri	декември

MACEDONIAN

MACEDONIAN

Seasons

summer	le-to	лето
autumn	e-sen	есен
winter	zi-ma	зима
spring	pro-let	пролет

Present

today	de-nes	денес
this morning	o-va ut-ro	ова утро
tonight	ve-cher-va	вечерва
this week	o-va-a ne-de-la	оваа недела
this year	o-va-a go-di-na	оваа година
now	se-ga	сега

Past

yesterday	vche-ra	вчера
day before yesterday	zav-che-ra	завчера
yesterday morning	vche-ra na-ut-ro	вчера наутро
last night	si-no-kya	синоќа
last week	mi-na-ta-ta	минатата
	ne-de-la	недела
last year	mi-na-ta-ta	минатата
	go-di-na	година

Future

tomorrow	ut-re	утре
day after tomorrow	zad-ut-re	задутре
tomorrow morning	ut-re na-ut-ro	утре наутро
tomorrow afternoon/	ut-re po-plad-ne/	утре попладне/
evening	ve-cher	вечер
next week	sled-na-ta	следната
	ne-de-la	недела
next year	sled-na-ta	следната
	go-di-na	година

During the Day

afternoon	po-plad-ne	попладне
dawn; early morning	zo-ra/ra-no ut-ro	зора/рано утро
day	den	ден
midday	plad-ne	пладне
midnight	pol-noky	полноќ
morning	ut-ro	утро
night	noky	ноќ
sunrise	iz-grev	изгрев
sunset	za-lez	залез

NUMBERS & AMOUNTS

0	nu-la	нула		6	shest	шест
1	e-den	еден		7	se-dum	седум
2	dva	два		8	o-sum	осум
3	tri	три		9	de-vet	девет
4	che-ti-ri	четири		10	de-set	десет
5	pet	пет		11	e-di-na-e-set	единаесет

12	dva-na-e-set	дванаесет
13	tri-na-e-set	тринаесет
14	che-ti-ri-na-e-set	четиринаесет
15	pet-na-e-set	петнаесет
16	shes-na-e-set	шеснаесет
17	se-dum-na-e-set	седумнаесет
18	o-sum-na-e-set	осумнаесет
19	de-vet-na-e-set	деветнаесет
20	dva-e-set	дваесет
21	dva-e-set i e-den	дваесет и еден
22	dva-e-set i dva	дваесет и два
30	tri-e-set	триесет
40	che-ti-ri-e-set	четириесет
50	pe-de-set	педесет
60	she-e-set	шеесет
70	se-dum-de-set	седумдесет
80	o-sum-de-set	осумдесет
90	de-ve-de-set	деведесет
100	sto	сто
one million	e-den mi-li-on	еден милион

1st	prv	прв
2nd	vtor	втор
3rd	tret	трет
1/4	ed-na chet-vr-ti-na	една четвртина
1/3	ed-na tre-ti-na	една третина
1/2	ed-na po-lo-vi-na	една половина
3/4	tri chet-vr-ti-ni	три четвртини

Useful Words

Enough!	do-vol-no!	Доволно!
a little (amount)	mal-ku	малку
few	ne-kol-ku	неколку
too much	pre-mno-gu	премногу
double	dup-lo	дупло
dozen	du-zi-na	дузина
less	po-mal-ku	помалку
many	mno-gu	многу
more	po-ve-kye	повеќе
once	ed-nash	еднаш
pair	par	пар
per cent	pro-cent	процент
some	ne-kol-ku	неколку
twice	dva-pa-ti	двапати

ABBREVIATIONS

Д-р	Dr
ЕЗ	European Community
Г./Г-ѓa/Г-ца	Mr/Mrs/Ms
гр/кг	gram/kilogram
ч/мин/сек	hours/minutes/seconds
ЛК	ID
ОН	United Nations
САД	USA
СИДА	AIDS
С/Ј	North/South
СОС	SOS
ВБ	United Kingdom

EMERGENCIES

Help!	upo-mosh!	Помош!
It's an emergency.	it-no e	Итно е.
Go away!	o-de-te si!	Одете си!
Thief!	kra-dets!	Крадец!
I've been robbed.	me op-lyach-ka-a	Ме опљачкаа
I've been raped.	me si-lu-va-a	Ме силуваа.
I'm lost.	se za-gu-biv	Се загубив.
I'm sorry.	zhal mi e	Жал ми е.
I apologise.	se iz-vi-nu-vam	Се извинувам.
Call ...!	vik-ne-te ...!	Викнете ...!
a doctor	le-kar	лекар
an ambulance	br-za po-mosh	брза помош
the police	po-li-tsi-ya	полиција

There's been an accident.
se slu-chi ne-sre-kya — Се случи несреќа.

I'll call the police.
kye vik-nam po-li-tsi-ya — Ќе викнам полиција.

Where's the police station?
ka-de e po-li-tsis-ka-ta sta-ni-tsa? — Каде е полициската станица?

I'm ill.
yas sum bo-len/bo-lna — Јас сум болен/болна. (m/f)

Could you help me please?
mo-zhe li da mi po-mog-ne-te ve mo-lam? — Може ли да ми помогнете, ве молам?

Could I please use the telephone?
mo-zhe li da te-le-fo-ni-ram? — Може ли да телефонирам?

Where are the toilets?
ka-de se to-a-le-ti-te? — Каде се тоалетите?

I didn't realise I was doing anything wrong.
ne mis-lev de-ka pra-vam nesh-to po-gresh-no — Не мислев дека правам нешто погрешно.

MACEDONIAN

I want to contact my
embassy/consulate.
   sa-kam da se ya-vam
   vo mo-ya-ta
   am-ba-sa-da/mo-yot
   kon-zu-lat

Сакам да се јавам
во мојата
амбасада/мојот
конзулат.

I have medical insurance.
   i-mam zdrav-stve-no
   o-si-gu-ru-va-nye

Имам здравствено
осигурување.

My possessions are insured.
   mo-i-te ra-bo-ti se
   o-sí-gu-ra-ni

Моите работи се
осигурани.

My ... was stolen.	mo-yot/*mo-ya-ta* ... e u-kra-den	Мојот/Мојата ... е украден. (m/f)
I've lost my ...	za-gu-biv ...	Загубив ...
bags	gi za-gu-biv mo-i-te tor-bi	ги загубив моите торби.
handbag	ya za-gu-biv mo-ya-ta rach-na chan-ta	ја загубив мојата рачна чанта.
money	gi za-gu-biv pa-ri-te	ги загубив парите.
travellers cheques	gi za-gu-biv pat-nich-ki-te che-ko-vi	ги загубив патничките чекови.
passport	go za-gu-biv pa-so-shot	го загубив пасошот.
wallet	pa-rich-nik	паричник.

POLISH

QUICK REFERENCE

| Hello. | djen *do*-bri | Dzień dobry. |
| Goodbye. | do vee-*dze*-nya | Do widzenia. |

Yes./No.	tak/nye	Tak./Nie.
Excuse me.	pshe-*pra*-sham	Przepraszam.
May I?	chi *mo*-ge?	Czy mogę?
Sorry.	pshe-*pra*-sham	Przepraszam.
Please.	*pro*-she	Proszę.
Thank you.	djen-*koo*-ye	Dziękuję
You're welcome.	*pro*-she	Proszę.
Where's the ...?	gdje yest ...?	Gdzie jest ...?
What time is it?	*ktoo*-ra (yest) go-*djee*-na?	Która (jest) godzina?

I'd like a ...	po-*pro*-she ...	Poproszę ...
room	po-kooy	pokój
ticket to ...	bee-let do ...	bilet do ...
one-way ticket	*bee*-let *fyed*-nom *stro*-ne	bilet w jedną stronę
return ticket	*bee*-let po-*vrot*-ni	bilet powrotny

I (don't) understand.
    (nye) ro-*zoo*-myem   (Nie) rozumiem.
Do you speak English?
    chi pan/*pa*-nee *moo*-vee   Czy pan/pani mówi po
    po an-*gyel*-skoo?   angielsku?
Where are the toilets?
    gdje som to-a-*le*-ti?   Gdzie są toalety?
Turn left/right.
    pro-she *skren*-cheech   Proszę skręcić w
    fle-vo/*fpra*-vo   lewo/prawo.
Go straight ahead.
    pro-she ye-hach da-ley *pros*-to   Proszę jechać dalej prosto.
How much is it ...?
    ee-le to kosh-*too*-ye?   Ile to kosztuje?

1	*ye*-den	jeden	6	sheshch	sześć
2	dva	dwa	7	*she*-dem	siedem
3	tshi	trzy	8	*o*-shem	osiem
4	*chte*-ri	cztery	9	*dje*-vyench	dziewięć
5	pyench	pięć	10	*dje*-shench	dziesięć

POLISH

Polish, along with Czech and Slovak, is a western variety of the group of Slavonic languages, which covers a dozen languages spoken in a number of Central and Eastern European countries, including Russia, the Ukraine, Bulgaria, Serbia, Croatia, and the Czech and Slovak republics. The group is a branch of the large Indo-European family of languages which includes English, Greek and Latin, and has its distant origins back in ancient Sanskrit.

Although Polish is a language with a long, if obscure, history, its written form didn't actually develop until the Middle Ages. In medieval Poland, Latin was the lingua franca and the language used by the Crown's state offices, administration and the Church. The oldest known text in Polish, the song *Bogurodzica, 'Mother of God'*, was reputedly written in the 13th century and was the national anthem until the 18th century.

It wasn't until the Renaissance period that the Polish language came into wider use. The invention of printing contributed to the spread of books; the first printed text in Polish was published in 1475. During the course of the 16th century, Latin became largely dominated by Polish in both its spoken and written form. Polish literature began to develop at a remarkable pace and saw its first major achievements, with a range of Polish literature published.

The Latin alphabet was adapted to write the Polish language, but in order to represent the complex sounds of the tongue, a number of consonant clusters and diacritical marks were applied. In effect, the visual appearance of Polish is pretty fearsome for people from outside the Slavic circle, and undoubtedly it's not the world's easiest language to master. It has a complicated grammar, with word endings changing depending on case, number and gender, and its rules abound in exceptions. Yet, it's not the most difficult language either. Despite its bewildering appearance, Polish script is phonetic, largely consistent, and has a logical structure.

Today, Polish is the official language of Poland and is spoken by over 99 percent of the country's population of 39 million.

It's also spoken by roughly up to 10 million Poles scattered all over the world, with the largest Polish emigre community living in the USA.

Save for a few tiny areas, Polish has no pronounced regional dialects or variations, and sounds pretty much the same the breadth and width of the country. Understandably, there are some minor regional differences in the language's sound and melody, which locals can distinguish but for outsiders won't be noticeable.

Ideally, everyone who wants to travel in Poland should know some basic Polish – the more you know the easier your travel is likely to be and the more you'll get out of your time in the country. Enjoy your travels!

PRONUNCIATION

Unlike English, Polish is essentially a phonetic language, which means that there's a consistent relationship between pronunciation and spelling. In other words, a letter or a cluster of letters is always pronounced the same way. For example, Polish *a* has one pronunciation rather than the numerous pronunciations we find in English, such as the 'a' in 'cake', 'art' and 'all'.

Following are the transliterations used in this phrasebook to imitate their pronunciation. Consonants not mentioned here are pronounced as they are in English.

SUBJECT PRONOUNS		
SG		
I	ya	ja
you	ti	ty
he	on	on
she	ona	ona
it	ono	ono
PL		
we	mi	my
you	vi	wy
they (m; m+f)	oni	oni
they (f; m+f+neut)	one	one

POLISH

Transliterations
Vowels
Polish vowels are of roughly even length.

a   as the 'u' in 'cut'
e   as the 'e' in 'ten'
ee   similar to the 'i' in 'marine' but shorter
em   as the 'em' in 'emblem'
en   as the 'en' in 'engage'
i   as the 'i' in 'bit'
o   as the 'o' in 'not'
oo   as the 'u' in 'put'
om   as the 'om' in 'tomb'
on   as the 'on' in 'bond'

POLISH ALPHABET					
a	a	e	e	rz	zh/sh
ą	on/om	ę	en/em/e	s	s
b	b/p	g	g/k	sz	sh
c	ts	h	h	ś	sh
ć	ch	i	ee	u	oo
ch	h	j	y	w	v/f
cz	ch	ł	w	y	i
d	d/t	ń	n	z	z/s
dz	dz	o	o	ź	zh
dź	dj	ó	oo	ż	zh
dż	dj	r	r	szcz	shch

POLISH

Consonants

ch	as the 'ch' in 'church'
dj	as the 'j' in 'jam'
dz	as the 'ds' in 'adds up'
g	as the 'g' in 'get'
h	as the 'ch' in the Scottish 'loch'
n	as the 'ni' in 'onion'
r	always trilled
s	as the 's' in 'sin'
shch	as the 'shch' in 'fresh cheese'
ts	as the 'ts' in 'its'
w	as the 'w' in 'wine'
y	as the 'y' in 'yet'
zh	as the 's' in 'pleasure';
	as the 's' in 'pleasure', but softer

QUESTIONS

How?	yak?	Jak?
What?	tso?	Co?
When?	*kye*-di?	Kiedy?
Where?	gdje?	Gdzie?
Which?	*ktoo*-ri?	Który?
Who?	ktoo?	Kto?
Why?	dla-*che*-go?	Dlaczego?

Stress

As a rule, the stress falls on the second-last syllable of a word. In some words of foreign origin (mostly from Latin and Greek), stress falls on to the third-last syllable:

music	*moo*-zi-ka	*muzyka*
university	oo-nee-*ver*-si-tet	*uniwersytet*

GREETINGS & CIVILITIES

It's a good idea to use greetings whenever you approach someone. *Dzień dobry*, 'good morning/afternoon', is good in any situation, at any time of the day until evening. In more informal encounters with friends and the people you know well, and particularly with young people, *cześć*, 'hi', is commonly used as both a greeting or when saying goodbye.

Top Useful Phrases

Hello.	djen *do*-bri	*Dzień dobry.*
Hi.	cheshch	*Cześć.*
Goodbye.	do vee-*dze*-nya	*Do widzenia.*
Bye.	cheshch	*Cześć.*
See you later.	do zo-ba-*che*-nya	*Do zobaczenia.*
Good evening.	do-bri *vye*-choor	*Dobry wieczór.*
Goodnight.	do-*bra*-nots	*Dobranoc.*
Yes./No.	tak/nye	*Tak./Nie*
Excuse me.	pshe-*pra*-sham	*Przepraszam.*
Please.	*pro*-she	*Proszę.*
Thank you	djen-*koo*-ye	*Dziękuję*
(very much).	(*bar*-dzo)	(*bardzo*).
You're welcome.	*pro*-she	*Proszę.*
Excuse me; Sorry.	pshe-*pra*-sham	*Przepraszam.*
May I; Do you mind?	chi *mo*-ge?	*Czy mogę?*

Forms of Address

Poland is still very much a traditional territory where formal forms of address predominate, particularly among strangers. It's best (and safest) to use *pan*, 'Mr/Sir', and *pani*, 'Mrs/Madam', unless you're among friends or hanging around with younger people, where informality is the norm.

Mr	pan/pa-*no*-vye	*Pan/Panowie* (sg/pl)
Mrs	pa-nee/pa-nye	*Pani/Panie* (sg/pl)
Miss	pan-na/pan-ni	*Panna/Panny* (sg/pl)
Mr & Mrs	pan-stfo	*Państwo*
ladies and gentlemen	pan-stfo	*Państwo*

To strike up a conversation with someone in a formal situation, it's usual to start with *proszę pana* (lit: please, sir) or *proszę pani* (lit: please, madam).

POLISH

SMALL TALK
Meeting People

How are you?

   yak she pan/*pa*-nee ma?   *Jak się pan/pani ma?* (pol)

Fine, thanks. And you?

   djen-*koo*-ye, *do*-bzhe   *Dziękuję, dobrze.*

   ee pan/*pa*-nee?   *I pan/pani?* (pol)

My name's ...

   na-*zi*-vam she ...   *Nazywam się ... + surname* (pol)

   mam na *ee*-mye ...   *Mam na imię ... + first name* (inf)

I'm pleased to meet you.

   mee-wo mee *pa*-na/   *Miło mi pana/*

   pa-nyom *poz*-nach   *panią poznać.* (pol)

Do you live here?

   chi pan/*pa*-nee too   *Czy pan/pani tu*

   myesh-ka?   *mieszka?* (pol)

WHATS NEW?!

Polish has a number of expressions roughly equivalent to the English 'how are you' or 'what's new'. The following list features some of the most common ones.

They can be used interchangeably, and each is OK in any informal situation. Except for the last one, they're also suitable for most formal occasions. They don't require any specific answer other than just *Dziękuję, dobrze,* 'fine, thanks'.

tso *swi*-hach?	*Co słychać?*
tso no-*ve*-go?	*Co nowego?*
tso do-*bre*-go?	*Co dobrego?*
yak *zdro*-vye?	*Jak zdrowie?*
yak *ee*-dje?	*Jak idzie?*
yak *le*-chee?	*Jak leci?*

Occupations

What's your occupation?
  ya-kee yest *pa*-na/*pa*-nee   *Jaki jest pana/pani*
  za-voot?   *zawód?*

PAN & PANI
Remember that the terms *pan* and *pani* are polite ways of addressing a man or woman respectively.

I'm a/an ...	*yes*-tem ...	*Jestem* ...
artist	ar-*tis*-tom	*artystą* (m)
	ar-*tist*-kom	*artystką* (f)
businessperson	biz-nes-*me*-nem	*biznesmenem* (m)
	biz-nes-*men*-kom	*biznesmenką* (f)
doctor	le-*ka*-zhem	*lekarzem* (m)
	le-*kar*-kom	*lekarką* (f)
engineer	een-zhi-*nye*-rem	*inżynierem*
lawyer	prav-*nee*-kyem	*prawnikiem* (m)
	prav-*neech*-kom	*prawniczką* (f)
mechanic	me-ha-*nee*-kyem	*mechanikiem*
nurse	pye-leng-*nya*-zhem	*pielęgniarzem* (m)
	pye-leng-*nyar*-kom	*pielęgniarką* (f)
office worker	pra-tsov-*nee*-kyem	*pracownikiem*
	byoo-*ro*-vim;	*biurowym* (m)
	pra-tsov-*nee*-tsom	*pracownicą*
	byoo-*ro*-vom	*biurową* (f)
scientist	na-oo-*kof*-tsem	*naukowcem*
student	stoo-*den*-tem	*studentem* (m)
	stoo-*dent*-kom	*studentką* (f)
teacher	na-oo-chi-*che*-lem	*nauczycielem* (m)
	na-oo-chi-*chel*-kom	*nauczycielką* (f)
waiter	kel-*ne*-rem	*kelnerem* (m)
	kel-*ner*-kom	*kelnerką* (f)

I'm unemployed.
  yes-tem bez-ro-*bot*-ni/a   *Jestem bezrobotny/a.*

Nationalities

Where are you from?
skont pan/*pa*-nee po-*ho*-djee/yest?		*Skąd pan/pani pochodzi/jest?* (pol)

I'm from ...	*yes*-tem s ...	*Jestem z ...*
Australia	a-woos-*tra*-lyee	*Australii*
Canada	ka-*na*-di	*Kanady*
England	*an*-glee	*Anglii*
Europe	ew-*ro*-pi	*Europy*
Ireland	eer-*lan*-dyee	*Irlandii*
the USA	*sta*-noof zye-dno-*cho*-nih	*Stanów Zjednoczonych*

Religion

What's your religion?
ya-*kye*-go yest pan/*pa*-nee viz-*na*-nya?	*Jakiego jest pan/pani wyznania?* (pol)

I'm not religious.
yes-tem nye-vye-*zhon*-tsi/a	*Jestem niewierzący/a.*

I'm ...	*yes*-tem ...	*Jestem ...*
Buddhist	bood-*dis*-tom	*buddystą* (m)
	bood-*dist*-kom	*buddystką* (f)
Catholic	ka-to-*lee*-kyem	*katolikiem* (m)
	ka-to-*leech*-kom	*katoliczką* (f)
Hindu	heen-doo-*ees*-tom	*hinduistą* (m)
	heen-doo-*eest*-kom	*hinduistką* (f)
Jewish	*zhi*-dem	*żydem* (m)
	zhi-*doof*-kom	*żydówką* (m)
Muslim	moo-zoow-ma-*nee*-nem	*muzułmaninem* (m)
	moo-zoow-*man*-kom	*muzułmanką* (f)

Family

Are you married?
chi yest pan zho-*na*-ti?		*Czy jest pan żonaty?* (m)
chi yest *pa*-nee za-*men*-zhna?		*Czy jest pani zamężna?* (f)

I'm single.
yes-tem ka-va-*le*-rem/*pan*-nom	*Jestem kawalerem/panną.* (m/f)

I'm married.
 yes-tem zho-*na*-ti/   *Jestem żonaty/*
 za-*men*-zhna   *zamężna.* (m/f)
How many children do you have?
 ee-le pan/*pa*-nee ma *dje*-chee?   *Ile pan/pani ma dzieci?*
We don't have any children.
 nye *ma*-mi *dje*-chee   *Nie mamy dzieci.*

aunt	*chot*-ka	*ciotka*
brother	brat	*brat*
child	*djets*-ko	*dziecko*
children	*dje*-chee	*dzieci*
daughter	*tsoor*-ka	*córka*
family	ro-*djee*-na	*rodzina*
father	*oy*-chets	*ojciec*
grandfather	*dja*-dek	*dziadek*
grandmother	*bap*-ka	*babka*
husband	monsh	*mąż*
mother	*mat*-ka	*matka*
parents	ro-*djee*-tse	*rodzice*
sister	*shos*-tra	*siostra*
son	sin	*syn*
uncle	*voo*-yek	*wujek*
wife	*zho*-na	*żona*

Feelings

I'm sorry. (condolence)	*pshi*-kro mee	*Przykro mi.*
I'm sorry. (regret)	zha-*woo*-ye	*Żałuję.*
I'm afraid.	o-*ba*-vyam she	*Obawiam się.*
I'm cold/hot.	yest mee *zheem*-no/ go-*ron*-tso	*Jest mi zimno/ gorąco.*
I'm in a hurry.	*spye*-she she	*Spieszę się.*
I'm right.	mam *ra*-tsye	*Mam rację.*
I'm well.	*choo*-ye she *do*-bzhe	*Czuję się dobrze.*

POLISH

I'm ...	*yes*-tem ...	*Jestem ...*
angry	zwi/a	*zły/a*
grateful	*vdjench*-ni/a	*wdzięczny/a*
happy	shchen-*shlee*-vi/a	*szczęśliwy/a*
hungry	*gwod*-ni/a	*głodny/a*
sad	*smoot*-ni/a	*smutny/a*
sleepy	*shpyon*-tsi/a	*śpiący/a*
thirsty	spra-*gnyo*-ni/a	*spragniony/a*
tired	zmen-*cho*-ni/a	*zmęczony/a*
worried	za-nye-po-ko-*yo*-ni/a	*zaniepokojony/a*

BREAKING THE LANGUAGE BARRIER

Do you speak English?
    chi pan/*pa*-nee *moo*-vee   *Czy pan/pani mówi po*
    po an-*gyel*-skoo?   *angielsku?*

| Yes, I do. | tak, *moo*-vye | *Tak, mówię.* |
| No, I don't. | nye, nye *moo*-vye | *Nie, nie mówię.* |

Does anyone here speak English?
    chi ktosh too *moo*-vee po   *Czy ktoś tu mówi po*
    an-*gyel*-skoo?   *angielsku?*

Do you understand?
    chi pan/*pa*-nee ro-*zoo*-mye? *Czy pan/pani rozumie?*

I (don't) understand.
    (nye) ro-*zoo*-myem   *(Nie) rozumiem.*

Please speak more slowly.
    pro-she *moo*-veech *vol*-nyey *Proszę mówić wolniej.*

Please repeat that.
    pro-she to pof-*too*-zhich   *Proszę to powtórzyć.*

Please write it down.
    pro-she to na-*pee*-sach   *Proszę to napisać.*

BODY LANGUAGE

Body language in Poland is much the same as in most Western countries, so can be easily understood. For example, 'yes' is commonly indicated by nodding the head down and up, while 'no' is expressed by shaking the head from side to side.

PAPERWORK

address	*a*-dres	adres
age	vyek	wiek
date of birth	*da*-ta oo-ro-*dze*-nya	data urodzenia
date of expiry	*da*-ta vazh-*nosh*-chee	data ważności
date of issue	*da*-ta vi-*da*-nya	data wydania
driver's licence	*pra*-vo *yaz*-di	prawo jazdy
given names	ee-*myo*-na	imiona
marital status	stan tsi-*veel*-ni	stan cywilny
single	ka-*va*-ler	kawaler (m)
	pan-na	panna (f)
married	zho-*na*-ti	żonaty (m)
	za-*men*-zhna	zamężna (f)
nationality	na-ro-*do*-voshch	narodowość
passport	*pash*-port	paszport
passport number	*noo*-mer pash-*por*-too	numer paszportu
place of birth	*myey*-stse oo-ro-*dze*-nya	miejsce urodzenia
profession	*za*-voot	zawód
purpose of visit	tsel vee-*zi*-ti	cel wizyty
business	*pra*-tsa	praca
tourism	too-ris-*ti*-ka	turystyka
sex	pwech	płeć
signature	*pot*-pees	podpis
surname	naz-*vees*-ko	nazwisko
visa	*vee*-za	wiza

GETTING AROUND

Where's the ...?	gdje yest ...?	*Gdzie jest ...?*
bus station	*dvo*-zhets	*dworzec*
	aw-to-boo-*so*-vi	*autobusowy*
city centre	*tsen*-troom	*centrum*
road to ...	*dro*-ga do ...	*droga do ...*
train station	*dvo*-zhets ko-le-*yo*-vi	*dworzec kolejowy*

How do I get there?
    yak she tam *dos*-tach?   *Jak się tam dostać?*
Is it far from here?
    chi to da-*le*-ko stont?   *Czy to daleko stąd?*
Please show me (on the map).
    pro-she mee po-*ka*-zach   *Proszę mi pokazać (na mapie).*
    (na *ma*-pye)

Directions

Go straight ahead.	*pro*-she eeshch *pros*-to	*Proszę iść prosto.*
Turn left/right	*pro*-she *skren*-cheech	*Proszę skręcić w*
at the ...	*fle*-vo/*fpra*-vo na ...	*lewo/prawo na ...*
next corner	nay-*bleesh*-shim	*najbliższym*
	ro-goo	*rogu*
traffic lights	*shfya*-twah	*światłach*
roundabout	*ron*-dje	*rondzie*
end of the street	*kon*-tsoo oo-*lee*-tsi	*końcu ulicy*

behind	za	*za*
in front of	pshet	*przed*
far	da-*le*-ko	*daleko*
near	*blees*-ko	*blisko*
opposite	na-pshe-*cheef*-ko	*naprzeciwko*
here	too	*tu*
there	tam	*tam*

POLISH

north	*poow*-nots	*północ*
south	po-*wood*-nye	*południe*
east	fs-hoot	*wschód*
west	*za*-hoot	*zachód*

Booking Tickets

Where can I buy a ticket?
    gdje *mo*-ge *koo*-peech *bee*-let? *Gdzie mogę kupić bilet?*

I want to go to ...
| htse po-*ye*-hach do ... | *Chcę pojechać do ...* (bus, train) |
| htse po-*le*-chech do ... | *Chcę polecieć do ...* (plane) |

I'd like ...	po-*pro*-she ...	*Poproszę ...*
a one-way ticket	*bee*-let *fyed*-nom *stro*-ne	*bilet w jedną stronę*
a return ticket	*bee*-let po-*vrot*-ni	*bilet powrotny*
two tickets	dva *bee*-le-ti	*dwa bilety*

| 1st class | *pyer*-fshom *kla*-se | *pierwszą klasę* |
| 2nd class | *droo*-gom *kla*-se | *drugą klasę* |

Is there a discount for ...?	chi yest *zneesh*-ka dla ...?	*Czy jest zniżka dla ...?*
children	*dje*-chee	*dzieci*
pensioners	ren-*chees*-toof	*rencistów*
students	stoo-*den*-toof	*studentów*

Bus

Poland's intercity buses are cheap but rather slow. Buses mostly service medium and short-distance regional routes (long-distance travel is faster and more convenient by train).

Which bus goes to ...?
| *ktoo*-ri aw-*to*-boos | |
| *ye*-dje do ...? | *Który autobus jedzie do ...?* |

Does this bus go to ...?
| chi ten aw-*to*-boos | |
| *ye*-dje do ...? | *Czy ten autobus jedzie do ...?* |

How often do buses go to ...?
    yak *chen*-sto *ho*-dzom
    aw-to-*boo*-si do ...?
    Jak często chodzą
    autobusy do ...?

What time does the
bus leave/arrive?
    o *ktoo*-rey ot-*ho*-djee/
    pshi-*ho*-djee aw-to-boos?
    O której odchodzi/
    przychodzi autobus?

Please let me know
when we get to ...
    pro-she mi po-*vye*-djech gdi
    do-ye-*dje*-mi do ...
    Proszę mi powiedzieć gdy
    dojedziemy do ...

What time's	o *ktoo*-rey yest ...	*O której jest ...*
the ... bus?	aw-*to*-boos?	*autobus?*
first	*pyer*-fshi	*pierwszy*
last	os-*tat*-ni	*ostatni*
next	nas-*temp*-ni	*następny*

Train

Railway networks and trains are administered by the Polish State
Railways, commonly referred to as *PKP*. Services include EuroCity
(EC), InterCity (IC), express (Ex), fast and ordinary.

Which platform does the train
leave from?
    sktoo-*re*-go pe-*ro*-noo
    ot-*yesh*-dja po-chonk?
    Z którego peronu odjeżdża
    pociąg?

What station is this?
    ya-ka to *sta*-tsya?
    Jaka to stacja?

Does this train stop at ...?
    chi ten *po*-chonk
    za-tshi-*moo*-ye she f ...?
    Czy ten pociąg zatrzymuje się
    w ...?

I want to get off at ...
    htse *vi*-shonshch f ...
    Chcę wysiąść w ...

Is this seat free?
    chi to *myey*-stse yest *vol*-ne?
    Czy to miejsce jest wolne?

... train	*po*-chonk ...	*pociąg ...*
fast	pos-*pyesh*-ni	*pospieszny*
long-distance	da-le-ko-*byezh*-ni	*dalekobieżny*
slow	o-so-*bo*-vi	*osobowy*
suburban	pod-*myey*-skee	*podmiejski*

Taxi

Are you free?
  chi yest pan/*pa*-nee *vol*-ni/a?   *Czy jest pan/pani wolny/a?*
How much does it cost to go to ...?
  ee-le ben-dje kosh-*to*-vach do ...?   *Ile będzie kosztować do ...?*

Please take me to the/this ...	*pro*-she mnye za-*vyeshch* ...	*Proszę mnie zawieźć ...*
address	pot ten *a*-dres	*pod ten adres*
airport	na lot-*nees*-ko	*na lotnisko*
city centre	do *tsen*-troom	*do centrum*
hotel	do *te*-go ho-*te*-loo	*do tego hotelu*
train station	na *dvo*-zhets ko-le-*yo*-vi	*na dworzec kolejowy*

Continue straight ahead.
  pro-she ye-hach *da*-ley *pros*-to   *Proszę jechać dalej prosto.*
The next street to the left/right.
  nas-*temp*-na oo-*lee*-tsa na *le*-vo/*pra*-vo   *Następna ulica na lewo/prawo.*
Please stop at the corner.
  pro-she she za-*tshi*-mach na *ro*-goo   *Proszę się zatrzymać na rogu.*
Please stop here.
  pro-she she too za-*tshi*-mach   *Proszę się tu zatrzymać.*
Please wait here.
  pro-she too za-*che*-kach   *Proszę tu zaczekać.*

POLISH

Car

Where can I rent a car?
    gdje *mo*-ge vi-po-*zhi*-chich   *Gdzie moge wypożyczyć*
    sa-*mo*-hoot?   *samochód?*
How much is it daily/weekly?
    ee-le kosh-*too*-ye *djen*-nye/   *Ile kosztuje dziennie/*
    ti-god-*nyo*-vo?   *tygodniowo?*
Does that include insurance?
    chi oo-bes-pye-*che*-nye   *Czy ubezpieczenie*
    yest vlee-*cho*-ne?   *jest wliczone?*
Where's the nearest petrol station?
    gdje yest nay-*bleesh*-sha   *Gdzie jest najbliższa stacja*
    sta-tsya ben-zi-*no*-va?   *benzynowa?*
Can I park here?
    chi *mozh*-na too par-*ko*-vach?   *Czy można tu parkować?*
I need a mechanic.
    pot-she-*boo*-ye me-ha-*nee*-ka   *Potrzebuję mechanika.*

air	po-*vyet*-she	*powietrze*
battery	a-koo-moo-*la*-tor	*akumulator*
brakes	ha-*mool*-tse	*hamulce*
drivers licence	*pra*-vo *yaz*-di	*prawo jazdy*
engine	*sheel*-neek	*silnik*
garage	*var*-shtat	*warsztat*
motorway	aw-to-*stra*-da	*autostrada*
oil	*o*-ley	*olej*
self-service	sa-mo-op-*swoo*-ga	*samoobsługa*
speed limit	o-gra-nee-*che*-nye	*ograniczenie*
	prent-*kosh*-chee	*prędkości*
tyre	o-*po*-na	*opona*
... petrol	ben-*zi*-na ...	*benzyna ...*
leaded	o-wo-*vyo*-va	*ołowiowa*
regular	*zvik*-wa	*zwykła*
unleaded	be-so-wo-*vyo*-va	*bezołowiowa*

ACCOMMODATION

Where can I find a ...?	gdje *mo*-ge *zna*-leshch ...?	*Gdzie mogę znaleźć ...?*
camping ground	*kam*-peenk	*camping*
guesthouse	pen-*syo*-nat	*pensjonat*
hotel	*ho*-tel	*hotel*
motel	*mo*-tel	*motel*
youth hostel	sro-*nees*-ko mwo-dje-*zho*-ve	*schronisko młodzieżowe*

What's the address?
ya-kee yest *a*-dres?   *Jaki jest adres?*

At the Hotel

Do you have any rooms available?
chi som *vol*-ne po-*ko*-ye?   *Czy są wolne pokoje?*

How much does it cost per night?
ee-le kosh-*too*-ye za nots?   *Ile kosztuje za noc?*

I'd like a bed in a dorm.
po-*pro*-she o *woosh*-ko   *Poproszę o łóżko w sali*
fsa-lee zbyo-*ro*-vey   *zbiorowej.*

I'd like a ... room.	po-*pro*-she o *po*-kooy ...	*Poproszę o pokój ...*
single	yed-no-o-so-*bo*-vi	*jednoosobowy*
double	dvoo-o-so-*bo*-vi	*dwuosobowy*

I want a room with a ...	po-*pro*-she o *po*-kooy s ...	*Poproszę o pokój z ...*
bathroom	wa-*zhen*-kom	*łazienką*
shower	prish-*ni*-tsem	*prysznicem*
window	*ok*-nem	*oknem*

Can I see it?
chi *mo*-ge go zo-*ba*-chich?   *Czy mogę go zobaczyć?*

Are there any others?
chi som *een*-ne?   *Czy są inne?*

POLISH

Where's the bathroom?
    gdje yest wa-*zhen*-ka?   *Gdzie jest łazienka?*
Is there hot water (all day)?
    chi yest *chep*-wa *vo*-da   *Czy jest ciepła woda (przez*
    (pshes *tsa*-wi djen)?   *cały dzień)?*
Is there a discount for
children/students?
    chi yest *ya*-kash *zneesh*-ka   *Czy jest jakaś zniżka dla*
    dla *dje*-chee/stoo-*den*-toof?   *dzieci/studentów?*
It's fine. I'll take it.
    do-bzhe. *vez*-me go   *Dobrze. Wezmę go.*

Requests & Complaints

Can I deposit my valuables here?
    chi *mozh*-na too zde-po-*no*-   *Czy można tu zdeponować*
    vach *zhe*-chi var-tosh-*cho*-ve?   *rzeczy wartościowe?*
Can I use the telephone?
    chi *mozh*-na sko-*zhis*-tach   *Czy można skorzystać*
    ste-le-*fo*-noo?   *z telefonu?*
I can't open/close the
window/door.
    nye *mo*-ge ot-*fo*-zhich/   *Nie mogę otworzyć/*
    zam-knonch *ok*-na/dzhvee   *zamknąć okna/drzwi.*
The toilet doesn't flush.
    vo-da she nye *spoosh*-cha   *Woda się nie spuszcza.*
There's no hot water.
    nye ma *chep*-wey *vo*-di   *Nie ma ciepłej wody.*

AROUND TOWN

Where's a/the ...?	gdje yest ...?	*Gdzie jest ...?*
bank	bank	*bank*
city centre	*tsen*-troom	*centrum*
consulate	kon-*soo*-lat	*konsulat*
embassy	am-ba-*sa*-da	*ambasada*
police station	pos-te-*roo*-nek	*posterunek*
	po-*lee*-tsyee	*policji*
post office	*poch*-ta	*poczta*
public telephone	aw-*to*-mat	*automat*
	te-le-fo-*neech*-ni	*telefoniczny*
public toilet	to-a-*le*-ta	*toaleta publiczna*
	poo-*bleech*-na	
tourist	*byoo*-ro	*biuro informacji*
information	een-for-*ma*-tsyee	*turystycznej*
office	too-ris-*tich*-ney	

What time does it
open/close?

   o *ktoo*-rey she ot-*fye*-ra/   *O której się otwiera/*
za-*mi*-ka?   *zamyka?*

SIGNS

CIĄGNĄĆ	PULL
NIE PALIĆ	NO SMOKING
OTWARTE	OPEN
PCHAĆ	PUSH
TOALETY	TOILETS
WEJŚCIE	ENTRANCE
WSTĘP WOLNY	FREE ADMISSION
WSTĘP WZBRONIONY	NO ENTRY
WYJŚCIE	EXIT
WYJŚCIE AWARYJNE/	EMERGENCY EXIT
BEZPIECZEŃSTWA	
WZBRONIONY	PROHIBITED
ZAMKNIĘTE	CLOSED
ZAREZERWOWANY	RESERVED

POLISH

At the Post Office

I want to buy ...	htse *koo*-peech ..	*Chcę kupić ...*
postcards	poch-*toof*-kee	*pocztówki*
stamps	*znach*-kee	*znaczki*

How much does it cost
to send this to ...?

ee-le kosh-*too*-ye vi-*swa*-nye   *Ile kosztuje wysłanie*
te-go do ...?   *tego do ...?*

Where can I collect poste
restante mail?

gdje *mo*-ge o-*de*-brach post   *Gdzie mogę odebrać poste*
res-*tant?*   *restante?*

Is there any mail for me?

chi yest *ya*-kash   *Czy jest jakaś*
poch-ta dla mnye?   *poczta dla mnie?*

I want to send a ...	htse *vi*-swach ...	*Chcę wysłać ...*
letter	leest	*list*
parcel	*pach*-ke	*paczkę*

airmail	*poch*-ta lot-*nee*-cha	*poczta lotnicza*
envelope	ko-*per*-ta	*koperta*
letter	leest	*list*
mail box	*skshin*-ka poch-*to*-va	*skrzynka pocztowa*
parcel	*pach*-ka	*paczka*
postcode	kot poch-*to*-vi	*kod pocztowy*
post office	*poch*-ta	*poczta*
registered letter	leest po-le-*tso*-ni	*list polecony*
sender	na-*daf*-tsa	*nadawca*

Telephone

Could I please use the telephone?

chi *mo*-ge sko-*zhis*-tach   *Czy mogę skorzystać*
ste-le-*fo*-noo?   *z telefonu?*

I want to make a call to ...

htse za-*dzvo*-neech do ...   *Chcę zadzwonić do ...*

I want to make a
reverse-charges call.

htse za-*dzvo*-neech na kosht
a-bo-*nen*-ta

*Chcę zadzwonić na koszt
abonenta.*

The number is ...

to yest *noo*-mer ...

To jest numer ...

What's the area code for ...?

ya-kee yest *noo*-mer
kye-roon-*ko*-vi do ...?

*Jaki jest numer
kierunkowy do ...?*

It's engaged.

yest za-*yen*-te

Jest zajęte.

I've been cut off.

roz-won-*cho*-no mnye

Rozłączono mnie.

Can I speak to ...?

chi *mo*-ge *moo*-veech s ...?

Czy mogę mówić z ...?

Hello. (making a call) *ha*-lo *Halo.*
Hello. (answering a call) swoo-ham/*pro*-she *Słucham/Proszę.*

operator	te-le-fo-*nees*-ta	*telefonista* (m)
	te-le-fo-*neest*-ka	*telefonistka* (f)
phonecard	*kar*-ta te-le-fo-*neech*-na	*karta telefoniczna*
public	aw-*to*-mat	*automat*
telephone	te-le-fo-*neech*-ni	*telefoniczny*
telephone	te-*le*-fon	*telefon*
token	*zhe*-ton	*żeton*

Internet

Is there an Internet cafe
around here?

chi yest too *ya*-kash
ka-*vyar*-nyaeen-ter-ne-*to*-va?

*Czy jest tu jakaś kawiarnia
internetowa?*

I want to get access to the Internet.

shoo-kam dos-*tem*-poo do
een-ter-*ne*-too

*Szukam dostępu do
internetu.*

I want to check my email.

htse *sprav*-djeech *mo*-yom
poch-te e-lek-tro-*neech*-nom

*Chcę sprawdzić moją pocztę
elektroniczną.*

At the Bank

The usual place to change foreign cash in Poland is the *kantor,* or the private currency exchange office. They are ubiquitous in cities and towns and change most major currencies. They accept cash only, so if you want to change travellers cheques you'll need a *bank.*

Can I exchange money here?
  chi *mo*-ge too vi-*mye*-neech   *Czy mogę tu wymienić*
  pye-*nyon*-dze?   *pieniądze?*

I want to change ...	htse vi-*mye*-neech ...	*Chcę wymienić ...*
cash	go-*toof*-ke	*gotówkę*
foreign currency	*op*-tsom va-*loo*-te	*obcą walutę*
travellers cheques	*che*-kee	*czeki*
	po-*droozh*-ne	*podróżne*

ATM (automatic teller machine)	ban-*ko*-mat	*bankomat*
banknote	*ban*-knot	*banknot*
cash	go-*toof*-ka	*gotówka*
commission	pro-*vee*-zya	*prowizja*
credit card	*kar*-ta kre-di-*to*-va	*karta kredytowa*
currency	va-*loo*-ta	*waluta*
exchange rate	koors vi-*mya*-ni	*kurs wymiany*
money	pye-*nyon*-dze	*pieniądze*
signature	*pot*-pees	*podpis*
travellers cheque	chek po-*droozh*-ni	*czek podróżny*

Can I get a cash advance on
my credit card?
  chi *mo*-ge *dos*-tach za-*leech*-ke   *Czy mogę dostać zaliczkę na*
  na *mo*-yom *kar*-te kre-di-*to*-wom?   *moją kartę kredytową?*
The ATM has swallowed my card.
  ban-*ko*-mat *powk*-now   *Bankomat połknął*
  mo-yom *kar*-te   *moją kartę.*
What's the exchange rate?
  ya-kee yest koors vi-*mya*-ni?   *Jaki jest kurs wymiany?*

Can I use my credit card
in the automatic teller machine?

    chi *mo*-ge oo-*zhi*-vach *mo*-yom   *Czy mogę używać moją*
    kar-te kre-di-*to*-vom   *kartę kredytową*
    vban-ko-*ma*-che?   *w bankomacie?*

Is there a commission?

    chi yest *ya*-kash pro-*vee*-zya?   *Czy jest jakaś prowizja?*

INTERESTS & ENTERTAINMENT
Sightseeing

Can I get a guidebook/city map?

    chi dos-*ta*-ne pshe-*vod*-neek/   *Czy dostanę przewodnik/*
    plan *mya*-sta?   *plan miasta?*

What's that?

    tso to yest?   *Co to jest?*

Is there an admission charge?

    chi *pwa*-chee she za fstemp?   *Czy płaci się za wstęp?*

Can I take photographs?

    chi *mo*-ge *ro*-beech *zdyen*-cha?   *Czy mogę robić zdjęcia?*

art gallery	ga-*le*-rya *shtoo*-kee	*galeria sztuki*
botanic gardens	o-groot bo-ta-*neech*-ni	*ogród botaniczny*
castle	*za*-mek	*zamek*
cathedral	ka-*te*-dra	*katedra*
cemetery	*tsmen*-tash	*cmentarz*
church	*kosh*-choow	*kościół*
concert hall	*sa*-la kon-tser-*to*-va	*sala koncertowa*
monastery	*klash*-tor	*klasztor*
monument	*pom*-neek	*pomnik*
museum	*moo*-ze-oom	*muzeum*
old town	*sta*-re *mya*-sto	*stare miasto*
old town square	*ri*-nek	*rynek*
palace	*pa*-wats	*pałac*
stadium	*sta*-dyon	*stadion*
tourist	*byoo*-ro	*biuro informacji*
information	een-for-*ma*-tsyee	*turystycznej*
office	too-ris-*tich*-ney	
university	oo-nee-*ver*-si-tet	*uniwersytet*

POLISH

Going Out

What's on tonight?

tso *gra*-yom djeesh vye-*cho*-rem? *Co grają dziś wieczorem?*

Are there any tickets for ...?

chi som bee-*le*-ti na ...? *Czy są bilety na ...?*

I feel like going to a cinema/theatre.

mam o-*ho*-te pooyshch do *kee*-na/te-*a*-troo *Mam ochotę pójść do kina/teatru.*

Is there a jazz club around here?

chi yest too gdjesh kloop dje-*zo*-vi? *Czy jest tu gdzieś klub jazzowy?*

Where can you go to hear folk music?

gdje too *mozh*-na pos-*woo*-hach *moo*-zi-kee loo-*do*-vey? *Gdzie tu można posłuchać muzyki ludowej?*

What a great concert/film!

tso za fspa-*nya*-wi *kon*-tsert/ feelm! *Co za wspaniały koncert/ film!*

band	*groo*-pa / *zes*-poow	*grupa/zespół*
cinema	*kee*-no	*kino*
comedy	ko-*me*-dya	*komedia*
concert	*kon*-tsert	*koncert*
documentary	feelm	*film*
	do-koo-men-*tal*-ni	*dokumentalny*
drama	*dra*-mat	*dramat*
orchestra	or-*kyes*-tra	*orkiestra*
performance	pshet-sta-*vye*-nye	*przedstawienie*
play	*shtoo*-ka (te-a-*tral*-na)	*sztuka (teatralna)*
show	*spek*-takl	*spektakl*

POLISH

Sports & Interests

What do you do in your
spare time?

    tso *ro*-beesh *vvol*-nim   *Co robisz w wolnym*
    cha-she?   *czasie?* (inf)

Which kind of music do you like?

    ya-kom *moo*-zi-ke *loo*-beesh?   *Jaką muzykę lubisz?* (inf)

Do you like sport?

    chi *loo*-beesh sport?   *Czy lubisz sport?* (inf)

What sport do you play?

    ya-kee sport oo-*pra*-vyash?   *Jaki sport uprawiasz?* (inf)

Do you like ...?   chi *loo*-beesh ...?   *Czy lubisz ...?* (inf)

I like ...	*loo*-bye ...	*Lubię ...*
arts	*shtoo*-ke	*sztukę*
athletics	lek-ko-a-tle-*ti*-ka	*lekkoatletyka*
basketball	ko-shi-*koof*-ka	*koszykówka*
dance	*ta*-nyets	*taniec*
film	*kee*-no	*kino*
horseriding	*yaz*-da *kon*-na	*jazda konna*
literature	lee-te-ra-*too*-re	*literaturę*
music	*moo*-zi-ke	*muzykę*
photography	fo-to-*gra*-fye	*fotografię*
skiing	nar-*char*-stfo	*narciarstwo*
soccer	*peew*-ka *nozh*-na	*piłka nożna*
sports	sport	*sport*
swimming	pwi-*va*-nye	*pływanie*
tennis	*te*-nees	*tenis*
theatre	*te*-atr	*teatr*
travel	po-*droo*-zhe	*podróże*
TV	te-le-*vee*-zye	*telewizję*

Festivals

Wielkanoc vyel-*ka*-nots
Easter (March/April)
Easter is one of Poland's most important religious feasts.
Celebrations start on Palm Sunday (*Niedziela Palmowa*) and
go for the whole Holy Week (*Wielki Tydzień*) until Easter
Monday (*Poniedziałek Wielkanocny*). A solemn breakfast on
Easter Sunday (*Niedziela Wielkanocna*) features consecrated
food, including painted Easter eggs (*jajka wielkanocne*).

Święto Konstytucji 3-go Maja
shfyen-to kon-sti-*too*-tsyee tshe-*che*-go *ma*-ya
3 May Constitution Day
commemorates the constitution of 1791, passed in Warsaw
on the 3 May. It was the world's first fully liberal constitution
after the one in the USA.

Boże Ciało bo-zhe *cha*-wo
Corpus Christi (a Thursday in May or June)
this important religious day features church masses and proces-
sions all over the country, with the most elaborate celebrations
taking place in Łowicz, near Warsaw

Wniebowzięcie vnye-bo-*vzhen*-che
Assumption (15 August)
another major religious day, it culminates at Częstochowa,
Poland's spiritual capital, where mass pilgrimages from all
around the country come for this holy day

Święto Zmarłych shfyen-to *zmar*-wih
All Souls' Day (1 November)
a day of remembrance and prayer for the souls of the dead,
when people visit cemeteries to leave flowers, wreaths and lit
candles on the graves of relatives

Święto Niepodległości shfyen-to nye-pod-leg-*wosh*-chee
Independence Day (11 November)
held to commemorate 11 November 1918, when Poland regained
its independence after 123 years under foreign occupation

POLISH

Boże Narodzenie　　　　　*bo*-zhe na-ro-*dze*-nye
　　Christmas (25 December)
　　the most celebrated day is Christmas Eve (*Wigilia*), featuring a
　　solemn family supper which traditionally consists of 12 courses.
　　　After the meal, Santa Claus (*Święty Mikołaj*) hands out gifts
　　from under the Christmas tree (*choinka*). Many people then
　　go to church for midnight mass (*pasterka*).

IN THE COUNTRY
Weather

What's the weather like?
　　ya-ka yest po-*go*-da?　　　　*Jaka jest pogoda?*
The weather's fine/bad.
　　yest *wad*-nye/*bzhit*-ko　　　*Jest ładnie/brzydko.*
What a lovely day!
　　tso za tsoo-*dov*-ni djen!　　*Co za cudowny dzień!*
What's the weather
forecast for tomorrow?
　　ya-ka yest pro-*gno*-za　　　*Jaka jest prognoza pogody na*
　　po-*go*-di na *yoo*-tro?　　　　*jutro?*

Today it's ...	djeesh yest ...	*Dziś jest ...*
Tomorrow it'll be ...	*yoo*-tro *ben*-dje ...	*Jutro będzie ...*
cloudy	poh-*moor*-nye	*pochmurnie*
cold	*zheem*-no	*zimno*
hot	go-*ron*-tso	*gorąco*
sunny	swo-*nech*-nye	*słonecznie*
warm	*chep*-wo	*ciepło*
windy	*vyech*-nye	*wietrznie*

POLISH

climate	*klee*-mat	*klimat*
cloud	*hmoo*-ra	*chmura*
fog	mgwa	*mgła*
forecast	pro-*gno*-za	*prognoza*
frost	mroos	*mróz*
hail	grat	*grad*
heat	*oo*-paw	*upał*
ice	loot	*lód*
lightning	bwis-ka-*vee*-tsa	*błyskawica*
rain	deshch	*deszcz*
snow	shnyek	*śnieg*
storm	*boo*-zha	*burza*
sun	*swon*-tse	*słońce*
sunrise	fs-hoot *swon*-tsa	*wschód słońca*
sunset	za-hoot *swon*-tsa	*zachód słńca*
temperature	tem-pe-ra-*too*-ra	*temperatura*
thunder	gzhmot	*grzmot*
weather	po-*go*-da	*pogoda*
wind	vyatr	*wiatr*

Camping

Is there a campsite nearby?
    chi yest *ya*-keesh *kam*-peenk   *Czy jest jakiś camping w*
    fpob-*lee*-zhoo?   *pobliżu?*

Where's the nearest campsite?
    gdje yest nay-*bleesh*-shi   *Gdzie jest najbliższy camping?*
    kam-peenk?

Where can we pitch our tent?
    gdje *mozh*-na *roz*-beech   *Gdzie można rozbić namiot?*
    na-myot?

How much is it for a ...?	*ee*-le kosh-*too*-ye za ...?	*Ile kosztuje za ...?*
car	sa-*mo*-hoot	*samochód*
caravan	pshi-*che*-pe	*przyczepę*
night	nots	*noc*
person	o-*so*-be	*osobę*
tent	*na*-myot	*namiot*

camping	*kam*-peenk	*camping*
campsite	*kam*-peenk	*camping*
caravan (trailer)	pshi-*che*-pa	*przyczepa*
	(kam-peen-*go*-va)	*(campingowa)*
mattress	ma-*te*-rats	*materac*
penknife	stsi-*zo*-rik	*scyzoryk*
sleeping bag	*shpee*-voor	*śpiwór*
tent	*na*-myot	*namiot*
torch (flashlight)	la-*tar*-ka	*latarka*

FOOD

Poland has for centuries been a cosmopolitan country, and its food has been influenced by various cuisines. The Jewish, Lithuanian, Belarusian, Ukrainian, Russian, Hungarian and German traditions have all made their mark. Polish food is hearty and filling – with thick soups and sauces, potatoes and dumplings – and is rich in meat, if not in vegetables.

Vegetarian Meals

I'm a vegetarian.

yes-tem ya-*ro*-shem/   *Jestem jaroszem/*
ya-*rosh*-kom   *jaroszką.* (m/f)

I don't eat chicken or fish.

nye *ya*-dam *dro*-byoo   *Nie jadam drobiu*
a-nee rip   *ani ryb.*

Do you have any
vegetarian dishes?

chi som ya-*kyesh da*-nya   *Czy są jakieś dania*
yar-skye?   *jarskie?*

Does this dish have meat?

chi to *da*-nye za-*vye*-ra   *Czy to danie zawiera*
myen-so?   *mięso?*

Can I get this
without meat?

chi *mo*-ge to *dos*-tach bes   *Czy mogę to dostać bez*
myen-sa?   *mięsa?*

POLISH

MENU DECODER

Appetisers

barszcz (czerwony) ...	beetroot broth ...
ukraiński	with beans and potatoes
zabielany	with sour cream
z pasztecikiem	with a savoury pastry filled with minced meat
z uszkami	with small, ravioli-style dumplings stuffed with meat
befsztyk tatarski	raw minced sirloin served with onion, raw egg yolk and often chopped dill cucumber
botwinka	summertime soup made from the stems and leaves of baby beetroot
bukiet z jarzyn	mixed raw and pickled vegetables
grzyby (marynowane)	(marinated) wild mushrooms
kapuśniak	sauerkraut soup with potatoes
krupnik	thick barley soup with a variety of vegetables and small chunks of meat
jajko w majonezie	boiled egg in mayonnaise
łosoś wędzony	smoked salmon
mizeria	sliced, fresh cucumber in sour cream
sałatka jarzynowa	salad made with potato, vegetable and mayonnaise
zapiekanka	half bread roll with cheese and mushrooms, baked and served hot
zupa ...	... soup
cebulowa	onion
grochowa	lentil
jarzynowa	vegetable
ogórkowa	dill cucumber
pomidorowa	tomato
rybna	fish
ziemniaczana	potato

Main Meals

bigos	thick stew made of sauerkraut, cabbage and various kinds of meat and seasonings
gołąbki	cabbage leaves stuffed with minced beef and rice
kaczka ...	duck ...
pieczona	roasted
z jabłkami	roasted and stuffed with apples

MENU DECODER

karp ...	... carp
po grecku	served cold in an onion and tomato sauce
kurczak ...	... chicken
pieczony	roasted
z rożna	spit-roasted
naleśniki	crepes served with various fillings
pasztecik	savoury pastry stuffed with minced meat
pierogi ...	dumplings ...
ruskie	with soft, white cheese and potatoes
z kapustą i grzybami	with sauerkraut and wild mushrooms
z serem	with cottage cheese
placki kartoflane/	pancakes made with grated potatoes,
ziemniaczane	egg and flour. Usually served with
	sour cream and/or sugar.
polędwica pieczona	roasted sirloin steak
pyzy	potato dumplings, steamed
sałatka ...	... salad
jarzynowa	potato, vegetable and mayonnaise
owocowa	fruit
z pomidorów	tomato
schab pieczony	roasted pork seasoned with prunes
sos ...	... sauce/gravy
chrzanowy	horseradish
grzybowy	mushroom
pomidorowy	tomato
zrazy zawijane	beef rolls stuffed with mushrooms and/or
	bacon, stewed and served in a
	sour-cream sauce
sztuka mięsa	boiled beef served with horseradish

Desserts

budyń	milk pudding
ciastko	pastry; small cake
gofry	waffles
jabłecznik	apple strudel
keks	fruit cake
knedle	dumplings filled with plums, cherries or apples
lody	ice cream
makowiec	poppyseed strudel
melba	ice cream with fruit and whipped cream
szarlotka	apple cake
tort	cream cake

POLISH

Breakfast

Polish breakfast usually includes bread with butter, cheese, jam, and sausage or ham. Eggs are fairly popular, and can be prepared in a variety of guises such as soft-boiled, fried and scrambled. All this is washed down with a glass of tea or a cup of coffee with milk.

bacon	*bo*-chek	*boczek*
bread	hlep	*chleb*
butter	*ma*-swo	*masło*
cheese	ser	*ser*
ham	*shin*-ka	*szynka*
jam	djem	*dżem*
margarine	mar-ga-*ri*-na	*margaryna*
sausage	kyew-*ba*-sa	*kiełbasa*
toast	*gzhan*-ka	*grzanka*
eggs	*yay*-ka	*jajka*
fried eggs	*yay*-ka sa-*dzo*-ne	*jajka sadzone*
hard/soft-boiled egg	*yay*-ko na	*jajko na*
	tfar-do/*myenk*-ko	*twardo/miękko*
scrambled eggs	ya-yech-*nee*-tsa	*jajecznica*

Non-Alcoholic Drinks

black coffee	*char*-na *ka*-va	*czarna kawa*
coffee (with milk)	*ka*-va (*zmle*-kyem)	*kawa (z mlekiem)*
herbal tea	her-*ba*-ta zho-*wo*-va	*herbata ziołowa*
tea with milk	ba-*var*-ka	*bawarka*
tea ...	her-*ba*-ta ...	*herbata ...*
with sugar	*stsoo*-krem	*z cukrem*
without sugar	bes *tsoo*-kroo	*bez cukru*
with a slice of lemon	stsi-*tri*-nom	*z cytryną*
juice	sok	*sok*
milk	*mle*-ko	*mleko*
(mineral) water	*vo*-da	*woda*
	(mee-ne-*ral*-na)	*(mineralna)*

Alcoholic Drinks

Cheers!	na *zdro*-vye!	*Na zdrowie!*
beer	*pee*-vo	*piwo*
brandy	*ko*-nyak	*koniak*
champagne	*sham*-pan	*szampan*
liqueur	*lee*-kyer	*likier*
mulled beer/	*gzha*-nyets *spee*-va	*grzaniec z piwa/wine*
wine	*zvee*-na	
plum brandy	shlee-vo-*vee*-tsa	*śliwowica*
rum	room	*rum*
vodka	*voot*-ka	*wódka*
... wine	*vee*-no ...	*wino ...*
dry	vi-*trav*-ne	*wytrawne*
red	cher-*vo*-ne	*czerwone*
sweet	*swot*-kye	*słodkie*
white	*bya*-we	*białe*

NA ZDROWIE!

Vodka is Poland's national drink, and Poles claim it was invented here. Polish vodka comes in a number of colours and flavours, from very sweet to extra-dry.

bimber	*beem*-ber	home-distilled vodka
jarzębiak	ya-*zhem*-byak	vodka flavoured with rowanberry
myśliwska	mish-*leef*-ska	vodka flavoured with juniper berries
nalewka	na-*lef*-ka	home-made spirit made from vodka flavoured with herbs and berries
wiśniówka	veesh-*nyoof*-ka	cherry-flavoured vodka
wódka (f)	*voot*-ka	vodka
żubrówka	zhoo-*broof*-ka	bison vodka (flavoured with grass from the Białowieża forest on which bison feed)
żytnia	*zhit*-nya	dry vodka

POLISH

AT THE MARKET

Basics

bread	hlep	chleb
butter	*ma*-swo	masło
cheese	ser	ser
egg	*yay*-ko	jajko
flour	*mon*-ka	mąka
ham	*shin*-ka	szynka
margarine	mar-ga-*ri*-na	margaryna
milk	*mle*-ko	mleko
salt	sool	sól
sugar	*tsoo*-kyer	cukier
yogurt	*yo*-goort	jogurt

Meat & Poultry

beef	vo-wo-*vee*-na	wołowina
chicken	*koor*-chak	kurczak
ham	*shin*-ka	szynka
lamb	ba-ra-*nee*-na	baranina
meat	*myen*-so	mięso
pork	vyep-sho-*vee*-na	wieprzowina
sausage	kyew-*ba*-sa	kiełbasa
turkey	*een*-dik	indyk
veal	che-len-*chee*-na	cielęcina

Seafood

fish	*ri*-ba	ryba
lobster	*ho*-mar	homar
mussels	*maw*-zhe	małże
oysters	os-*tri*-gee	ostrygi
shrimp	kre-*vet*-ka	krewetka

Vegetables

(green) beans	fa-*so*-la	fasola
	shpa-*ra*-go-va	(szparagowa)
beetroot	boo-*ra*-kee	buraki
cabbage	ka-*poos*-ta	kapusta

AT THE MARKET

capsicum	pa-*pri*-ka	papryka
carrot	*mar*-hef	marchew
cauliflower	ka-*la*-fyor	kalafior
celery	*se*-ler	seler
cucumber	o-*goo*-rek	ogórek
lettuce	sa-*wa*-ta	sałata
onion	tse-*boo*-la	cebula
peas	*gro*-shek	groszek
potato	*zhem*-nyak	ziemniak
	kar-*to*-fel	kartofel
pumpkin	*di*-nya	dynia
spinach	*shpee*-nak	szpinak
tomato	po-*mee*-dor	pomidor
vegetables	va-*zhi*-va	warzywa
	ya-*zhi*-ni	jarzyny

Fruit

apple	*yap*-ko	jabłko
apricot	mo-*re*-la	morela
banana	*ba*-nan	banan
fig	*fee*-ga	figa
grape	vee-no-*gro*-no	winogrono
lemon	tsi-*tri*-na	cytryna
orange	po-ma-*ran*-cha	pomarańcza
peach	bzhos-*kfee*-nya	brzoskwinia
pear	*groosh*-ka	gruszka
plum	*shleef*-ka	śliwka
wild stawberry	po-*zhom*-ka	poziomka

Herbs, Spices & Condiments

garlic	*chos*-nek	czosnek
ginger	*eem*-beer	imbir
parsley	pyet-*roosh*-ka	pietruszka
pepper	pyepsh	pieprz
salt	sool	sól

POLISH

SHOPPING

English	Pronunciation	Polish
Where's the ...?	gdje yest ...?	*Gdzie jest ...?*
bakery	pye-*kar*-nya	*piekarnia*
bookshop	kshen-*gar*-nya	*księgarnia*
chemist	ap-*te*-ka	*apteka*
delicatessen	de-lee-ka-*te*-si	*delikatesy* (pl)
greengrocer	sklep o-vo-*tso*-vo va-*zhiv*-ni	*sklep owocowo-warzywny*
grocer	sklep spo-*zhif*-chi	*sklep spożywczy*
laundry	*pral*-nya	*pralnia*
stationers	sklep pa-pyer-*nee*-chi	*sklep papierniczy*

Do you have ...?		
chi som ...?		*Czy są ...?*
Can I pay by credit card?		
chi *mo*-ge za-*pwa*-cheech *kar*-tom kre-di-*to*-vom?		*Czy mogę zapłacić kartą kredytową?*

Essential Groceries

English	Pronunciation	Polish
bread	hlep	*chleb*
butter	*ma*-swo	*masło*
cheese	ser	*ser*
chocolate	che-ko-*la*-da	*czekolada*
eggs	*yay*-ka	*jajka*
flour	*mon*-ka	*mąka*
fruit	o-*vo*-tse	*owoce*
ham	*shin*-ka	*szynka*
margarine	mar-ga-*ri*-na	*margaryna*
matches	za-*paw*-kee	*zapałki*
milk	*mle*-ko	*mleko*
salt	sool	*sól*
shampoo	*sham*-pon	*szampon*
soap	*mi*-dwo	*mydło*
sugar	*tsoo*-kyer	*cukier*
toilet paper	*pa*-pyer to-a-le-*to*-vi	*papier toaletowy*
toothpaste	*pas*-ta do *zem*-boof	*pasta do zębów*
washing powder	*pro*-shek do *pra*-nya	*proszek do prania*
yogurt	*yo*-goort	*jogurt*

POLISH

Souvenirs

amber	*boor*-shtin	*bursztyn*
glassware	shkwo	*szkło*
handicrafts	vi-*ro*-bi shtoo-kee	*wyroby sztuki*
	loo-*do*-vey	*ludowej*
jewellery	bee-zhoo-*te*-rya	*biżuteria*
posters	pla-*ka*-ti	*plakaty*

Clothing

belt	*pa*-sek	*pasek*
bra	byoos-*to*-nosh	*biustonosz*
clothing	oo-*bra*-nye	*ubranie*
coat	pwashch	*płaszcz*
dress	soo-*kyen*-ka	*sukienka*
jacket	*koor*-tka	*kurtka*
jumper (sweater)	*sfe*-ter	*sweter*
shirt	ko-*shoo*-la	*koszula*
shoes	*boo*-ti	*buty*
skirt	spood-*nee*-tsa	*spódnica*
socks	skar-*pet*-kee	*skarpetki*
trousers	*spod*-nye	*spodnie*
T-shirt	pot-ko-*shool*-ka	*podkoszulka*
underpants (men's)	*slee*-pi	*slipy*
underpants (women's)	*fee*-gee	*figi*

Materials

ceramic	tse-ra-*mee*-ka	*ceramika*
cotton	ba-*veoo*-na	*bawełna*
glass	shkwo	*szkło*
gold	*zwo*-to	*złoto*
leather	*skoo*-ra	*skóra*
linen	*pwoot*-no	*płótno*
silk	*yet*-vap	*jedwab*
silver	*sre*-bro	*srebro*
wood	*dzhe*-vo	*drzewo*
wool	*veoo*-na	*wełna*

Colours

black	*char*-ni	czarny
blue	nye-*byes*-kee	niebieski
brown	bron-*zo*-vi	brązowy
green	zhe-*lo*-ni	zielony
orange	po-ma-ran-*cho*-vi	pomarańczowy
pink	roo-*zho*-vi	różowy
purple	fyo-le-*to*-vi	fioletowy
red	cher-*vo*-ni	czerwony
white	*bya*-wi	biały
yellow	*zhoow*-ti	żółty

Toiletries

comb	*gzhe*-byen	grzebień
condoms	pre-zer-va-*ti*-vi/	prezerwatywy
	kon-*do*-ni	kondony
moisturiser	krem	krem
	na-veel-zha-*yon*-tsi	nawilżający
razor	ma-*shin*-ka do	maszynka do
	go-*le*-nya	golenia
sanitary napkins	pot-*pas*-kee	podpaski
	hee-gye-*neech*-ne	higieniczne
shaving cream	krem do go-*le*-nya	krem do golenia
tampons	tam-*po*-ni	tampony
toothbrush	shcho-*tech*-ka do	szczoteczka do

Photography

Can I have this film processed here?
chi *mo*-ge too vi-*vo*-wach   *Czy mogę tu wywołać*
ten feelm?   *ten film?*

How much is it to process this film?
ee-le kosh-*too*-ye vi-vo-*wa*-nye   *Ile kosztuje wywołanie*
te-go *feel*-moo?   *tego filmu?*

When will it be ready?
kye-di *ben*-dje go-*to*-vi?   *Kiedy będzie gotowy?*

I need new batteries for this camera.
    pot-she-*boo*-ye *no*-ve ba-*te*-rye   *Potrzebuję nowe baterie*
    do *te*-go a-pa-*ra*-too   *do tego aparatu.*
My camera doesn't work.
    mooy a-*pa*-rat nye *dja*-wa   *Mój aparat nie działa.*

battery	ba-*te*-rya	*bateria*
B&W film	feelm char-no-*bya*-wi	*film czarno-biały*
camera	a-*pa*-rat (fo-to-gra-*feech*-ni)	*aparat (fotograficzny)*
colour film	feelm ko-lo-*ro*-vi	*film kolorowy*
enlargement	po-vyenk-*she*-nye	*powiększenie*
lens	o-*byek*-tiv	*obiektyw*
light meter	shvya-*two*-myesh	*światłomierz*
slides	*slay*-di	*slajdy*
videotape	*tash*-ma vee-*de*-o	*taśma video*

Stationery & Publications

Is there an English-language
bookshop here?
    chi yest too kshen-*gar*-nya   *Czy jest tu księgarnia*
    an-glo-yen-*zich*-na?   *anglojęzyczna?*

book	*kshon*-shka	*książka*
city map	plan *mya*-sta	*plan miasta*
dictionary	*swov*-neek	*słownik*
envelope	ko-*per*-ta	*koperta*
magazine	ma-*ga*-zin	*magazyn*
map	*ma*-pa	*mapa*
newspaper	ga-*ze*-ta	*gazeta*
paper	*pa*-pyer	*papier*
pen (ballpoint)	dwoo-*go*-pees	*długopis*
pencil	o-*woo*-vek	*ołówek*
postcard	poch-*toof*-ka	*pocztówka*

Smoking

A packet of cigarettes, please.
po-*pro*-she *pach*-ke
pa-pye-*ro*-soof

*Poproszę paczkę
papierosów.*

Are these cigarettes strong or mild?
chi te pa-pye-*ro*-si som
mots-ne chi wa-*god*-ne?

*Czy te papierosy są mocne czy
łagodne?*

Do you have a light?
chi *mo*-ge *pro*-sheech o *o*-gyen?

Czy moge prosić o ogień.

Please don't smoke here.
pro-she too nye *pa*-leech

Proszę tu nie palić.

Can I smoke here?
chi *mo*-ge too *pa*-leech?

Czy moge tu palić?

cigarettes	pa-pye-*ro*-si	*papierosy*
cigarette paper	bee-*boow*-ka do	*bibułka do*
	pa-pye-*ro*-soof	*papierosów*
lighter	za-pal-*neech*-ka	*zapalniczka*
matches	za-*paw*-kee	*zapałki*
pipe	*fay*-ka	*fajka*
tobacco	*ti*-ton	*tytoń*
with filter	*sfeel*-trem	*z filtrem*
without filter	bes *feel*-tra	*bez filtra*

Sizes & Comparisons

also	*tak*-zhe	*także*
enough	vis-*tar*-chi	*wystarczy*
big	*doo*-zhi/a	*duży/a*
less	mnyey	*mniej*
a little bit	*tro*-he	*trochę*
more	*vyen*-tsey	*więcej*
much/many	*doo*-zho	*dużo*
small	*ma*-wi/a	*mały/a*
too little	za *ma*-wo	*za mało*
too much/many	za *doo*-zho	*za dużo*

HEALTH

Where's the	gdje yest nay-	*Gdzie jest naj-*
nearest ...?	*bleesh*-shi/a ...?	*bliższy/a ...?*
chemist	ap-*te*-ka	*apteka*
dentist	den-*tis*-ta	*dentysta*
doctor	*le*-kash	*lekarz*
hospital	*shpee*-tal	*szpital*

I'm sick.
   yes-tem *ho*-ri/a   *Jestem chory/a.*
My friend is sick.
   mooy pshi-*ya*-chel yest *ho*-ri   *Mój przyjaciel jest chory.*
   mo-ya pshi-ya-*choow*-ka yest *ho*-ra   *Moja przyjaciółka jest chora.*
It hurts here.
   too-tay mnye *bo*-lee   *Tutaj mnie boli.*
I'm pregnant.
   yes-tem *fchon*-zhi   *Jestem w ciąży.*

Parts of the Body

My ... hurts.	*bo*-lee mnye ...	*Boli mnie ...*
ankle	*kos*-tka	*kostka*
arm	*ra*-mye	*ramię*
back	*ple*-tsi	*plecy*
chest	pyersh	*pierś*
ear	*oo*-ho	*ucho*
eye	*o*-ko	*oko*
finger	*pa*-lets	*palec*
foot	*sto*-pa	*stopa*
hand	*ren*-ka	*ręka*
head	*gwo*-va	*głowa*
heart	*ser*-tse	*serce*
knee	ko-*la*-no	*kolano*
leg	*no*-ga	*noga*
mouth	*oos*-ta	*usta*
muscle	*myen*-shen	*mięsień*
nose	nos	*nos*
shoulder	*ra*-mye	*ramię*
skin	*skoo*-ra	*skóra*
stomach	zho-*won*-dek	*żołądek*
throat	*gar*-dwo	*gardło*

POLISH

Ailments

I'm ill.	*yes*-tem *ho*-ri/a	*Jestem chory/a.* (m/f)
I feel nauseous.	mam *mdwosh*-chee	*Mam mdłości.*
I've been vomiting.	vi-myo-to-*va*-wem/wam	*Wymiotowałem/łam.* (m/f)
I can't sleep.	nye *mo*-ge spach	*Nie mogę spać.*

I have (a/an) ...	mam ...	*Mam ...*
allergy	oo-choo-*le*-nye	*uczulenie*
cold	pshe-zhem-*bye*-nye	*przeziębienie*
constipation	zat-far-*dze*-nye	*zatwardzenie*
cough	*ka*-shel	*kaszel*
diarrhoea	bye-*goon*-ke/roz-vol-*nye*-nye	*biegunkę/rozwolnienie*
fever	go-*ronch*-ke	*gorączkę*
headache	bool *gwo*-vi	*ból głowy*
indigestion	nye-*strav*-noshch	*niestrawność*
infection	za-ka-*zhe*-nye	*zakażenie*
lice	fshi	*wszy*
low/high blood pressure	*nees*-kye/vi-*so*-kye cheesh-*nye*-nye	*niskie/wysokie ciśnienie*
migraine	mee-*gre*-ne	*migrenę*
pain	bool	*ból*
sore throat	bool *gar*-dwa	*ból gardła*
sprain	zveeh-*nyen*-che	*zwichnięcie*
stomachache	bool zho-*won*-tka	*ból żołądka*
travel sickness	ho-*ro*-be lo-ko-mo-*tsiy*-nom	*chorobę lokomocyjną*
venereal disease	ho-*ro*-be ve-ne-*rich*-nom	*chorobę weneryczną*
worms	ro-*ba*-kee	*robaki*

POLISH

At the Chemist

Where's the nearest (all-night) chemist?

gdje yest nay-*bleesh*-sha (tsa-wo-*nots*-na) ap-*te*-ka? — *Gdzie jest najbliższa (całonocna) apteka?*

Please give me something for ...

po-*pro*-she tsosh na ... — *Poproszę coś na ...*

antibiotic	an-ti-*byo*-tik	*antybiotyk*
antiseptic	an-ti-*sep*-tik	*antyseptyk*
aspirin	as-pee-*ri*-na	*aspiryna*
bandage	*ban*-dash	*bandaż*
Band-aids	plas-ter zo-pa-*troon*-kyem	*plaster z opatrunkiem*
condom	pre-zer-va-*ti*-va/ *kon*-don	*prezerwatywa/ kondon*
contraceptive	*shro*-dek an-ti-kon-tsep-*tsiy*-ni	*środek antykoncepcyjny*
cough medicine	lek na *ka*-shel	*lek na kaszel*
laxative	*shro*-dek pshe-chish-cha-*yon*-tsi	*środek przeczyszczający*
painkiller	*shro*-dek pshe-cheef-boo-*lo*-vi	*środek przeciwbólowy*
sleeping pills	*prosh*-kee na-*sen*-ne	*proszki nasenne*

At the Dentist

I have a toothache.	*bo*-lee mnye zomp	*Boli mnie ząb.*
I have a cavity.	mam *djoo*-re	*Mam dziurę.*

I've lost a filling.

vi-*pad*-wa mee *plom*-ba — *Wypadła mi plomba.*

I've broken my tooth.

zwa-maw mee she zomp — *Złamał mi się ząb.*

My gums hurt.

djon-swa mnye *bo*-lom — *Dziąsła mnie bolą.*

I don't want it extracted.

nye htse go *vir*-vach — *Nie chcę go wyrwać.*

Please give me an anaesthetic.

pro-she o znye-choo-*le*-nye — *Proszę o znieczulenie.*

TIME & DATES

What time is it?
   ktoo-ra (yest) go-*djee*-na?   *Która (jest) godzina?*
It's one o'clock.
   (yest) *pyer*-fsha   *(Jest) pierwsza.*
It's ten o'clock.
   (yest) dje-*shon*-ta   *(Jest) dziesiąta.*
Half past one.
   fpoow do *droo*-gyey   *Wpół do drugiej.*

in the morning	*ra*-no	*rano*
in the afternoon	po po-*wood*-nyoo	*po południu*
in the evening	vye-*cho*-rem	*wieczorem*
at night	*vno*-tsi	*w nocy*

Days

Monday	po-nye-*dja*-wek	*poniedziałek*
Tuesday	*fto*-rek	*wtorek*
Wednesday	*shro*-da	*środa*
Thursday	*chfar*-tek	*czwartek*
Friday	*pyon*-tek	*piątek*
Saturday	so-*bo*-ta	*sobota*
Sunday	nye-*dje*-la	*niedziela*

Months

January	*sti*-chen	*styczeń*
February	*loo*-ti	*luty*
March	*ma*-zhets	*marzec*
April	*kfye*-chen	*kwiecień*
May	may	*maj*
June	*cher*-vyets	*czerwiec*
July	*lee*-pyets	*lipiec*
August	*sher*-pyen	*sierpień*
September	*vzhe*-shen	*wrzesień*
October	pazh-*djer*-neek	*październik*
November	lees-*to*-pat	*listopad*
December	*groo*-djen	*grudzień*

Seasons

spring	*vyos*-na	*wiosna*
summer	*la*-to	*lato*
autumn	*ye*-shen	*jesień*
winter	*zee*-ma	*zima*

Present

now	*te*-ras	*teraz*
today	djeesh/*djee*-shay	*dziś/dzisiaj*
this morning	djeesh *ra*-no	*dziś rano*
this afternoon	djeesh po po-*wood*-nyoo	*dziś po południu*
tonight	djeesh vye-*cho*-rem	*dziś wieczorem*
this week	ftim ti-*god*-nyoo	*w tym tygodniu*
this month	ftim mye-*shon*-tsoo	*w tym miesiącu*
this year	ftim *ro*-koo	*w tym roku*

Past

yesterday	*fcho*-ray	*wczoraj*
day before yesterday	pshet-*fcho*-ray	*przedwczoraj*
yesterday ...	*fcho*-ray ...	*wczoraj ...*
morning	*ra*-no	*rano*
afternoon	po po-*wood*-nyoo	*po południu*
last ...	*vzesh*-wim ...	*w zeszłym ...*
week	ti-*god*-nyoo	*tygodniu*
month	mye-*shon*-tsoo	*miesiącu*
year	*ro*-koo	*roku*

Future

tomorrow	*yoo*-tro	*jutro*
day after tomorrow	po-*yoo*-tshe	*pojutrze*
tomorrow ...	*yoo*-tro ...	*jutro ...*
morning	*ra*-no	*rano*
afternoon	po po-*wood*-nyoo	*po południu*
evening	vye-*cho*-rem	*wieczorem*

next ...	*fpshish*-wim ...	*w przyszłym ...*
week	ti-*god*-nyoo	*tygodniu*
month	mye-*shon*-tsoo	*miesiącu*
year	*ro*-koo	*roku*

During the Day

dawn	shfeet	*świt*
day	djen	*dzień*
early	*fchesh*-nye	*wcześnie*
hour	go-*djee*-na	*godzina*
midnight	*poow*-nots	*północ*
morning	*ra*-no	*rano*
night	nots	*noc*
noon	po-*wood*-nye	*południe*
sunrise	fs-hoot *swon*-tsa	*wschód słońca*
sunset	*za*-hoot *swon*-tsa	*zachód słońca*

NUMBERS & AMOUNTS

0	*ze*-ro	*zero*
1	*ye*-den	*jeden*
2	dva	*dwa*
3	tshi	*trzy*
4	*chte*-ri	*cztery*
5	pyench	*pięć*
6	sheshch	*sześć*
7	*she*-dem	*siedem*
8	*o*-shem	*osiem*
9	*dje*-vyench	*dziewięć*
10	*dje*-shench	*dziesięć*
11	ye-de-*nash*-che	*jedenaście*
12	dva-*nash*-che	*dwanaście*
13	tshi-*nash*-che	*trzynaście*
14	chter-*nash*-che	*czternaście*
15	pyent-*nash*-che	*piętnaście*
16	shes-*nash*-che	*szesnaście*
17	she-dem-*nash*-che	*siedemnaście*
18	o-shem-*nash*-che	*osiemnaście*
19	dje-vyet-*nash*-che	*dziewiętnaście*

20	dva-*djesh*-cha	*dwadzieścia*
21	dva-*djesh*-cha ye-den	*dwadzieścia jeden*
22	dva-*djesh*-cha dva	*dwadzieścia dwa*
30	tshi-*djesh*-chee	*trzydzieści*
40	chter-*djesh*-chee	*czterdzieści*
50	pyen-*dje*-shont	*pięćdziesiąt*
60	shesh-*dje*-shont	*sześćdziesiąt*
70	she-dem-*dje*-shont	*siedemdziesiąt*
80	o-shem-*dje*-shont	*osiemdziesiąt*
90	dje-vyen-*dje*-shont	*dziewięćdziesiąt*
100	sto	*sto*
101	sto *ye*-den	*sto jeden*
110	sto *dje*-shench	*sto dziesięć*
1000	*ti*-shonts	*tysiąc*
10,000	*dje*-shench ti-*shen*-tsi	*dziesięć tysięcy*
100,000	sto ti-*shen*-tsi	*sto tysięcy*
one million	*mee*-lyon	*milion*

Useful Words

dozen	*too*-zheen	*tuzin*
few	*keel*-ka	*kilka*
less	mnyey	*mniej*
a little (amount)	nye-*doo*-zho	*niedużo*
many/much	*doo*-zho	*dużo*
more	*vyen*-tsey	*więcej*
once	ras	*raz*
percent	*pro*-tsent	*procent*
some	*tro*-he	*trochę*
too little	za *ma*-wo	*za mało*
too much/many	za *doo*-zho	*za dużo*
twice	dva *ra*-zi	*dwa razy*

POLISH

ABBREVIATIONS

al	avenue
dr	doctor
godz	hour
itp	etc
LOT	LOT Polish Airlines
min	minute
ONZ	United Nations
PKP	Polish State Railways
PKS	Polish State Bus Company
PTSM	Polish Youth Hostel Association
PTTK	Polish Tourist Association
PZM	Polish Motoring Association
ul	street

EMERGENCIES

Help!	ra-*toon*-koo!;	*Ratunku!*;
	po-*mo*-tsi!;	*Pomocy!*;
	na *po*-mots!	*Na pomoc!*
Stop!	stach!	*Stać!*
Go away!	*pro*-she o-deyshch!	*Proszę odejść!* (pol)
	o-deych!	*Odejdź!* (inf)
Thief!	zwo-djey!	*Złodziej!*
Fire!	po-zhar!;	*Pożar!*;
	pa-lee she!	*Pali się!*
Watch out!	*pro*-she oo-*va*-zhach!	*Proszę uważać!* (pol)
	oo-*va*-zhay!	*Uważaj!* (inf)

Call a/an ...!	*pro*-she *vez*-vach ...!	*Proszę wezwać ...!*
ambulance	ka-*ret*-ke	*karetkę*
doctor	le-*ka*-zha	*lekarza*

I'm ill.
    yes-tem *ho*-ri/a   *Jestem chory/a.*

My friend is ill.
    mooy pshi-*ya*-chel yest *ho*-ri   *Mój przyjaciel jest chory.*
    mo-ya pshi-ya-*choow*-ka   *Moja przyjaciółka jest chora.*
    yest *ho*-ra

I have medical insurance.
    mam oo-bes-pye-*che*-nye   *Mam ubezpieczenie medyczne.*
    me-*dich*-ne

Please call the police!
    pro-she *vez*-vach po-*lee*-tsye!   *Proszę wezwać policję!*

Where's the police station?
    gdje yest pos-te-*roo*-nek   *Gdzie jest posterunek policji?*
    po-*lee*-tsyee?

It's an emergency.
    to yest *na*-gwi pshi-*pa*-dek   *To jest nagły przypadek.*

Could you help me please?
    pro-she mee *po*-moots?   *Proszę mi pomóc.*

I'm lost.
    zgoo-*bee*-wem/wam she   *Zgubiłem/łam się.* (m/f)

Where are the toilets?
    gdje som to-a-*le*-ti?   *Gdzie są toalety?*

POLISH

Dealing with the Police

I want to report a/an ...	htse *zgwo*-sheech ...	*Chcę zgłosić ...*
accident	vi-*pa*-dek	*wypadek*
attack	na-pat	*napad*
loss	*zgoo*-be	*zgubę*
theft	*kra*-djesh	*kradzież*

I've lost ...	zgoo-*bee*-wem/wam ...	*Zgubiłem/łam* (m/f) ...
My ... has/have been stolen.	skra-*djo*-no mee ...	*Skradziono mi ...*
backpack	*ple*-tsak	*plecak*
camera	a-*pa*-rat (fo-to-gra-*feech*-ni)	*aparat (fotograficzny)*
car	sa-*mo*-hoot	*samochód*
credit card	*kar*-te kre-di-*to*-vom	*kartę kredytową*
money	pye-*nyon*-dze	*pieniądze*
passport	*pash*-port	*paszport*
travellers cheques	*che*-kee po-*droozh*-ne	*czeki podróżne*
wallet	*por*-tfel	*portfel*

I've been assaulted.	na-pad-*nyen*-to na mnye	*Napadnięto na mnie.*
I've been robbed.	o-bra-bo-*va*-no mnye	*Obrabowano mnie.*
I've been raped.	zgvaw-*tso*-no mnye	*Zgwałcono mnie.*
My possessions are insured.	*mo*-ye *zhe*-chi son oo-bes-pye-*cho*-ne	*Moje rzeczy są ubezpieczone.*

POLISH

ROMANIAN

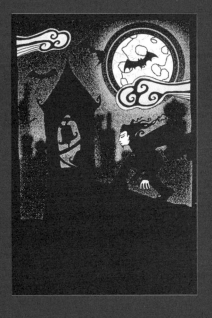

ROMANIAN

QUICK REFERENCE

English	Pronunciation	Romanian
Yes./No.	*dah/nu*	Da./Nu.
Hello.	*bu-nă zi-uah*	Bună ziua.
Goodbye.	*lah re-ve-de-re*	La revedere.
Excuse me.	*sku-zah-tsi-mă*	Scuzaţi-mă.
May I?	*se poah-te?*	Se poate?
Do you mind?	*per-mi-te-tsi?*	Permiteţi?
Sorry.	*î-mi pah-re rău*	Îmi pare rău.
Please.	*vă rog*	Vă rog.
Thank you.	*mul-tsu-mesk*	Mulţumesc.
You're welcome.	*ku plă-che-re*	Cu plăcere.
Where's ...?	*un-de es-te ...?*	Unde este ...?
What time is it?	*kît e cheah-sul?*	Cît e ceasul?
How much is it?	*kît kos-tă?*	Cît costă?
How do I get to ...?	*kum ah-zhung lah ...?*	Cum ajung la ...?

Turn left/right at the ...	*în-toahr-che lah* stîn-gah/ dreahp-tah lah ...	Întoarce la stînga/ dreapta la ...
next corner	*ur-mă-to-rul kolts*	următorul colţ
traffic lights	*se-mah-for*	semafor

Go straight ahead.
du-te drept î-nah-in-te Du-te drept înainte.
Where are the toilets?
un-de es-te to-ah-le-tah? Unde este toaleta?
I (don't) understand.
eu (nu) în-tse-leg Eu (nu) înţeleg.
Do you speak English?
vor-bitsi en-gle-zah? Vorbiţi engleza?

I'd like a ...	*ahsh do-ri ...*	Aş dori ...
single room	*o kah-me-ră de o per-soah-nă*	o cameră de o persoană
one-way ticket	*un bi-let dus*	un bilet dus
return ticket	*un bi-let dus în-tors*	un bilet dus-întors

1	*u-nu*	unu	6	*shah-se*	şase
2	*doi*	doi	7	*shahp-te*	şapte
3	*trei*	trei	8	*opt*	opt
4	*pah-tru*	patru	9	*no-uă*	nouă
5	*chinchi*	cinci	10	*ze-che*	zece

Romanian belongs to the group of Romance languages, the modern descendants of Latin which include French, Italian, Portuguese and Spanish. The Romanian language represents the present stage of evolution of the Latin spoken in the Danubian provinces, in the north-eastern part of the Roman Empire, since early Roman occupation. The transformation process of Latin into Romanian, between the 5th and 8th centuries AD, saw the development of the main characteristics of Romanian which distinguish it today.

The sounds of the Romanian language and its grammatical structure are mostly of Latin origin. Words of Latin origin are in widespread use to describe everyday concepts such as parts of the human body, various kinds of animals, food, natural phenomena, and notions concerning time.

Contact with other peoples, has resulted in words of Hungarian, Turkish, Greek and Bulgarian origin penetrating the Romanian vocabulary. However, Romanian's close connection to Latin has caused Romania to be considered a Latin island in a Slav sea. Romania has 22 million inhabitants, all of whom speak Romanian. The language is also spoken in areas of the former USSR, and there are half a million Romanian speakers in Hungary and around 200,000 in Bulgaria.

Romanian uses different forms of words to refer to men and women. As a rule, feminine forms of words are distinguished from masculine by the suffix *a* or *ă*. In this chapter, the two forms are generally separated by a slash. For example, *fermier/ă*, 'farmer', means that a male farmer is a *fermier* and a female farmer is a *fermieră*.

ROMANIAN

PRONUNCIATION

Romanian is written more or less as it's spoken, although a few letters are unfamiliar to English speakers. Pronunciation is particularly straightforward as each letter is always pronounced in the same way.

You'll discover that it's a very easy language to read, and Romanians will be very appreciative if you make an effort to speak the language.

Vowels

Double vowels, such as *ii* or *ee*, are pronounced as two distinct sounds.

a	ah	an 'ah' sound, as the 'a' in 'father'
ă	ă	as the 'a' in 'sofa'
e	e	as the 'e' in 'souffle'
i	i	as the 'i' in 'it'
î	î	purse your lips to say 'ee' but say 'oo'
o	o	as the 'o' in 'pot'
u	u	as the 'u' in 'pull'

Consonants

Double consonants such as 'nn', are pronounced as two distinct sounds. Consonants not described here are pronounced as in English.

c	ch	before 'e' and 'i', as the 'ch' in 'church';
	k	elsewhere, as the 'k' in 'king'
ch	k	always as the 'k' in 'king'
g	j	before 'e' and 'i', as the 'j' in 'jeans';
	g	elsewhere, as the 'g' in 'get'
gh	g	always as the 'g' in 'get'
r	r	trilled
ş	sh	as the 'sh' as in 'ship'
ţ	ts	as the 'ts' in 'cats'

ROMANIAN

Stress

There's no general rule for stress in Romanian. It falls on different syllables in different words, and just has to be learned.

SUBJECT PRONOUNS		
SG		
I	eu	*eu*
you (inf)	tu	*tu*
you (pol)	dum-neah-voahs-tră	*Dumneavoastră*
he/it	el	*el*
she	eah	*ea*
PL		
we	noi	*noi*
you (inf)	voi	*voi*
you (pol)	dum-neah-voahs-tră	*Dumneavoastră*
they (m)	ei	*ei*
they (f/neut)	ele	*ele*

Note that it's not always necessary to use subject pronouns as they are indicated on verb endings.

QUESTION WORDS		
How?	kum?	*Cum?*
What?	che?	*Ce?*
When?	kind?	*Cînd?*
Where?	un-de?	*Unde?*
Which?	ka-re?	*Care?*
Who?	chi-ne? ka-re?	*Cine? Care?*
Why?	de che?	*De ce?*

ROMANIAN

GREETINGS & CIVILITIES
Top Useful Phrases

Hello.	bu-nă zi-uah	*Bună ziua.*
Goodbye.	lah re-ve-de-re	*La revedere.*
Yes./No.	dah/nu	*Da./Nu.*
Excuse me.	sku-zah-tsi-mă	*Scuzaţi-mă.*
Please.	vă rog	*Vă rog.*
Thank you.	mul-tsu-mesk	*Mulţumesc.*
Many thanks.	mul-te mul-tsu-miri	*Multe mulţumiri.*

May I? Do you mind?	
se poah-te? per-mi-te-tsi?	*Se poate? Permiteţi?*
Sorry. (excuse me, forgive me)	
î-mi pah-re răů	*Îmi pare rău.*
That's fine. You're welcome.	
n-ah-vetsi pen-tru che.	*N-aveţi pentru ce.*
ku plă-che-re	*Cu plăcere.*

Greetings

Good morning.	bu-nă di-mi-neah-tsah	*Bună dimineaţa.*
Good afternoon.	bu-nă zi-uah	*Bună ziua.*
Good evening.	bu-nă seah-rah	*Bună seara.*
Good night.	no-ahp-te bu-nă.	*Noapte bună.*
How are you?	che mai fa-che-tsi?	*Ce mai faceţi?*
Well, thanks.	bi-ne, mul-zu-mesk	*Bine, mulţumesc.*

Forms of Address

Madam/Mrs	doahm-nah	*Doamna (Dna)*
Sir/Mr	domn	*Domn*
Mr ...	dom-nu(l) ...	*Domnu(l) ...*
Miss (Dşoara)	dom-ni-shoah-rah ...	*Domnişoara ...*
companion/ friend	pri-e-ten	*prieten*

Different forms are used when addressing someone directly:

Madam/Mrs	doahm-nă	*Doamnă* (sg)
	doahm-ne-lor	*Doamnelor* (pl)
Sir/Mr	dom-nu-le	*Domnule* (sg)
	dom-ni-lor	*Domnilor* (pl)
Miss	dom-ni-shoah-ră	*Domnişoară* (sg)
	dom-ni-shoah-re-lor	*Domnişoarelor* (pl)
companion/	pri-e-te-ne	*prietene* (sg)
friend	pri-e-te-ni-lor	*prietenilor* (pl)

SMALL TALK
Meeting People

What's your name?
    kum vă nu-mitsi?   *Cum vă numiţi?*

My name's ...
    nu-me-le meu es-te ...   *Numele meu este ...*

I'd like to introduce you to ...
    ash do-ri să vă pre-zint ...   *Aş dori să vă prezint ...*

Pleased to meet you.
    sînt în-kîn-taht să vă   *Sînt încîntat să vă cunosc.*
    ku-nosk

How old are you?
    che vîr-stă ah-vetsi?   *Ce vîrstă aveţi?*
    kîtsi ahni ah-vetsi?   *Cîţi ani aveţi?*

I'm ... years old.
    (eu) ahm ... ahni   *(Eu) am ... ani.*

ROMANIAN

Nationalities

Where are you from?
de un-de sîn-tetsi? *De unde sînteţi?*

I'm from ...	sînt din ...	Sînt din ...
Australia	ah-us-trah-li-ah	*Australia*
Canada	kah-nah-dah	*Canada*
England	ahn-gli-ah	*Anglia*
Ireland	ir-lahn-dah	*Irlanda*
New Zealand	nouah ze-e-lahn-d	*Noua Zeelandă*
Scotland	sko-tsi-ah	*Scoţia*
United States	stah-te-le u-ni-te	*Statele Unite*
Wales	tsah-ra gah-li-lor	*ţara Galilor*

Occupations

What do you do?
ku che vă o-ku-pahtsi? *Cu ce vă ocupaţi?*

I'm unemployed.
sînt sho-mer *Sînt şomer.*

WHATS NEW?!

• The arrival of a guest is signified by a spider in the home – the bigger the spider, the more important the guest.

• It's bad luck to kiss or shake hands across a threshold.

• On the streets, expect good luck if someone crosses your path with a pail of water.

ROMANIAN

I'm a/an ...	(eu) sînt ...	(Eu) sînt ...
artist	ahr-tist/ă	artist/ă
businessman	om de ah-fah-cheri	om de afaceri
businesswoman	fe-mei-ah de ah-fah-cheri	femeia de afaceri
doctor	dok-tor/me-dik	doctor/medic
computer programmer	pro-grah-mah-tor	programator
engineer	in-ji-ner/ă	inginer/ă
farmer	fer-mi-er/ă	fermier/ă
journalist	zi-ah-rist/ă	ziarist/ă
lawyer	ah-vo-kaht/ă	avocat/ă
manual worker	mun-chi-tor/ mun-chi-toah-re	muncitor/ muncitoare (m/f)
mechanic	me-kah-nik	mecanic
nurse	ah-sis-tent/ă me-di-kahl/ă	asistent/ă medical/ă
office worker	funk-tsi-o-nahr/ă	funcționar/ă
scientist	cher-che-tă-tor/ shti-in-tsi-fik	cercetător/ științific
student	stu-dent/ă	student/ă
teacher	pro-fe-sor/ pro-fe-soah-ră	profesor/ profesoară (m/f)
waiter	kel-ner/kel-ne-ri-tsă	chelner/ chelneriță (m/f)
writer	skri-i-tor/ skri-i-toah-re	scriitor/ scriitoare (m/f)

Religion

What's your religion?
che re-li-ji-e ah-vetsi? *Ce religie aveți?*

I'm not religious.
nu sînt re-li-ji-os/ re-li-ji-oah-să *Nu sînt religios/ religioasă. (m/f)*

ROMANIAN

I'm ...	(eu) sînt ...	*Eu sînt ...*
Buddhist	bu-dist/ă	*budist/ă*
Catholic	kah-to-lik/ă	*catolic/ă*
Christian	kresh-tin/ă	*creştin/ă*
Hindu	hin-dus/ă	*hindus/ă*
Jewish	e-vre-u/e-vrei-kă	*evreu/evreică* (m/f)
Muslim	mu-sul-mahn/ă	*musulman/ă*

Family

Are you married?
   sîn-te-tsi kă-să-to-rit/ă   *Sînteţi căsătorit/ă?*

I'm single.
   nu sînt kă-să-to-rit/ă.   *Nu sînt căsătorit/ă.*

I'm married.
   sînt kă-să-to-rit/ă   *Sînt căsătorit/ă.*

How many children do
you have?
   kî-tsi ko-pii ah-vetsi?   *Cîţi copii aveţi?*

I don't have any children.
   nu ahm nichi un ko-pil   *Nu am nici un copil.*

I have a daughter/a son.
   ahm o fi-i-kă/un fiu   *Am o fiică/un fiu.*

brother	frah-te	*frate*
children	ko-pii	*copii*
daughter	fi-i-kă	*fiică*
family	fah-mi-li-e	*familie*
father	tah-tă	*tată*
grandfather	bu-nik	*bunic*
grandmother	bu-ni-kă	*bunică*
husband	sots	*soţ*
mother	mah-mă	*mamă*
sister	so-ră	*soră*
son	fi-u	*fiu*
wife	so-tsi-e	*soţie*

Feelings

I like ...
îmi *plah*-che ...   *Îmi place ...*
I don't like ...
nu-mi *plah*-che ...   *Nu-mi place ...*
I'm sorry. (condolence)
îmi *pah*-re rău   *Îmi pare rău.*
I'm grateful.
(eu) sînt re-ku-nos-kă-*tor*   *(Eu) sînt recunoscător.*

I'm ...	îmi es-te ...	*Îmi este ...*
cold	re-che	*rece*
hot	kahld	*cald*
hungry	foah-me	*foame*
thirsty	se-te	*sete*

I'm right	ahm drep-tah-te	*Am dreptate.*
I'm sleepy.	sînt som-no-ros/	*Sînt somnoros/*
	som-no-roah-să	*somnoroasă.* (m/f)

I'm ...	(eu) sînt ...	*(Eu) sînt ...*
angry	su-pă-raht/ă	*supărat/ă*
happy	fe-ri-chit/ă	*fericit/ă*
sad	trist/ă	*trist/ă*
tired	o-bo-sit/ă	*obosit/ă*
well	bi-ne	*bine*
worried	în-gri-zho-raht/ă	*îngrijorat/ă*

ROMANIAN

BREAKING THE LANGUAGE BARRIER

Do you speak English?
    vor-bitsi en-gle-zah?   *Vorbiţi engleza?*

Does anyone speak English?
    vor-besh-te chi-ne-vah en-gle-zah?   *Vorbeşte cineva engleza?*

I don't speak ...
    nu vor-besk ...   *Nu vorbesc ...*

I (don't) understand.
    eu (nu) în-tse-leg   *Eu (nu) înţeleg.*

Could you speak more slowly, please?
    ah-tsi pu-teah vor-bi mahi rahr?   *Aţi putea vorbi mai rar?*

Could you repeat that?
    ah-tsi pu-teah re-pe-tah?   *Aţi putea repeta?*

How do you say ...?
    kum spu-netsi ...?   *Cum spuneţi ...?*

What does ... mean?
    che în-seahm-nă ...?   *Ce înseamnă ...?*

SIGNS	
CALD	HOT
DESCHIS	OPEN
FUMATUL INTERZIS	NO SMOKING
IEŞIRE (DE URGENŢĂ)	(EMERGENCY) EXIT
INCHIS	CLOSED
INFORMAŢII	INFORMATION
INTERZIS	PROHIBITED
INTRARE	ENTRANCE
INTRAREA INTERZISĂ	NO ENTRY
INTRARE LIBERĂ	FREE ADMISSION
NU FUMAŢI	NO SMOKING
NU INTRAŢI	NO ENTRY
RECE	COLD
TOALETA	TOILETS
RESERVAT	RESERVED

ROMANIAN

BODY LANGUAGE

There are no aspects of body language that are likely to cause confusion – the 'body talk' of Romanians doesn't differ from that of most other Europeans. It's worth remembering, though, that it's often expected of Romanian men to kiss the hand of a woman they meet.

PAPERWORK

address	ah-dre-sah	*adresa*
age	vîr-stah	*vîrsta*
birth certificate	cher-ti-fi-kaht de nahsh-te-re	*certificat de naştere*
date of birth	dah-tah nahsh-te-rii	*data naşterii*
driver's licence	per-mis de kon-du-che-re	*permis de conducere*
identification	le-ji-ti-ma-tsi-e (de i-den-ti-tah-te)	*legitimaţie (de identitate)*
marital status	stah-tu-tul mah-tri-mo-ni-ahl	*statutul matrimonial*
name	nu-me(le)	*nume(le)*
nationality	nah-tsi-o-nah-li-tah-teah	*naţionalitatea*
passport	pah-shah-port	*paşaport*
passport number	nu-mă-rul pah-shah-por-tu-lui	*numărul paşaportului*
place of birth	lo-kul nahsh-te-rii	*locul naşterii*
profession	pro-fe-si-ah	*profesia*
reason for travel	mo-ti-vul kă-lă-to-ri-ei	*motivul călătoriei*
religion	re-li-ji-ah	*religia*
sex	se-xul	*sexul*
visa	vi-zah	*viza*

ROMANIAN

GETTING AROUND

What time does the ... leave/arrive?	lah che o-ră pleah-kă/ so-sesh-te ...?	*La ce oră pleacă/soseşte ...?*
aeroplane	ah-vi-o-nul	*avionul*
boat	vah-po-rul	*vaporul*
bus	ahu-to-bu-zul	*autobuzul*
train	tre-nul	*trenul*
tram	trahm-vah-iul	*tramvaiul*

Directions

Where's ...?
 un-de es-te ...? *Unde este ...?*
How do I get to ...?
 kum ah-zhung lah ...? *Cum ajung la ...?*
Is it far/close by?
 es-te de-pahr-te/ *Este departe/*
 ah-proah-pe de ah-ichi? *aproape de aici?*
Can I walk there?
 pot să merg pe zhos *Pot să merg pe jos pînă*
 pî-nă ah-ko-lo? *acolo?*
Can you show me (on the map)?
 pu-tetsi să-mi ah-ră-tahtsi *Puteţi să-mi arătaţi*
 (pe hahr-tă)? *(pe hartă)?*
Are there other means of getting there?
 sînt ahl-te mize-loah-che *Sînt alte mijloace*
 de trahn-sport pen-tru *de transport pentru*
 ah-zhun-je ah-ko-lo? *ajunge acolo?*
I want to go to ...
 vreahu sămerg lah ... *Vreau să merg la ...*
Go straight ahead.
 du-te drept î-nah-in-te *Du-te drept înainte.*
It's further down.
 es-te mai de-pahr-te *Este mai departe.*

Turn left/right ...	în-toahr-che lah stîn-gah/dreahp-tah ...	*Întoarce la stînga/ dreapta la ...*
at the next corner	lah ur-mă-to-rul kolts	*la următorul colţ*
at the traffic lights	lah se-mah-for	*la semafor*

behind	în spah-te-le	*în spatele*
far	de-pahr-te	*departe*
in front of	în fah-tsah	*în faţa*
near	ah-proah-pe	*aproape*
opposite	o-pus	*opus*

north	nord/miah-ză-noahp-te	*nord/miazănoapte*
south	sud/miah-ză-zi	*sud/miazăzi*
east	est/ră-să-rit/o-ri-ent	*est/răsărit/orient*
west	vest/a-pus/ ok-chi-dent	*vest/apus/ occident*

Booking Tickets

Where can I buy a ticket?
  un-de pot kum-pă-*rah* un bi-*let?*   *Unde pot cumpăra un bilet?*
I want to go to ...
  vreahu să merg lah ...   *Vreau să merg la ...*
I'd like to book a seat to ...
  ahsh do-*ri* săre-*serv* un loc lah ...   *Aş dori să rezerv un loc la ...*
Can I get a stand-by ticket?
  pot pri-*mi* un bi-*let* în   *Pot primi un bilet în*
  pi-*chioah*-re?   *picioare?*

ROMANIAN

I'd like ...	ahsh do-*ri* ...	*Aş dori ...*
a one-way ticket	un bi-*let* dus	*un bilet dus*
a return ticket	un bi-*let* dus	*un bilet dus-*
	în-*tors*	*întors*
two tickets	do-uă bi-*le*-te	*două bilete*
... fare	bi-let ...	*bilet ...*
child's	pen-tru ko-pii	*pentru copii*
pensioner	pen-si-o-nahri	*pensionari*
student	pen-tru stu-den-tsi	*pentru studenţi*
1st class	klah-sah în-tîi	*clasa întîi*
2nd class	klah-sah ah douah	*clasa a doua*

Bus

Where's the bus stop?
un-de es-te stah-tsi-ah de
ahu-to-buz?
Unde este staţia de autobuz?

Which bus goes to ...?
kah-re ahu-to-buz merje lah ...? *Care autobuz merge la ...?*

Does this bus go to ...?
ah-chest ahu-to-buz
merje lah ...?
Acest autobuz merge la ...?

How often do buses pass by?
kît de des trec ahu-to-bu-ze-le? *Cît de des trec autobuzele?*

Could you let me know when
we get to ...?
potsi să-mi spui kînd
ah-zhun-jem lah ...?
Poţi să-mi spui cînd ajungem la ...?

I want to get off!
vreahu să ko-bor! *Vreau să cobor!*

What time's the ... bus?	kînd es-te ... ahu-to-buz?	*Cînd este ... autobuz?*
first	pri-mul	*primul*
last	ul-ti-mul	*ultimul*
next	ur-mă-to-rul	*următorul*

ROMANIAN

Train & Metro

Which line takes me to ...?
    kah-re li-ni-e du-che lah ...?   *Care linie duce la ...?*
What's the next station?
    kah-re es-te ur-mă-toah-   *Care este următoarea stație?*
    reah stah-tsi-e?
Is this the right platform for ...?
    ah-ches-tah es-te   *Acesta este peronul*
    pe-ro-nul pen-tru ...?   *pentru ...?*
Is that seat taken?
    lo-kul es-te o-ku-paht?   *Locul este ocupat?*
I want to get off at ...
    vreahu să ko-bor lah ...   *Vreau să cobor la ...*

SIGNS	
IEȘIRE	WAY OUT
METROU	METRO/UNDERGROUND
PERON NR.	PLATFORM NUMBER
SCHIMB	CHANGE (coins)
SPRE/PE AICI	THIS WAY TO

Taxi

Can you take me to ...?
    pu-tetsi să mă du-chetsi lah ...?   *Puteți să mă ducețila ...?*
Please take me to ...
    vă rog, du-che-tsi-mă lah ...   *Vă rog, ducețimă la ...*
How much does it cost to go to ...?
    kît kos-ta dru-mul pî-nă lah ...?   *Cît costa drumul pînă la ...?*
Here's fine, thank you.
    ah-ichi es-te bi-ne,   *Aici este bine, mulțumesc.*
    mul-tsu-mesk
The next corner, please.
    ur-mă-to-rul kolts, vă rog   *Următorul colț, vă rog.*

ROMANIAN

Continue!	kon-ti-nu-ahtsi!	*Continuați!*
Stop here!	o-presh-te!	*Oprește!*

The next street to the left/right.
    ur-mă-toah-reah   *Următoarea*
    strah-dă lah stîn-gah/dreahp-tah   *stradă la stînga/dreapta.*
Please slow down.
    vă rog, în-che-ti-nitsi   *Vă rog, încetiniți.*
Please wait here.
    vă rog, ahsh-tep-tahtsi ah-ichi   *Vă rog, așteptați aici.*

Car

Where can I rent a car?
    un-de pot în-ki-ri-ah   *Unde pot închiria*
    o mah-shi-nă?   *o mașină?*
How much is it daily/weekly?
    kît kos-tă pe zi/   *Cît costă pe zi/*
    pe săp-tă-mî-nă?   *pe săptămînă?*
Does that include insurance/
mileage?
    in-klu-de shi   *Include și*
    ah-si-gu-rah-reah/kos-tul   *asigurarea/costul*
    ki-lo-me-trah-zhu-lui?   *kilometrajului?*
Where's the next petrol station?
    un-de es-te ur-mă-toah-   *Unde este următoarea*
    reah stah-tsi-e de ben-zi-nă?   *stație de benzină?*
How long can I park here?
    pen-tru kît timp pot   *Pentru cît timp pot*
    pahr-kah ah-ichi?   *parca aici?*
Does this road lead to ...?
    es-te ah-ches-tah   *Este acesta*
    dru-mul spre ...?   *drumul spre ...?*
I need a mechanic.
    ahm ne-vo-ie de un   *Am nevoie de un*
    me-ka-nik   *mecanic.*

ROMANIAN

air (for tyres)	ah-er	*aer*
battery	bah-te-ri-e/ ah-ku-mu-lah-tor	*baterie/* *acumulator*
brakes	frî-ne	*frîne*
clutch	bor-nă/kle-mă/ în-ki-ză-tor/ku-plă	*bornă/clemă/* *închizător/cuplă*
driver's licence	per-mis de kon-du-che-re	*permis de* *conducere*
engine	mo-tor	*motor*
lights	lu-mini	*lumini*
oil	u-lei	*ulei*
petrol	ben-zi-nă	*benzină*
puncture	pah-nă (pah-nă de kah-u-chiuk)	*pană (pană de* *cauciuc)*
radiator	rah-di-ah-tor	*radiator*
road map	hahr-tă ru-ti-e-ră	*hartă rutieră*
tyres	kah-u-chiu-kuri	*cauciucuri*
windscreen	pahr-briz (jeahm)	*parbriz (geam)*

SIGNS

AUTOSTRADA	FREEWAY
CEDEAZA TRECEREA	GIVE WAY
FAČRA PLUMB	UNLEADED
GARAJ	GARAGE
INVALIZI	DISABLED
MECANIC	MECHANIC
NORMAL	NORMAL
OCOLIRE/OCOL/DEVIERE	DETOUR
NU INTRAŢI	NO ENTRY
NU PARCAŢI	NO PARKING
REPARAŢII	REPAIRS
SENS UNIC	ONE WAY

ROMANIAN

ACCOMMODATION

Where's a	un-de es-te un	*Unde este un*
... hotel?	ho-tel ...?	*hotel ...?*
cheap	ief-tin	*ieftin*
clean	ku-raht	*curat*
good	bun	*bun*
nearby	ah-pro-pi-aht	*apropiat*

What's the address?
kah-rei ah-dre-sah?   *Care-i adresa?*

Could you write the address, please?
po-tsi să-mi skrii   *Poţi să-mi scrii*
adresa, te rog?   *adresa, te rog?*

At the Hotel

Do you have any rooms available?
ah-vetsi kah-me-reh li-be-reh?   *Aveţi camere libere?*

I'd like ...	ahsh do-ri ...	*Aş dori ...*
a single room	o kah-me-ră de o	*o cameră de o*
	per-soah-nă	*persoană*
a double room	o kah-me-ră du-blă	*o cameră dublă*
to share a dorm	ah îm-păr-tsi un	*a împărţi un*
	dor-mi-tor	*dormitor*
a bed	un paht	*un pat*

I want a room	vreahu o ka-me-ră	*Vreau o cameră*
with a ...	ku ...	*cu ...*
bathroom	bah-ie	*baie*
shower	dush	*duş*
window	fe-reahs-tră	*fereastră*

How much is it per (night/person?)
kît kos-tă (pe noap-te/   *Cît costă (pe noapte/*
de per-soah-nă?)   *de persoană?)*

Can I see it?
pot să văd?   *Pot să văd?*

Are there any others?
    mahi sînt shi ahl-te-le?   *Mai sînt şi altele?*
Can I see the bathroom?
    pot să văd bah-iah?   *Pot să văd baia?*
Is there a reduction for
students/children?
    ex-is-tă re-du-che-re   *Există reducere pentru*
    pen-tru stu-den-tsi/ko-pii?   *studenţi/copii?*
Does it include breakfast?
    în-klu-de mi-kul de-zhun?   *Include micul dejun?*
Is there hot water all day?
    es-te ah-pă kahl-dă   *Este apă caldă*
    toah-tă zi-uah?   *toată ziua?*
It's fine, I'll take it.
    es-te în re-gu-lă, îl (o) iahu   *Este în regulă, îl (o) iau.*
I'd like to pay the bill.
    ahsh do-ri să plă-tesk no-tah/   *Aş dori să plătesc nota./*
    ahsh do-ri a-ki-tah   *Aş dori achita*
    no-tah de plah-tă   *nota de plată.*

Requests & Complaints

Do you have a safe where
I can leave my valuables?
    ah-vetsi un seif un-de pot   *Aveţi un seif unde pot*
    lă-sah vah-lo-ri-le/   *lăsa valorile/*
    luc-ru-ri-le de prets?   *lucrurile de preţ?*
Can I use the telephone?
    pot fo-lo-si te-le-fo-nul?   *Pot folosi telefonul?*
I can't open/close the window.
    nu pot des-ki-de/în-ki-de   *Nu pot deschide/închide*
    fe-reahs-trah   *fereastra.*
I've locked myself out of my room.
    m-ahm în-ku-iaht în   *M-am incuiat în*
    ah-fah-rah kah-me-rei   *afara camerei.*
The toilet won't flush.
    to-ah-le-tah nu funk-tsi-o-neah-ză   *Toaleta nu funcţionează.*

ROMANIAN

AROUND TOWN

I'm looking for
a/the ...

	kah-ut ...	Caut ...
art gallery	gah-le-ri-ah de ahr-tă	*galeria de artă*
bank	o bahn-kă	*o bancă*
church	bi-se-ri-kah	*biserica*
city centre	chen-trul	*centrul*
	o-rah-shu-lui	*oraşului*
... embassy	ahm-bah-sah-dah ...	*ambasada ...*
... hotel	ho-te-lul ...	*hotelul ...*
market	piah-tsah	*piaţa*
museum	mu-ze-ul	*muzeul*
police	po-li-tsi-ah	*poliţia*
post office	posh-tah	*poşta*
public toilet	o to-ah-le-tă	*o toaletă*
	pu-bli-kă	*publică*
telephone centre	chen-trah-lah	*centrala*
	te-le-fo-ni-kă	*telefonică*
tourist	bi-roul de	*biroul de*
information	in-for-mah-tsii	*informaţii*
office	pen-tru tu-rism	*pentru turism*

What time does it open/close?
kînd/lah che o-ră se
des-ki-de/în-ki-de?

Cînd/la ce oră se deschide
închide?

For directions, see the Getting Around section, page 370.

ROMANIAN

At the Post Office

I'd like some stamps.
    ahsh do-ri kî-te-vah tim-bre   *Aş dori cîteva timbre.*

How much is the postage?
    kît es-te tah-xah posh-tah-lă?   *Cît este taxa poştală?*

I'd like to send a/an ...	ahsh do-ri să tri-mit ...	*Aş dori să trimit ...*
aerogram	skri-soah-re ex-pres	*scrisoare expres*
letter	o skri-soah-re	*o scrisoare*
parcel	unco-let posh-tahl	*un colet poştal*
postcard	o kahr-te posh-tah-lă	*o carte poştală*
telegram	o te-le-grah-mă	*o telegramă*
airmail	posh-tă ah-e-ri-a nă	*poştă aeriană*
envelope	un plik	*un plic*
mail box	ku-ti-e posh-tah-lă	*cutie poştală*
parcel	pah-ket	*pachet*
registered mail	skri-soah-re re-ko-mahn-dah-tă	*scrisoare recomandată*
surface mail	skri-soah-re sim-plă	*scrisoare simplă*

Telephone

To call abroad you must wait 30 to 45 minutes for your request, because Romania is not connected to the international direct telephone system.

I want to ring ...	
ahsh do-ri să sun ...	*Aş dori să sun ...*
The number is ...	
nu-mă-rul es-te ...	*Numărul este ...*
I want to speak for three minutes.	
vreahu să vor-besk trei mi-nu-te	*Vreau să vorbesc trei minute.*
How much does a three-minute call cost?	
kît kos-tă o kon-vor-bi-re de trei mi-nu-te?	*Cît costă o convorbire de trei minute?*

ROMANIAN

I'd like to speak to (Mr Perez).
   ahsh do-ri să vor-besk ku
   (dom-nul perez)
I want to make a reverse-charges phone call.
   ahsh do-ri o kon-vor-bi-re
   ku tah-xă in-ver-să
It's engaged.
   es-te o-ku-paht
I've been cut off.
   ahm fost în-tre-rupt/ă

*Aş dori să vorbesc cu
(domnul Perez).*

*Aş dori o convorbire
cu taxă inversă.*

Este ocupat.

Am fost întrerupt/ă.

Internet

Where can I get Internet access?
   un-de pot să ob-tsin
   ak-ches lah in-ter-net?
How much is it per hour?
   cît se plă-tesh-te pe o-ră?
I want to check my email.
   ash vreah să văd dah-că
   ahm pri-mit un i-meil

*Unde pot să obţin
acces la internet?*

Cît se plăteşte pe oră?

*Aş vrea să văd dacă
am primit un e-mail.*

DID YOU KNOW ... Gregore Pintea Viteazul is Romania's most famous outlaw. He prowled the country's highways in the 17th century, accumulating wealth by robbing the poor. However, he fell in love with a peasant woman, and following her death was so broken-hearted he gave away his riches, henceforth stealing only from the rich to give to the poor.

At the Bank

It's difficult to transfer money from your bank to a bank in Romania, so you should take sufficient money with you.

ROMANIAN

I want to exchange some
(money/travellers cheques).
    vreauh să skimb (che-vah   *Vreau să schimb (ceva*
    bahni/che-ku-ri)   *bani/cecuri).*
What's the exchange rate?
    kah-re es-te rah-tah de   *Care este rata de*
    schimb?   *schimb?*
How many lei per dollar?
    kîtsi lei pen-tru un do-lahr?   *Cîți lei pentru un dolar?*

bankdraft	bi-let de bahn-kă po-li-tsă	*bilet de bancă poliță*
banknotes	bahnk-no-te	*bancnote*
cashier	kah-si-er	*casier*
coins	mo-ne-de	*monede*
credit card	kahr-te de kre-dit	*carte de credit*
exchange	skimb vah-lu-tahr	*schimb valutar*
loose change	mă-runt/mă-run-tsish	*mărunt/mărunțiș*
signature	sem-nă-tu-ră	*semnătură*

INTERESTS & ENTERTAINMENT
Sightseeing

Do you have a guidebook/
local map?
    ah-vetsi un jid/   *Aveți un ghid/*
    o hahr-tă lokah-lă?   *o hartă locală?*
What are the main attractions?
    kah-re sînt prin-chi-   *Care sînt principalele*
    pah-le-le ah-trahk-tsii?   *atracții?*
What's that?
    che es-te ah-cheahs-tah?   *Ce este aceasta?*

ROMANIAN

How old is it?
kît de ve-ki/ve-ke es-te?   *Cît de vechi/veche este?* (m/f)
Can I take photographs?
pot fo-to-grah-fi-ah?   *Pot fotografia?*
What time does it open/close?
kînd se des-ki-de/în-ki-de?   *Cînd se deschide/închide?*

ancient	veki/ahn-tik	*vechi/antic*
archaeological	ahr-he-o-lo-jik	*arheologic*
beach	plah-zhă	*plajă*
building	klă-di-re	*clădire*
castle	kahs-tel	*castel*
cathedral	kah-te-drah-lă	*catedrală*
church	bi-se-ri-kă	*biserică*
concert hall	sah-lă de kon-chert	*sală de concert*
library	bi-bli-o-te-kă	*bibliotecă*
main square	piah-tsa prin-chi-pah-lă	*piaţa principală*
market	piah-tsa/ bah-zahr/hah-lă	*piaţa/bazar/hală*
monastery	mă-năs-ti-re	*mănăstire*
monument	mo-nu-ment	*monument*
mosque	mos-ke-e	*moschee*
old city	ve-kiul o-rahsh	*vechiul oraş*
palace	pah-laht	*palat*
opera house	o-pe-rah	*opera*
ruins	ru-i-ne	*ruine*
stadium	stah-di-on	*stadion*
statues	stah-tui	*statui*
temple	tem-plu	*templu*
university	u-ni-ver-si-tah-te	*universitate*

ROMANIAN

Going Out

What's there to do in the evenings?
    che se poah-te fah-che   *Ce se poate face*
    seah-rah?   *seara?*

Are there any nightclubs?
    sînt dis-ko-techi?   *Sînt discoteci?*

Are there places where you
can hear local folk music?
    sînt lo-kuri un-de se   *Sînt locuri unde se*
    poah-te ahs-kul-tah   *poate asculta*
    mu-zi-kă po-pu-lah-ră?   *muzică populară?*

cinema	chi-ne-mah	*cinema*
concert	kon-chert	*concert*
nightclub	dis-ko-te-kă	*discotecă*
theatre	teah-tru	*teatru*

Sports & Interests

What sports do you play?
    ce sport prahk-ti-katsi?   *Ce sport practicaţi?*
What are your interests?
    ce vă in-te-re-seah-ză?/   *Ce vă interesează?/*
    ce pre-fe-rahtsi?   *Ce preferaţi?*

art	ahr-tă	*artă*
basketball	bas-ket	*baschet*
chess	shahh	*şah*
collecting things	să fak ko-lek-tsi-e	*să fac colecţie*
dancing	dahn-suri	*dansuri*
food	ah-li-men-te	*alimente*
football	fot-bal	*fotbal*
hiking	tu-rism	*turism*
martial arts	ahr-tă mi-li-tah-ră	*arte marţiale*
meeting friends	în-tîl-ni-ri ku	*întîlniri cu prieteni*
	pri-e-teni	

ROMANIAN

movies	fil-me/chi-ne-mah	*filme/cinema*
music	mu-zi-kă	*muzică*
nightclubs	klu-buri de noahp-te	*cluburi de noapte*
photography	fo-to-grah-fi-e-re	*fotografiere*
reading	chi-ti-re de kärtsi	*citire de cărţi*
shopping	să fahk kum-pă-ră-turi	*să fac cumpărături*
skiing	ski	*schi*
swimming	înot	*înot*
tennis	te-nis	*tenis*
travelling	kă-lă-to-ri-e	*călătorie*
TV/videos	să mă uit lah te-le-vi-zor/ vi-de-o	*să mă uit la televizor/ video*
visiting friends	vi-zi-te lah pri-e-teni	*vizite la prieteni*
walking	să ies lah plim-bah-re/ să mă plimb	*să ies la plimbare/ să mă plimb*

DID YOU KNOW ...

MGM's original *Tarzan the Ape Man* (1932) was born in Timişoara. Billed by the movie-makers as 'the only man in Hollywood who can act without clothes', Johnny Weissmüller (1904-84) was also a five-time Olympic swimming gold medalist.

Festivals

Tânjaua de pe Mara Festival
   traditional folk festival to celebrate the first ploughing of
   spring, held in Hoteni, Maramureş
Bucharest Carnival
   street carnival held in the last weekend of May

International Chamber Music Festival
concerts take place during July in Braşov and Bran

Târgul de fete
Girls' Fair – traditional match-making festival held around
20 July in Mount Găina, Avram Iancu

Medieval Days
two-week medieval arts, crafts and music festival held in
August in the streets of Sighişoara

Sâmbra oilor
major pastoral festival held in September to mark the
transhumanţă, or 'coming down' of the sheep from the
mountains; held in and around Bran

Ontoi Decembre
National Unity Day – On 1 December, 1918
the final unification of Valachia and Moldova with
Transylvania was announced in the town of Alba Iulia

De la Colind la Stea
International Christmas festival held in Brasov

IN THE COUNTRY
Weather

What's the weather like?
    kum es-te tim-pul?   *Cum este timpul?*

The weather's ...	tim-pul es-te ...	*Timpul este ...*
today.	ahzi	*azi.*
Will it be ...	vah fi ...	*Va fi ...*
tomorrow?	mîi-ne?	*mîine?*
cloudy	no-ros	*noros*
cold	re-che	*rece*
foggy	che-tsos	*ceţos*
frosty	je-ros	*geros*
hot	kahld	*cald*
raining	plo-ios	*ploios*
sunny	în-so-rit	*însorit*
windy	ku vînt	*cu vînt*
snowing	nin-je	*ninge*

ROMANIAN

Camping

Am I allowed to camp here?
    pot să kahm-pez ah-ichi?   *Pot să campez aici?*
Is there a campsite nearby?
    ah-vetsi vre-un kahm-ping   *Aveţi vreun camping*
    în ah-pro-pi-e-re?   *în apropiere?*

backpack	ruk-sahk	*rucsac*
can opener	des-ki-ză-tor	*deschizător*
	de kon-ser-ve	*de conserve*
compass	bu-so-lă/kom-pas	*busolă/compas*
crampons	krahm-poah-ne	*crampoane*
firewood	lem-ne de fok	*lemne de foc*
gas cartridge	lahm-pă ku gaz	*lampă cu gaz*
hammock	hah-mahk	*hamac*
ice axe	pi-o-let	*piolet*
mattress	sahl-teah	*saltea*
penknife	bri-cheag	*briceag*
rope	frîn-ji-e/sfoah-ră	*frînghie/sfoară*
tent	kort	*cort*
tent pegs	tsă-rush	*ţăruş*
torch (flashlight)	lahn-ter-nă	*lanternă*
sleeping bag	sahk de dor-mit	*sac de dormit*
stove	so-bă/kup-tor	*sobă/cuptor*
water bottle	plos-kă	*ploscă*

FOOD

For Romanians, the working day begins at 7 am and ends at 3 to 3.30 pm. People generally have a break *(pauză de masă)* when they eat a sandwich or snack, or drink coffee, but they don't leave their offices. Lunch is usually taken at 4 pm. Most eating places in Romania have recognisable names, such as 'snack bar'. Here are some others:

ROMANIAN

restaurant cu autoservire	self-service restaurant	
bufet lacto	milk bar	
restaurant de categoria întîi	1st class restaurant	
restaurant de lux	deluxe restaurant	
restaurant lactovegetarian	vegetarian restaurant	

breakfast	mi-kul de-zhun	*micul dejun*
lunch	prînz/de-zhun	*prînz/dejun*
dinner	chi-nă	*cină*

Vegetarian Meals

Vegetarian restaurants are not common and often have a very small menu.

I'm a vegetarian.
    eu sînt ve-je-tah-ri-ahn   *Eu sînt vegetarian.*
I don't eat meat.
    eu nu mă-nînk kahr-ne   *Eu nu mănînc carne.*
I don't eat chicken, fish or ham.
    eu nu mă-nînk pui,   *Eu nu mănînc pui,*
    pesh-te shi shun-kă   *peşte şi şuncă.*

Breakfast & Dinner

A Romanian breakfast consists of a selection of the following foods, with tea, milk, and white or black coffee. Dinner very much resembles breakfast, although without black coffee.

bread	pîi-ne	*pîine*
butter	unt	*unt*
cheese	brîn-ză	*brînză*
jam	jem	*gem*
marmalade	mahr-me-lah-dă	*marmeladă*
salami	sah-lahm	*salam*
... eggs	... ouă	*... ouă*
fried	pră-ji-te	*prăjite*
poached	o-ki-uri	*ochiuri*
soft/hard boiled	fi-er-te moi/tah-ri	*fierte moi/tari*

ROMANIAN

MENU DECODER

Soups
Ciorbă means sour soup and is typical of many Romanian dishes.

ciorbă de ...	chior-bă de ...	soup, made with ...
burtă	bur-tă	a small amount of vegetables and a large amount of beef tripe
fasole	fah-so-le	beans
perişoare	pe-ri-shoa-re	vegetables and balls of minced meat
peşte	pesh-te	fish
văcuţă	vă-ku-tsă	vegetables and beef
supă ...	su-pă ...	clear soup with ...
de cartofi	de kahr-tofi	potato
de legume	de le-gu-me	vegetables
cu tăieţei	ku tă-ie-tsei	vermicelli or noodles (Transylvania)

Salads

salată ...	sah-lah-tă ...	... salad
de boeuf	de boeuf	cold beef
de castraveţi	de kahs-trah-vetsi	cucumber
de vinete	de vi-ne-te	eggplant
orientală	o-ri-en-tah-lă	oriental
verde cu roşii	ver-de ku ro-shii	lettuce and tomato

Main Meals
sarmale   sahr-mah-le
  stuffed cabbage with minced pork meat, rice, spices. Each leaf of cabbage (fresh or sour) is stuffed with this mixture, rolled up, and usually served with sour cream and *hominy*, *mămăligă* (coarsely ground maize flour). The *hominy* is served also with cottage cheese/fresh cheese, *brînză*, and sour cream or milk.

friptură de porc cu salată   frip-tu-ră de pork ku sa-lah-tă
  roasted pork with vegetable salad

Desserts

biscuits	bis-ku-itsi	*biscuiți*
cake	pră-ji-tu-ră	*prăjitură*
dessert	de-sert	*desert*
doughnuts	go-goshi	*gogoși*
ice cream	în-je-tsah-tă	*înghețată*
pancakes	clă-ti-te	*clătite*
pastry	pro-du-se de pah-ti-se-ri-e	*produse de patiserie*
pie	plă-chin-tă	*plăcintă*
pudding	bu-din-kă	*budincă*
stewed fruit	kom-pot	*compot*
sweet biscuit	pish-kot/bis-ku-it	*pișcot/biscuit*

Non-Alcoholic Drinks

black coffee	kah-feah	*cafea*
white coffee	kah-feah ku lahp-te	*cafea cu lapte*
tea	cheahi	*ceai*
ice	jeah-tsă	*gheață*
fruit juice	suk de fruk-te	*suc de fructe*
milk	lahp-te	*lapte*
mineral water	ah-pă mi-ne-rah-lă	*apă minerală*
soda	si-fon	*sifon*
soft drinks	bă-u-turi ră-ko-ri-toah-re	*băuturi răcoritoare*
(boiled) water	ah-pă (fi-ahr-tă)	*apă fiartă*

Alcoholic Drinks

beer	be-re	*bere*
black/white	neah-gră/blon-dă	*neagră/blondă*
brandy	tsui-kă	*țuica*
cognac	ko-niahk	*coniac*
liqueur	li-kior	*lichior*
plum brandy	tsui-kă	*țuică*
(very strong)		
wine	vin	*vin*
red wine	vin ro-shu	*vin roșu*
white wine	vin alb	*vin alb*
whisky	uis-ki	*whisky*

ROMANIAN

AT THE MARKET

Staples

cereal	pah-ni-fi-kah-te	panificate
cheese	brîn-ză	brînză
chocolate	chio-ko-lah-tă	ciocolată
eggs	ouă	ouă
flour	fă-i-nă	făină
honey	mi-e-re	miere
margarine	mahr-gah-ri-nă	margarină
marmalade	mahr-me-lah-dă/jem	marmeladă/gem
milk	lahp-te	lapte
olive oil	unt-de-lemn	untdelemn
pepper	pi-per	piper
rice	o-rez	orez
salt	sah-re	sare
spaghetti	spah-ghe-te	spaghete
sugar	zah-hăr	zahăr
yogurt	iah-urt	iaurt

Meat & Poultry

beef	vah-kă	vacă
chicken	pui	pui
beefsteak	bif-tek	biftec
duck	rah-tsă	rață
ham	shun-kă	șuncă
hamburger	hahm-bur-ger	hamburgher
lamb	cahr-ne de mi-el	carne de miel
sausage	kîr-nahtsi	cîrnați
turkey	kur-kahn	curcan
veal	kahr-ne de vi-tsel	carne de vițel

Vegetables

beetroot	sfek-lă	sfeclă
(green) beans	fah-so-le (ver-de)	fasole (verde)
cabbage	vahr-ză	varză
capsicum	ahr-dei	ardei
carrot	mor-kovi	morcovi
cauliflower	ko-no-pi-dă	conopidă

ROMANIAN

AT THE MARKET

chillies	ahr-dei iu-te	ardei iute
cucumber	kahs-trah-ve-te	castravete
garlic	us-tu-roi	usturoi
lettuce	sah-lah-tă ver-de	salată verde
mushroom	chiu-per-kă	ciupercă
onion	cheah-pă	ceapă
peas	mah-ză-re	mazăre
potato	kahr-tof	cartof
spinach	spah-nak	spanac
tomato	ro-shii	roşii
zucchini	do-vle-chei	dovlecei

Seafood
fish	pesh-te	peşte
lobster	rah-chi/krah-bi	raci/crabi
mussels	sko-ichi	scoici
oysters	stri-dii	stridii
shrimp	kre-ve-te	crevete

Pulses
broad beans	bob	bob
chickpeas	nă-ut	năut
kidney beans	fah-so-le	fasole
lentils	lin-te	linte

Fruit
apples	me-re	mere
apricot	ka-i-se	caise
bananas	bah-nah-ne	banane
fig	smo-ki-ne	smochine
grapes	stru-guri	struguri
kiwifruit	ki-vi	kiwi
lemon	lă-mîi	lămîi
oranges	por-to-kah-le	portocale
peaches	pi-er-sishi	piersici
pear	pe-re	pere
plums	pru-ne	prune
strawberry	kăp-shuni	căpşuni

ROMANIAN

SHOPPING

Where's the nearest ...?	un-de e chel mahi ah-pro-pi-aht ...?	*Unde e cel mai apropiat ...?*
bookshop	li-brǎ-ri-e	*librărie*
camera shop	mah-gah-zin pen-tru mah-te-ri-ah-le fo-to-gra-fi-che	*magazin pentru materiale fotografice*
chemist	fahr-mah-chi-e	*farmacie*
clothing store	mah-gah-zin de îm-brǎ-kǎ-min-te	*magazin de îmbrăcăminte*
delicatessen	de-li-kah-te-se	*delicatese*
general store	mah-gah-zin u-ni-ver-sahl	*magazin universal*
laundry	spǎ-lǎ-to-ri-e	*spălătorie*
market	piah-tsǎ	*piață*
newsagency/ stationers	ki-oshk de zi-ah-re	*chioșc de ziare*
shoeshop	mah-gah-zin de în-kǎl-tsǎ-min-te	*magazin de încălțăminte*
souvenir shop	mah-gah-zin de kah-do-uri	*magazin de cadouri*
supermarket	su-per-mahr-ket	*supermarket*
green grocer	ah-pro-zahr	*aprozar*

How much (is it)?
  kît kos-tǎ?   *Cît costă?*
Do you accept credit cards?
  ahk-chep-tahtsi kǎr-tsi   *Acceptați cărți*
  de kre-dit?   *de credit?*

Essential Groceries

I'd like ...	ash do-ri ...	*Aş dori ...*
cheese	brîn-ză	*brînză*
chocolate	chio-ko-lah-tă	*ciocolată*
honey	mi-e-re	*miere*
margarine	mahr-gah-ri-nă	*margarină*
marmalade	mahr-me-lah-dă, jem	*marmeladă, gem*
matches	ki-brit (ki-bri-turi)	*chibrit (chibrituri)*
milk	lahp-te	*lapte*
shampoo	shahm-pon	*şampon*
soap	să-pun	*săpun*
toilet paper	hîr-ti-e i-ji-e-ni-kă	*hîrtie igienică*
toothpaste	pahs-tă de din-tsi	*pastă de dinţi*
washing powder	de-ter-jent	*detergent*

For more groceries, see the At the Market section on page 390.

Souvenirs

earrings	cher-chei	*cercei*
embroidered blouses	blu-ze ku bro-de-ri-e	*bluze cu broderie*
embroidered tablecloths	fe-tse de mah-să ku bro-de-ri-e	*feţe de masă cu broderie*
glassware	stik-lă-ri-e	*sticlărie*
handicraft	ahr-ti-zah-naht	*artizanat*
necklace	ko-li-er	*colier*
pottery	o-bi-ek-te de o-lă-rit; o-bi-ek-te din che-rah-mi-kă	*obiecte de olărit; obiecte din ceramică*
black pottery vases	vah-ze din che-rah-mi-kă neah-gră	*vaze din ceramică neagră*
ring	i-nel	*inel*
rug	kahr-pe-tă/ko-vor	*carpetă/covor*
(china) trinket	bi-be-lo-uri (din por-tse-lan)	*bibelouri (din porţelan)*

ROMANIAN

Clothing

clothing	îm-bră-kă-min-te/ hahi-ne	îmbrăcăminte/ haine
coat	pahl-ton	palton
dress	ro-ki-e	rochie
jacket	zhah-ke-tă	jachetă
jumper (sweater)	pu-lo-ver	pulovăr
shirt	tri-kou/kă-mah-shă	tricou/cămaşă
shoes	pahn-to-fi	pantofi
skirt	fus-tă	fustă
trousers	pahn-tah-loni	pantaloni
underwear	len-zhe-ri-e/ru-fă-ri-e de korp	lenjerie/rufărie de corp

Materials

What's it made of?

din che (fel de mah-te-ri-al) e fă-kut?

Din ce (fel de material) e făcut?

cotton	bum-bahk	bumbac
handmade	luk-ru mah-nu-ahl; lu-kraht de mî-nă; mah-nu-ahl	lucru manual; lucrat de mînă; manual
leather	pi-e-le	piele
of brass	din bronz/ah-lah-mă	din bronz/alamă
of gold	din ah-ur	din aur
of silver	din ahr-jint	din argint
pure alpaca wool	ahl-pah-ka pu-ră i-nox	alpaca pură inox
silk	mă-tah-se	mătase
wool	lî-nă	lînă

Toiletries

comb	pi-ep-ten (pi-ep-te-ne)	pieptén (pieptene)
condoms	pre-zer-vah-ti-ve	prezervative
deodorant	de-o-do-rahnt	deodorant
hairbrush	pe-ri-e de	perie de păr

ROMANIAN

moisturiser	kre-mă hi-drah-tahn-tă	*cremă hidratantă*
razor	lah-mă	*lamă*
sanitary napkins	sher-ve-tse-le i-ji-e-ni-che	*şerveţele igienice*
shampoo	shahm-pon	*şampon*
shaving cream	kre-mă de rahs	*cremă de ras*
soap	să-pun	*săpun*
sunscreen	kre-mă de soah-re	*cremă de soare*
tampons	tahm-poah-ne	*tampoane*
tissues	sher-ve-tse-le	*şerveţele*
toilet paper	hîr-ti-e i-jiŕni-kă	*hîrtie igienică*
toothbrush	pe-ri-e de din-tsi	*perie de dinţi*
toothpaste	pahs-tă de din-tsi	*pastă de dinţi*
scissors	foahr-fe-kă	*foarfecă*

Colours

black	ne-gru	*negru*
blue	ahl-bahs-tru	*albastru*
brown	mah-ro	*maro*
green	ver-de	*verde*
pink	roz	*roz*
purple	pur-pu-riu	*purpuriu*
red	ro-shu	*roşu*
white	ahlb	*alb*
yellow	gahl-ben	*galben*

Stationery & Publications

map	hahr-tă	*hartă*
newspaper	zi-ahr	*ziar*
paper	hîr-ti-e	*hîrtie*
pen (ballpoint)	sti-(pix)	*stilou (pix)*
English-language ...	în en-gle-ză	*... în engleză*
newspaper	zi-ah-re	*ziare*
novels	ro-mah-ne	*romane*

Photography

How much is it to process this film?
    kît du-reah-ză de-ve-lo-   *Cît durează developarea*
    pah-reah fil-mu-lui?   *filmului?*
When will it be ready?
    kînd vah fi gah-tah?   *Cînd va fi gata?*
I'd like a film for this camera.
    ahsh do-ri un film pen-tru   *Aş dori un film pentru*
    ah-chest ah-pah-raht   *acest aparat.*

B&W (film)	ahlb-ne-gru	*alb-negru*
camera	ah-pah-raht	*aparat*
	fo-to-grah-fik/	*fotografic/*
	fo-to-ah-pah-raht	*fotoaparat*
colour (film)	ko-lor (film)	*color (film)*
film	film	*film*
flash	blits	*bliţ*
lens	o-bi-ek-tiv	*obiectiv*
light meter	fo-to-met-ru	*fotometru*

Smoking

Do you smoke?
    fu-mah-tsi?   *Fumaţi?*
Please don't smoke.
    vă rog, nu fu-mahtsi   *Vă rog, nu fumaţi.*

ROMANIAN

ROMANIAN

A packet of cigarettes.
 un pah-ket de tsi-gări   *Un pachet de ţigări.*
Are these cigarettes strong/mild?
 ah-ches-te tsi-gări sînt   *Aceste ţigări sînt*
 tahri/slah-be?   *tari/slabe?*
Do you have a light?
 ah-ve-tsi un fok?   *Aveţi un foc?*

cigarette papers	fo-i-tsă de tsi-gah-ră	*foiţă de ţigară*
cigarettes	tsi-gah-ri	*ţigări*
filtered	ku fil-tru	*cu filtru*
lighter	slah-be/u-shoah-re	*slabe/uşoare*
matches	ki-bri-turi	*chibrituri*
menthol	men-to-lah-te	*mentolate*
pipe	pi-pă	*pipă*
tobacco (pipe)	tu-tun	*tutun*

Sizes & Comparisons

small	mik	*mic*
big	mah-re	*mare*
heavy	greu	*greu*
light	u-shor	*uşor*
more	mahi mult	*mai mult*
less	mahi pu-tsin	*mai puţin*
too much/many	preah mult/mul-te	*prea mult/multe*

ROMANIAN

HEALTH

Every Romanian village and town has a health facility. In the cities there are hospitals and clinics. The prices for medicines are quite low.

Where's the ...?	un-de es-te ...?	*Unde este ...?*
chemist	fahr-mah-chis-tul	*farmacistul*
dentist	den-tis-tul	*dentistul*
doctor	dok-to-rul	*doctorul*
hospital	spi-tah-lul	*spitalul*

I'm sick.
    sînt bol-nav   *Sînt bolnav.*
My friend is sick.
    pri-e-te-nul meu es-te bol-nahv   *Prietenul meu este bolnav.*
What's the matter?
    kah-re es-te pro-ble-mah?/   *Care este problema?/*
    che s-ah în-tîm-plaht?   *Ce s-a întîmplat?*
Where does it hurt?
    che vă doah-re?   *Ce vă doare?*
It hurts here.
    mă doah-re ah-ichi   *Mă doare aici.*

Parts of the Body

My ... hurts.	mă doah-re ...	*Mă doare ...*
ankle	glez-nah	*glezna*
arm	brah-tsul	*braţul*
back	spah-te-le	*spatele*
chest	piep-tul	*pieptul*
ear	u-re-keah	*urechea*
eye	o-kiul	*ochiul*
finger	de-je-tul	*degetul*
foot	lah-bah pi-chio-ru-lui	*laba piciorului*
hand	mî-nah	*mîna*
head	kah-pul	*capul*

ROMANIAN

heart	i-ni-mah	*inima*
leg	pi-chio-rul	*piciorul*
mouth	gu-rah	*gura*
nose	nah-sul	*nasul*
ribs	koahs-te-le	*coastele*
skin	pie-leah	*pielea*
spine	ko-loah-nah	*coloana*
	ver-te-brah-lă	*vertebrală*
teeth	din-tsii	*dinţii*
throat	jî-tul	*gîtul*

Ailments

I have (a/an) ...	eu ahm ...	*Eu am ...*
allergy	o ah-ler-ji-e	*o alergie*
anaemia	ah-ne-mi-e	*anemie*
burn	o ahr-su-ră	*o arsură*
cold	o ră-cheah-lă	*o răceală*
constipation	kon-sti-pah-tsi-e	*constipaţie*
cough	o se	*o tuse*
diarrhoea	di-ah-ree	*diaree*
fever	fe-bră	*febră*
headache	o du-re-re de kahp	*o durere de cap*
hepatitis	he-pah-ti-tă	*hepatită*
indigestion	in-di-ges-ti-e	*indigestie*
infection	o in-fek-tsi-e	*o infecţie*
influenza	gri-pă	*gripă*
lice	pă-duki	*păduchi*
low/high	hi-po	*hipo/*
blood pressure		*hipertensiune*
pain	o du-re-re	*o durere*
sore throat	du-re-re de jît	*durere de gît*
sprain	o ră-su-chi-re	*o răsucire*
stomachache	o du-re-re de	*o durere de*
	sto-mahk	*stomac*
sunburn	ahr-su-ră de soah-re	*arsură de soare*
venereal disease	o boah-lă ve-ne-ri-kă	*o boală venerică*
worms	vier-mi in-tes-ti-nahli	*viermi intestinali*

ROMANIAN

Useful Words & Phrases

I've been vaccinated.
(eu) ahm fost vahk-chi-naht/ă   *(Eu) am fost vaccinat/ă*
I have my own syringe.
(eu) ahm si-rin-gă pro-pri-e   *(Eu) am siringă proprie.*
I feel better/worse.
(eu) mă simt mahi bi-ne/răul.   *(Eu) mă simt mai bine/rău.*

accident	ahk-chi-dent	*accident*
addiction	nahr-ko-mah-ni-e	*narcomanie*
antibiotics	ahn-ti-bi-o-ti-che	*antibiotice*
bite	mush-kă-tu-ră/	*mușcătura*
blood pressure	ten-si-u-ne	*tensiune*
blood test	tes-tul sîn-je-lui	*testul sîngelui*
injection	in-zhek-tsi-e	*injecție*
injury	rah-nă/le-zi-u-ne	*rană/leziune*
menstruation	men-stru-ah-tsi-e	*menstruație*
nausea	greah-tsă/ră-u de mah-re	*greață/rău de mare*
oxygen	o-ksi-jen	*oxigen*
wound	plah-gă/rah-nă	*plagă/rană*

At the Chemist

I need medication for ...
ahm ne-vo-ie de   *Am nevoie de*
me-di-kah-men-te   *medicamente*
pen-tru ...   *pentru ...*
I have a prescription.
ahm o re-tse-tă   *Am o rețetă.*

antiseptic	ahn-ti-sep-tik	*antiseptic*
aspirin	ahs-pi-ri-nă	*aspirină*
bandage	bahn-dahzh	*bandaj*
contraceptive	kon-trah-chep-ti-ve	*contraceptive*
medicine	me-di-kah-ment	*medicament*
vitamins	vi-tah-mi-ne	*vitamine*

ROMANIAN

At the Dentist

I have a toothache.
    ahm o du-re-re de din-tsi   *Am o durere de dinți.*
I've lost a filling.
    mi-ah că-zut o plom-bă   *Mi-a căzut o plombă.*
I've broken a tooth.
    mi-ahm spahrt un din-te   *Mi-am spart un dinte.*
My gums hurt.
    mă dor jin-ji-i-le   *Mă dor gingiile.*
I don't want it extracted.
    nu vreahu să o ex-trahg   *Nu vreau să o extrag.*
Please give me an anaesthetic.
    vă rog, dah-tsi-mi un   *Vă rog, dați-mi un*
    ah-nes-te-zik   *anestezic.*

TIME & DATES

Romanians use both the 12-hour and 24-hour clocks. The 24-hour clock is the more formal system used in print and conversation. Telling the time is very simple! You only need to state the hour then the minutes, and between the hour and minutes you say *și* (and). For example, 4.05 is *patru și cinci*.

What time is it?
    kît e cheah-sul?   *Cît e ceasul?*
What date is it today?
    che dah-tă es-te ahs-tăzi?   *Ce dată este astăzi?*

It's ... am/pm.   es-te ... ah-em/pe-em   *Este ... am/pm.*

in the morning   di-mi-neah-tsah   *dimineața*
in the afternoon   du-pă-ah-miah-zah   *după-amiaza*
in the evening   seah-rah   *seara*

ROMANIAN

Days

Monday	lu-ni	*luni*
Tuesday	mahr-tsi	*marţi*
Wednesday	mier-kuri	*miercuri*
Thursday	zhoi	*joi*
Friday	vi-neri	*vineri*
Saturday	sîm-bă-tă	*sîmbătă*
Sunday	du-mi-ni-kă	*duminică*

Months

January	iah-nu-ah-ri-e	*ianuarie*
February	fe-bru-ah-ri-e	*februarie*
March	mahr-ti-e	*martie*
April	ah-pri-li-e	*aprilie*
May	mahi	*mai*
June	iu-ni-e	*iunie*
July	iu-li-e	*iulie*
August	ahu-gust	*august*
September	sep-tem-bri-e	*septembrie*
October	ok-tom-bri-e	*octombrie*
November	no-iem-bri-e	*noiembrie*
December	de-chem-bri-e	*decembrie*

Seasons

summer	vah-ră	*vară*
autumn	toahm-nă	*toamnă*
winter	iahr-nă	*iarnă*
spring	pri-mă-vah-ră	*primăvară*

Present

today	ahs-tăzi	*astăzi*
this morning	ahzi di-mi-neah-tsă	*azi dimineaţă*
tonight	în noahp-teah ah-cheahs-tah	*în noaptea aceasta*
this week	săp-tă-mî-nah ah-cheahs-ta	*săptămîna aceasta*
this year	ah-nul ah-ches-ta	*anul acesta*
now	ah-kum	*acum*

ROMANIAN

Past

yesterday	ier-i	*ieri*
day before yesterday	ah-lahl-tă-ier-i	*alaltăieri*
yesterday morning	ieri di-mi-neah-tsa	*ieri dimineața*
last ...	... tre-ku-tă	*... trecută*
night	noahp-teah	*noaptea*
week	săp-tă-mî-nah	*săptămîna*

Future

tomorrow	mîi-ne	*mîine*
day after tomorrow	poi-mîi-ne	*poimiine*
tomorrow ...	mîi-ne ...	*mîine ...*
morning	di-mi-neah-tsa	*dimineață*
afternoon	du-pă-ah-miah-ză	*după-amiază*
evening	seah-ră	*seară*
next week	săp-tă-mî-nah vi-i-toah-re	*săptămîna viitoare*
next year	ah-nul vi-i-tor	*anul viitor*

During the Day

afternoon	du-pă-ah-miah-ză	*după-amiază*
dawn	în zori	*în zori*
day	zi	*zi*
early	de-vre-me	*devreme*
midday	ah-miah-ză	*amiază*
midnight	mie-zul nop-tsii	*miezul nopții*
morning	di-mi-naeh-tsah	*dimineața*
night	noahp-teah	*noaptea*
sunrise	ră-să-rit	*răsărit*
sunset	ahs-fin-tsit/ah-pus	*asfințit/apus*

ROMANIAN

NUMBERS & AMOUNTS

0	ze-ro	*zero*
1	u-nu	*unu*
2	doi	*doi*
3	trei	*trei*
4	pah-tru	*patru*
5	chin-chi	*cinci*
6	shah-se	*şase*
7	shahp-te	*şapte*
8	opt	*opt*
9	no-uă	*nouă*
10	ze-che	*zece*

20	do-uă-ze-chi	*douăzeci*
30	trei-ze-chi	*treizeci*
40	pah-tru-ze-chi	*patruzeci*
50	chinchi-ze-chi	*cincizeci*
60	shahi-ze-chi	*şaizeci*
70	shahp-te-ze-chi	*şaptezeci*
80	opt-ze-chi	*optzeci*
90	no-uă-ze-chi	*nouăzeci*
100	o su-tă	*o sută*
1000	o mi-e	*o mie*
one million	un mi-li-on	*un milion*

ROMANIAN

Useful Words

Enough!	des-tul!	*Destul!*
a little (amount)	pu-tsin	*puţin*
double	du-blu	*dublu*
a dozen	o du-zi-nă	*o duzină*
few	chî-te-vah	*cîteva*
less	pu-tsin	*puţin*
many	mul-tsi/mul-te	*mulţi/multe*
more	mahi mult/mul-tă	*mai mult/multă*
once	o dah-tă	*o dată*
per cent	pro-chent	*procent*
some	kî-te-vah	*cîteva*
too much	preah mult	*prea mult*
twice	de două ori	*de două ori*

ABBREVIATIONS

C.E.	*Comunitatea Europeană*	EU
Dl	*Domnul*	Mr
D-na	*Doamna*	Mrs
D-şoara	*Domnişoara*	Miss
e.n./î.e.n.	*era noastră/înaintea erei*	AD/BC
N/S	*Nord/Sud*	North/South
O.N.U.	*Organizaţia Naţiunilor Unite*	United Nations
Str	*strada*	Street

ROMANIAN

EMERGENCIES

Help! ah-zhu-tor! *Ajutor!*

It's an emergency.
es-te o ur-jen-tsă *Este o urgenţă.*

There's been an accident.
ah fost un ahk-chi-dent *A fost un accident.*

Call a doctor!
ke-mahtsi un dok-tor! *Chemaţi un doctor!*

Call an ambulance!
ke-mahtsi o ahm-bul-ahn-tsa/ *Chemaţi o ambulanţă/*
sahl-vah-re! *salvare!*

Call the police!
ke-mahtsi po-li-tsi-ah! *Chemaţi poliţia!*

I've been raped.
ahm fost vi-o-lah-tă *Am fost violată.*

I've been robbed.
ahm forst zhe-fu-i-t/ă *Am fost jefuit/ă.*

Where's the police station?
un-de es-te po-li-tsi-ah? *Unde este Poliţia?*

Go away!
du-te!/pleah-kă! *Du-te!/Pleacă!*

I'll call the police.
ahm să kem po-li-tsi-ah *Am să chem poliţia.*

Thief!
Hots!/tîl-hahr! *Hoţ!/Tîlhar!*

I'm/My friend is ill.
eu sînt/pri-e-te-nul *Eu sînt/Prietenul*
meu es-te bol-nahv *meu este bolnav.*

I'm lost.
sînt pier-dut. *Sînt pierdut.*

Where are the toilets?
un-de es-te to-ah-le-tah? *Unde este toaleta?*

Could you help me, please?
m-ahtsi pu-teah ah-zhu-tah? *M-aţi putea ajuta?*

May I use the telephone?
 pot fo-lo-si te-le-fo-nul?   *Pot folosi telefonul?*
I'm sorry. I apologise.
 imi pah-re rău.   *Imi pare rău.*
 imi cher sku-ze.   *Imi cer scuze.*
I didn't realise I was doing
anything wrong.
 nu mi-ahm daht seah-mah   *Nu mi-am dat seama*
 kă fahk che-vah rău   *că fac ceva rău.*
I didn't do it.
 nu ahm fă-ku-to eu   *Nu am făcut-o eu.*

I want to contact my
embassy/consulate.
 ahsh do-ri să vin în   *Aş dori să vin*
 kon-tahkt ku   *în contact cu*
 ahm-bah-sah-dah/   *ambasada/*
 kon-su-lah-tul   *consulatul.*
I speak English.
 (eu) vor-besk en-gle-zah   *(Eu) vorbesc engleza.*
I have medical insurance.
 (eu) ahm ah-si-gu-rah-re   *(Eu) am asigurare*
 me-di-kah-lă   *medicală.*
My possessions are insured.
 lu-kru-ri-le me-le sînt   *Lucrurile mele sînt*
 ah-si-gu-rah-te   *asigurate.*

ROMANIAN

My ... was stolen.	... meu/meah a fost fu-raht/ă	... meu/mea a fost furat/ă (m/f)
I've lost my ...	ahm pier-dut ...	Am pierdut ...
bags	bah-gah-zhe-le me-le	bagajele mele
handbag	po-she-tă/jeau-tă/ bah-gah-jul de mină	poşetă/geantă/ bagajul de mină
money	bah-nii mei	banii mei
travellers cheques	che-ku-ri-le de că-lă-to-ri-e	cecurile de călătorie
passport	pah-shah-por-tul meu	paşaportul meu
wallet	por-to-fel	portofel

SERBIAN

QUICK REFERENCE

SERBIAN

Hello.	zdr-avoo	Zdravo.
Goodbye.	do vii-dje-enya	Do viđenja.
Yes./No.	daa/ne	Da/Ne.
Excuse me.	izz-vii-nite	Izvinite.
May I?	da li mo-gu?	Da li mogu?
Sorry. (excuse me/ forgive me)	paa-rdon	Pardon.
Please.	mo-lim	Molim.
Thank you.	hvaa-la	Hvala.
You're welcome.	ne-ma na che-emu	Nema na čemu.
What time is it?	ko-liko ye saa-ti?	Koliko je sati?
Where's ...?	gde ye ...?	Gde je ...?
Go straight ahead.	idii-te praa-vo naa-pre-ed	Idite pravo napred.

Turn left/right at the ...	skre-nite le-vo/ de-esno ...	Skrenite levo/ desno
next corner	na sle-detchem ug-glu	na sledecem uglu
traffic lights	kod se-ma-fo-ra	kod semafora

I'd like a ...	zhe-lim ...	Želim ...
single room	so-bu sa ye-dniim	sobu sa jednim
one-way ticket	kaa-rtu u ye-dnom praa-vcu	kartu u jednom pravcu
return ticket	pov-raa-tnu kaa-rtu	povratnu kartu

Where are the toilets? gde su to-aleti?	Gde su toaleti?
How much is it? ko-li-ko ko-shta?	Koliko košta?
I (don't) understand. ya (ne) raa-zuu-mem	Ja (ne) razumem.
Do you speak English? go-vo-rite li eng-le-ski?	Govorite li engleski?

1	ye-dan	jedan	6	shest	šest
2	dva	dva	7	se-dam	sedam
3	tr-ri	tri	8	osaam	osam
4	che-tiri	cetiri ·	9	de-vet	devet
5	pet	pet	10	de-set	deset

Serbian belongs to the South Slavonic language group, together with Croation, Slovenian, Macedonian and Bulgarian.

The earliest Serbian literature dates from the 9th century when Cyril and Methodius, two monks who were familiar with the Slav dialect of Macedonia, were sent to Moravia by the Byzantian Emperor to preach Christianity to the inhabitants. The two missionaries set about translating the Scriptures and prayer books, but first they needed a script to reproduce the sounds of the Slav dialect. Thus, the Glagolitic alphabet came about.

Two of Cyril's students from Ohrid, Kliment and Naum, replaced the Glagolitic script with the Cyrillic script, named in honour of their master. The Cyrillic alphabet was adopted wherever Christian Slav-Orthodox rites were followed. With the splitting of the Roman Empire into the Catholic West under the aegis of Rome and the Orthodox East under Byzantium, came the major division of the alphabet: the Cyrillic was adopted by those belonging to the Orthodox church, and the Roman alphabet by the Roman Catholics. This is why the Serbs in Belgrade use the Cyrillic alphabet, while the Croats in Zagreb use the Roman alphabet.

In this phrasebook, we've used the Roman alphabet, which will be understood by all educated locals. As signs and street names in Serbia are printed mainly in the Cyrillic script, we've used Cyrillic for signs.

PRONUNCIATION

In Serbian almost every word is written exactly as it's pronounced.
Every letter represents a single sound. There are 30 letters in the
Serbian version of the Roman alphabet, as well as in the Cyrillic
alphabet.

Roman	Cyrillic	Transliteration
A a	A a	a/aa
B b	Б б	b
V v	В в	v
G g	Г г	g
D d	Д д	d
Đ đ	Т ђ	dj
E e	E e	e
Ž ž	Ж ж	zh
Z z	З з	z
I i	И и	i/ii
J j	J j	y
K k	К к	k
L l	Л л	l
Lj lj	Љ љ	ly
M m	М м	m
N n	Н н	n
Nj nj	Њ њ	ny
O o	О о	o
P p	П п	p
R r	Р р	r
S s	С с	s
T t	Т т	t
Ć ć	Щ џ	tch
U u	У у	u/uu
F f	Ф ф	f
H h	Х х	h
C c	Ц ц	ts
Č č	Ч ч	ch
Dž dž	Џ џ	dzh
Š š	Ш ш	sh

SERBIAN

Vowels

a/aa	as the 'a' in 'rather'
e	as the 'ea' in 'bear'
i	as the 'i' in 'machine'
o	as the 'o' in 'shore'
u/uu	as the 'u' in 'put'

Consonants

ch	as the 'ch' in 'chop'
dj	as the 'du' in 'verdure'
dzh	as the 'j' in 'just'
g	as the 'g' in 'got'
ly	as the 'lli' in 'million'
ny	as the 'ny' in 'canyon'
r	as the 'r' in 'rock'
s	as the 's' in 'sin'
tch	as the 'tch' in 'catch'
ts	as the 'ts' in 'cats'
y	as the 'y' in 'young'
zh	as the 's' in 'pleasure'

SERBIAN

SUBJECT PRONOUNS		
SG		
I	yaa	ja
you (inf)	tii	ti
you (pol)	vii	Vi
he/she/it	on/ona/ono	on/ona/ono
PL		
we	mii	mi
you	vii	vi
they (m/f/neut)	oni/one/ona	oni/one/ona

SERBIAN

Stress

Generally, in complex words, the emphasis is on the first syllable. In some cases, such as in words with a prefix, the stress is on the middle syllable. The last syllable of a word is never stressed. Inflected words do not always have the same stress in all their inflections.

QUESTION WORDS		
How?	kaa-ko?	Kako?
When?	kaa-da?	Kada?
Where?	gdee?	Gde?
Which?	ko-yii?	Koji?
Who?	ko?	Ko?
Why?	zaa-shto?	Zašto?

GREETINGS & CIVILITIES
Top Useful Phrases

Hello.	zdr-avoo	Zdravo.
Goodbye.	do vii-dje-enya	Do viđenja.
Yes./No.	daa/ne	Da./Ne.
Excuse me.	izz-vii-nite	Izvinite.
May I? Do you mind?	da li mo-gu?	Da li mogu?
Sorry. (excuse me)	paa-rdon	Pardon.
Forgive me.	op-pro-stite	Oprostite.
Please.	mo-lim	Molim.
Thank you.	hvaa-la	Hvala.
Many thanks.	puu-no hvaa-la	Puno hvala.
That's fine.	u re-du ye	U redu je.
You're welcome.	ne-ma na che-emu	Nema na čemu.

Greetings

Good morning.	do-bro yuu-tro	Dobro jutro.
Good afternoon.	do-bar daa-n	Dobar dan.
Good evening.	do-bro ve-che	Dobro vece.
Good night.	laa-ku no-tch	Laku noc.
How are you?	kaa-ko ste?	Kako ste?
Well, thanks.	do-bro, hvaa-la	Dobro, hvala.

Forms of Address

Madam/Mrs	go-spo-gya	*Gospoda*
Sir/Mr	go-spo-din	*Gospodin*
Miss	go-spo-djitsa	*Gospodica*
companion	dru-zhe	*druže* (m)
	drug-a-rice	*drugaritse* (f)
friend	pri-ya-tely-u	*prijatelju*

SMALL TALK
Meeting People

What's your name?
  kaa-ko se zo-ve-te?   *Kako se zovete?*
My name's ...
  zo-vem se ...   *Zovem se ...*
I'd like to introduce you to ...
  da vas upo-znam sa ...   *Da Vas upoznam sa ...*
Pleased to meet you.
  draa-go mi ye   *Drago mi je.*
How old are you?
  ko-liko go-dina imaa-te?   *Koliko godina imate?*
I'm ... years old.
  imaam ... go-dina   *Imam ... godina.*

Nationalities

Where are you from?
  odaa-kle ste?   *Odakle ste?*

I'm from ...	ya saa-m iz ...	*Ja sam iz ...*
Australia	auu-staa-liye	*Australije*
Canada	kaa-nade	*Kanade*
England	enn-gle-ske	*Engleske*
Ireland	irr-ske	*Irske*
New Zealand	no-vog ze-landa	*Novog Zelanda*
Scotland	shko-tske	*Škotske*
the USA	ame-rike	*Amerike*
Wales	vel-sa	*Velsa*

SERBIAN

Occupations

What do you do?

	shtaa ste po zaa-nii-manyu?	*Šta ste po zanimanju?*

I'm (a/an) ...	yaa sam ...	*Ja sam ...*
artist	ume-tnik	*umetnik*
businessperson	u bii-znisu	*u biznisu*
computer programmer	pro-gra-meer	*programer*
unemployed	ne-za-po-slen	*nezaposlen* (m)
	ne-za-po-slena	*nezaposlena* (f)
doctor	le-kar	*lekar*
engineer	inn-zhe-nyer	*inženjer*
farmer	zem-lyo-raad-nik	*zemljoradnik*
journalist	no-vinar	*novinar*
lawyer	praa-vnik	*pravnik*
manual worker	raa-dnik	*radnik*
mechanic	me-haa-ni-ch-ar	*mehanicar*
nurse	bol-ni-char	*bolnicar* (m)
	me-di-tsii-nska se-estra	*medicinska sestra* (f)
office worker	sluuzh-be-nik	*službenik*
scientist	naa-uch-nik	*naucnik*
student	stuu-dent	*student*
teacher	utcii-tely	*ucitelj* (m)
	uchii-telyitsa	*uciteljica* (f)
waiter	ke-lner	*kelner* (m)
	ke-lneritsa	*kelnerica* (f)
writer	pii-sats	*pisac*

Family

Are you married?

daa-li ste ozhe-enyeni/ udaa-ti?	*Da li ste oženjeni/ udati?* (m/f)

I'm single.

ya sam saa-mats/saa-mitsa	*Ja sam samac/samica.* (m/f)

I'm married.

ya sam ozhe-enyen/udaa-ta	*Ja sam oženjen/udata.* (m/f)

I'm ...	yaa sam ...	*Ja sam ...*
divorced	raz-ve-den	*razveden* (m)
	raz-ve-de-na	*razvedena* (f)
separated	ras-tav-lyen	*rastavljen* (m)
	ras-tav-lye-na	*rastavljena* (f)
widowed	u-do-vats	*udovac* (m)
	u-do-vi-tsa	*udovica* (f)

How many children do you have?
ko-liko de-etse imaa-te?   *Koliko dece imate?*
I don't have any children.
ne-mam de-etse   *Nemam dece.*
I have a daughter/son.
imaam tche-rku/sii-na   *Imam cerku/sina.*
How many brothers/
sisters do you have?
**ko-liko braa-tche/ses-stara   *Koliko brace/sestara imate?*
imaa-te?**
Do you have a boyfriend/
girlfriend?
imaa-te li de-chka/de-evoyku?   *Imate li decka/devojku?*

SERBIAN

brother	braa-ta	*brata*
children	de-etse	*dece*
daughter	tche-rku	*cerku*
family	po-ro-ditsu	*porodicu*
father	otsa	*oca*
grandfather	de-du	*dedu*
grandmother	ba-bu	*babu*
husband	suu-pruga/muuzha	*supruga/muža*
mother	maa-yku	*majku*
sister	se-stru	*sestru*
son	sii-na	*sina*
wife	suup-ruu-gu/zhe-nu	*suprugu/ženu*

Religion

What's your religion?
  ko-ye ste vere?   *Koje ste vere?*
I'm not religious.
  nii-sam re-li-gii-ozan   *Nisam religiozan.*

I'm...	yaa sam...	*Ja sam...*
Buddhist	buu-dist-a	*Budista* (m)
	bu-dist-kinya	*Budistkinja* (f)
Christian	hrish-tcha-nin	*Hrišćanin* (m)
	hrish-tcha-nka	*Hrišćanka* (f)
Catholic	kaa-to-lik	*Katolik* (m)
	kaa-tolki-nya	*Katolkinja* (f)
Orthodox	pra-vo-slaa-van	*Pravoslavan* (m)
	pra-vo-slav-na	*Pravoslavna* (f)
Hindu	hiin-dus	*Hindus* (m)
	hind-uski-nya	*Hinduskinja* (f)
Jewish	yev-rey-in	*Jevrejin* (m)
	yev-rey-ka	*Jevrejka* (f)
Muslim	mus-li-man	*Musliman* (m)
	mus-li-man-ka	*Muslimanka* (f)

Useful Phrases

Sure!	svaa-kaa-ko!	*Svakako!*
Just a minute.	saa-mo tre-nu-taak	*Samo trenutak.*

It's (not) important.
  to ye (nii-ye) vaazh-noo   *To je (nije) važno.*
It's (not) possible.
  to ye (ne)mo-guu-tche   *To je (ne)moguce.*
Wait!
  saa-che-kay-te!   *Sacekajte!*
Good luck!
  sre-tchno!   *Srecno!*

Feelings

I (don't) like ...	(ne) vo-lim ...	*(Ne) volim ...*

I'm ...	me-ni ...	*Meni ...*
cold	hla-dno/zi-ma	*hladno/zima*
right	ye do-bro	*je dobro*
sleepy	se spaa-va	*se spava*

SERBIAN

I'm ...	ya sam ...	*Ja sam ...*
angry	lyuut	*ljut* (m)
	lyuu-ta	*ljuta* (f)
happy	sre-tchaan	*srecan* (m)
	sre-tchna	*srecna* (f)
hungry	glaa-dan	*gladan* (m)
	glaa-dna	*gladna* (f)
in a hurry	u zhur-bi	*u žurbin* (m)
	zhu-rim	*žurim* (f)
sad	tuu-zhaa-n	*tužan* (m)
	tuu-zhn-a	*tužna* (f)
thirsty	zhe-dan	*žedan* (m)
	zhe-dna	*žedna* (f)
tired	umor-an	*umoran* (m)
	umor-na	*umorna* (f)
well	do-bro	*dobro*
worried	zaa-brii-nut	*zabrinut* (m)
	zaa-brii-nut-a	*zabrinuta* (f)

I'm sorry.	zhaa-o mi ye	*Žao mi je.*
I'm grateful.	zaa-hvaa-lan/	*Zahvalan/*
	zaa-hvaa-lna sam	*Zahvalna sam.* (m/f)

PAPERWORK

address	adre-esa	*adresa*
age	staa-rost	*starost*
birth certificate	kr-rshte-ni-tsa	*krštenica*
business	poo-slov-no	*poslovno*
date of birth	daa-tum ro-dje-nya	*datum rodenja*
driver's licence	vo-zaa-chka do-zvo-la	*vozacka dozvola*
holiday	od-mor	*odmor*
identification	ide-enti-fii-kaa-tsiya	*identifikacija*
marital status	braa-chno sta-anye	*bracno stanje*
name	ime	*ime*
nationality	naa-tsii-o-naa-lnost	*nacionalnost*
passport	paa-sosh	*pasoš*
passport number	bro-y pa-asosha	*broj pasoša*
place of birth	me-esto ro-dje-nya	*mesto rodenja*
profession	zaa-ni-maa-nye	*zanimanje*
reason for travel	raa-zlog puu-to-vanya	*razlog putovanja*
religion	re-lii-giya	*religija*
sex	pol	*pol*
tourist card	tu-ris-tich-ka kar-ta/	*turistička*
	le-gi-ti-ma-tsiya	*karta/legitimacija*
visa	vii-za	*viza*

BREAKING THE LANGUAGE BARRIER

Do you speak English?
> go-vo-rite li eng-le-ski?   *Govorite li engleski?*

Does anyone speak English?
> go-vo-ri li ne-ko eng-le-ski?   *Govori li neko engleski?*

I (don't) understand.
> ya (ne) raa-zuu-mem   *Ja (ne) razumem.*

Could you speak more slowly, please?
> go-vo-ri-te po-la-ko, mo-lim?   *Govorite polako, molim?*

Could you repeat that?
> mo-lim vas, po-no-vii-te?   *Molim vas, ponovite?*

Please write that down.
> mo-lim vas, naa-pi-shii-te mi   *Molim vas, napišite mi.*

SERBIAN

How do you say ...?
  kaa-ko se kaa-zhe ...?   *Kako se kaže ...?*
What does ... mean?
  shtaa znaa-chi ...?   *Šta znaci ...?*

BODY LANGUAGE

Lively gestures and a wide range of facial expressions are common for both sexes. Lifting up both hands with open palms is often used as a reinforcement of verbal communication. As with most other European cultures, Serbs favour 'face-to-face' relationships.

Avoiding direct eye contact can be seen as a sign of weakness or insincerity. Nodding the head up and down signals 'yes' and shaking it left to right signals 'no'.

SERBIAN

SIGNS	
ВРУЋЕ/ХЛАДНО	HOT/COLD
ЗАБРАЊЕНО	PROHIBITED
ЗАБРАЊЕНО ПУШЕЊЕ	NO SMOKING
ЗАТВОРЕНО	CLOSED
ИЗЛАЗ	EXIT
ИЗЛАЗ ЗА СЛУЧАЈ ОПАСНОСТИ	EMERGENCY EXIT
ИНФОРМАЦИЈЕ	INFORMATION
ОПАСНОСТ	DANGER
ОТВОРЕНО	OPEN
РЕЗЕРВИСАНО	RESERVED
ТЕЛЕФОН	TELEPHONE
ТОАЛЕТИ	TOILETS
УЛАЗ	ENTRANCE
УЛАЗ СЛОБОДАН	FREE ADMISSION
УЛАЗ ЗАБРАЊЕН	NO ENTRY
УПОЗОРЕЊЕ	WARNING
ХЛАДНО	COLD

GETTING AROUND

What time does the ... leave/arrive?	kaa-da ... po-lazi/do-lazi?	Kada ... polazi/dolazi?
aeroplane	avii-on	avion
boat	brod	brod
city bus	auto-bus graa-dski	autobus gradski
intercity bus	auto-bus me-djuu-graa-dski	autobus medugradski
train	voz	voz
tram	traam-vaay	tramvaj

SERBIAN

Directions

Where's ...?
gde ye ...? *Gde je ...?*

How do I get to ...?
kaa-ko da stii-gnem do ...? *Kako da stignem do ...?*

Is it far from here?
ye li daa-le-ko od-davde? *Je li daleko odavde?*

Can I walk there?
mo-gu li pe-e-shii-tse? *Mogu li pešice?*

Can you show me
(on the map)?
mo-zhete li mi po-kaa-zati *Možete li mi pokazati*
(na kaa-rti)? *(na karti)?*

I want to go to ...
zhe-lim da odem u ... *Želim da odem u ...*

Go straight ahead.
idii-te praa-vo naa-pre-ed *Idite pravo napred.*

It's two blocks down.
to ye dvaa blo-ka odaa-vde *To je dva bloka odavde.*

Turn left/right ...	skre-nite le-vo/de-esno ...	Skrenite levo/desno ...
at the next corner	na sle-detchem ug-glu (cho-sh-ku)	Na sledecem uglu (cošku)
at the traffic lights	kod se-ma-fo-ra	kod semafora

behind/in front of	iza/is-pred	*iza/ispred*
far/near	daa-leko/blii-zu	*daleko/blizu*
opposite	pre-eko	*preko*

north	see-ver	*Sever*
south	yug	*Jug*
east	is-tok	*Istok*
west	zaa-pad	*Zapad*

Booking Tickets

Where can I buy a ticket?
  gde mo-gu da ku-pim   *Gde mogu da kupim*
  kaa-rtu?   *kartu?*
I want to go to ...
  zhe-lim da od-em u ...   *želim da odem u ...*
Do I need to book?
  dali mi ye pot-re-bna   *Da li mi je potrebna*
  re-zer-vaa-tsiya?   *rezervacija?*
Can I get a stand-by ticket?
  mo-gu li do-biti kaa-rtu bez   *Mogu li dobiti kartu bez*
  re-ezer-vaa-tsiye?   *rezervacije?*

I'd like ...	zhe-lim ...	*Želim ...*
a one-way ticket	kaar-tu u ye-dnom praa-vcu	*kartu u jednom pravcu*
a return ticket	pov-raa-tnu kaa-rtu	*povratnu kartu*
two tickets	dve kaa-rte	*dve karte*
tickets for all of us	kaa-rte za sve naas	*karte za sve nas*
a student's fare	stu-dent-sku tse-enu	*studentsku cenu*
a child's fare	detchyu tse-nu	*decju cenu*
a pensioner's fare	pen-zio-ner-sku tse-nu	*penzionersku cenu*

| 1st class | pr-rvu klaa-su | *prvu klasu* |
| 2nd class | druu-gu klaa-su | *drugu klasu* |

SERBIAN

SERBIAN

Bus & Tram

Where's the bus stop?
gde ye auto-bus-ska sta-nitsa?   *Gde je autobuska stanica?*

Which bus goes to ...?
ko-yi auto-buus ide za ...?   *Koji autobus ide za ...?*

Does this bus go to ...?
ide li ovaa-y auto-buus za ...?   *Ide li ovaj autobus za ...?*

How often do buses pass by?
ko-li-ko che-sto nai-laze   *Koliko cesto nailaze*
au-to-busi?   *autobusi?*

Could you let me know
when we get to ...?
mo-zhe-ee li mi re-tchi   *Možete li mi reci*
kada stii-zhemo u ...?   *kada stižemo u ...?*

I want to get off!   zhe-lim da sii-djem!   *Želim da sidem!*

What time's   kaa-da po-lazi ...   *Kada polazi ...*
the ... bus?   auto-buus?   *autobus?*
  first   pr-rvi   *prvi*
  last   pos-le-dnyi   *poslednji*
  next   sle-detchi   *sledeci*

SIGNS	
АУТОМЕХАНИЧАР	MECHANIC
АУТОПУТ	FREEWAY
БЕЗОЛОВНИ	UNLEADED
ГАРАЖА	GARAGE
ДАЈТЕ ПРЕДНОСТ	GIVE WAY
ДЕТУР-ОБИЛАЗНИ ПУТ	DETOUR
ЗАБРАЊЕНО ПАРКИРАЊЕ	NO PARKING
ЗАБРАЊЕН УЛАЗ	NO ENTRY
ЈЕДНОСМЕРНО	ONE WAY
НОРМАЛНО	NORMAL
ПОПРАВКЕ	REPAIRS
САМОПОСЛУЖИВАЊЕ	SELF SERVICE
СТОП	STOP
СУПЕР	SUPER

Train & Metro

Which line takes me to ...?
    ko-ya lii-niya ide za ...?   *Koja linija ide za ...?*
What's the next station?
    ko-ya ye sle-detcha staa-nii-tsa?   *Koja je sledeca stanica?*
The train leaves from platform ...
    voz po-lazi sa ... pe-rona   *Voz polazi sa ... perona.*
Is this the right platform for ...?
    daa-li ye ovo pe-ron za ...?   *Dali je ovo peron za ...?*
Is this seat taken?
    daa-li ye ovo se-di-sh-te   *Dali je ovo sedšte*
    zauu-zeto?   *zauzeto?*

dining car	va-gon res-to-ran	*vagon restoran*
express	eks-spres	*ekspres*
local	lo-kaal-ni	*lokalni*
sleeping car	ko-la za spaa-va-nye	*kola za spavanje*

SERBIAN

THEY MAY SAY ...

puu-no ye	It's full.
voz kaa-sni/	The train is delayed/
ye ukii-nut	cancelled.
kaa-sni ... saa-ti	There's a delay of ... hours.
puu-tnii-tsi mo-rayu ...	Passengers must ...
da pro-me-ne voz	change trains
da pro-me-ene pe-ron	change platforms

Taxi

Can you take me to ...?
    mo-zhete li me odve-sti do ...?   *Možete li me odvesti do ...?*
Please take me to ...
    mo-lim vas, odve-zite   *Molim vas, odvezite*
    me do ...   *me do ...*
How much does it
cost to go to ...?
    ko-liko ko-shta vo-zhnya do ...?   *Koliko košta vožnja do ...?*

SERBIAN

Here's fine, thank you.
  ov-vde-e iz-laa-zim, hvaa-la   *Ovde izlazim, hvala.*
The next corner, please.
  na sle-de-tchem   *Na sledećem*
  ug-glu, mo-lim   *uglu, molim.*
Continue!
  pro-duu-zhii-te!   *Produžite!*
The next street to the left/right.
  sle-detcha u-lii-tsa le-vo/de-sno *Sledeca ulica levo/desno.*
Stop here!
  staa-ni-te ov-vde-e!   *Stanite ovde!*
Please, slow down.
  uspo-ri-te, mo-lim   *Usporite, molim.*
Please, wait here.
  saa-tche-kayte ov-de-e, mo-lim   *Sacekajete ovde, molim.*

Car

Where can I hire a car?
  gde mo-gu da   *Gde mogu da*
  naa-djem ren-taa-kar?   *nadem rent-a-car?*
How much is it daily/weekly?
  ko-liko ko-shta dne-vno/   *Koliko košta dnevno/*
  ne-de-lyno?   *nedeljno?*
Does that include
insurance/mileage?
  da li ye uklyuu-che-no   *Da li je ukljuceno*
  osii-gu-raanye/kilo-me-trazha?   *Osiguranje/kilometraža?*
Where's the next petrol station?
  gde-e ye sle-de-tcha   *Gde je sledeca*
  ben-zii-nska staa-nitsa?   *benzinska stanica?*
How long can I park here?
  ko-li-ko duu-go mo-gu ov-de   *Kako dugo mogu ovde*
  da paar-kii-ram?   *da parkiram?*
Does this road lead to ...?
  daa-li ov-vay puut vo-di do ...? *Da li ovaj put vodi do ...?*
I need a mechanic.
  tre-ba mi me-haa-ni-chaar   *Treba mi mehanicar.*

air (for tyres)	vaa-zdugh	*vazduh*
battery	akuu-muu-laa-tor	*akumulator*
brakes	ko-chnii-tse	*kocnice*
clutch	kuu-pluung	*kuplung*
driver's licence	vo-zaa-ch-ka doz-vo-la	*vozacka dozvola*
engine	maa-shii-na	*mašina*
lights	sve-etla	*svetla*
oil	ulye	*ulje*
petrol	ben-zii-na	*benzina*
puncture	pro-buu-she-no	*probušeno*
radiator	raa-dii-yator	*radijator*
road map	auu-to-kaa-rta	*auto-karta*
tyres	guu-me	*gume*
windscreen	ve-tro-bran	*vetrobran*

SERBIAN

SIGNS	
АУТОБУСКА СТАНИЦА	BUS STOP
ВОЗНИ РЕД	TIMETABLE
ДОЛАСЦИ	ARRIVALS
ЖЕЛЕЗНИЧКА СТАНИЦА	TRAIN STATION
ПОДЗЕМНИ ПРОЛАЗ	SUBWAY
ПОЛАСЦИ	DEPARTURES
ПРОДАЈА КАРАТА	TICKET OFFICE
ПРТЉАГ	BAGGAGE COUNTER
РЕГИСТРАЦИЈА	CHECK-IN COUNTER
СТАНИЦА	STATION
ЦАРИНА	CUSTOMS

ACCOMMODATION

Where's a ...?	gde-e imaa ...?	*Gde ima ...?*
cheap hotel	ye-ftin ho-tel	*jeftin hotel*
clean hotel	chii-st ho-tel	*cist hotel*
good hotel	do-bar ho-tel	*dobar hotel*
nearby hotel	ho-tel u blii-zini	*hotel u blizini*

What's the address?
ko-ya ye adre-sa?   *Koja je adresa?*
Could you write the address, please?
mo-liim vas, naa-pi-shi-te   *Molim vas, napišite*
mi adre-su?   *mi adresu?*

At the Hotel

Do you have any rooms available?
da li imaa-te   *Da li imate*
slo-bo-dnih so-ba?   *slobodnih soba?*

I'd like ...	zhe-lim ...	*Želim ...*
a single room	so-bu sa ye-dniim kre-ve-tom	*sobu sa jednim krevetom*
a double room	so-bu sa duu-plim kre-ve-tom	*sobu sa duplim krevetom*
a room with a bathroom	so-bu sa kuu-pa-atilom	*sobu sa kupatilom*
to share a dorm	kre-vet u stuu-den-tskom do-mu	*krevet u studen-tskom domu*
a bed	kre-vet	*krevet*

I want a room with a ...	zhe-lim so-bu sa ...	*Želim sobu sa ...*
bathroom	kuu-paa-tii-lom	*kupatilom*
shower	tuu-shom	*tušom*
window	pro-zo-rom	*prozorom*

SERBIAN

I'm going to stay for ...	ostaa-tchu ...	*Ostacu ...*
one day	ye-dan daan	*jedan dan*
two days	dva daa-na	*dva dana*
one week	ye-dnu ne-delju	*jednu nedelju*

How much is it
per night/person?
    ko-lii-ko ko-shta za ye-dnu   *Koliko košta za jednu*
    no-tch/po oso-bi?   *noc/po osobi?*
Can I see it?
    mo-gu li da po-glee-dam?   *Mogu li da pogledam?*
Are there any others?
    da li imate druu-ge so-be?   *Da li imate druge sobe?*
Is there a reduction for
students/children?
    ima li po-puust za   *Ima li popust za*
    stuu-de-nte/de-etsu?   *studente/decu?*
It's fine, I'll take it.
    u re-du ye, uze-tchu ye   *U redu je, uzecu je.*
I'd like to pay the bill.
    zhe-lim da pla-tim ra-chun   *Želim da platim racun.*

SERBIAN

Requests & Complaints

Do you have a safe where
I can leave my valuables?
    imaa-te li seef gde mo-gu da   *Imate li sef gde mogu da*
    ostaa-vim vre-dne stvaa-ri?   *ostavim vredne stvari?*
Is there somewhere to
wash clothes?
    mo-gu li neg-de da   *Mogu li negde da*
    ope-rem ve-sh?   *operem veš?*
Can I use the telephone?
    mo-gu li da tele-fo-niram?   *Mogu li da telefoniram?*

The room needs to be cleaned.
 so-bu tre-ba ochiis-tii-ti *Sobu treba ocistiti.*
I can't open/close the window.
 ne mo-gu da ot-tvo-rim/ *Ne mogu da otvorim/*
 zat-vo-rim pro-zor *zatvorim prozor.*
I've locked myself out of
my room.
 zaa-luu-pi-la su mi se vraa-ta *Zalupila su mi se vrata.*
The toilet won't flush.
 to-alet/klo-zet ne *Toalet/klozet ne*
 pu-shta vo-du *pušta vodu.*

AROUND TOWN

I'm looking traa-zhim ... *Tražim ...*
for a/the ...

art gallery	gaa-le-riyu	*galeriju*
bank	baa-nku	*banku*
church	tsr-rkvu	*crkvu*
city centre	tse-ntar graa-da	*centar grada*
... embassy	... ambaa-saa-du	*... ambasadu*
my hotel	moy ho-tel	*moj hotel*
market	pii-yaa-cu	*pijacu*
museum	muu-zey	*muzej*
police	mi-lii-tsiyu	*miliciju*
post office	po-shtu	*poštu*
public toilet	yaa-vni toaa-let/	*javni toalet/*
	klo-zet	*klozet*
telephone centre	yaa-vni tele-fon	*javni telefon*
tourist	tuu-rii-sti-chki	*turisticki*
information	bii-ro	*biro*
office		

What time does it open/close?
 kaa-da se otvaa-ra/zaa-tvaa-ra? *Kada se otvara/zatvara?*

For directions, see the Getting Around section, page 422.

SERBIAN

At the Post Office

I'd like to send a/an ...	zhe-lim da po-shaa-lyem ...	*Želim da pošaljem ...*
aerogram	aero-gram	*aerogram*
letter	pii-smo	*pismo*
parcel	paa-ket	*paket*
postcard	raaz-gle-dnitsu	*razglednicu*
telegram	te-le-gram	*telegram*

I'd like some stamps.

zhe-lim po-shte-nske maa-rke   *Želim poštanske marke.*

How much is the postage?

ko-liko ko-shta po-shtaa-rina?   *Koliko košta poštarina?*

airmail	avii-onski	*avionski*
envelope	ko-ve-rat	*koverat*
mailbox	po-shtaa-nsko saa-ndu-che	*poštansko sanduce*
registered mail	pre-po-ruu-cheno pii-smo	*preporuceno pismo*
surface mail	obii-chno pii-smo	*obicno pismo*

SERBIAN

TURKISH HERITAGE

The name 'Sarajevo' comes from 'saraj', Turkish for 'palace'. Sarajevo is one of the most Oriental cities in Europe, retaining the essence of its history with mosques, markets and the picturesque old Turkish bazaar called Baščaršija. When the Turks finally withdrew, half a century of Austro-Hungarian domination began.

SERBIAN

Telephone

I want to ring ...
    zhe-elim da te-le-fo-niram ...   *Želim da telefoniram ...*
The number is ...
    broy ye ...   *Broj je ...*
I want to speak for
three minutes.
    zhe-lim da go-vo-rim   *Želim da govorim*
    tri mii-nuta.   *tri minuta.*
How much does each
extra minute cost?
    ko-liko ko-shta svaa-ki   *Koliko košta svaki*
    do-datni mii-nut?   *dodatni minut?*
I'd like to speak
to (Mr Perez).
    zhe-lim go-vo-rim sa   *Želim da govorim sa*
    (gos-po-dinom pe-ritchem)   *(Gospodinom Pericem).*
I want to make a reverse-
charges phone call.
    zhe-lim da tele-fo-nii-ram na   *Želim da telefoniram na*
    nyii-ghov raa-chuun   *njihov racun.*
It's engaged.
    zauu-zeto ye   *Zauzeto je.*
I've been cut off.
    pre-kii-nuli su me   *Prekinuli su me.*

Internet

Where can I get Internet access?
    gde mo-gu da na-djem   *Gde mogu da nađem*
    inter-net?   *internet?*
How much is it per hour?
    ko-li-ko ko-shta na sat   *Koliko košta na sat?*
I want to check my email.
    ho-tchu da pro-ve-rim   *Hoću da proverim*
    moj e-mail   *moj email.*

At the Bank

I want to	zhe-lim da	*Želim da*
exchange some ...	raa-zmenim ...	*razmenim ...*
money	no-vats	*novac*
travellers cheques	put-niich-ke che-ko-ve	*putničke čekove*

What's the exchange rate?
  ko-yi ye kuurs?   *Koji je kurs?*

How many ... per dollar?
  ko-liko dii-nara za   *Koliko dinara za*
  ye-dan do-lar?   *jedan dolar?*

Can I have money transferred
here from my bank?
  mo-gu li da pre-baa-tsim   *Mogu li da prebacim*
  no-vats iz mo-ye u   *novac iz moje u*
  ovu baa-nku?   *ovu banku?*

How long will it take to arrive?
  ko-liko vre-mena tre-ba da   *Koliko vremena treba da*
  stii-gne?   *stigne?*

Has my money arrived yet?
  daa-li ye stii-gao moy no-vats?   *Da li je stigao moj novac?*

SERBIAN

bankdraft	baa-nkovni chek	*bankovni cek*
banknotes	nov-chaa-nitsa	*novcanica*
cashier	blaa-gaa-ynik	*blagajnik*
coins	me-talni no-vats	*metalni novac*
credit card	kre-ditna kaa-rta	*kreditna karta*
exchange	raa-zme-na	*razmena*
loose change	sii-tan no-vac	*sitan novac*
signature	pot-pis	*potpis*

INTERESTS & ENTERTAINMENT
Sightseeing

Do you have a guidebook?
da li ima-te vo-dich? *Da li imate vodič?*

Do you have a local map?
da li ima-te kar-tu gra-da? *Da li imate mapu grada?*

What are the main attractions?
ko-ye su glaa-vne *Koje su glavne*
zaa-nii-mlyivosti? *zanimljivosti?*

What's that?
shtaa ye ovo? *Šta je to?*

Can I take photographs?
da-li smem da sli-kam? *Da li smem da slikam?*

ancient	staa-ro	*staro*
archaeological	ar-rhe-o-lo-shko	*arheološko*
beach	plaa-zha	*plaža*
building	zgraa-da	*zgrada*
castle	zaa-mak	*zamak*
cathedral	kaa-te-draa-la	*katedrala*
church	tsr-rkva	*crkva*
concert hall	kon-cer-rtna	*koncertna*
	dvo-rana	*dvorana*
library	bii-blii-oo-te-ka	*biblioteka*
main square	glaa-veni trrg	*glavni trg*
market	pii-yatsa	*pijaca*
monastery	maa-na-stiir	*manastir*
monument	spo-me-nik	*spomenik*
mosque	dzhaa-miya	*džamija*
old city	staa-ri graad	*stari grad*
opera house	ope-ra	*opera*
palace	paa-laa-ta	*palata*
ruins	ruu-she-vine	*ruševine*
stadium	staa-dion	*stadion*
statues	staa-tue	*statue*
synagogue	sii-na-go-ga	*sinagoga*
university	unii-verzii-tet	*univerzitet*

SERBIAN

Going Out

What's there to do
in the evenings?

    gde mo-zhe da se izaa-dje   *Gde može da se izade*
    uve-che?   *uvece?*

Are there any nightclubs?

    da li ov-vde iima dii-sko?   *Da li ovde ima disko?*

Are there places where you
can hear local folk music?

    imaa li gde da se sluu-sha   *Ima li gde da se sluša*
    lokaa-lna naa-ro-dna   *lokalna narodna*
    muu-zii-ka?   *muzika?*

How much does it cost
to get in?

    ko-li-ko ko-shta ulaa-znitsa?   *Koliko košta ulaznica?*

cinema	bio-skop	*bioskop*
concert	ko-ntsert	*koncert*
nightclub	dii-sko-te-ka	*diskoteka*
theatre	po-zo-rishte	*pozorište*

SERBIAN

Festivals

The most important religious festivals celebrated in Serbia are:

Božić   **bo-shithc**
    Christmas Day, which falls on 7 January, according to the old
    calendar

Sveti Sava   **svee-ti saa-va**
    St Sava's day, 25 January, is particularly celebrated by school
    children. The son of the Serbian ruler in 13th century, St Sava,
    became the founder of the Serbian Orthodox church and the
    founder of Serbian literature.

Uskrs   **us-krs**
    Easter Day

SERBIAN

Vidovdan   vii-dov-dan
St Vitus Day, 28 June, is a very important festival, commemorating the fateful Kosovo battle in 1389 when, defeated by the Ottoman Turks, the Serbs lost their medieval kingdom

Sports & Interests

What sports do you play?
ko-yim spor-to-vi-ma   *Kojim sportovima*
se ba-vi-te   *se bavite?*
What are your interests?
shta vas zaa-ni-ma?   *Šta vas zanima?*

art	ume-tn-ost	*umetnost*
basketball	ko-shar-ka	*košarka*
chess	sha-gh	*šah*
collecting things	sku-plya-nye stva-ri	*skupljanje stvari*
dancing	ples	*ples*
food	hraa-na	*hrana*
football	fud-baal	*fudbal*
hiking	pla-nii-na-re-nye	*planinarenje*
martial arts	bo-ri-la-chke	*borilacke*
	ve-shti-ne	*veštine*
meeting friends	dru-zhe-nye	*druženje*
movies	fil-mo-vi	*filmovi*
music	muu-zi-ka	*muzika*
nightclubs	no-tchni klu-bo-vi	*nocni klubovi*
photography	fo-to-gra-fi-ya	*fotografija*
reading	chi-taa-nye	*citanje*
shopping	ku-po-vi-na	*kupovina*
skiing	skii-ya-nye	*skijanje*
swimming	pli-va-nye	*plivanje*
tennis	ten-nis	*tenis*
travelling	pu-to-va-nye	*putovanje*
TV/videos	te-le-vii-zii-ya/vi-deo	*televizija/video*
visiting friends	po-se-te/see-dely-ke	*posete/sedeljke*
walking	she-tnye	*šetnje*

IN THE COUNTRY
Weather

What's the weather like?
kaa-kvo ye vre-eme? *Kakvo je vreme?*

Will it be ...	da li tche su-tra	*Da li ce sutra*
tomorrow?	bi-ti ...?	*biti ...?*
The weather is	vre-eme da-nas ye ...	*Vreme danas je ...*
... today.		
cloudy	oblaa-chno	*oblacno*
cold	hlaa-dno	*hladno*
foggy	maa-glo-vito	*maglovito*
frosty	mraa-z	*mraz*
hot	vruu-tche	*vruce*
raining	kii-sho-vi-to	*kišovito*
	(pa-da ki-sha)	*(pada kiša)*
snowing	sne-eg (pa-da sne-eg)	*sneg (pada sneg)*
sunny	suu-nchaa-no	*suncano*
windy	ve-tro-vito	*vetrovito*

SERBIAN

Camping

Am I allowed to camp here?
da li mo-gu da kaam-pu-jem *Da li mogu da kampujem*
ov-vde-e? *ovde?*

Is there a campsite nearby?
da li ima kaa-mping u *Da li ima kamping u*
blii-zii-ni? *blizini?*

backpack	raa-nats	*ranac*
can opener	otvaa-raa-ch za	*otvarac za*
	kon-ze-rve	*konzerve*
compass	ko-mpas	*kompas*
crampons	kram-po-ni	*kramponi*
firewood	dr-rva za og-gre-ev	*drva za ogrev*
gas cartridge	bo-tsa sa plii-nom	*boca sa plinom*
hammock	le-zha-lyka	*ležaljka*

ice axe	se-kii-ra	*sekira*
mattress	duu-shek	*dušek*
penknife	no-zhitch	*nožic*
rope	uzhe	*uže*
tent	shaa-tor	*šator*
tent pegs	ko-chii-tchi za shaa-tor	*kocici za šator*
torch (flashlight)	dzhe-pna lam-pa (ba-te-ri-ya)	*dzepna lampa (baterija)*
sleeping bag	vre-tcha za spaa-vaa-nye	*vreca za spavanje*
stove	pe-tch	*pec*
water bottle	flaa-sha za vo-du	*flaša za vodu*

SERBIAN

FOOD

Cooking in this region illustrates the effect of history and geography. Food from northern Croatia and Vojvodina (northern Yugoslavia) has an unmistakable Hungarian flavour, while Italian pasta and risotto have both crossed the Adriatic. Places along the coast and larger restaurants in the interior of the country also serve fish specialities.

Serbian cooking is typically very rich, with most meals consisting of highly seasoned meats. Lunches tend to be more interesting than dinners, as locals generally take their main meal at midday.

Main towns and resorts have plenty of attractive restaurants, many privately run, where you can eat well at any time. Many restaurants provide *meni*, a lunchtime set menu for the day which includes soup and a main course.

breakfast	do-ruu-chak	*dorucak*
lunch	ruu-chaak	*rucak*
dinner	ve-che-ra	*vecera*

MENU DECODER

Starters

ajvar	ayvar	a spicy mixture of fried peppers and eggplant, chopped and seasoned with garlic, salt, vinegar and cooking oil. Try this spread on bread.
burek	bu-urek	a flaky pastry with layers of cheese, spinach or minced meat. Try burek with yoghurt, it's delicious.
dalmatinski pršut	dalmatinski prshut	lightly smoked ham
užicka pršuta	uzh-ich-ka pr-shu-ta	beef smoked until it's hard
gibanica	gi-ba-ni-tsa	dish made of layers of filo pastry filled with *kajmak* (the cream from boiled milk, salted and kept over a period of time), mixed with eggs and white cheese and baked in the oven
kacamak	ka-cha-mak	a paste-like entree made of ground maize, cooked in salt water, and eaten with white cheese
kajmak	kay-mak	a Serbian speciality, this is a kind of cheese butter made out of the salted cream from boiled milk. Try it on bread instead of butter.
pihtije	pigh-ti-ye	jellied pork or duck with garlic – highly recommended
pita	pi-ta	a flaky pastry filled with a combination of spinach, cheese and eggs
pogačice sa čvarcima	pogachitse sa chvartsima	a kind of oven-baked cake, similar to scones, containing pieces of fried pork fat

SERBIAN

SERBIAN

MENU DECODER

Main Dishes

Main meals are usually served with finely chopped raw onion and are accompanied by salads, such as *šopska salata* shop-ska sa-la-ta which consists of red and green peppers, cucumber and lettuce.

pljeskavica	plyeskavitsa	grilled minced meat, usually a mixture of pork, beef and lamb
pljeskavica (sa kajmakom)	plyeskavitsa (sa kaymakom)	as above, with kajmak
ražnjići	razhnyitchi	small cubes of pork grilled on a skewer
ćevapčići	tchevapchitchi	minced pork, beef or lamb shaped into small sausages then grilled
punjene paprike	punyene paprike	peppers stuffed with minced beef or pork and rice in a fresh tomato sauce
djuvec	dju-ve-ech	an oven-cooked mixture of eggplant, carrot, potato, rice and meat topped with grated cheese

Desserts

Serbian cakes tend to be very rich and sweet:

doboš rorta	do-bosh tor-ta	cake of Hungarian origin, garnished with coffee and caramel
štrudla	sht-rud-la	a fantastic blend of pastry and fruit
sa jabukama	sa ya-bu-ka-ma	with apples
sa trešnjama	sa tre-shnya-ma	with cherries
baklava	ba-kla-va	a flaky pastry with nuts, soaked in sugar syrup

Vegetarian Meals

I'm a vegetarian.
  ya sam ve-geta-ri-yanats/
  ve-geta-rii-yanka

*Ja sam vegetarijanac/
vegetarijanka.* (m/f)

I don't eat meat.
  ne ye-dem me-so

Ne jedem meso.

I don't eat chicken, fish or ham.
  ne ye-dem pi-letche me-so,
  rii-bu ni shun-ku

*Ne jedem pilece meso,
ribu ni šunku.*

Non-Alcoholic Drinks

In Serbia, *Turska Kava* 'Turkish coffee' served black, is a must for any coffee lover.

(black/white) coffee	(tsr-na/be-la) ka-fa	*(crna/bela) kafa*
tea	chay	*čaj*
with sugar	sa she-tche-rom	*sa šećerom*
fruit juice	vo-tchni sok	*vocni sok*
hot chocolate	vru-tcha cho-ko-la-da	*vruća čokolada*
mineral water	mi-ner-al-na vo-da	*mineralna voda*
soft drink	bez-alko-hol-no pi-tche	*bezalkoholno piće*
(boiled) water	(pro-ku-va-na) vo-da	*(prokuvana) voda*

SERBIAN

Alcoholic Drinks

This is a great vine-growing country. Table wines are widely available and are very cheap. In restaurants you can order wine in jugs of various sizes. Local wines change names according to their colour:

red wine	tsr-no	*crno*
white wine	be-lo	*belo*
rosé	ru-zhi-tsa	*ružica*

All local spirits are extremely strong. The generic name for most distilled drinks is *rakija*, which means 'brandy', though you'll usually be given *šljivovica*, plum brandy.

beer	pi-vo	*pivo*
brandy	ra-ki-ya	*rakija*
plum brandy	shlyi-vo-vi-tsa	*šljivovica*
red wine	tsr-no vi-no	*crno vino*
rosé	ru-zhi-tsa	*ružica*
white wine	be-lo vi-no	*belo vino*

At the Market

How much is it?
   ko-li-ko ko-shta? — *Koliko košta?*

Could you lower the price?
   mo-zhe-te li smaa-nyiti tse-nu? — *Možete li smanjiiti cenu?*

I don't have much money.
   ne-mam mno-go no-vtsa — *Nemam mnogo novca.*

Staple Foods

bread	gh-leb	*hleb*
butter	pu-ter	*puter*
cereal	zhi-ta-ri-tse	*žitarice*
cheese	sir	*sir*
chocolate	cho-ko-la-du	*cokoladu*
eggs	ya-ya	*jaja*
flour	bra-shno	*brašno*
honey	me-ed	*med*
margarine	maar-ga-rin	*margarin*
marmalade	maar-me-la-du	*marmeladu*
milk	mle-ko	*mleko*
olive oil	ma-sli-no-vo ulye	*maslinovo ulje*
pasta	tes-te-ni-ne	*testenine*
pepper	bii-ber	*biber*
rice	pi-ri-nach	*pirinač*
salt	so	*so*
sugar	she-tcher	*šecer*
yoghurt	yo-gurt	*jo-gurt*

Meat & Fish

beef	go-ve-di-na	*govedina*
chicken	pi-le-ti-na	*piletina*
ham	shun-ku	*šunku*
hamburger	ham-bur-ger	*hamburger*
lamb	yag-nye-ti-na	*jagnjetina*
lobster	ja-stog	*jastog*
meat	me-so	*meso*
mussels	mu-shu-le	*mušule*
oysters	shkoly-ke	*školjke*
pork	svi-nye-ti-na	*svinjetina*
sausage	ko-ba-si-tsa	*kobasica*
shrimp	ra-chi-tch	*račić*
turkey	tchu-re-ti-na	*ćuretina*
veal	te-le-ti-na	*teletina*

SERBIAN

Fruit

apple	ya-bu-ka	*jabuka*
apricot	kay-si-ya	*kajsija*
banana	ba-na-na	*banana*
fig	smok-va	*smokva*
grapes	grozh-dje	*grožđe*
kiwifruit	ki-vi	*kivi*
lemon	li-mun	*limun*
orange	po-mo-ran-dzha	*pomorandža*
peach	bres-kva	*breskva*
pear	kru-shka	*kruška*
plum	shlyi-va	*šljiva*
strawberry	ya-go-da	*jagoda*

Vegetables

(green) beans	bo-ra-ni-ya	*boranija*
beetroot	tsve-kla	*cvekla*
broad beans	bo-ra-ni-ya	*boranija*
cabbage	ku-pus	*kupus*
carrot	shar-ga-re-pa	*šargarepa*
capsicum (red/green)	pa-pri-ka	*paprika*
cauliflower	kar-fi-ol	*karfiol*
celery	tse-ler	*celer*
chickpeas	leb-leb-li-ye	*lebleblije*
chillies	lyu-te pap-ri-chi-tse	*ljute papričice*
cucumber	kra-sta-vats	*krastavac*

eggplant	pla-vi pat-li-dzhan	*plavi patlidžan*
garlic	be-li luk	*beli luk*
ginger	djum-bir	*djumbir*
kidney beans	pa-suly	*pasulj*
lentils	so-chi-vo	*sočivo*
lettuce	ze-le-na sa-la-ta	*zelena salata*
mushrooms	pe-chur-ke	*pečurke*
onion	tsr-ni luk	*crni luk*
peas	gra-shak	*grašak*
potato	krom-pir	*krompir*
spinach	spa-natch	*spanać*
tomato	pa-ra-dajz	*paradjz*
vegetables	po-vr-tche	*povrće*
zucchini	tik-vi-tse	*tikvice*

SHOPPING

How much is it?
    ko-li-ko ko-shta?   *Koliko košta?*
Where is the nearest ...?
    gde je naj-bli-zha ...?   *Gde je najbliža ...?*

bookshop	knyii-zhaa-ra	*knjižara*
camera shop	raa-dnja za	*radnja za*
	fo-to-apaa-rate	*fotoaparate*
clothing store	raa-dnya za ode-tchu	*radnja za odecu*
delicatessen	de-li-kaa-tes	*delikates*
general store	rob-naku-tcha	*robna kuca*
laundry	pe-rii-onitsa	*perionica*
market	pii-yats	*pijac*
newsagency	ki-osk za no-vi-ne	*kiosk za novine*
stationers	knyii-zhaa-ra	*knjižara*
chemist	apo-teka	*apoteka*
shoeshop	obu-tcha	*obuca*
souvenir shop	suu-ve-nii-ri	*suveniri*
supermarket	samo-pos-lu-ga	*samoposluga*
green grocer	pii-lyar-ni-tsa	*piljarnica*

Do you accept credit cards?
    da li mo-gu da plaa-tim   *Da li mogu da platim*
    kre-dit kaar-tom?   *kredit kartom?*

Clothing

clothing	ode-tcha/ode-lo	*odeca/odelo*
coat	kaa-put	*kaput*
dress	haa-lyii-na	*haljina*
jacket	saa-ko	*sako*
jumper (sweater)	dzhe-emper	*džemper*
shirt	ko-shuu-lya	*košulja*
shoes	tsii-pele	*cipele*
skirt	suu-knya	*suknja*
trousers	pann-ta-lo-ne	*pantalone*

SERBIAN

SERBIAN

Essential Groceries

I'd like ...	zhe-lim ...	želim ...
batteries	ba-te-ri-ye	baterije
bread	gh-leb	hleb
butter	pu-ter	puter
cheese	sir	sir
chocolate	cho-ko-la-du	cokoladu
honey	me-ed	med
margarine	maar-ga-rin	margarin
marmalade	maar-me-la-du	marmeladu
matches	shi-bi-tse	šibice
milk	mle-ko	mleko
shampoo	sham-pon	šampon
soap	sa-pun	sapun
toilet paper	to-a-let pa-pir	toalet papir
toothpaste	paas-tu za zu-be	pastu za zube
washing powder	de-ter-dzhe-ent	deterdžent

Toiletries

condoms	ko-ndom	kondomi
deodorant	de-zo-do-rans	dezodorans
hairbrush	che-tka za ko-su	cetka za kosu
moisturiser	kre-ma za te-lo	krema za telo
razor	brii-yach	brijac
sanitary napkins	hi-gi-yen-ske ulo-shke	higijenske uloške
shampoo	shaam-pon	šampon
shaving cream	kre-ma za brii-yanye	krema za brijanje
soap	saa-pun	sapun
sunscreen	kre-ma za sun-cha-nye	krema za suncanje
tampons	taam-po-ni	tamponi
tissues	pa-pi-rne ma-ra-mi-tse	papirne maramice
toilet paper	to-aletni paa-pir	toaletni papir
toothbrush	chet-kii-tsa za zuu-be	cetkica za zube
toothpaste	paa-sta za zuu-be	pasta za zube

Souvenirs

Woven rugs, *ćilim*, (similar to Turkish ones) can be found in markets and in special shops called 'Narodna Radinost', which means 'Folk handwork'. Various objects made of copper and other metals (such as ashtrays, coffee pots, decorative plates) can also be found in these shops, as well as beautiful garments with needle-work, belts and knitted woollen jackets.

earrings	miin-djuu-she	*minduše*
handicraft	ruu-chni rad	*rucni rad*
necklace	ogr-rlitsa	*ogrlica*
pottery	grn-nchariya	*grncarija*
ring	prs-sten	*prsten*
rug	tchii-lim	*ćilim*

Materials

What's it made of?

od che-ga ye o-vo na-prav-lye-no? *Od čega je ovo napravljeno?*

cotton	paa-muk	*pamuk*
handmade	ruu-chni raad	*rucni rad*
leather	ko-zha	*koža*
of copper	od baa-kra	*od bakra*
of gold	od zlaa-ta/zlaa-tno	*od zlata/zlatno*
of silver	od sre-bra/sree-br-no	*od srebra/srebrno*
silk	svii-la	*svila*
wool	vuu-na	*vuna*

Colours

black	tsr-rna	*crna*
blue	plaa-va	*plava*
brown	braa-on	*braon*
green	ze-lena	*zelena*
orange	na-ran-dzhaa-sta	*narandžasta*
pink	ro-ze	*roze*
purple	lyuu-bii-chaa-sta	*ljubicasta*
red	tsr-ve-na	*crvena*
white	be-ela	*bela*
yellow	zhuu-ta	*žuta*

SERBIAN

Stationery & Publications

map	kaa-rta	*karta*
newspaper/novels	no-vine knyii-ge	*novine/knjige*
(in English)	(na een-ngle-skom)	*(na Engleskom)*
paper	paa-pir	*papir*
pen (ballpoint)	he-mii-yska	*hemijska*
scissors	maa-kaze	*makaze*

Photography

How much is it to process
this film?
    ko-liko ko-shta da   *Kolko košta da*
    se raaz-vii-ye   *se razvije*
    ovay fii-lm?   *ovaj film?*
When will it be ready?
    kada tche bii-ti go-tov?   *Kada ce biti gotov?*
I'd like a film for this camera.
    zhe-lim fii-lm za ovaay   *Želim film za ovaj*
    apaa-rat?   *aparat.*

B&W (film)	tsr-rno be-eli	*crno-beli*
camera	fo-to apaa-rat	*foto aparat*
colour (film)	u bo-yi	*u boji*
film	fii-lm	*film*
flash	bliits	*blic*
lens	obye-ktiv	*objektiv*
light meter	sve-t-lo-sni indii-kator	*svetlosni indikator*

SERBIAN

Smoking

A packet of cigarettes, please.	kuu-tii-yu tsii-gaa-re-ta, mo-lim	*Kutiju cigareta, molim.*
Are these cigarettes strong/mild?	da-li su ove tsi-ga-re-te ya-ke/bla-ge?	*Da li su ove cigarete jake/blage?*
Do you have a light?	imaa-te li upaa-lyach?	*Imate li upaljac?*
Do you smoke?	da li pu-shi-te?	*Da li pušite?*
Please don't smoke.	mo-lim vas da ne pu-shi-te	*Molim vas da ne pušite.*

cigarette papers	paa-pir za tsii-gaa-re-te	*papir za cigarete*
cigarettes	tsii-gaa-re-te	*cigarete*
filtered	sa fiil-te-rom	*sa filterom*
lighter	upaa-lyach	*upaljac*
matches	shii-bii-tse	*šibice*
menthol	me-ntol	*mentol*
pipe	luu-lu	*lulu*
tobacco (pipe)	duu-van	*duvan*

SERBIAN

SIGNS

ЗАБРАЊЕНО ПУШЕЊЕ	NO SMOKING

Sizes & Comparisons

small	maa-li	*mali*
big	ve-lii-ki	*veliki*
heavy	te-zhak	*težak*
light	laa-gan	*lagan*
more	vii-she	*više*
less	maa-nye	*manje*
too much/many	pre-vii-she	*previše*

SERBIAN

HEALTH

Where's the ...?	gde ye ...?	*Gde je ...?*
chemist	apo-teka	*apoteka*
dentist	zuu-bar	*zubar*
doctor	le-kar	*lekar*
hospital	bo-lnitsa	*bolnica*

I'm sick.
   bo-le-stan/bo-le-sna sam   *Bolestan/Bolesna sam.* (m/f)
My friend is sick.
   moy prii-ya-te-ly ye bo-le-stan/   *Moj prijatelj je bolestan.* (m)
   mo-ya pri-iya-te-lyitsa   *Moja prijateljica*
   ye bo-le-sna   *je bolesna.* (f)
Could I see a female doctor?
   da li mo-gu da vii-dim le-kaa-rku? *Da li mogu da vidim lekarku?*

Parts of the Body

ankle	chlaa-nak	*clanak*
arm	ruu-ka	*ruka*
back	le-dja	*leda*
chest	gruu-di	*grudi*
ear	uvo	*uvo*
eye	oko	*prst*
foot	sto-palo	*stopalo*
hand	ruu-ka	*ruka*
head	glaa-va	*glava*
heart	sr-rtse	*srce*
leg	no-ga	*noga*
mouth	us-sta	*usta*
nose	nos	*nos*
ribs	re-bra	*rebra*
skin	ko-zha	*koža*
spine	kii-chma	*kicma*
stomach	sto-mak	*stomak*
teeth	zuu-bi	*zubi*
throat	gr-rlo	*grlo*

It hurts here.   bo-li me ov-vde-e   *Boli me ovde .*

Ailments

I have a/an...	bo-li me ...	*Boli me ...*
allergy	aler-gii-ya	*alergija*
anaemia	ane-miya	*anemija*
blister	pl-lik	*plik*
burn	ope-ko-tina	*opekotina*
cold	naa-zeb	*nazeb*
constipation	kon-stii-paa-tsiya	*konstipacija*
cough	kaa-shaly	*kašalj*
diarrhoea	pro-liv	*proliv*
fever	gro-zni-tsa	*groznica*
headache	glaa-vo-bo-lya	*glavobolja*
indigestion	lo-she vaa-renye	*loše varenje*
infection	inn-fe-ktsiya	*infekcija*

SERBIAN

influenza	griip	*grip*
lice	vaa-shke	*vaške*
low/high blood	nii-zak/vii-sok kr-rvni	*nizak/visok*
pressure	prii-tisak	*krvni pritisak*
pain	bol	*bol*
sore throat	upaa-lu gr-rla	*upala grla*
sprain	uga-nuu-tche	*uganuce*
stomachache	bo-lovi u sto-maku	*bolovi u*
		stomaku
sunburn	ope-koti-ne od	*opekotine od*
	su-ntsa	*sunca*
venereal disease	ve-ne-ri-chna bo-lest	*venericna*
		bolest
worms	glii-ste	*gliste*

SERBIAN

At the Chemist

I need medication for ...
    tre-ba mi lek za ...   *Treba mi lek za ...*
I have a prescription.
    imaam re-tsept   *Imam recept.*

antibiotics	antii-bii-otii-tsi	*antibiotici*
antiseptic	antii-se-ptii-k	*antiseptik*
bandage	zaa-voy	*zavoj*
contraceptive	sre-dstva za	*sredstva za*
	kon-tra-tse-ptsiyu	*kontracepciju*
medicine	lek	*lek*
vitamins	vitaa-mini	*vitamini*

At the Dentist

I have a toothache.
    imaam zubo bo-lya   *Imam zubobolju.*
I've lost a filling.
    is-pa-la mi je plom-ba   *Ispala mi je plomba.*
I've broken a tooth.
    slo-mio mi se zuub   *Slomio mi se zub.*
My gums hurt.
    bo-le me de-sni   *Bole me desni.*
I don't want it extracted.
    ne zhe-lim da se vaa-di   *Ne želim da se vadi.*
Please give me an anaesthetic.
    mo-lim vas, daa-yte mi   *Molim vas, dajte mi*
    ane-ste-ziyu   *anesteziju.*

TIME & DATES

What date is it today?
   ko-yi ye daa-nas daa-tum?   *Koji je danas datum?*
What time is it?
   ko-liko ye saa-ti?   *Koliko je sati?*

It's ... am/pm.	saa-da ye ... saa-ti	*Sada je ... sati.*
It's 9 am.	sa-da je de-vet	*Sada je devet*
	uyu-tru	*ujutru.*
It's 1.30 pm.	sa-da je po-la dva	*Sada je pola dva*
	po-podne	*popodne*
in the morning	uyuu-tro	*ujutro*
in the afternoon	po-po-dne	*popodne*
in the evening	uve-eche	*uvece*

SERBIAN

Days

Monday	po-ne-de-lyak	*ponedeljak*
Tuesday	uto-rak	*utorak*
Wednesday	sre-eda	*sreda*
Thursday	chet-vr-rtak	*cetvrtak*
Friday	pe-tak	*petak*
Saturday	suu-bota	*subota*
Sunday	ne-de-elya	*nedelja*

Months

January	yaa-nu-ar	*januar*
February	feb-ruu-ar	*februar*
March	maart	*mart*
April	app-ril	*april*
May	may	*maj*
June	yuu-ni	*juni*
July	yuu-li	*juli*
August	avguu-st	*avgust*
September	sep-te-mbar	*septembar*
October	okto-bar	*oktobar*
November	no-ve-mbar	*novembar*
December	de-tse-mbar	*decembar*

SERBIAN

Seasons

summer	le-eto	*leto*
autumn	ye-sen	*jesen*
winter	zii-ma	*zima*
spring	pro-le-etche	*prolece*

Present

today	daa-nas	*danas*
this morning	yuu-tros	*jutros*
tonight	ve-che-ras	*veceras*
this week	ove ne-delye	*ove nedelje*
this year	o-ve go-dine	*ove godine*
now	saa-da	*sada*

Past

yesterday	yuu-che	*juče*
the day before yesterday	prek-yuu-che	*prekjuče*
yesterday morning	yuu-che uyuu-tro	*juce ujutro*
last night	sii-notch	*sinoc*
last week	pro-shla ne-delya	*prošla nedelja*
last year	pro-shla go-dina	*prošla godina*

Future

tomorrow	suu-tra	*sutra*
day after tomorrow	pre-ko-suu-tra	*prekosutra*
tomorrow morning	suu-tra uyuu-tro	*sutra ujutro*
tomorrow afternoon/ evening	suu-tra po-po-dne/ uve-che	*sutra popodne uvece*
next week	iduu-tche ne-delye	*iduce nedelje*
next year	iduu-tche go-dii-ne	*iduce godine*

During the Day

afternoon	po-po-dne	*popodne*
dawn	zo-ra	*zora*
day	dan	*dan*
early	raa-no	*rano*
midday	po-dne	*podne*
midnight	po-notch	*ponoc*
morning	yuu-tro	*jutro*
night	no-tch	*noc*
sunrise	sva-nu-tche	*svanuce*
sunset	zaa-laa-zak suu-ntsa	*zalazak sunca*

NUMBERS & AMOUNTS
Numbers

0	nuu-la	*nula*
1	ye-dan	*jedan*
2	dva	*dva*
3	tr-ri	*tri*
4	che-tiri	*cetiri*
5	pet	*pet*
6	shest	*šest*
7	se-dam	*sedam*
8	osaam	*osam*
9	de-vet	*devet*
10	de-set	*deset*
11	jeedaa-naa-est	*jedanaest*
12	dvaa-naa-est	*dvanaest*
13	trii-naa-est	*trinaest*
14	che-tr-naa-est	*cetrnaest*
15	pet-naa-est	*petnaest*
16	shes-naa-est	*šesnaest*
17	seedaa-mnaa-est	*sedamnaest*
18	osaa-mnaa-est	*osamnaest*
19	deeve-at-naa-est	*devetnaest*
20	dvaa-de-set	*dvadeset*
21	dvaa-de-set i ye-dan	*dvadeset i jedan*
22	dvaa-de-set i dva	*dvadestet i dva*
30	trii-de-set	*trideset*

SERBIAN

40	chetr-de-set	*cetrdeset*
50	pe-de-set	*pedeset*
60	shez-de-set	*šezdeset*
70	se-dam-de-set	*sedamdeset*
80	osaam-de-set	*osamdeset*
90	de-ve-de-set	*devedeset*
100	sto	*sto*
1000	hii-lyada	*hiljada*
one million	ye-dan mii-lion	*jedan milion*

Useful Words

a little (amount)	maa-lo	*malo*
double	duu-plo	*duplo*
dozen	tuu-tse	*tuce*
Enough!	do-sta!	*Dosta!*
few	ne-ko-liko	*nekoliko*
less	maa-nye	*manje*
many	mno-go	*mnogo*
more	vii-she	*više*
once	ye-dnom	*jednom*
pair	par	*par*
per cent	pro-tse-enat	*procenat*
some	ne-shto	*nešto*
too much	pre-vii-she	*previše*
twice	dva-puu-t	*dvaput*

SERBIAN

ABBREVIATIONS

Roman	Cyrillic	
EZ	Е.З.	European Community
LK	Л.К.	ID
G-din	Г-дин	Mr
G-dja	Г-ђа	Mrs
G-djica	Г-ђица	Ms
Ul.	Ул.	Street/Road
VB	В.Б.	United Kingdom
OUN	ОУН	United Nations
SAD	САД	USA

EMERGENCIES

Help!	upo-motch!	*Upomoc!*
Go away!	be-zhi-te!	*Bežite!*
Thief!	lo-pov!	*Lopov!*
It's an emergency!	hii-tno ye!	*Hitno je!*

SIGNS

МИЛИЦИЈА	POLICE
ПОЛИЦИЈСКА СТАНИЦА	POLICE STATION

SERBIAN

There's been an accident!
  do-go-dii-la se nes-re-etcha!   *Dogodila se nesreca!*
Call a doctor!
  po-zo-vii-te le-kaa-ra!   *Pozovite lekara!*
Call an ambulance!
  po-zo-vii-te hii-tnu po-omotch!   *Pozovite hitnu pomoc!*
Call the police!
  po-zo-vii-te mii-lii-tsiyu!   *Pozovite miliciju!*
I've been raped.
  sii-lo-vana sam   *Silovana sam.*
I've been robbed!
  pok-ra-den/pok-ra-dena sam!   *Pokraden/Pokradena sam!* (m/f)
Where's the police station?
  gde ye staa-nitsa mii-lii-tsi-ye?   *Gde je stanica milicije?*
I'm ill.
  bo-le-stan/bo-le-sna sam   *Bolestan/Bolesna sam.* (m/f)
I'm lost.
  izgu-bio/izgu-bila sam se   *Izgubio/Izgubila sam se.* (m/f)
Where are the toilets?
  gde su to-aleti?   *Gde su toaleti?*
Could you help me, please?
  mo-zhete li mi po-motchi?   *Možete li mi pomoci?*
Could I please use the
telephone?
  mo-gu li da te-le-fo-niram?   *Mogu li da telefoniram?*

SERBIAN

I'm sorry. I apologise.
  zhaa-o mi ye.   *Žao mi je. Izvinjavam se.*
  izvii-nya-vaam se
I didn't do it.
  ya nii-sam to   *Ja nisam to uradio/*
  uraa-dio/uraa-dila   *uradila.* (m/f)
I want to contact my
embassy/consulate.
  zhe-lim da   *Želim da*
  kon-ta-ktii-ram mo-yu   *kontaktiram moju*
  amba-sa-du/moy kon-zuu-lat   *ambasadu/moj konzulat.*
I have medical insurance.
  imaam zraav-stve-no   *Imam zdravstveno*
  osii-guu-ranye   *osiguranje.*

My ... was	mo-y ... ye ukraa-den	*Moj ... je ukraden.* (m)
stolen.	mo-ya ... ye ukraa-dena	*Moja ... je ukradena.* (f)
I've lost my ...	izguu-bio/izguu-bila	*Izgubio/Izgubila*
	sam ...	*sam ... (m/f)*
bags	mo-ye to-rbe	*moje torbe*
handbag	ruu-tchnu to-rbu	*rucnu torbu*
money	moy no-vats	*moj novac*
travellers	mo-ye puu-tnii-chke	*moje putnicke*
cheques	che-kove	*cekove*
passport	moy paa-sosh	*moj pasoš*
wallet	nov-cha-nik	*novčanik*

SLOVAK

QUICK REFERENCE

Hello.	doh-bree dyien	*Dobrý deň.*
Goodbye.	doh vidyeny-nyiah	*Do videnia.*
Yes./No.	aa-noh/nyieh	*Áno./Nie.*
Excuse me.	prepaach-tyeh	*Prepáčte.*
May I?	smyiem?	*Smiem?*
Sorry.	prepaach-tyeh	*Prepáčte*
Please.	proh-seem	*Prosím.*
Thank you.	dyakuh-yem	*Ďakujem.*
You're welcome.	proh-seem	*Prosím.*
What time is it?	koly-koh yeh hoh-dyeen?	*Koľko je hodín?*
Where's the ...?	gdyeh yeh ...?	*Kde je ...?*

Where are the toilets?
dyeh soo tuh zaa-khodih?   *Kde sú tu záchody?*
Go straight ahead.
poh-krachuy-tyeh v yaz-dyeh!   *Pokračujte v jazde!*
Turn to the left/right.
za-boch-tyeh   *Zabočte*
vlyah-voh/fprah-voh   *vľavo/vpravo.*
I don't understand.
nyeh-rozuh-miehm   *Nerozumiem.*
Do you speak English?
hovoh-ree-tyeh poh ahnglits-kih?   *Hovoríte po anglicky?*
How much is it?
koly-koh toh stoh-yee?   *Koľko to stojí?*

I'd like ...	poh-trebuhyem ...	*Potrebujem ...*
a single room	yednoh-luozhkoh-voo izbuh	*jednolôžkovú izbu*
a ticket	leas-tok	*lístok*
one-way	yednoh-smernee	*jednosmerný*
return	spyiatoch-nee	*spiatočný*

1	yeh-den	*jeden*	6	shesty	*šesť*
2	dvah	*dva*	7	seh-dyem	*sedem*
3	trih	*tri*	8	oh-sem	*osem*
4	shtih-rih	*štyri*	9	dye-vety	*deväť*
5	pety	*päť*	10	dye-sahty	*desať*

SLOVAK

SLOVAK

The Slovak language belongs to the Western branch of the Slavonic languages, and is the standard language of the six million people living in Slovakia, as well as nearly two million people living beyond the country's borders.

Slovak evolved between the 9th and the 15th centuries, and was associated with the development of a national Slovak culture at a time when Slovakia's territory and the surrounding regions were dominated by Latin at all levels – religious, administrative and literary. In the 17th century Slovakia was at the eastern border of Christian Europe, and the rules of Slovak were written down for the first time. However, Slovak didn't emerge as a uniform literary language until the mid-19th century, during the course of a national revival.

The language that bears the closest resemblance to Slovak is Czech. This should come as no surprise, since ties between the two countries date back to the 9th century and the Great Moravian Empire, where one common language (Old Church Slavonic) was in use. Although modern Slovak and Czech are, in general, mutually understandable, it's advisable not to substitute one for the other. The linguistic territory of each language includes many regional dialects, and these form a continuum across present and past political boundaries, so that, for example, the East Slovak dialect is closer to the West Ukrainian dialect than to the standard Czech language.

PRONUNCIATION

Slovak is written as it sounds, and isn't as difficult as it looks. It may help to remember that Slovak makes use of only four diacritical marks. The most common are – é, which lengthens a vowel, and ď, which softens a vowel. The other two are limited to the letters ä and ô.

Vowels

Slovak has six short and five long vowels and one long and one short semi-vowel. It's important to observe their different pronunciation, as detailed below, since vowel length may determine the meaning of a word.

Short Vowels		Long Vowels	
a	as the 'u' in 'cup'	*á*	as the 'a' in 'father'
ä	as the 'a' in 'fat'		
e	as in 'bed'	*é*	as the 'ea' in 'bear'
i	as the 'i' in 'machine'	*í*	as the 'ee' in 'feet'
o	as in 'pot'	*ó*	as the 'o' in 'shore'
u	as the 'oo' in 'book'	*ú*	as the 'u' in 'flute'
y	as the 'i' in 'bit'	*ý*	as the 'ee' in 'feet'

Vowel Combinations

There are four vowel combinations in Slovak:

ia	as the 'i' in 'machine' followed by the 'u' in 'cup'
ie	as the 'i' in 'machine' followed by the 'e' in 'bed'
iu	as the 'i' in 'machine' followed by the 'oo' in 'book'
ô	as the 'wa' in 'swan'

Consonants

Consonants not described are pronounced as they are in English.

c	as the 'ts' in 'lots';
	as the 'ch' in Scottish 'loch'
č	as the 'ch' in 'China'
dz	as the 'ds' in 'roads'

dž	as the 'j' in 'jeans'
ď, ť, ň, ľ	followed by a 'y' sound, as in 'during', 'tutor', 'new', 'lure'
h	as the 'h' in 'hand' but pronounced more forcefully
j	as the 'y' in 'yes'
k, p, t	pronounced without a puff of air following
ĺ, ŕ	semi-vowels, found in words such as *stĺp, vŕba, tŕň* (very hard to pronounce)
q, w, x	only exist in words of foreign origin and are pronounced approximately as in their original language
r	trilled
š	as the 'sh' in 'shoe'

Stress

Stress always falls on the first syllable, but is far less strong than in other languages. Slovak doesn't allow two consecutive long syllables, and avoids heavy emphasis on any word. This is why Slovak speakers refer to their language lovingly as *ľúbozvučná slovenčina*, 'sweet sounding Slovak', in recognition of its melodious quality.

SLOVAK

SUBJECT PRONOUNS		
SG		
I	yah	*ja*
you (inf)	tih	*ty*
you (pol)	vih	*Vy*
he/she/it	ohn/ohnah/ohnoh	*on/ona/ono*
PL		
we	mih	*my*
you	vih	*vy*
they (m)	onyih	*oni*
they (f)	onih	*ony*

GREETINGS & CIVILITIES
Top Useful Phrases

Hello.	doh-bree dyien	*Dobrý deň.*
Goodbye.	doh vidyeny-nyiah	*Do videnia.*
Yes./No.	aa-noh/nyieh	*Áno./Nie.*
Excuse me.	prepaach-tyeh	*Prepáčte.*
May I?	smyiem?	*Smiem?*
Do you mind?	dovoh-leetyeh?	*Dovolíte?*
Sorry. (Forgive me.)	prepaach-tyeh, proh-seem	*Prepáčte, prosím.*
Please.	proh-seem	*Prosím.*
Thank you.	dyakuh-yem	*Ďakujem.*
Many thanks.	dyakuh-yem vely-mih pek-neh	*Ďakujem veľmi pekne.*
That's fine.	nyieh yeh zah cho	*Nie je za čo.*
You're welcome.	proh-seem	*Prosím.*

Greetings

Good morning.	doh-brair raano	*Dobré ráno.*
Good afternoon.	doh-bree dyeny	*Dobrý deň.*
Good evening.	doh-bree veh-cher	*Dobrý večer.*
Good night.	doh-broo nots	*Dobrú noc.*
How are you?	akoh sah maa-tyeh?	*Ako sa máte?*
Well, thanks.	dyakuh-yem dobreh	*Ďakujem, dobre.*

Forms of Address

Madam/Mrs/Ms	pah-nyih	*pani*
Sir/Mr	paan	*pán*
Miss	slech-nah	*slečna*
friend	pryiah-tyely	*priateľ* (m)
	pryiah-tyely-kah	*priateľka* (f)

SLOVAK

SMALL TALK
Meeting People
What's your name?
akoh sah voh-laa-tyeh? *Ako sa voláte?*

My name's ...
voh-laam sah ... *Volám sa ...*

I'd like to introduce you to ...
dovoly-tyeh abih som *Dovolte, aby som Vás*
vaas predstah-vil totoh yeh ... *predstavil. Toto je ...*

Pleased to meet you.
tyeshee mah *Teší ma.*

How old are you?
koly-koh maa-teh rokohw? *Kolko máte rokov?*

Nationalities
Where are you from? **odkyialy styeh?** *Odkial ste?*

I'm from ...	som z ...	Som z ...
Australia	ahwstraa-lyieh	Austrálie
Canada	kanah-dih	Kanady
England	anglitz-kah	Anglicka
Ireland	eer-skah	Írska
New Zealand	novair-hoh	Nového
	zair-landuh	Zélandu
Scotland	shkawht-skah	Škótska
USA	oo-es-ah	USA
	(spoyeh-neekh	(Spojených
	shtaa-tohw	štátov
	ameritz-keekh)	amerických)
Wales	wheyl-suh	Walesu

SLOVAK

Occupations
What do you do?
choh robee-tyeh? *Čo robíte?*

I'm unemployed.
som nyeh-zah-mest-nah-nee/ *Som nezamestnaný/*
nyeh-zah-mest-nah-naa *nezamestnaná.* (m/f)

I'm a/an ...	(yah) som ...	*(Ja) som ...*
artist	oomeh-lets	*umelec* (m)
	oomel-kinya	*umelkyňa* (f)
businessperson	podnyih-kah-tyely	*podnikateľ* (m)
	podnyih-kah-tyely-kah	*podnikateľka* (f)
computer	proh-grah-maa-tor	*programátor* (m)
programmer	proh-grah-maa-tor-kah	*programátorka* (f)
doctor	dok-tor	*doktor* (m)
	dok-tor-kah	*doktorka* (f)
engineer	inzhih-nyier	*inžinier* (m)
	inzhih-nyier-kah	*inžinierka* (f)
farmer	roly-nyeek	*roľník* (m)
	roly-nyeech-kah	*roľníčka* (f)
journalist	novih-naar	*novinár* (m)
	novih-naar-kah	*novinárka* (f)
lawyer	praav-nyik	*právnik* (m)
	praav-nyich-kah	*právnička* (f)
manual worker	robot-nyeek	*robotník* (m)
	robot-nyeech-kah	*robotníčka* (f)
mechanic	mekhah-nik	*mechanik* (m)
	mekhah-nich-kah	*mechanička* (f)
nurse	osheh-trovah-tyely	*ošetrovateľ* (m)
	osheh-trovah-tyely-kah	*ošetrovateľka* (f)
office worker	oorad-nyeek	*úradník* (m)
	oorad-nyeech-kah	*úradníčka* (f)
scientist	vedyets-kee	*vedecký*
	pratsov-nyeek	*pracovník* (m)
	vedyets-kaa	*vedecká*
	pratsov-nyeech-kah	*pracovníčka* (f)
student	shtuh-dent	*študent* (m)
	shtuh-dent-kah	*študentka* (f)
teacher	oochih-tyely	*učiteľ* (m)
	oochih-tyely-kah	*učiteľka* (f)
waiter	chash-nyeek	*čašník* (m)
	chash-nyeech-kah	*čašníčka* (f)
writer	spisoh-vah-tyely	*spisovateľ* (m)
	spisoh-vah-tyely-kah	*spisovateľka* (f)

Religion

What's your religion?
akair-hoh styeh (vyieroh)   *Akého ste (viero-)vyznania?*
viznah-nyiah?

I'm not religious.
som bez viznah-nyiah   *Som bez vyznania.*

I'm ...	(yah) som ...	*(Ja) som ...*
Buddhist	boodhih-stah	*budhista* (m)
	bood-hist-kah	*budhistka* (f)
Catholic	kahtoh-leek	*katolík* (m)
	kahtoh-leech-kah	*katolíčka* (f)
Protestant	evanyieh-lik	*evanjelik* (m)
	evanyieh-lich-kah	*evanjelička* (f)
Christian	kres-tyan	*kresťan* (m)
	kres-tyan-kah	*kresťanka* (f)
Hindu	hindoo-istah	*hinduista* (m)
	hindoo-ist-kah	*hinduistka* (f)
Jewish	zhid	*žid* (m)
	zhidohv-kah	*židovka* (f)
Muslim	mos-lim	*moslim* (m)
	mos-lim-kah	*moslimka* (f)

Family

Are you married?
steh zhenah-tee/   *Ste ženatý/*
vidah-taa?   *vydatá?* (m/f)

I'm single.
som slobod-nee/   *Som slobodný/*
slobod-naa   *slobodná.* (m/f)

I'm married.
som zhenah-tee/   *Som ženatý/*
vidah-taa   *vydatá.* (m/f)

How many children do you have?
koly-koh maa-tyeh dyeh-tyee?   *Koľko máte detí?*

I don't have any children.
nye-maam dyeh-tih   *Nemám deti.*

I have a daughter/son.
maam tsair-ruh/sinah   *Mám dcéru/syna.*

brother	braht	*brat*
daughter	tsair-rah	*dcéra*
family	rodyih-nah	*rodina*
father	oh-tyets	*otec*
grandfather	stah-ree oh-tyets	*starý otec*
grandmother	stah-raa mat-kah	*stará matka*
husband	man-zhel	*manžel*
mother	mat-kah	*matka*
sister	seh-strah	*sestra*
son	sin	*syn*
wife	manzhel-kah	*manželka*

Feelings

I'm ...

cold/hot	yeh mih zimah/ tyep-loh	*Je mi zima/ teplo.*
hungry	maam hlahd	*Mám smäd.*
in a hurry	ponaa-hlyam sah	*Ponáhľam sa.*
right	maam prahv-duh	*Mám pravdu.*
sleepy	som ospah-lee/ ospah-laa	*Som ospalý/ ospalá.* (m/f)
thirsty	maam smed	*Mám smäd.*

I'm ...

angry	hnye-vaam sah	*Hnevám sa.*
happy	som shtyast-nee/ shtyast-naa	*Som štastný/ štastná.* (m/f)
sad	som smut-nee/ smut-naa	*Som smutný/ smutná.* (m/f)
tired	som oonah-vehnee/ oonah-vehnaa	*Som unavený/ unavená.* (m/f)
well	tsee-tyim sah dob-reh	*Cítim sa dobre.*
worried	ohbaa-vam sah	*Obávam sa.*

SLOVAK

I like ...
    maam raad/radah...   *Mám rád/rada ... (m/f)*

I don't like ...
    nyeh-maam raad/radah...   *Nemám rád/rada ... (m/f)*

I'm sorry. (condolence)
    lyutuh-yem   *Ľutujem.*

I'm grateful.
    som vdyach-nee/vdyach-naa   *Som vďačný/vďačná. (m/f)*

BREAKING THE LANGUAGE BARRIER

Do you speak English?
    hovoh-ree-tyeh poh   *Hovoríte po anglicky?*
    ahnglits-kih?

Does anyone (here)
speak English?
    hovoh-ree (tuh)   *Hovorí (tu)*
    nyiek-toh poh ahnglits-kih? *niekto po anglicky?*

I speak a little ...
    yah hovoh-reehm   *Ja hovorím trocha (po) ...*
    tro-kha (poh) ...

I (don't) understand.
    (nyeh-)rozuh-miehm   *(Ne)rozumiem.*

Could you speak more
slowly, please?
    muoh-zhetyeh proh-seem *Môžete prosím*
    hoh-vohrity pohmal-shyieh? *hovoriť pomalšie?*

Could you repeat that?
    muoh-zhetyeh toh zopa-kovaty? *Môžete to zopakovať?*

How do you say ...?
    akoh sah povyieh?   *Ako sa povie ...?*

BODY LANGUAGE

The body language or gesticulation of Slovaks has nothing typical which might distinguish them from other Eastern Europeans.

SLOVAK

PAPERWORK

address	adreh-sah	*adresa*
age	vek	*vek*
date of birth	daatum	*dátum narodenia*
	naroh-dyenyiah	
driver's licence	vodyich-skee	*vodičský*
	preh-oo-kahz	*preukaz*
identification	preh-oo-kahz	*preukaz*
	totozh-nostih	*totožnosti*
marital status	(rohdyin-nee) stav	*(rodinný) stav*
name	menoh	*meno*
nationality	naarod-nosty	*národnosť*
passport	tses-tohv-nee pahs	*cestovný pas*
passport number	cheesloh tses-tohv-	*číslo cestovného*
	nairhoh pahsuh	*pasu*
place of birth	myiestoh	*miesto*
	naroh-dyenyiah	*narodenia*
profession	povoh-lanyieh	*povolanie*
religion	vyieroh-vizna-nyieh	*vierovyznanie*
reason for travel	oochel tses-tih	*účel cesty*
business	ob-khod-nee stick	*obchodný styk*
holiday	doh-voh-len-kah/	*dovolenka/*
	praazd-nyi-nih	*prázdniny*
sex	poh-hlavyieh	*pohlavie*
tourist card	toorist itskee	*turistický*
	preh-oo-kahz	*preukaz*
visa	veezum	*vízum*

SLOVAK

QUESTION WORDS

How?	ah-koh?	*Ako?*
When?	kedy?	*Kedy?*
Where?	gdyeh?	*Kde?*
Which?	ktoh-ree?	*Ktorý?*
Who?	gdoh?	*Kto?*
Why?	preh-choh?	*Preèo?*

GETTING AROUND

What time does the ... leave/arrive?	kedih ot-khaa-dzah/ pri-khaa-dzah ...?	*Kedy odchádza/ prichádza ...?*
aeroplane	lyieh-tadloh	*lietadlo*
boat	lody	*loď*
city/	mest-skee/	*mestský/*
intercity bus	medzih-mest-skee owtoh-buhs	*medzimestský autobus*
train	vlakh	*vlak*
tram	elek-trich-kah	*električka*

Directions

Where's ...?
gdyeh yeh ...?   *Kde je ...?*

How do I get to ...?
akoh sah dostah-
nyem doh ...?   *Ako sa dostanem do ...?*

Is it far/closeby?
yeh toh od-tyialy-toh
dya-lekoh/bleez-koh?   *Je to odtiaľto ďaleko/blízko?*

Can I walk there?
daa sah tam easty peshih?   *Dá sa tam ísť peši?*

Can you show me (on the map)?
muo-zhetyeh mih
uh-kaazaty (nah mapeh)?   *Môžete mi ukázať (na mape)?*

I want to go to ...
khtsehm easty doh ...   *Chcem ísť do ...*

Are there other means of getting there?
akoh sah tam
daa eshtyeh dos-taty?   *Ako sa tam dá ešte dostať?*

Go straight ahead.
khody-tyeh rovnoh dya-lay   *Choďte rovno ďalej.*

It's two blocks down.
soo toh od-tyialy-toh
dveh uhlih-tse   *Sú to odtiaľto dve ulice.*

SLOVAK

Turn left/right	zaboch-tyeh vlya-voh/	*Zabočte vľavo/*
at the ...	fpra-voh nah ...	*vpravo na ...*
next corner	nasleh-duh-	*nasledu*
	yootsom rohuh	*júcom rohu*
traffic lights	krizho-vatkeh	*križovatke*
	zoh svetlah-mih	*so svetlami*

behind	zah	*za*
far	dyah-leh-koh	*ďaleko*
near	bleez-koh	*blízko*
in front of	pred	*pred*
opposite	oh-protyih	*oproti*

Booking Tickets

Where can I buy a ticket?

gdyeh sih muo-zhem koo-pity	*Kde si môžem kúpiť*
tses-tohv-nee leas-tok?	*cestovný lístok?*

I want to go to ...

| **khtsem easty do ...** | *Chcem ísť do ...* |

Do I need to book?

potreh-buyem	*Potrebujem*
myies-tyenkuh?	*miestenku?*

I'd like ...	proh-seem sih ...	*Prosím si ...*
a one-way ticket	yednoh-smernee leas-tok	*jednosmerný lístok*
a return ticket	spyiatoch-nee leas-tok	*spiatočný lístok*
two tickets	dvah least-kih	*dva lístky*
tickets for all of us	least-kih preh naas fshet-keekh	*lístky pre nás všetkých*
a student's fare	shtudent-skee leas-tok	*študentský lístok*
a child's fare	dyet-skee leas-tok	*detský lístok*
pensioner's fare	leas-tok preh duo-khod-tsohw	*lístok pre dôchodcov*

1st class	prvaa tryieh-dah	*prvá trieda*
2nd class	dru-haa tryieh-dah	*druhá trieda*

SIGNS

HORÚCA/STUDENÁ (VODA)	HOT/COLD (WATER)
INFORMÁCIE	INFORMATION
NÚDZOVÝ VÝCHOD	EMERGENCY EXIT
OTVORENÉ/ZATVORENÉ	OPEN/CLOSED
REZERVOVANÉ	RESERVED
TELEFÓN	TELEPHONE
VCHOD	ENTRANCE
VOĽNÝ (BEZPLATNÝ) VSTUP	FREE ADMISSION
VÝCHOD	EXIT
ZÁCHODY/WC/TOALETY	TOILETS
ZAKÁZANÉ	PROHIBITED
ZÁKAZ FAJČENIA	NO SMOKING
ZÁKAZ VSTUPU/VSTUP ZAKÁZANÝ	NO ENTRY

Bus & Tram

Where's the bus/tram stop?
gdyeh yeh tuh zas-taavkah
owtoh-buhsuh/elek-trichkih?

Kde je tu zastávka autobusu/električky?

Which bus goes to ...?
ktoh-reem owtoh-buhsom
sah dos-tanyem doh ...?

Ktorým autobusom sa dostanem do ...?

Does this bus go to ...?
idyeh tentoh owtoh-buhs
doh ...?

Ide tento autobus do ...?

How often do buses pass by?
akoh chas-toh tuh yaz-dyiah
owtoh-buhsih?

Ako často tu jazdia autobusy?

Could you let me know
when we get to ...?
muo-zhetyeh mah proh-seem
upoh-zornyity kedih
buh-dyemeh v ...?

Môžete ma prosím upozorniť keď budeme v ...?

SLOVAK

I want to get off!

khtsem vih-stoopyity!		*Chcem vystúpiť!*

What time's
the ... bus?

kedih pree-dyeh ...		*Kedy príde ...*
owtoh-buhs?		*autobus?*
first	pr-vee	*prvý*
last	poh-slednee	*posledný*
next	nasleh-duhyoo-tsih	*nasledujúci*

Train & Metro

dining car	yedaa-lenskee vozeny	*jedálenský vozeň*
express	eks-pres/reekh-lick	*expres/rýchlik*
local	lokaal-nih vlakh	*lokálny vlak*
sleeping car	spah-tsee vozeny	*spací vozeň*

Which line takes me to ...?
  ktoh-rohw lin-kohw sah   *Ktorou linkou sa*
  dos-tahnyem doh ...?   *dostanem do ...?*
What's the next station?
  akoh sah volaa   *Ako sa volá nasledujúca*
  nah-sleduh-yoo-tsah   *stanica?*
  stanyi-tsah?
Is this the right platform for ...?
  yeh toh spraav-neh   *Je to správne*
  naah-stupish-tyeh doh ...?   *nástupište do ...?*

Taxi

Can you take me to ...?
  muo-zhetyeh mah   *Môžete ma*
  zavyiesty doh ...?   *zaviesť do ...?*
Please take me to ...
  zavestyeh mah   *Zavezte ma*
  proh-seem doh ...   *prosím do ...*
How much does it cost to go to ...?
  koly-koh toh budyeh   *Koľko to bude*
  staaty doh ...?   *stáť do ...?*

Here's fine, thank you.
 potyialy-toh toh stachee   *Potiaľ to to stačí.*

The next corner, please.
 azh poh nai-blizh-shee rokh   *Až po najbližší roh,*
 proh-seem   *prosím.*

The next street to the left/right.
 nah-sleduyoo-tsa ulitsa   *Nasledujúca ulica*
 vlyah-voh/fprah-voh   *vľavo/vpravo.*

Stop here, please.
 zah-stavtyeh tuh proh-seem   *Zastavte tu, prosím.*

Please wait here.
 pochkay-tyeh tuh proh-seem   *Počkajte tu, prosím.*

Car

Where can I hire a car?
 gdyeh sih muo-zhem   *Kde si môžem*
 preh-nayaty owtoh?   *prenajať auto?*

How much is it daily/weekly?
 koly-koh toh stoh-yee nah   *Koľko to stojí na*
 dyeny/nah teezh-dyeny?   *deň/na týždeň?*

Does that include insurance/
mileage?
 yeh v tse-nyeh za-hrnuh-tai   *Je v cene zahrnuté*
 poh-istyeh-nyieh/   *poistenie/*
 kiloh-metraazh?   *kilometráž?*

Where's the next petrol station?
 gdyeh yeh nai-blizh-shyieh   *Kde je najbližšie*
 benzee-novair cher-pahd-loh?   *benzínové čerpadlo?*

How long can I park here?
 akoh dlhoh tuh muo-zhem   *Ako dlho tu môžem*
 par-kovaty?   *parkovať?*

Does this road lead to ...?
 veh-dyieh taa-toh tses-tah   *Vedie táto cesta do ...?*
 doh ...?

I need a mechanic.
 potreh-buyem pomots   *Potrebujem pomoc*
 owtoh-mekhah-nikah   *automechanika.*

SLOVAK

It's not working.
  neh-fuhn-guhyeh toh   *Nefunguje to.*

air (for tyres)	stlah-cheh-nee	*stlačený*
	vz-dukh/	*vzduch/*
	kom-preh-sor	*kompresor*
battery	bah-tair-ryiah	*batéria*
brakes	brz-dih	*brzdy*
clutch	spoy-kah	*spojka*
driver's licence	voh-dyich-skee	*vodičský*
	preh-oo-kaz	*preukaz*
engine	moh-tor	*motor*
lights	sveht-laa	*svetlá*
oil	aw-ley	*olej*
petrol (gas)	ben-zeenuh	*benzínu*
puncture	deh-fekt	*defekt*
radiator	khlah-dyich	*chladič*
road map	owtoh-mapah	*automapa*
tyres	pneu-mah-tikih	*pneumatiky*
windscreen	pred-nair skloh	*predné sklo*

ON THE ROAD

AUTOOPRAVY	**REPAIRS**
AUTOOPRAVOVŇA	**GARAGE/**
	WORKSHOP
DAJ PREDNOSŤ V	**GIVE WAY**
JAZDE	
DIAĽNICA	**FREEWAY**
JEDNOSMERNÁ	**ONE WAY**
DOPRAVA/	
PREMÁVKA	
NATURÁL	**UNLEADED**
OBCHÁDZKA	**DETOUR**
SAMOOBSLUHA	**SELF SERVICE**
ZÁKAZ PARKOVANIA	**NO PARKING**
ZÁKAZ VJAZDU	**NO ENTRY**

SLOVAK

ACCOMMODATION

Where's a ... hotel?	gdyeh yeh ... hoh-tel?	*Kde je ... hotel?*
cheap	lats-nee	*lacný*
clean	chis-tee	*čistý*
good	dob-reeh	*dobrý*
nearby	nah-blees-kuh	*nablízku*

At the Hotel

Do you have any rooms available?
| maa-tyeh voly-nair izbih? | *Máte voľné izby?* |

I'd like ...	poh-tre-buh-yem ...	*Potrebujem ...*
a single room	yednoh-luozhkoh-voo izbuh	*jednolôžkovú izbu*
a double room	izbuh preh dveh ohsoh-bih	*izbu pre dve osoby*
to share a dorm	(spoloch-noo) izbuh nah uhbitov-nyih	*(spoločnú) izbu na ubytovni*
a bed	pos-tyely	*posteľ*

I want a room with a ...	muo-zhetyeh mih daty izbuh ...	*Môžete mi dať izbu ...*
bathroom	s koo-pelynyohw	*s kúpeľňou*
shower	zoh spr-khohw	*so sprchou*
window	s oknom	*s oknom*

I'm going to stay for ...	zoh-stanyem tuh ...	*Zostanem tu ...*
one day	yeden dyeny	*jeden deň*
two days	dvah dnyih	*dva dni*
one week	yeden teezh-dyeny	*jeden týždeň*

How much is it per night/person?
| koly-koh toh stoh-yee nah dyeny/oh-sobuh? | *Koľko to stojí na deň/osobu?* |

Can I see it, please?
| muo-zhem toh proh-seem vi-dyiety? | *Môžem to (prosím) vidieť?* |

SLOVAK

Are there any others?
  maa-tyeh eshtyeh ih-nair   *Máte ešte iné na výber?*
  nah vee-ber?
Is there a reduction for
(students/children)?
  mah-yoo (shtuden-tyih/   *Majú (študenti/deti) zľavu?*
  dyetyih) zlyah-vuh?
It's fine, I'll take it.
  doh-breh, beh-ryiem toh   *Dobre, beriem to.*

SLOVAK

Requests & Complaints

Do you have a safe where I can
leave my valuables?
  maa-tyeh treh-zor (saife)   *Máte trezor (safe) na*
  nah uh-lozheh-nyieh   *uloženie cenností?*
  tsen-nos-tyee?
Is there somewhere to wash clothes?
  muo-zhem sih nyiegdyeh   *Môžem si niekde oprať*
  opraty obleh-chenyieh?   *oblečenie?*
Can I use the telephone?
  muo-zhem poh-uzheevaty   *Môžem používať telefón?*
  teleh-fawn?
I've locked myself out of my room.
  vim-kohl/vim-klah   *Vymkol/Vymkla*
  som sah z izbih   *som sa z izby. (m/f)*

AROUND TOWN

I'm looking for a/the ...	hlyah-daam ...	*Hľadám ...*
art gallery	galair-ryiuh	*galériu*
bank	bankuh	*banku*
church	kostol	*kostol*
city (centre)	stred (tsen-truhm)	*stred (centrum)*
	mestah	*mesta*
... embassy	shtaat-neh	*štátne*
	zastuh- pityehly-stvoh ...	*zastupiteľstvo ...*
market	trkh	*trh*
museum	moo-zeum	*múzeum*
police	polee-tsyiuh	*políciu*
post office	posh-tuh	*poštu*
public toilet	vereih-nair	*verejné*
	zaa-khodih	*záchody*
telephone	teleh-fawn-nuh	*telefónnu*
centre	tsentraa-luh	*centrálu*
tourist	infor-mahchnair	*informačné*
information	stredyis-koh preh	*stredisko pre*
office	turis-tohw	*turistov*

What time does it open/close?	
oh koly-kay otvaa-rahyoo/ zah-tvaa-rahyoo?	*O koľkej otvárajú/zatvárajú?*

At the Post Office

I'd like to send a/an ...	khtsel/khtseh-lah bih som pos-laty ...	*Chcel/Chcela by som poslať...* (m/f)
aerogram	airoh-grahm	*aerogram*
letter	list	*list*
parcel	bah-leak	*balík*
postcard	pohlyad-nitsu	*pohľadnicu*
telegram	teleh-grahm	*telegram*

I'd like some stamps.

khtsel/khtseh-lah bih som	*Chcel/Chcela by som*
koo-pit znaam-kih	*kúpiť známky. (m/f)*

How much is the postage?

koly-koh yeh posh-tohv-nair?	*Koľko je poštovné?*

airmail	letyets-kaa posh-tah	*letecká pošta*
envelope	obaal-kah	*obálka*
mailbox	poshtoh-vaa	*poštová*
	skhraan-kah	*schránka*
registered mail	dopoh-ruche-nyeh	*doporučene*
surface mail	obichai-nohw	*obyčajnou*
	posh-tohw	*poštou*

Telephone

I want to ring ...

khtsem teleh-fohnoh-vaty ...	*Chcem telefonovať ...*

The number is ...

chees-loh yeh	*Číslo je ...*

I want to make a reverse-charges call.

khtsem teleh-fohnoh-vaty	*Chcem telefonovať na účet*
nah ooh-chet volah-nair-	*volaného čísla.*
hoh chees-lah	

It's engaged.

yeh op-sadyeh-nair	*Je obsadené.*

How much does a three-minute call cost?

koly-koh stoh-yee troi-	*Koľko stojí trojminútový*
minoo-tohvee hoh-vor?	*hovor?*

I'd like to speak to (Mr Perez).

muo-zhem hoh-vohrity	*Môžem hovoriť s (pánom*
s (paa-nom pe-re-zom)?	*Perezom)?*

I've been cut off.

muoy hoh-vor bol	*Môj hovor bol prerušený.*
preh-rushe-nee	

Internet

Where can I get Internet access?
gdyeh yeh tuh inter-net
gdis-poh-zee-tsyih?

*Kde je tu internet k
dispozícii?*

How much is it per hour?
koly-koh toh stoh-yee nah
hoh-dyi-nuh?

Koľko to stojí na hodinu?

I want to check my email.
khtsem sih skon-troh-
loh-vaty e-mail

*Chcem si skontrolovaš
e-mail.*

At the Bank

I want to exchange some (money/
travellers cheques).
khtsem vih-meh-nyihty
(peh-nyiah-zeh/tses-tohv-nair
shekih)

*Chcem vymeniť (peniaze/
cestovné šeky).*

What's the exchange rate?
akee yeh vee-men-nee kurz?

Aký je výmenný kurz?

How many crowns per US dollar?
koly-koh koh-roohn
dostah-nyem zah yeden
doh-laar?

*Koľko korún dostanem
za jeden
dolár?*

bankdraft	bankoh-vaa zmen-kah	*banková zmenka*
banknotes	bankov-kih	*bankovky*
cashier	poklad-nyeek	*pokladník* (m)
	poklad-nyeech-kah	*pokladníčka* (f)
coins	min-tseh	*mince*
credit card	ooveh-rohvaa	*úverová*
	(kredit-naa) kartah	*(kreditná) karta*
exchange	zmeh-naa-reny	*zmenáreň*
signature	(vlastnoh-ruchnee)	*(vlastnoručný)*
	pod-pis	*podpis*

SLOVAK

INTERESTS & ENTERTAINMENT
Sightseeing

Do you have a guidebook/local map?
maa-tyeh tses-tohv-noo pree-ruchkuh/myiest-nuh mapuh?	*Máte cestovnú príručku/ miestnu mapu?*

What are the main attractions?
akair soo tuh turist-itskair za-ooyee-mah-vostih?	*Aké sú tu turistické zaujímavosti?*

What's that?
cho yeh toh?	*Čo je to?*

How old is it?
akoh yeh toh stah-rair?	*Ako je to staré?*

Can I take photographs?
muo-zhem fotoh-gra- foh-vaty?	*Môžem fotografovat?*

ancient	staroh-bilee/	*starobylý*
archaeological	arkheoloh-ghi-tskee	*archeologický*
castle	hrad/zaa-mok	*hrad/zámok*
cathedral	kateh-draalah	*katedrála*
church	kostol	*kostol*
concert hall	kon-tsert-naa syieny	*koncertná sieň*
library	knyizh-nyitsa	*knižnica*
main square	hlav-nair-naa-mestyieh	*hlavné námestie*
market	trkh	*trh*
monastery	klaash-tor	*kláštor*
monument	pah-mat-nyeek	*pamätník*
old city	stah-raa chasty mestah	*stará časť mesta*
palace	palaats	*palác*
opera house	operah	*opera*
ruins	zroo-tsa-nyihnih	*zrúcaniny*
statues	sokhih	*sochy*
temple	khraam	*chrám*
university	uhnih-ver-zitah	*univerzita*

SLOVAK

Going Out

What's there to do in the evenings?
    kam sah daa easty vecher?   *Kam sa dá ísť večer?*
Are there any nightclubs
around here?
    soo tuh diskoh-taihkih?   *Sú tu diskotéky?*
Are there places where you can
hear local folk music?
    daa sah tuh nyieh-gdyeh   *Dá sa tu niekde ísť počúvať*
    easty pochoo-vaty   *ľudovú hudbu?*
    lyudoh-voo hoodbuh?
How much does it cost to get in?
    koly-koh yeh vstup-nair?   *Koľko je vstupné?*

cinema	kinah	*kina*
concert	kon-tsert	*koncert*
nightclub	diskoh-taihkuh	*diskotéku*
theatre	dyivah-dlah	*divadla*

SLOVAK

Sports & Interests

What sports do you play?
    a-keehm shpor-tohm   *Akým športom sa venujete?*
    sah veh-nuh-yeh-tyeh?
What are your interests?
    a-keeh maa-tyieh zaau-yee-mih?   *Aké máte záujmy?*

SLOVAK

art	uh-meh-nyieh	*umenie*
basketball	basket-bahl	*basketbal*
chess	shah-khih	*šachy*
collecting things	zbeh-rah-telyi-stvoh	*zberateľstvo*
dancing	tah-nyets	*tanec*
food	yed-loh	*jedlo*
football	foot-bahl	*futbal*
hiking	peshyiuh tuh-ris-tih-kuh	*pešiu turistiku*
martial arts	boh-yo-veh uh-meh-nyiah	*bojové umenia*
meeting friends	streh-taah-vahtyi sah s pryia-tyiel-mih	*stretávať sa s priateľmi*
movies	fil-mih	*filmy*
music	hood-booh	*hudbu*
nightclubs	notch-neh kloo-bih	*nočné kluby*
photography	phoh-toh-graphoh-vah-nyieh	*fotografovanie*
reading	chee-tah-nyieh	*čítanie*
shopping	nah-kooh-poh-vah-nyieh	*nakupovanie*
skiing	lee-zhoh-vah-nyieh	*lyžovanie*
swimming	plaah-vah-nyieh	*plávanie*
tennis	tennis	*tenis*
travelling	tses-toh-vah-nyieh	*cestovanie*
TV/videos	teh-leh-vee-zyiuh/vih-deh-aah	*televíziu/videá*
visiting friends	nah-vshteh-voh-vatyih pryia-tyie-low	*navštevovať priateľov*
walking	preh-khaah-tz-kih	*prechádzky*

Festivals
State Holidays

Cyril a Metod, vierozvestovia
  (July 5) Sts Cyril and Methodius (Apostles) Day

Deň ústavy SR
  (September 1) Constitution Day (1992)

Nový rok a Vznik SR
  (January 1) New Year and Establishment of the Slovak
  Republic (1993)

Výročie Slovenského národného povstania
  (August 29) Slovak National Uprising Anniversary (1944)

Religious Holidays

Druhý sviatok vianočný
  (December 26) Boxing Day

Prvý sviatok vian očný
  (December 25) Christmas Day

Sedembolestná Panna Mária, patrónka Slovenska
  (September 15) Our Lady of Sorrows Day

Štedrý deň
  (December 24) Christmas Eve

Sviatok práce
  (May 1) Labour Day

Traja králi; Zjavenie Pána
  (January 6) Epiphany; Orthodox Christmas Day

Veľkonočný pondelok
  Easter Monday

Veľký piatok
  Easter Friday

Všetkých svätých
  (November 1) All Saints Day

SLOVAK

IN THE COUNTRY
Weather

What's the weather like?

akair yeh pocha-syieh?		*Aké je počasie?*

The weather's ... today.	dnyes yeh ...	*Dnes je ...*
Will it be ... tomorrow?	budyeh zai-trah ...?	*Bude zajtra ...?*
cloudy	zamrah-chenair	*zamračené*
cold	zimah	*zima*
foggy	hmlis-toh	*hmlisto*
frosty	mraaz	*mráz*
hot	horoo-tsoh	*horúco*
raining	pr-shaty	*pršať*
snowing	snyeh-zhity	*snežiť*
sunny	sl-nyech-noh	*slnečno*
windy	vetyer-noh	*veterno*

Camping

Am I allowed to camp here?

muo-zhem tuh stanoh-vaty?		*Môžem tu stanovať?*

Is there a campsite nearby?

yeh tuh nableez-kuh taaboh-riskoh?		*Je tu nablízku táborisko?*

backpack	plets-nyiak	*plecniak*
can opener	otvaa-rach nah konzer-vih	*otvárač na konzervy*
compass	kom-pahs	*kompas*
crampons	skobih	*skoby*
firewood	palivoh-vair dreh-voh	*palivové drevo*
gas cartridge	naa-plny doh plinoh-vairhoh vahrih-cha	*náplň do plynového variča*
hammock	(visuh-tair) luozh-koh	*(visuté) lôžko* (lit: hanging bed)

SLOVAK

ice axe	horoh-lezets-kee	*horolezecký*
	cha-kan	*čakan*
mattress	mah-trahts	*matrac*
penknife	vretskoh-vee nuozh	*vreckový nôž*
rope	poh-vraz/lanoh	*povraz/lano*
tent	stahn	*stan*
tent pegs	stahno-vair kolee-kih	*stanové kolíky*
torch (flashlight)	bater-kah	*baterka*
sleeping bag	spah-tsee vahk	*spací vak*
stove	varich	*varič*
water bottle	flah-sha nah voduh	*fľaša na vodu*

FOOD

Food in Slovakia reflects the myriad of influences which has shaped this part of Europe. During your stay you'll find dishes you may have appreciated elsewhere, such as Austrian strudel, Czech dumplings, German sauerkraut, French crepes and Hungarian goulash, but you'll always find them prepared with a special Slovak touch.

Modern Slovak cooks haven't forgotten traditional recipes – they're well worth discovering!

breakfast	ranyai-kih	*raňajky*
lunch	obed	*obed*
dinner	vecheh-rah	*večera*

Vegetarian Meals

Apart from salads, it may be difficult to find food entirely without meat or meat product.

I'm a vegetarian.
   (yah) som veghe-tahryiaan   *(Ja) som vegetarián.*
I don't eat meat.
   nyeh-yem masoh   *Nejem mäso.*
I don't eat chicken, fish or ham.
   nyeh-yem kurah-tsyieh   *Nejem kuracie*
   masoh ribih ahnyih shun-kuh   *mäso, ryby ani šunku.*

Vegetarian dishes are detailed in the Menu Decoder, page 489.

MENU DECODER

Starters & Snacks

hlávkový šalát s oštiepkom
  hlaah-vko-veeh sha-laat z osh-tyiep-kom
  green salad with sheep cheese

husacia pečeň
  huh-sah-tsyiah peh-tcheny
  goose liver

kurací šalát s majonézou
  kuh-rah-tseeh sha-laat z mayio-neh-zohw
  chicken salad with mayonnaise

obložený chlebíček
  ob-loh-zhe-neeh khle-bee-check
  open sandwich

praženica
  prah-zheh-nitsa
  scrambled eggs

salámový tanier s oblohou
  sah-laah-moh-vee tanyier z oblo-hohw
  salami platter with fresh/pickled vegetables

šalátová misa
  sha-laa-toh-vaah mih-sah
  salad niçoise

s údeným lososom
  z ooh-dyie-neem loh-soh-sohm
  smoked salmon

syrový tanier
  sih-roh-vih tah-nyier
  cheese platter

Main Meals

a s mandľovou plnkou
  ah s mand-lyioh-vow pln-kohw
  turkey breast stuffed with mushrooms and almonds

cigánska pečienka
  tsih-ghan-skah peh-chyien-kah
  gypsy style grilled beef; a very common dish on Slovak menus, which denotes quick preparation similar to barbecuing

kapor na víne
kah-por nah vee-nyieh
carp braised in wine

kurací paprikáš
kuh-rah-tseeh pah-prih-kaash
chicken braised in red (paprika) sauce

morčacie prsíčka na hríboch
mor-chah-tsyieh pr-seech-kah nah hree-bokh

roštenka so šunkou vajcoma
roh-shtyien-kah zoh shun-kohw ah vay-tzoh-ma
roast beef with ham and eggs

vyprážané rybacie filé
vih-praa-zha-neh rih-bah-tsyieh fih-leh
fillet of fish fried in breadcrumbs

zajac na smotane
zah-yats nah smoh-tah-nyieh
rabbit/hare in a cream sauce

Vegetarian Dishes

karfiolový nákyp
kar-phyio-loh-veeh naah-kip
cauliflower souffle

vyprážaný syr s tatarskou omáčkou
vih-praah-zhah-neeh sihr tah-tar-skohw oh-maatch-kohws
fried cheese with tartare sauce

zeleninové rizoto
zeh-leh-nyi-noh-veh rizo-toh
risotto with vegetables

*špagety/makaróny
na taliansky spôsob*
shpah-gheh-tih/mah-kah-roh-nih
nah ta-lyian-skih spwoh-sohb
spaghetti or macaroni with tomato sauce and cheese

SLOVAK

SLOVAK

Soups

chicken soup	kuh-rah-tsyiah poh-lyiev-kah	*kuracia polievka*
fish soup	rih-bah-tsyiah poh-lyiev-kah	*rybacia polievka*
pheasant soup	poh-lyiev-kah z bah-zhan-tah	*polievka z bažanta*
vegetable soup	zeh-leh-nyi-noh-veh poh-lyiev-kih	*zeleninové polievky*

with ...	s ...	s ...
dumplings	kned-leetch-kah-mih	*knedlíčkami*
gnocchi	hah-loosh-kah-mih	*haluškami*
rice	rih-zhow	*ryžou*

Side Dishes

bread and pastry	khlyieb ah peh-chih-voh	*chlieb a pečivo*
potato chips	zeh-myiah-koh-veh hrah-nol-kih	*zemiakové hranolky*
roast potatoes	oh-peh-kah-neh zeh-myiah-kih	*opekané zemiaky*

Desserts

apple strudel	yah-bl-koh-veeh zaah-vin	*jablkový závin*
bread pudding	zhem-lyiov-kah	*žemľovka*
cherry souffle	cheh-resh-nyio-vah booh-blah-nyi-nah	*čerešňová bublanina*
chestnut cream	gahsh-tah-noh-veh pih-reh	*gaštanové pyré*
chocolate gateau	choh-koh-laah-doh-vaah tor-tah	*čokoládová torta*
doughnuts	shish-kih	*šišky*
fruit cake	oh-vots-neeh (bis-kup-skeeh) khle-bee-check	*ovocný (biskupský) chlebíček*

rice souffle	rih-zhoh-veeh naah-kip	*ryžový nákyp*
chocolate roulade	choh-koh-laah-doh-vaah roh-laah-dah	*čokoládová roláda*
shortbread	maass-loh-veh (drob-neh cha-yoh-veh) peh-chi-voh	*maslové (drobné čajové) pečivo*

INCOGNITO

Many Slovak dishes have names that don't offer a clue as to what's in them. One that all Slovaks know is *Španielsky vtáčik* (lit: Spanish Birds), but it is actually beef rolled up with bacon and gherkins, served with rice and sauce.

Another is *Moravský*, 'Moravian Sparrow', which is a fist-sized piece of roasted pork. Other common dishes are *Katúv šleh*, 'The Executioner's Lash', which is thinly sliced pieces of pork, capsicum and tomato in a sauce, or *Tajemstvo*, 'A Secret', which is ham wrapped around a slice of cheese in breadcrumbs.

But even the Slovaks will need to ask about the following: *Meč krále Jiřího*, 'King George's Sword', *Tajemství Petra Voka*, Peter Voka's Mystery', *Bašta nadlesního Karáska*, 'Ranger' Karasek's Meal, and *Kotlík rytíre*, 'The Kettle of Rimbaba the Knight'.

SLOVAK

Staples

bread	khlyieb	*chlieb*
butter	mahs-loh	*maslo*
cereal	oh-bil-nyi-noh-vair kah-sheh	*obilninové kaše*
cheese	sihr	*syr*
chocolate	choh-koh-laah-duh	*čokoládu*
eggs	vai-tsyiah	*vajcia*
flour	mooh-kuh	*múku*
margarine	mar-gah-reen	*margarín*
marmalade	mar-meh-laah-duh	*marmeládu*
milk	mlyieh-koh	*mlieko*
(olive) oil	(olih-voh-veeh) oh-lei	*(olivový) olej*
pasta	ches-toh-vee-nee	*cestoviny*
pepper	tchyier-neh koh-reh-nyieh	*čierne korenie*
rice	rih-zhah	*ryža*
salt	sol	*soľ*
sugar	tzuh-kor	*cukor*
yogurt	yoh-guhrt	*jogurt*

Salads

beetroot	tzwick-loh-veeh	*cviklový*
cabbage	kah-puss-toh-veeh	*kapustový*
celeriac and carrot	zeh-leh-roh-veeh s mrk-vohw	*zelerový s mrkvou*
cucumber	ooh-hor-koh-veeh	*uhorkový*
lettuce	hlaav-koh-veeh	*hlávkový*
mixed	z myie-shah-nyiey zeh-leh-nyi-nih	*miešanej zeleniny*
potato	zeh-myiah-koh-veeh	*zemiakový*
sauerkraut	zoh suh-doh-vey (kiss-lei) kah-puss-tih	*zo sudovej (kyslej) kapusty*
tomato	ray-tchyia-koh-veeh/ pah-rah-dai-koh-veeh	*rajčiakový/ paradajkový*

SLOVAK

Non-Alcoholic Drinks

carbonated water	saw-dah	*sóda*
... coffee	... kaah-vah	... *káva*
Turkish	two-rets-kaah	*turecká*
Vienna	vyieh-dyien-skaah	*viedenská*
espresso	es-preh-soh	*espresso*
fruit juice	oh-vots-naah	*ovocná*
	shtyah-vah	*šťava*
hot chocolate	vah-reh-naah	*varená čokoláda*
	choh-koh-laah-dah	
tea	chai	*čaj*
... water	... voh-dah	... *voda*
boiled	preh-vah-reh-naa	*prevarená*
mineral	mi-neh-raal-nah	*minerálna*

Alcoholic Drinks

Slovak wine is good and cheap and there are some excellent sparkling wines. Popular brands include *Tokay* from South Slovakia, and *Kláštorné* (a red) and *Venušíno čáro* (a white), both from the Carpathians north of Bratislava.

Special drinks to try are *demänovka*, a bittersweet Slovak liqueur slightly sweetened with honey, and *slivovice*, 'plum brandy'. *Grog* – rum with hot water and sugar – is a great pick-me-up.

... beer	pih-voh ...	*pivo ...*
bottled	flush-koh-veh	*fľaškové*
draught	cha-poh-vah-neh	*čapované*
... wine	vee-noh ...	*víno ...*
white	byieh-leh	*biele*
red	tcher-veh-neh	*červené*
young (green) wine	bur-chyiak	*burčiak*
liqueurs	lih-keh-rih	*likéry*
spirits	deh-stihl-laah-tih	*destiláty*

SLOVAK

AT THE MARKET

Basics

bread	khlyieb	chlieb
butter	mahs-loh	maslo
cereal	oh-bil-nyi-noh-vair kah-sheh	obilninové kaše
cheese	sihr	syr
chocolate	choh-koh-laah-duh	čokoládu
eggs	vai-tsyiah	vajcia
flour	mooh-kuh	múku
margarine	mar-gah-reen	margarín
marmalade	mar-meh-laah-duh	marmeládu
milk	mlyieh-koh	mlieko
(olive) oil	(olih-voh-veeh) oh-lei	(olivový) olej
pasta	ches-toh-vee-nee	cestoviny
pepper	tchyier-neh koh-reh-nyieh	čierne korenie
rice	rih-zhah	ryža
salt	sol	soľ
sugar	tzuh-kor	cukor
yogurt	yoh-guhrt	jogurt

Meat & Poultry

ham	shoon-kuh	so šunku
hamburger	ham-bur-gehr	hamburger
lamb	yah-nyah-tsye meh-soh	jahňacie mäso
pork	braf-choh-vair meh-soh	bravčové mäso
sausage	kloh-baa-sah	klobása
turkey	moh-ryak	moriak
veal	tye-lya-tsye meh-soh	teľacie mäso

Seafood

lobster	braf-choh-vair meh-soh	morský rak
mussels	moosh-leh	mušle
oysters	ooh-strih-tseh	ustrice
shrimp	kreh-veh-tah	kreveta

Vegetables

bean	fah-zoo-loh-vaah	fazuľová
beetroot	tsvick-lah	cvikla
... capsicum	... pap-rih-kah	... paprika
green	zeh-leh-naa	zelená
red	cher-veh-naa	červená

AT THE MARKET

cabbage	kah-poos-tah	*kapusta*
carrot	mrh-kvah	*mrkva*
cauliflower	kahr-fih-ohl	*karfiol*
celery	zeh-lehr	*zeler*
chillies	feh-feh-rawn-kih	*feferónky*
cucumber	ooh-hor-kah	*uhorka*
eggplant	bah-klah-zhaan	*baklažán*
garlic	tses-nuck	*cesnak*
leek	poh-roh-vaah	*pórová*
lettuce	hlaav-koh-vee shah-laat	*hlávkový šalát*
mushrooms	hree-bih	*hríby*
onion	tsih-buh-lyah	*cibuľa*
pea	hraash	*hráš*
potato	zeh-myi-ak	*zemiak*
spinach	shpeh-naaht	*špenát*
tomato	pah-rah-day-kah	*paradajka*
vegetables	zeh-leh-nyi-nah	*zelenina*
zucchini	tyek-vitch-kih	*tekvičky*

Pulses

broad beans	fah-zoo-leh	*fazule*
chick peas	tsih-zr-nah	*cizrna*
kidney beans	vlash-skair fah-zoo-leh	*vlašské fazule*
lentils	sho-sho-vih-tsah	*šošovica*

Fruit

apple	yah-bl-koh	*jablko*
apricot	mar-hoo-lyah	*marhuľa*
banana	bah-naan	*banán*
figs	fih-gah	*figa*
grapes	hroz-noh	*hrozno*
kiwifruit	kih-vih	*kivi*
lemon	tsit-rawn	*citrón*
orange	poh-mah-rahnch	*pomaranč*
peach	bros-kih-nyah	*broskyňa*
pear	hroosh-kah	*hruška*
plum	slif-kah	*slivka*
strawberry	ya-hoh-dah	*jahoda*

SHOPPING

camera shop	fotoh (potreh-bih)	*foto (potreby)*
chemist (pharmacy)	lekaa-reny	*lekáreň*
clothing store	odyeh-vih	*odevy*
delicatessen	lahuod-kih	*lahôdky*
general store	ob-khod zoh zmyiesha-neem tovah-rom	*obchod so zmiešaným tovarom*
greengrocer	zele-nyinah ah ovoh-tsyieh	*zelenina a ovocie*
laundry	praa-chov-nya	*práčovňa*
market	trkh	*trh*
newsagency	novih-nih ah chahso-pisih	*noviny a časopisy*
stationer's	pahpyier-nitstvoh	*papiernictvo*
shoeshop	obuv	*obuv*
souvenir shop	darche-kih/suveh-neerih	*darčeky/suveníry*
supermarket	samoh-obslu-hah	*samoobsluha*

How much is it?
    koly-koh toh stoh-yee?   *Koľko to stojí?*
Do you accept credit cards?
    muo-zhem plah-tyity   *Môžem platiť úverovou*
    ooveh-rovohw kar- tohw?   *kartou?*

SLOVAK

Essential Groceries

I'd like ...	muo-zhem doh-staht ...	*Môžem dostať...*
bread	khlyieb	*chlieb*
butter	mahs-loh	*maslo*
cheese	sihr	*syr*
chocolate	choh-koh-laah-duh	*čokoládu*
eggs	vai-tsyiah	*vajcia*
honey	med	*med*
margarine	mar-gah-reen	*margarín*
marmalade	mar-meh-laah-duh	*marmeládu*
matches	zaah-pal-kih	*zápalky*
milk	mlyieh-koh	*mlieko*
shampoo	shahm-pawn	*šampón*
soap	mid-loh	*mydlo*
toilet paper	zaa-khoh-doh-veeh/	*záchodový/*
	toah-let-neeh pah-pyier	*toaletný papier*
toothpaste	zuhb-nooh pas-tuh	*zubnú pastu*
washing powder	praah-shock nah	*prášok na*
	prah-nyieh	*pranie*

Souvenirs

Popular souvenirs in Slovakia are wood carvings, lace and embroidery, glass and leather goods.

earrings	naa-ush-nyitse	*náušnice*
handicrafts	umelets-koh-	*umelecko-*
	pryieh-mihsel-nair	*priemyselné*
	veerob-kih	*výrobky*
necklace	naahr-dyelnyeek	*náhrdelník*
pottery	kerah-mikah	*keramika*
ring	prs-tyeny	*prsteň*
rug	prih-kreev-kah/	*prikrývka/*
	pokroh-vets	*pokrovec*

SLOVAK

Clothing

coat	kah-baat	*kabát*
dress	shah-tih	*šaty*
jacket	sakoh	*sako*
jumper	sveh-ter	*sveter*
shirt	kosheh-lyah	*košeľa*
shoes	topaan-kih	*topánky*
skirt	suk-nyah	*sukňa*
trousers	nohah-vitseh	*nohavice*
underwear	byeh-lih-zeny	*bielizeň*

It's too big/small.
yeh toh pree-lish	*Je to príliš veľké/malé.*
vely-kair/mah-lair	

Materials

of brass	moh-sadz	*mosadz*
cotton	bavl-nah	*bavlna*
of gold	zlatoh	*zlato*
handmade	ruch-naa veeroh-bah	*ručná výroba*
leather	kozha	*koža*
silk	hod-vaab	*hodváb*
of silver	stryieh-broh	*striebro*
wool	vl-nah	*vlna*

Colours

black	chyier-nah	*čierna*
blue	behlah-saa/mod-raa	*belasá/modrá*
brown	hnyeh-daa	*hnedá*
green	zeleh-naa	*zelená*
orange	orahn-zhohvaa	*oranžová*
pink	ruzhoh-vaa	*ružová*
purple	nakhoh-vaa	*nachová*
red	cherveh-naa	*červená*
white	byieh-lah	*biela*
yellow	zhl-taa	*žltá*

SLOVAK

Toiletries

comb	hreh-beny	*hrebeň*
condoms	prezer-vahtee-vih/	*prezervatívy/*
	kon-doh-mih	*kondómy*
deodorant	dezoh-dorant/	*dezodorant/*
	deoh-dorant	*deodorant*
hairbrush	kefah nah vlasiĥ	*kefa na vlasy*
moisturiser	hidrah-touch-nee	*hydratačný*
	krairm	*krém*
shaving cream	krairm nah	*krém na*
	holeh-nyieh	*holenie*
sunscreen	krairm zoh sl-netch-	*krém so slnečným*
	neehm fil-trom	*filtrom*
tampons	tahm-pohnih	*tampóny*
tissues	vrets-kohw-kih	*vreckovky*
toothbrush	zub-naa kef-kah	*zubná kefka*

SLOVAK

Stationery & Publications

map	mahpah	*mapa*
newspaper	novih-nih	*noviny*
paper	pah-pyier	*papier*
pen (ballpoint)	peh-roh	*pero*
scissors	nozhnih-tse	*nožnice*
English-	... v anglich-tyinyeh	*... v angličtine*
language ...		
newspaper	novih-nih	*noviny*
novels	beleh-tryiah	*beletria*

Photography

How much is it to process
this film?

   koly-koh stoh-yee   *Koľko stojí vyvolanie*
   vivoh-lanyieh   *tohto filmu?*
   tokh-toh fill-muh?

When will it be ready?

   kedih toh buh-dyeh   *Kedy to bude hotové?*
   hotoh-vair?

I'd like a film for this camera.

   maa-tyeh film doh tokh-toh   *Máte film do tohto*
   fotoh-ahpah-raa-tuh?   *fotoaparátu?*

B&W (film)	chyier-noh-byielih film	*čiernobiely film*
camera	fotoh-ahpah-raat	*fotoaparát*
colour (film)	fareb-nee film	*farebný film*
film	film	*film*
flash	blesk	*blesk*
lens	obyek-teev	*objektív*
light meter	ekspoh-zih-mehter	*expozimeter*

Smoking

A packet of cigarettes, please.

   bahlee-chek tsiga-ryiet   *Balíček cigariet,*
   proh-seem   *prosím.*

Are these cigarettes
strong/mild?

   soo toh sil-nair/ yem-nair   *Sú to silné/jemné*
   tsiga-retih?   *cigarety?*

Do you smoke?

   fy-chee-tyeh?   *Fajčíte?*

Do you have a light?

   maa-teh zaa-palkih/   *Máte zápalky/zapaľovač?*
   zapah-lyoh-vach

Please don't smoke

   nye-fy-chithy proh-seem.   *Nefajčiť prosím.*

SLOVAK

cigarette papers	tsiga-retoh-vair	*cigaretové*
	pah-pyieh-reh	*papiere*
cigarettes	tsiga-retih	*cigarety*
filtered	tsiga-retih s fil-trom	*cigarety s filtrom*
lighter	zapah-lyoh-vach	*zapaľovač*
matches	zaa-palkih	*zápalky*
menthol cigarettes	mentoloh-vair	*mentolové*
	tsiga-retih	*cigarety*
pipe	fy-kah	*fajka*
tobacco (pipe)	fy-koh-vee tabak	*fajkový tabak*

Sizes & Comparisons

small	mah-lee	*malý*
big	vely-kee	*veľký*
heavy	tyazh-kee	*tažký*
light	lyakh-kee	*ľahký*
more	vyiats	*viac*
less	meh-nyeay	*menej*

HEALTH

Where's the ...?	gdyeh yeh ...?	*Kde je ...?*
chemist	lekaar-nyik	*lekárnik*
dentist	zoob-nee lekaar	*zubný lekár*
doctor	dok-tor/lekaar	*doktor/lekár*
hospital	nyemots-nyitsah	*nemocnica*

SLOVAK

It hurts here.
    tuh mah boh-lee   *Tu ma bolí.*
I'm sick.
    som kho-ree/kho-raa   *Som chorý/chorá.* (m/f)
My friend is sick.
    muoy pryiah-tyely yeh kho-ree   *Môj priateľ je chorý.* (m)
    moh-yah pryiah-tyely-kah   *Moja priateľka je chorá.* (f)
    yeh kho-raa

Parts of the Body

My ... hurts.	boh-lee mah ...	*Bolí ma ...*
ankle	chleh-nok	*členok*
arm	ruh-kah	*ruka*
back	hr-baat	*chrbát*
chest	hrudyi	*hruď*
ear	ukhoh	*ucho*
eye	okoh	*oko*
finger	prst	*prst*
foot	noh-hah/kho-dyid-loh	*noha/chodidlo*
hand	ruh-kah	*ruka*
head	hlah-vah	*hlava*
leg	noh-hah	*noha (celá)*

Ailments

I have (a/an) ...		
allergy	maam aler-ghiuh	*Mám alergiu.*
blister	maam otlahk	*Mám otlak.*
burn	maam popaa-leh-nyinuh	*Mám popáleninu.*
cold	maam naad-khuh	*Mám nádchu.*
constipation	maam zaap-khuh	*Mám zápchu.*
cough	maam kah-shely	*Mám kašeľ.*
diarrhoea	maam hnach-kuh	*Mám hnačku.*
fever	maam horooch-kuh	*Mám horúčku.*
headache	bohlee mah hla-vah	*Bolí ma hlava.*
hepatitis	maam zhl-touch-kuh	*Mám žltačku.*
(low/high) blood pressure	maam (nyeez-kih/visoh-kee) krv-nee tlak	*Mám (nízky/vysoký) krvný tlak.*
pain	maam boles-tyih	*Mám bolesti.*
sore throat	bohlee mah hrd-loh	*Bolí ma hrdlo.*
stomachache	bohlee mah zhaloo-dok	*Bolí ma žalúdok.*
veneral disease	maam pohlav-noo khoro-buh	*Mám pohlavnú chorobu.*
worms	maam chrev-neekh parah-zitohw	*Mám črevných parazitov.*

SLOVAK

At the Chemist

I need medication for ...
    potreh-buyem lyiek nah ...   *Potrebujem liek na ...*
I have a prescription.
    maam lekaar-skih   *Mám lekársky*
    pred-pis(reh-tsept)   *predpis(recept).*

antibiotics	antih-biyoh-tihkaa	*antibiotiká*
antiseptic	anti-septih-khum	*antiseptikum*
aspirin	aspih-reen	*aspirín*
bandage	ob-vaz	*obväz*
contraceptives	proh-stryied-kih	*prostriedky proti*
	protih pocha-tyiuh	*počatiu*
medicine	lyiek	*liek*
vitamins	vitah-meanih	*vitamíny*

At the Dentist

I have a toothache.
    boh-lyiah mah zoobih   *Bolia ma zuby.*
I've lost a filling.
    vih-padlah mih plom-bah   *Vypadla mi plomba.*
I've broken a tooth.
    zloh-mil sa mih zoob   *Zlomil sa mi zub.*
My gums hurt.
    boh-lyiah mah dyas-naa   *Bolia ma ďasná.*
I don't want it extracted.
    nyeh-khtsem sih toh   *Nechcem si to nechať*
    nyeh-khaty vih-trh-nooty   *vytrhnúť.*
Please give me an anaesthetic.
    uh-mrrt-vityeh mih toh   *Umŕtvite mi to, prosím.*
    proh-seem

SLOVAK

TIME & DATES

What date is it today?
  koly-kairhoh yeh dnyes?   *Kolkého je dnes?*
What time is it?
  koly-koh yeh hoh-dyeen?   *Koľko je hodín?*

Telling the time takes three forms in Slovak:

- 1 o'clock takes the singular form of the verb 'to be' and the singular form of 'hour'

  It's one o'clock.
    yeh jeh-dnah hodih-nah
    Je jedna hodina.
    (lit: it-is one hour)

- 2, 3 and 4 o'clock use the plural form of the verb 'to be' and the plural form of 'hour'

  It's two/three/four o'clock.
    soo dveh/trih/shtih-rih hodyih-nih
    Sú dve/tri/štyri hodiny.
    (lit: they-are two/three/four hours)

- 5 o'clock onwards uses the singular form of the verb 'to be' and plural form of 'hour'

  It's five o'clock.
    yeh petyih hoh-dyeen
    Je päť hodín.
    (lit: it-is five hours)

in the morning
  dopoh-luh-dnyah/   *dopoludnia/*
  pred-poluh-dnyeem   *predpoludním*
in the afternoon
  popoh-ludnyee   *popoludní*
in the evening
  veh-cher   *večer*

Days

Monday	pon-dyelok	*pondelok*
Tuesday	uh-torok	*utorok*
Wednesday	stre-dah	*streda*
Thursday	shtvr-tok	*štvrtok*
Friday	piah-tok	*piatok*
Saturday	soboh-tah	*sobota*
Sunday	nye-dye-lya	*nedeľa*

Months

January	yanooh-aar	*január*
February	februh-aar	*február*
March	maretz	*marec*
April	apreel	*apríl*
May	maai	*máj*
June	yoon	*jún*
July	yool	*júl*
August	ow-goost	*august*
September	septem-behr	*september*
October	oktoh-behr	*október*
November	nohvem-behr	*november*
December	detzem-behr	*december*

Seasons

summer	letoh	*leto*
autumn	yeseny	*jeseň*
winter	zimah	*zima*
spring	yahr	*jar*

Present

now	teras	*teraz*
this morning	dnyes raa-noh	*dnes ráno*
today	dnyes	*dnes*
tonight	dnyes veh-cher	*dnes večer*
this week/year	tentoh teezh-dyeny/rok	*tento týždeň/ rok*

SLOVAK

Past

yesterday	fcheh-rah	*včera*
day before yesterday	pred-fcheh-rom	*predvčerom*
last night	minuh-loo notz	*minulú noc*
last week/year	minuh-lee teezh-dyeny/rok	*minulý týždeň/rok*

Future

tomorrow	zai-trah	*zajtra*
day after tomorrow	poh-zai-trah	*pozajtra*
tomorrow morning	zai-trah raa-noh	*zajtra ráno*
next week	buhdoo-tzi teezh-dyeny	*budúci týždeň*
next year	buhdoo-tzi rok	*budúci rok*

During the Day

afternoon	popoh-ludnyie	*popoludnie*
dawn	ooh-svit	*úsvit*
day	dyeny	*deň*
early morning	skoh-roh raa-noh	*skoro ráno*
midday	poluh-dnyie	*poludnie*
midnight	pol-notz	*polnoc*
morning	raa-noh	*ráno*
night	notz	*noc*
sunrise	vee-khod sln-kah	*východ slnka*
sunset	zaa-pad sln-kah	*západ slnka*

NUMBERS & AMOUNTS

0	noolah	*nula*
1	yeh-den	*jeden*
2	dvah	*dva*
3	trih	*tri*
4	shtih-rih	*štyri*
5	pety	*päť*
6	shesty	*šesť*
7	seh-dyem	*sedem*
8	oh-sem	*osem*
9	dye-vety	*deväť*
10	dye-sahty	*desať*
20	dvah-tsahty	*dvadsať*
30	trih-tsahty	*tridsať*
40	shtih-rih-tsahty	*štyridsať*
50	pety-dyeh-syiat	*päťdesiat*
60	shez-dyeh-syiat	*šesťdesiat*
70	seh-dyem-dyeh-syiat	*sedemdesiat*
80	oh-sem-dyeh-syiat	*osemdesiat*
90	dye-vaty-dyeh-syiat	*deväťdesiat*
100	stoh	*sto*
1000	tyih-seetz	*tisíc*
10 000	dye-sahty tyih-seetz	*desaťtisíc*
100 000	stoh tyih-seetz	*stotisíc*
one million	milih-yawhn	*milión*

SLOVAK

Useful Words

Enough!	dosty!/stah-cheeh!	*Dosť!/Stačí!*
double	dvoy-moh	*dvojmo*
dozen	tuhtzet	*tucet*
few	maa-loh	*málo*
less	meh-nyay	*menej*
a little bit	troh-khuh	*trochu*
many	mnohoh/veh-lyah	*mnoho/veľa*
more	vyiah-tzyey	*viacej*
once	yeden-kraat/yeden raz	*jedenkrát/jeden raz*
pair	paar	*pár*
percent	per-tzen-toh	*percento*
some	nyieh-koly-koh	*niekoľko*
too much	pree-lish veh-lyah	*príliš veľa*
twice	dvah-kraat/dvah razih	*dvakrát/dva razy*

ABBREVIATIONS

atď.	etcetera
cm/m/km	cm/m/km(s)
D.P.H.	GST (VAT)
EÚ	European Union
h.(hod.)/min./sek.	hr(s)/min/sec
nám	square
nábr	Quay
n.l./pr. n.l.	AD/BC
OSN	UN
Sev./Juž./Záp./Vých.	North/South/West/East
Sk (slovenská koruna)	crown (unit of currency)
ŠPZ	Car Reg No.
SR	Slovak Republic
t.č.	at present (now)
tel. č.	telephone number
t.j.	i.e.
t.r.	this year
ul.	street

EMERGENCIES

Help!	pomots!	*Pomoc!*
Thief!	zlodyey!	*Zlodej!*

Call ...	zah-voh-lai-tyeh ...	*Zavolajte ...*
a doctor	leh-kaa-rah	*lekára*
an ambulance	zaa-khran-kuh	*záchranku*
the police	poh-lee-tsyuh	*políciu*

It's an emergency.
  treh-bah pomots · *Treba pomoc.*

There's been an accident.
  stalah sah nyeh-hodah · *Stala sa nehoda.*

Where's the police station?
  gdyeh yeh poli-tsai-naa · *Kde je policajná stanica?*
  stanyih-tsa?

Go away!
  khody prech! · *Choď preč!* (sg)
  khody-tyeh prech! · *Choďte preč!* (pl)

I'll call the police.
  zahvoh-laam polee-tsyiuh · *Zavolám políciu.*

I'm ill.
  (yah) som khoree/khoraa · *(Ja) som chorý/chorá.* (m/f)

My friend is ill.
  muoy pryia-tyely yeh khoree · *Môj priateľ je chorý.* (m)
  moya pryia-tyely-kah yeh khoraa · *Moja priateľka je chorá.* (f)

I'm lost.
  nye-viznaahm sah tuh · *Nevyznám sa tu.*

Where are the toilets?
  dyeh soo tuh zaa-khodih? · *Kde sú tu záchody?*

Could you help me, please?
  muo-zhetye mih proh-seem · *Môžete mi prosím pomôct?*
  poh-muotsty?

Could I please use the telephone?
  muo-zhem proh-seem · *Môžem prosím*
  pohw-zhity teleh-fawn? · *použiť telefón?*

I'm sorry. I apologise.
  prepaach-tyeh proh-seem   *Prepáčte, prosím.*
I didn't do it.
  yah som toh nyeh-oorobil/   *Ja som to neurobil/*
  nyeh-oorobilah   *neurobila.* (m/f)
I want to contact my embassy/
consulate.
  khtsehm hoh-vohrityi zoh   *Chcem hovoriťso*
  zastuh-pityely-stvom   *zastupiteľstvom*
  svoh-yey krayih-nih   *svojej krajiny.*
I have medical insurance.
  maam nyemotsen-skair   *Mám nemocenské poistenie.*
  poh-istyenyieh
My possessions are insured.
  moyah batoh-zhinah yeh   *Moja batožina je poistená.*
  poh-istyenaa

My ... was stolen.   ookrad-lih mih   *Ukradli mi ...*
I've lost my ...   strahtyil/   *Stratil/Stratila*
  strahtyil-lah som ...   *som ... (m/f)*

  bags   batoh-zhinuh   *batožinu*
  handbag   tash-kuh/kabel-kuh   *tašku/kabelku*
  money   penyiah-zeh   *peniaze*
  travellers cheques   tses-tohv-nair sheh-kih   *cestovné šeky*
  passport   tses-tohv-nee pahs   *cestovný pas*
  wallet   peh-nya-zhen-kah   *peňaženka*

SLOVENE

QUICK REFERENCE

Hello.	poz-drahw-lyei-ne	*Pozdravljeni.*
Goodbye.	nahs-vee-dan-yea	*Nasvidenje.*
Yes.	yah/dah	*Ja. (inf)/Da. (pol)*
No.	na	*Ne.*
Excuse me.	do-vo-lee-tei me, pro-sim	*Dovolite mi, prosim.*
Maybe	mo-gho-chei	*Mogoče.*
Sorry.	o-pro-stee-tei	*Oprostite.*
Please.	pro-sim	*Prosim.*
Thank you.	hvah-lah	*Hvala.*
You're welcome.	dob-ro-dosh-le!	*Dobrodošli!*
May I?	ah-le luh-ko?	*Ali lahko?*
What time is it?	ko-lick-ko yea oo-rah?	*Koliko je ura?*

Can I see the room?
   luh-ko vee-dim so-bo? — *Lahko vidim sobo?*

I (don't) understand.
   (nei) rah-zoom-mam — *(Ne) razumem.*

Do you speak English?
   go-vo-ree-tei ahn-glesh-ko? — *Govorite angleško?*

Where's the toilet?
   kye yea strah-neesh-chei/ve-tse? — *Kje je stranišče/WC?*

I want to go to ...
   zha-leem ee-te ... — *Szeretnék ...*

Turn left/right.
   o-bur-nee-tei — *Obrnite*
   le-vo/des-no — *levo/desno.*

Go straight ahead.
   poy-dee-tei nah-rahw-nost — *Pojdite naravnost*
   nah-pray — *naprej.*

How much is it ...?
   ko-lick-ko stah-ne? — *Koliko stane?*

one-way (ticket)	an-no-smer-nah (vo-zow-ne-tsah)	*enosmerna (vozovnica)*
return (ticket)	pow-raht-nah (vo-zow-ne-tsah)	*povratna (vozovnica)*

1	an-nah	*ena*	6	shest	*šest*
2	dve	*dve*	7	se-dehm	*sedem*
3	tree	*tri*	8	o-some	*osem*
4	shtee-re	*štiri*	9	de-vet	*devet*
5	pet	*pet*	10	de-set	*deset*

SLOVENE

SLOVENE

Slovene is the official language of the Republic of Slovenia. The forebears of today's Slovenians brought the language, with its roots in the Slavonic language, from their original homeland beyond the Carpathian Mountains.

The *Brižinski spomeniki* (Monuments of Freising) are the earliest known texts to be written in a language that reveals quite clear features of present-day Slovene. They date from the second half of the 10th century and were religious in content, relating two different forms of general confession, and a homily about sin and penitence.

The father of literary Slovene is Primož Trubar (1508-1586), a Protestant reformer and the first Slovenian writer who published his first book, *The Catechism*, at a printing house in Tübingen, Germany, in 1550. He was followed by Jurij Dalmatin who translated the Bible and published it in 1584.

Among other well-known Slovenian writers are the world-acclaimed poet France Prešeren (1800-1849), whose poems have been translated into the major world languages. Josip Jurčič and Ivan Tavčar are two of the best Slovenian representatives of literary realism. The works of Ivan Cankar (1876-1918), a great Slovenian playwright, are also translated into many languages.

Slovene is spoken in Slovenia by almost two million people, and in the countries where Slovenians have migrated, including the USA, Canada, Argentina, Brazil and Australia. It is also spoken by Slovenian minority groups in neighbouring countries. It is a uniform and rich language which has developed as a national tool of communication, and which, therefore, has a unificational and representative task.

Slovene uses Roman characters. Apart from singular and plural forms of words, Slovene also has a dual form, a rare characteristic in linguistics. The dual is used when referring to two persons or objects. The dual form has a special ending, for example:

one child	otro**k**
children	otro**ci**
two children	otro**ka**

I go	gre**m**
we go	gre**mo**
we two go	gre**va**

PRONUNCIATION
No sounds in Slovene are difficult for a speaker of English to learn. The Slovenian alphabet consists of 25 letters. Each letter has only one sound, with very few exceptions.

Vowels
a	as the 'u' in 'cut'
ê	as the 'a' in 'hat'
e	when unstressed, as the 'er' in 'opera'
é	as the 'e' in 'hey', but slightly longer
i	as the 'i' in 'ink'
ó	as the 'o' in 'or'
ò	as the 'o' in 'soft'
u	as the 'oo' in 'good'

Consonants
c	as the 'ts' in 'cats'
č	as the 'ch' in 'chocolate'
g	as the 'g' in 'gold'
j	as the 'y' in 'yellow'
r	a rolled 'r'
š	as the 'sh' in 'ship'
ž	as the 's' in 'pleasure'

SLOVENE

Stress

Slovene has free stress, which means there's no general rule for which syllable is stressed. It simply has to be learned.

SUBJECT PRONOUNS		
SG		
I	yus	jaz
you	tee	ti
he/she/it	on/o-nah	on/ona
PL		
we	mee	mi
you	vee	vi
they	o-ne/o-nei	oni/one

GREETINGS & CIVILITIES
Top Useful Phrases

Hi.	poz-drahw-lyei-ne/ poz-drahw-lyan	*Pozdravljeni/ Pozdravljen* (inf).
Goodbye.	nahs-vee-dan-yea	*Nasvidenje.*
Please.	pro-sim	*Prosim.*
Thank you (very much).	hvah-lah (le-pah)	*Hvala (lepa).*
You're welcome.	dob-ro-dosh-le!	*Dobrodošli!*
Yes.	yah/dah	*Ja.* (inf)/*Da.*
No.	na	*Ne.*
Maybe.	mo-gho-chei	*Mogoče.*
Excuse me.	do-vo-lee-tei me, pro-sim	*Dovolite mi, prosim.*
Sorry. (Forgive me.)	o-pro-stee-tei/ o-pro-ste	*Oprostite.* (pol)/ *Oprosti.* (inf)

Forms of Address

Mr	ghos-pod	*Gospod*
Mrs	ghos-pah	*Gospa*
(to a young woman)	ghos-po-deech-nah	*Gospodična*

SLOVENE

SMALL TALK

Good day.	do-bur dahn	*Dober dan.*
What's your name?	kah-ko vum jei e-me?	*Kako vam je ime?* (pol)
	kah-ko te jei e-me?	*Kako ti je ime?* (inf)
My name's ...	yus some ...	*Jaz sem ...*
Where are you from?	ot cought stei?	*Od kod ste?*
I'm from ...	some ez ...	*Sem iz ...*
Australia	ahws-trah-le-yea	*Avstralije*
the USA	ah-mair-re-kei	*Amerike*
UK	ve-le-ke	*Britanije Velike*
	bre-tah-ne-yea	
Do you like ...?	ah-le e-mah-tei	*Ali imate*
	rah-de ...?	*radi ...?*
I like it very much.	e-mahm za-lo rut	*Imam zelo rad.*
I don't like ...	nei mah-rahm ...	*Ne maram ...*
Just a minute.	sah-mo tran-noo-tehk	*Samo trenutek.*
May I?	ah-le luh-ko?	*Ali lahko?*
No problem.	braz prob-le-mah	*Brez problema.*
How do you say ... ?	kah-ko sei ra-chei ...?	*Kako se reče ...?*

Family

Are you married?
  stei po-row-chan-ne? — *Ste poročeni?*
I'm single.
  sahm-ski some — *Samski sem.* (m)
  sahm-skah some — *Samska sem.* (f)
I'm married.
  po-row-chan some — *Poročen sem.* (m)
  po-row-chan-nah some — *Poročena sem.* (f)
I have one child.
  e-mahm ann-nag-gah ot-raw-kah — *Imam enega otroka.*
I have two children.
  e-mahm dvah ot-raw-kah — *Imam dva otroka.*
I have three children.
  e-mahm tree ot-raw-kei — *Imam tri otroke.*

SLOVENE

brother	braht	*brat*
daughter	khchee	*hči*
father	ow-chei	*oče*
husband	mosh	*mož*
mother	mah-mah	*mama*
sister	sas-trah	*sestra*
son	sin	*sin*
wife	zhan-nah	*žena*

Occupations

What's your profession?
    cuy stei/se po pock-leet-soo?   *Kaj ste/si po poklicu?* (pol/inf)

I'm a tourist/student.
    some to-reest/shtoo-dent   *Sem turist/študent.*

businessperson	po-slow-nash	*poslovnež*
doctor	zdrahw-neek	*zdravnik* (m)
	zdraw-nee-tsah	*zdravnica* (f)
manual worker	de-lah-vats	*delavec* (m)
	de-lahw-kah	*delavka* (f)
computer	rah-choon-nahl-	*računalničar*
programmer	nee-char	
teacher	oo-cheat-tell	*učitelj* (m)
	oo-cheat-tell-lee-tsah	*učiteljica* (f)
waiter	nah-tah-car	*natakar* (m)
	nah-tah-car-ree-tsah	*natakarica* (f)
writer	pee-sah-tell	*pisatelj* (m)
	pee-sah-tell-lee-tsah	*pisateljica* (f)

SLOVENE

BREAKING THE LANGUAGE BARRIER

Do you speak English?
    go-vo-ree-tei ahn-glesh-ko?   *Govorite angleško?*
I understand.
    rah-zoom-mam   *Razumem.*
I (don't) understand.
    (nei) rah-zoom-mam   *(Ne) razumem.*
Could you repeat that, please?
    luh-ko po-no-vee-tei?   *Lahko ponovite?*

BODY LANGUAGE

Generally, Slovenes don't gesticulate when talking as much as the neighbouring Italians do. Slovenes nod for 'Yes', shake their heads for 'No' and shrug their shoulders for 'I don't know'. Beckoning is done with the pointer finger, palms up and other fingers folded.

SIGNS	
INFORMACIJE	INFORMATION
IZHOD	EXIT
ODPRTO/ZAPRTO	OPEN/CLOSED
POSTAJA	STATION
PREPOVEDANO	PROHIBITED
STRANIŠČE	TOILETS
VHOD	ENTRANCE
ŽELEZNIŠKA BLAGAJNA	TICKET OFFICE

PAPERWORK

date/place of birth	dah-toom krahj royst-vah	*datum/ kraj rojstva*
given name	e-me	*me*
male/female	mosh-ke/zhen-skah	*moški/ženska*
nationality	der-zhahw-lyahn-stvo	*državljanstvo*
passport	pot-ne leest	*potni list*
surname	pre-e-mack	*priimek*

SLOVENE

GETTING AROUND

I want to go to ...	zha-leem ee-te ...	*Želim iti ...*
What time does the ... leave?	k-die pel-yea ...?	*Kdaj pelje ...?*
bus	ahw-to-boos	*avtobus*
train	oo-lahk	*vlak*
boat/ferry	lahd-yah/trah-yect	*ladja/trajekt*

Can you tell me when we get to ...? me luh-ko po-ves-tei, k-die preed-dam-mo ...?	*Mi lahko poveste, kdaj pridemo ...?*
Stop here, please. oos-tah-vee-tei too-kai, pro-seem	*Ustavite tukaj, prosim.*
How long does the trip take? kah-ko dow-gho trah-yah po-to-vahn-yea?	*Koliko dolgo traja potovanje?*
Do I need to change? ah-le mo-rahm prei-se-ste?	*Ali moram presesti?*

THEY MAY SAY ...

oo-lahk e-mah zah-moo-do;
oo-lahk prei-he-te-vah
  The train is delayed/early.
oo-lahk pre-hah-yah prah-vo-chahs-no
  The train is on time.
vozh-nyah jei od-po-ve-dah-nah
  The train is cancelled.
prei-se-ste mo-rah-tei/mo-rah-tei
  You must change trains/platforms.
  nah droo-ghe pei-ron

SLOVENE

ticket	car-tah	*karta*
one-way (ticket)	an-no-smer-nah	*enosmerna*
	(vo-zow-ne-tsah)	*(vozovnica)*
return (ticket)	pow-raht-nah	*povratna*
	(vo-zow-ne-tsah)	*(vozovnica)*

I'd like to hire a ...	rud be nah-yew ...	*Rad bi najel ...*
bicycle	ko-lo	*kolo*
car	ahw-to	*avto*
guide	vo-dee-chah	*vodiča*
horse	con-yah	*konja*
motorcyle	mo-tor-no ko-lo	*motorno kolo*

SIGNS

AVTOBUSNO POSTAJALIŠČE	BUS STOP
CARINA	CUSTOMS
ODHODI	DEPARTURES
PRIHODI	ARRIVALS
ŽELEZNIŠKA POSTAJA	TRAIN STATION

Directions

How do I get to ...?
kah-ko pree-dam do ...?	*Kako pridem do ...?*

Is it near/far?
ah-le yea blee-zoo/dah-lach?	*Ali je blizu/daleč?*

What town/suburb is this?
kah-te-ro mes-to/	*Katero mesto/*
prad-mest-yea yea to?	*predmestje je to?*

What ... is this?	kah-te-rah ... yea to?	*Katera ... je to?*
road	tses-tah	*cesta*
street	oo-le-tsah	*ulica*
street number	oo-lich-nah	*ulična številka*
	shtei-veel-kah	

(Go) straight ahead.

(poy-dee-tei)		*(Pojdite) naravnost*
nah-pray	nah-rahw-nost	*naprej.*

(Turn) left/right ... (o-bur-nee-tei) *(Obrnite)*
at the ... **le-vo/des-no pre ...** *levo/desno pre ...*

traffic lights	**sei-mah-for-you**	*semaforju*
next/	**nah-sled-nyam/**	*naslednjem/*
second/	**droo-gam/**	*drugem/*
third corner	**tret-tyam o-veen-koo**	*tretjem ovinku*

behind	**zah (zah-die)**	*za (zadaj)*
opposite	**nahs-pro-te**	*nasproti*
here/there	**too/tum**	*too/tum*
everywhere	**pow-sod**	*povsod*
up/down	**zgho-rye/spo-die**	*zgoraj/spodaj*
north	**se-vur**	*sever*
south	**yoog**	*jug*
east	**ooz-hod**	*vzhod*
west	**zah-hod**	*zahod*

ACCOMMODATION

I'm looking for a/the ...	**eesh-chehm ...**	*Iščem ...*
camping ground	**kahm-pingh**	*kamping*
guesthouse	**ghos-teesh-chei**	*gostišče*
hotel	**ho-tell**	*hotel*
manager/	**de-rect-or-yah/**	*direktorja/*
owner	**lust-nee-kah**	*lastnika*
youth hostel	**po-cheet-nish-ke dom**	*počitniški dom*

What's the address?

kah-ko yea nah-slow?	*Kako je naslov?*

Please write it down.

pro-sim, nah-pee-she-tei	*Prosim, napišite*
nah-slow	*naslov.*

SLOVENE

Do you have a ...?	ah-le e-mah-tei pros-to ...?	*Ali imate prosto ...?*
bed	post-al-yaw	*posteljo*
cheap room	po-tse-ne so-bo	*poceni sobo*
single/ double room	an-no-post-al-no/ dvo-post-al-no so-bo	*enoposteljno/ dvoposteljno sobo*

How much is it per night/person?
    ko-le-ko stah-ne zah   *Koliko stane za*
    an-no noch/o-se-bo?   *eno noč/osebo?*

Is breakfast included?
    ah-le yea zy-turk ook-lyoo-chan?   *Ali je zajtrk vključen?*

Is service included?
    ah-le yea post-rezh-bah   *Ali je postrežba*
    ook-lyoo-chan-nah?   *vključena?*

Can I see the room?
    luh-ko vee-dim so-bo?   *Lahko vidim sobo?*

Where's the toilet?
    kye yea strah-neesh-chei/ve-tse?   *Kje je stranišče/WC?*

I'm/We're leaving now.
    dah-ness od-hi-ahm/od-hi-ah-mo   *Danes odhajam/odhajamo.*

Requests & Complaints

Do you have a safe (where I can leave my valuables)?
    e-mah-tei sef (kyer luh-ko   *Imate sef (kjer lahko*
    poo-steem drah-go-tsen-nos-te)?   *pustim dragocenosti)?*

Please wake me up at ...
    pro-seem,   *Prosim,*
    zboo-dee-tei mae ob ...   *zbudite me ob ...*

Do you have (a) ...?	ah-le e-mah-te ...?	*Ali imate ...?*
clean sheet	chees-to ur-yoo-ho	*čisto rjuho*
hot water	top-lo vo-do	*toplo vodo*
key	klooch	*ključ*
shower	toosh	*tuš*

SLOVENE

AROUND TOWN

Where's the/a ...?	kye yea ...?	*Kje je ...?*
bank	bahn-kah	*banka*
city centre	srei-deesh-chei mes-tah	*središče mesta*
consulate	con-zoo-laht	*konzulat*
embassy	ahm-bah-sah-dah	*ambasada*
exchange office	man-yahl-ne-tsah	*menjalnica*
post office	posh-tah	*pošta*
restaurant	rest-tau-rah-tsee-yah	*restavracija*
telephone centre	tel-lei-phon-skah	*telefonska*
	tsan-trah-lah	*centrala*
tourist	to-rees-tich-ne	*turistični*
information	in-for-mah-tseey-ski	*informaci*
office	oo-raht	*jski urad*

Post & Telecommunications

I want to make a telephone call.
rud be tel-lei-phon-near-ahw   *Rad bi telefoniral.*

How much is it for three minutes?
ko-leek-ko stah-nei-yaw   *Koliko stanejo*
tree me-noo-tei?   *tri minute?*

Where can I get Internet access?'
kye luh-ko pree-dam   *Kje lahko pridem*
doh inter-net-tah?   *do interneta?*

airmail	let-tahl-sko	*letalsko*
registered mail	pre-po-ro-chan-no	*priporočeno*
surface mail	nah-vahd-no	*navadno*

At the Bank

I'd like to change some ...	rud be zah-men-yahw ne-kai ...	*Rad bi zame njal nekaj ...*
money	dan-nahr-yah	*denarja*
travellers cheques	po-to-vahl-nih che-kow	*potovalnih čekov*

Can I have money transferred
here from my bank?
    luh-ko pran-ness-sam some   *Lahko prenesem sem*
    dan-nahr z moy-yea bahn-kei?   *denar z moje banke?*
How long will it take to arrive?
    k-die bo pre-shlo?   *Kdaj bo prišlo?*

INTERESTS & ENTERTAINMENT
Sightseeing

What time does it open/close?
    k-die sei odd-pra/zah-pra?   *Kdaj se odpre/zapre?*
Do you have a guidebook/local map?
    e-mah-tei vodd-neek/   *Imate vodnik/karto*
    car-to krah-yah?   *kraja?*
What is that?
    cuy yea to?   *Kaj je to?*
Can I take photographs?
    smem sleek-kah-tee?   *Smem slikati?*

abbey	**o-pah-tee-yah**	*opatija*
beach	**plah-zhah**	*plaža*
bridge	**most**	*most*
castle	**graht**	*grad*
cathedral	**stol-ne-tsah**	*stolnica*
church	**tser-coo**	*cerkev*
hospital	**ball-neesh-ne-tsah**	*bolnišnica*
island	**o-talk**	*otok*
lake	**ye-zei-ro**	*jezero*
main square	**glahw-ne turg**	*glavni trg*
market	**turzh-ne-tsa**	*tržnica*
old city (town)	**stah-ro mes-to**	*staro mesto*
palace	**pah-lah-chah**	*palača*
ruins	**roo-shei-vee-nei**	*ruševine*
sea	**mor-yea**	*morje*
square	**turg**	*trg*
tower	**stolp**	*stolp*

SLOVENE

Sports & Interests

What sports do you play?
**s kah-te-rim shport-tom
se ook-vahr-yahsh?**
*S katerim športom
se ukvarjaš?*

What are your interests?
**kah-te-rah zah-nee-mahn-yah
e-mahsh?**
*Katera zanimanja
imaš?*

art	oo-met-nost	*umetnost*
basketball	kosh-ahr-kah	*košarka*
chess	shahh	*šah*
collecting things	zbe-rah-tell-stvo	*zbirateljstvo*
dancing	ples	*ples*
food	hrah-nah	*hrana*
football	no-gho-met	*nogomet*
hiking	po-hod-nish-tvo	*pohodništvo*
martial arts	bo-reel-nei	*borilne*
	vash-chee-nei	*veščine*
meeting friends	sre-chahn-yah s	*srečanja s*
	pre-yah-tell-ye/	*prijatelji/*
	droo-zhan-yea	*druženje*
movies	feel-me/kee-no	*filmi/kino*
music	glahs-bah	*glasba*
nightclubs	noch-no zhiv-lyan-yea	*nočno življenje*
photography	pho-to-grah-fee-jah	*fotografija*
reading	brahn-yea	*branje*
shopping	nah-coo-po-vahn-yea	*nakupovanje*
skiing	smoo-chahn-yea	*smučanje*
swimming	plah-vahn-yea	*plavanje*
tennis	ten-nis	*tenis*
travelling	po-to-vahn-yah	*potovanja*
TV/videos	tel-lei-vee-ze-yah	*televizija/video*
visiting friends	o-bis-ko-vahn-yea	*obiskovanje*
	pre-yah-tell-yew	*prijateljev*
walking	sprei-ho-de	*sprehodi*

SLOVENE

FOOD

Slovenian cuisine is very similar to that of Austria and Italy, due to the proximity of the two countries and their historical interaction.

breakfast	zy-turk	*zajtrk*
lunch	ko-see-lo	*kosilo*
dinner	va-chair-yah	*večerja*
Cheers!	nah zdrahw-yea!	*Na zdravje!*

I'm hungry/thirsty.
lah-chehn/zhei-yehn some   *Lačen/žejen sem.*
Where can we get food?
kye sei do-be hrah-nah?   *Kje se dobi hrana?*
I'm vegetarian.
ve-ghe-tah-re-yahn-nets some   *Vegetarijanec sem.*
I don't eat ...
nei yem ...   *Ne jem ...*
How much is ...?
ko-lee-ko stah-nei ...?   *Koliko stane ...?*
I'd like the set lunch, please.
luh-ko do-beem   *Lahko dobim*
man-nee, pro-sim   *menu, prosim.*
Is service included in the bill?
ah-le yea nah-pit-nee-nah   *Ali je napitnina*
ook-lyoo-chan-nah?   *vključena?*
I'd like some ...
rud be ne-kai ...   *Rad bi nekaj ...*
Another, please.
shei an-krut, pro-sim   *Še enkrat, prosim.*
Waiter, the bill, please!
nah-tah-car, rah-choon pro-sim!   *Natakar, račun, prosim!*

hot/cold	to-puh/hlah-dehn	*topel/hladen*
restaurant	rest-tau-rah-tse-yah	*restavracija*
set menu	man-nee	*menu*
waiter	nah-tah-car	*natakar* (m)
	nah-tah-car-re-tsah	*natakarica* (f)
with/without	zeh/braz	*z/brez*

SLOVENE

Typical Dishes

soup	you-hah	*juha*
roast beef	gho-vei-yah pat-chen-kah	*goveja pečenka*
roast pork	sven-ska pat-chen-kah	*svinjska pečenka*
roast veal	tell-lech-yah pat-chen-kah	*telečja pečenka*
salad (mixed)	so-lah-tah (me-shun-nah)	*solata (mešana)*

Drinks

beer	pee-vo	*pivo*
fruit juice	sahd-ne sok	*sadni sok*
mineral water	me-na-rahl-nah vo-dah	*mineralna voda*
tea	chai	*čaj*
wine	vee-no	*vino*

SLURPING SLOVENES

The wine-growing regions of Slovenia and some of their better known products are:

- **Podravje** (in the east)
  - *Renski Rizling* — a true German Riesling
  - *Beli Pinot* — Pinot Blanc
  - *Traminec* — Traminer

- **Posavje** (in the south-east)
  - *Cviček* — a distinctly Slovenian light red

- **(coastal)**
  - *Teran* — a hearty red made from *Refok* grapes

SLOVENE

At the Market

How much is it?
ko-lick-ko stah-ne? *Koliko stane?*

It's too expensive for me.
pra-drah-gho yea zah-mae *Predrago je zame.*

I'd like ... grams/kilos.
rud be ... grah-mow/keel *Rad bi ... gramov/kil.*

Staples

bread	**krooh**	*kruh*
butter	**mah-slo**	*maslo*
cheese	**seer**	*sir*
chicken	**pish-chah-nehts**	*piščanec*
chocolate	**cho-ko-lah-do**	*čokolado*
coffee	**kah-vah**	*kava*
eggs	**yai-tsah**	*jajca*
fish	**ree-bei**	*ribe* (pl)
flour	**mo-ko**	*moko*
fruit	**sahd-yea**	*sadje*
ham	**slah-nee-no**	*slanino*
honey	**met**	*med*
margarine	**mahr-gah-ree-no**	*margarino*
marmalade	**mahr-mel-lah-do**	*marmelado*
meat	**mas-so**	*meso*
milk	**mle-ko**	*mleko*
olive oil	**ol-leew-no ol-yea**	*olivno olje*
pepper	**pop-per**	*poper*
pork	**svin-yee-nah**	*svinjina*
salt	**so**	*sol*
soup	**you-hah**	*juha*
sugar	**slaht-cor**	*sladkor*
yogurt	**yo-ghurt**	*jogurt*
vegetables	**zal-lan-yah-vah**	*zelenjava*

MENU DECODER

Soup

gobova kremna juha	mushroom soup
goveja juha z rezanci	beef broth with egg noodles
zelenjavna juha	vegetable soup

Meals

burek	sweet or savoury layered pastry
Dunajski zrezek	Wiener schnitzel
golaž	goulash
klobasa	sausage
kranjske klobase	sausages, usually served with *kislo zelje*
kislo zelje	sauerkraut (pickled cabbage)
njoki	potato dumplings
orehovi	walnut dumplings
paprikaš	chicken or beef stew
rižota	risotto
sirovi	cheese dumplings, a real delicacy
štruklji	dumplings
žlikrofi	ravioli-like dish

Desserts

gibanica	pastry filled with poppy seeds, walnuts, apple and/or sultanas and cheese, baked in cream
palačinke	thin pancakes filled with jam or nuts and topped with chocolate
potica	walnut roll
zavitek	strudel

SHOPPING

How much is it?	ko-lick-ko stah-ne?	*Koliko stane?*

bookshop	knee-gahr-nah	*knjigarna*
delicatessen	dell-leek-kah-tess-sah	*delikatesa*
food stall	stoy-ne-tsah	*stojnica*
grocery store	sah-mo-post-rezh-bah	*samopostrežba*
laundry/laundrette	prahl-neet-tsah	*pralnica*
market	turzh-ne-tsah	*tržnica*
supermarket	tur-go-veen-nah	*trgovina*
newsagency	key-yosk	*kiosk*

I'd like to buy it.
rud be coo-piw   *Rad bi kupil.*
It's too expensive for me.
pra-drah-gho yea zah-mei   *Predrago je zame.*
Can I look at it?
ah-le luh-ko pog-led-dahm   *Ali lahko pogledam?*
I'm just looking.
sah-mo gled-dahm   *Samo gledam.*

I'm looking for ...	eesh-chem ...	*Iščem ...*
a chemist	chis-steel-ne-tso	*čistilnico*
clothing	o-blah-chee-lah	*oblačila*
souvenirs	spo-meen-kei	*spominke*
book	knee-gah	*knjiga*
newspaper	chah-so-pees	*časopis*

Do you take travellers cheques?
ah-le oo-zah-mae-tei   *Ali vzamete*
po-to-vahl-nei che-kei?   *potovalne čeke?*
Do you have another colour/size?
ah-le e-mah-tei droo-gho   *Ali imate drugo*
bahr-vo/val-lick-kost?   *barvo/velikost?*

SLOVENE

Sizes & Comparisons

big/bigger	val-lick/vech-ye	*velik/večji*
small/smaller	my-hehn/mahn-she	*majhen/manjši*
more/less	vach/mun	*več/manj*
cheap/cheaper	po-tse-ne/tse-nay-she	*poceni/cenejši*

Essential Groceries

I'd like ...	rud be ...	*Rad bi ...*
batteries	bah-tear-ree-yea	*baterije*
cheese	seer	*sir*
chocolate	cho-ko-lah-do	*čokolado*
eggs	yai-tsah	*jajca*
honey	met	*med*
margarine	mahr-gah-ree-no	*margarino*
marmalade	mahr-mel-lah-do	*marmelado*
matches	oo-zhig-gahl-lee-tsei	*vžigalice*
milk	mle-ko	*mleko*
shampoo	shum-pown	*šampon*
soap	mee-lo	*milo*
sugar	slaht-cor	*sladkor*
toilet paper	toa-let-ne pah-peer	*toaletni papir*
toothpaste	zob-no cre-mo	*zobno kremo*
washing powder	prahl-ne prah-sheck	*pralni prašek*

HEALTH

I'm sick.

ball-lahn/bow-nah some   *Bolan/Bolna sem.* (m/f)

Where's the nearest dentist?

kye yea nahy-bleezh-ye   *Kje je najbližji*
zo-boz-drahw-neek?   *zobozdravnik?*

Where's the nearest
doctor/hospital?

kye yea nahy-bleezh-yah   *Kje je najbližja*
ball-neet-tsah?   *bolnica?*

I'm allergic to penicillin/antibiotics.
ah-lar-ghe-chan some nah   *Alergičen sem na*
pan-ne-tse-leen/   *penicilin/*
ahn-te-be-o-te-kei   *antibiotike.*

I'm diabetic/epileptic/asthmatic.
some de-ah-be-tick/   *Sem diabetik/*
ap-pe-lep-tick/ahst-mah-tick   *epileptik/astmatik.*

I've been vaccinated.
beew some tsep-lyan   *Bil sem cepljen.* (m)
be-lah some tsep-lyan-nah   *Bila sem cepljena.* (f)

Parts of the Body

arm	rock-kah	*roka*
back	her-bat	*hrbet*
chest	per-see	*prsi*
ear	oo-ho/oo-shess-sah	*uho/ušesa* (pl)
eye	ow-ko/ow-chee	*oko/oči* (pl)
foot	sto-pah-law	*stopalo*
hand	dlahn	*dlan*
leg	nog-gah	*noga*
nose	nos	*nos*
skin	ko-zhah	*koža*
stomach	tre-booh	*trebuh*

Useful Words

antiseptic	ahn-te-sep-tick/	*antiseptik/*
	rahz-coo-zhee-lo	*razkužilo*
aspirin	ahs-pe-reen	*aspirin*
condoms	con-do-me	*kondomi*
contraceptive	con-trah-tsep-tsey-sko	*kontracepcijsko*
	sret-stvo	*sredstvo*
diarrhoea	dree-skah	*driska*
medicine	zdrah-veel-lo	*zdravilo*
nausea	slah-bost	*slabost*
sunblock cream	cre-mah zah	*krema za*
	sohn-chan-yea	*sončenje*
tampons	tahm-pown-ne	*tamponi*

SLOVENE

TIME & DATES

When does (the) ... start?
k-die bo ...? *Kdaj bo ...?*
What time is it?
ko-lick-ko yea oo-rah? *Koliko je ura?*

It's ...	oo-rah yea ...	Ura je ...
1.15	chat-turt nah dve	četrt na dve (a quarter of two)
1.30	paul dvehh	pol dveh (a half of two)
1.45	tre chat-turt nah dve	tri četrt na dve (three-quarters of two)

in the morning	zyout-rye	*zjutraj*
in the evening	zva-chair	*zvečer*
all day	vuhs dahn	*ves dan*
every day	oo-suck dahn	*vsak dan*

yesterday	oo-chair-rye	*včeraj*
today	dah-ness	*danes*
tonight	no-tsoy	*nocoj*
tomorrow	you-tre	*jutri*
day after tomorrow	po-yoot-rish-nyam	*pojutrišnjem*

Days

Monday	po-ned-dell-yack	*ponedeljek*
Tuesday	tor-reck	*torek*
Wednesday	sre-dah	*sreda*
Thursday	chat-turt-tack	*četrtek*
Friday	pe-tack	*petek*
Saturday	saw-bo-tah	*sobota*
Sunday	ned-dell-yah	*nedelja*

SLOVENE

Months

January	**yahn-noo-ahr**	*januar*
February	**fab-roo-ahr**	*februar*
March	**mahr-rehts**	*marec*
April	**ahp-reel**	*april*
May	**my**	*maj*
June	**you-ney**	*junij*
July	**you-ley**	*julij*
August	**ahw-goost**	*avgust*
September	**sap-tam-bur**	*september*
October	**oc-to-bur**	*oktober*
November	**nov-vam-bur**	*november*
December	**dat-sam-bur**	*december*

Seasons

spring	**po-mlaht**	*pomlad*
summer	**po-let-yea**	*poletje*
autumn	**yea-sen**	*jesen*
winter	**zee-mah**	*zima*

NUMBERS & AMOUNTS

1	**an-nah**	*ena*
2	**dve**	*dve*
3	**tree**	*tri*
4	**shtee-re**	*štiri*
5	**pet**	*pet*
6	**shest**	*šest*
7	**se-dehm**	*sedem*
8	**o-some**	*osem*
9	**de-vet**	*devet*
10	**de-set**	*deset*
11	**an-nah-ist**	*enajst*
12	**dvah-nah-ist**	*dvanajst*
13	**tree-nah-ist**	*trinajst*
14	**shtee-re-nah-ist**	*štirinajst*
15	**pet-nah-ist**	*petnajst*

SLOVENE

16	shest-nah-ist	*šestnajst*
17	se-dehm-nah-ist	*sedemnajst*
18	o-some-nah-ist	*osemnajst*
19	de-vet-nah-ist	*devetnajst*
20	dvai-seht	*dvajset*
21	an-nah-in-dvai-seht	*enaindvajset*
22	dvah-in-dvai-seht	*dvaindvajset*
30	tree-de-seht	*trideset*
40	shtee-re-de-seht	*štirideset*
50	pet-de-seht	*petdeset*
60	shest-de-seht	*šestdeset*
70	se-dehm-de-seht	*sedemdeset*
80	o-some-de-seht	*osemdeset*
90	de-vet-de-seht	*devetdeset*
100	sto	*sto*
101	sto an-nah	*sto ena*
110	sto de-set	*sto deset*
1000	tee-soch	*tisoč*
one million	me-le-yon	*milijon*

Useful Words

Enough!	doh-vaull!	*Dovolj!*
too much/many	pra-vach	*preveč*
a little	mah-law	*malo*
a lot	vell-leek-ko	*veliko*

SLOVENE

EMERGENCIES

Help!	**nah po-moch!**	*Na pomoč!*
Go away!	**poy-dee-tei strahn!**	*Pojdite stran!*

Call a doctor/the police!
pok-lee-chit-tei zdrahw-nee-kah/ *Pokličite zdravnika/*
po-le-tsee-yaw! *policijo!*

I've been raped.
be-lah some po-see-lyan-nah *Bila sem posiljena.*

I've been robbed.
beew some or-rop-pahn *Bil sem oropan.*

I'm lost.
ez-goo-beew/ *Izgubil/*
ez-goo-bee-lah some sei *Izgubila sem se.* (m/f)

Could you please help me?
me luh-ko po-mah-gah-tei? *Mi lahko pomagate?*

I didn't do it.
te-gah nee-some nah-red-deew/ *Tega nisem naredil/*
nah-red-deal-lah *naredila.* (m/f)

I didn't realise I was doing
anything wrong.
nee-some ved-do/ved-dell-lah, *Nisem vedel/vedela,*
dah dell-lahm nah-ro-bei *da delam narobe.* (m/f)

I want to contact my
embassy/consulate.
ho-cham go-vau-ree-te z *Hočem govoriti z*
moy-yaw ahm-bah-sah-doh/z *mojo ambasado/z*
moy-yim con-zoo-lah-tom *mojim konzulatom.*

INDEX

MACEDONIAN 255

I
N
D
E
X